*Practically
Religious*

In memory of
Marie Reader 1910–1997
Ethel Yukie Tanabe 1915–1996

Contents

Contents ix

visit, and Robert Sharf of the University of Michigan, who gave us valuable comments.

We express our gratitude to Clark Chilson, Ikeuchi Fuki and Jay Sakashita for their help and encouragement. Ian Reader wishes to thank the Japan Foundation Research Committee for funds (JFEC grant 843) for a research visit to Japan in 1995, and the Leverhulme Trust for a grant that enabled him to carry out the survey of Shikoku pilgrims' prayer requests discussed in Chapter 5. George Tanabe gratefully acknowledges the support of the University of Hawai'i Japan Studies Endowment, which is funded by a grant from the Japanese government.

From the beginning this book has been the product of our mutual cooperation, which owes much to the changing pace of international travel as well as to new means of technology that enable authors on different sides of the globe to write together. It owes even more to the supportive atmospheres in which we both live. Here we owe an immense debt to our respective families for their support and for their toleration: to Dorothy, Rosie, and Philip Reader for providing a loving home life and for putting up with Ian's occasional and necessary visits to Hawai'i; and to Willa Tanabe for listening to our endless hours of discussion, for her perceptive comments, and especially for providing us with the book's title. Gen and Kelly Yee Tanabe were pleasant and insightful companions on many trips to temples and shrines. We also thank St. Pauli Girl for her inspirational qualities and spiritual nourishment.

Our final acknowledgment is one tinged with sadness. As we were working on the final stages of this book, both our mothers passed away: Ethel Tanabe in November 1996 and Marie Reader in June 1997. This book is dedicated to their memories, both in thanks for all they gave us and in gratitude for their long lives.

Acknowledgments

THE IDEA FOR THIS BOOK developed in 1992–1993 when Ian Reader spent a year as a Visiting Professor in Japanese Studies at the University of Hawai'i, where George Tanabe is based. Patricia Steinhoff, Director of the Center for Japanese Studies in the School of Hawaiian, Asian and Pacific Studies at that time, was instrumental in arranging this visit. It gave us the opportunity to explore the topic of practical benefits in the common religion of Japan, and our desire to write a book together was encouraged by Patricia Crosby, our editor at the University of Hawai'i Press. She nudged us beyond talking about our ideas over lunch into actually sitting down and writing about them. Thanks, Pat.

In conducting the research for this book we have visited numerous shrines and temples throughout Japan, and we wish to thank the many priests who assisted in our work by giving interviews, responding to our questions, and providing materials related to their institutions. We would like to thank the countless worshippers and visitors at various shrines and temples. They kindly accepted our often intrusive questioning of their actions and motivations, and patiently responded to such questioning.

We wish to thank our academic colleagues at the University of Stirling, the Nordic Institute of Asian Studies, and the University of Hawai'i for their support and tolerance of our obsession with the topic of practical benefits. We are grateful to the Society for the Study of Japanese Religions, especially its president, Jackie Stone, for inviting us to give a presentation at the 1996 meeting of the Association for Asian Studies in Hawai'i, and also to the audience at the talk for their responses and questions. We acknowledge the help of Abe Ryūichi of Columbia University, who arranged an important field

Introduction

MICHIKO WATANABE was an "office lady" in a major Japanese company. Normal company policy (as is so often the case in Japan) was to make all female employees retire when they got married or, if they failed to marry, to make them leave at the age of thirty. Michiko, however, loved her job and wished to continue working for the company as long as she could and, moreover, had no desire to get married. As her thirtieth birthday approached, she began to express her concerns over the impending loss of her job to friends, one of whom belonged to a new religious movement (*shin shūkyō*).[1] Extolling the efficacy of this religious group and its practices—which, she claimed, enabled its devotees to achieve any goal they wished—her friend persuaded her to go along to a meeting at this movement's local center. Attending the meeting and encountering several other women of a similar age, each of whom affirmed the positive nature of this religion, and listening to testimonies from members who told of practical benefits they had received as a result of their religious devotion, Michiko became convinced that this was a religion that might be able to help her out of her present predicament. She began to attend the meetings regularly, and got involved in special prayers and recitations both at home and at the weekly meetings. As colleagues and senior members of the religious group told her to do, she directed her prayers toward her wish to stay on at her company beyond her thirtieth birthday.

One day, some months before her birthday, she was summoned to the office of her section head. Believing she was about to be told she would have to leave the company, she entered in trepidation—only to hear her boss say that since she was a devoted and model worker, the company wanted her to stay on and become a senior in charge of training all new office lady employees. Michiko was overjoyed. In that

1

moment she realized the efficacy of her prayers and could see how
her involvement in the new religious movement had improved her
life. In that moment she recognized what her friend had told her and
what countless other adherents to new religions in Japan had
preached: proof of religious validity can be found through experience. She was convinced of the truth of her newfound religion because it had worked and solved her problem, and this deepened her
faith. Soon she was advocating its values to other friends and colleagues and advising them to come with her to meetings in order to
deal with their own problems and desires.

In various publications detailing the benefits that can accrue from
following their religious practices, numerous Japanese new religious
movements tell stories such as Michiko's and make it clear that direct,
immediate, and often material benefits flow from religious faith,
practice, and adherence to their tenets.[2] Such stories are commonplace among Japanese new religions and convey a readily understood
message for members and potential converts alike: here is a religion
that actually works, one that offers practitioners the hope of something beneficial and relevant to their daily lives. These immediate
benefits are known as *genze riyaku,* a term that can be translated as
"this-worldly benefits," "practical benefits in this lifetime," or simply
"practical benefits." As these three translations of the term are virtually synonymous, we use all of them in this book. At times *genze riyaku*
has also been translated as "this-worldly material benefits," but this
term can have a derogatory connotation, as if the only benefits sought
in the new religions are material.[3]

Although *genze riyaku* may cover any kind of good results, they are
generally understood to involve primarily material or physical gains
such as good health, healing, success, or, as in the case cited here,
personal advancement in one's life path, as well as less tangible
benefits such as an increased sense of personal well-being and freedom from problems. Such practical benefits have been widely regarded as an integral feature of the new religions and a crucial factor
in their appeal to a wide audience both in their initial stages of development and in their subsequent growth. The earliest religious
power of Nakayama Miki, for instance, the founder of the new religion Tenrikyō, was the apparent ability to grant safe childbirth to supplicants. It was this power, along with her ability to grant protection
against illnesses such as smallpox, that first drew people to her and
provided the catalyst for the formation of the group.[4]

Practical benefits have also been a constant target of the critiques
of the new religions made by priests and others associated with mainstream religious traditions, such as Buddhism, and by journalists in
the mass media. Accusing the new religions of being solely material-

istic in nature, such critics condemn them as being concerned with foolish superstition. From a psychological point of view, for example, Nakamura Kokyō attacked the new religion Ōmotokyō as "a frightful superstition unparalleled in the country."[5] Scholars too have joined in criticizing the new religions. In their book *Shinkō shūkyō*, Samoto Akio and Kotake Akira characterize the new religions as magical and ecstatic mass movements.[6] On the question of *genze riyaku* in particular, the Buddhist scholar Kikumura Norihiko argues that the term originally referred to spiritual benefits but Japanese folk beliefs corrupted the idea to include material pleasures.[7] The Nichiren scholar Asai Endō characterizes the new religions as being devoid of doctrine and having only methods for magical healing; he criticizes the Sōka Gakkai in particular for their understanding of practical benefits as actual proofs of the power of the *Lotus Sutra,* saying that their interpretation does not accord with what Nichiren himself wrote.[8] Studies carried out in the 1950s by Buddhist and Shinto scholars frequently characterized the new religions as being "doctrinally shallow, magical, and focused on this-worldly benefits."[9] Generally they portray the new religions and their adherents as interested in little other than material benefits obtained through magic rather than rational effort. This criticism implies that these are not true religions, a point emphasized by the terms often used to refer to them: *jakyō* (wrong religion), *ruiji shūkyō* (quasi-religion), and *shinko shūkyō* (new fad religion). Arai Ken has commented on the negative image that has surrounded new religions—especially as they were portrayed in the media in the prewar era—because of superstitious claims about their powers to heal the sick and confer all manner of worldly benefits.[10]

The critiques leveled against the new religions, through their focus on this-worldly benefits, have thus sought to depict them as not "real" or "true" religions but somehow false and corrupted—implying that "real" and "true" religions are not concerned with material or this-worldly benefits acquired through superstitious magic. True religion in this model involves genuine faith, spiritual salvation, creedal affirmation, and ethical rules of life. Although such critiques originated primarily in the Japanese situation from within a religiously oriented, predominantly Buddhist, academic milieu, they have to a great degree been reinforced by Western academic traditions. The textual-based origins of Western academic studies of religion, and of Buddhism in particular, have certainly played their part in this. From its beginnings in the nineteenth century, the Western study of Buddhism in India has had what Gregory Schopen calls a Protestant bias in having to find "true religion" located in scripture. So long as Buddhist studies scholars insist that "real Buddhism is textual Buddhism," then what is written in the texts as ideals must be understood as having taken place in actual practice—and, conversely, any idea or practice that cannot be found in scripture must be rejected as a historical impossibility.[11]

A major problem is that academic studies of religion have tended, especially from the nineteenth century onward, to emanate from a number of different sources. There is a particularly problematic split between anthropological and sociological studies on the one hand (which tend to focus on phenomena such as ritual, practice, and custom that are often visible apart from scriptural sources) and theological studies on the other with their focus on issues of creed, text, and doctrine. The latter, especially when related to the missionizing impulses of nineteenth-century Christianity, of which the academic-theological tradition was part, was concerned with differentiating between concepts of true and false religions and, through spreading the doctrines of "true religion," with rejecting what it saw as falsehood and superstition. The focus of anthropological study was thus relegated to the investigation of what from the theological viewpoint was seen as false and superstitious, while the study of "religion" proper was conceptualized within a theological, doctrinal, and faith-oriented framework. This tendency has naturally had repercussions on the subsequent development of the study of religion and religious cultures, as Schopen's point illustrates. While academic studies of religion have in many ways moved beyond the narrow theological parameters of the nineteenth century and now recognize the importance of practice and ritual, they have not always managed to resolve the problems created by early conceptualizations of "religion" within a basically Christian theological framework. Indeed, such is the concern over the potential theological (and culture-specific) implications of the term "religion" itself that scholars have begun to question the applicability of the term "religion" to non-Western cultures: since the term relates to creeds, beliefs, teachings, and doctrines, it is inappropriate as a term of analysis for situations where customs, practices, and other ritual actions may be the means of expressing underlying meanings that do not need affirmation in doctrinal forms.

While we recognize the problems caused by the term "religion," we do not concur with such concerns. In this book we are talking about a non-Western culture and are dealing largely with matters not of doctrine and teaching, not necessarily even of belief, but of practice and action. Thus we readily use the term "religion" to describe the issues we are talking about. We do this knowing full well that the topics we focus on—praying for worldly benefits and the various practices and concepts that surround it—may at times seem more closely associated with commerce, entertainment, and casual behavior than they are with the apparently traditional concerns of religion as a doctrinally oriented phenomenon. In our usage of the term "religion" we are, in effect, utilizing an English translation of a Japanese word, "shūkyō." The irony of this will not be lost on scholars aware that "shūkyō" is the term developed in the nineteenth century in Japan to refer to the English word "religion," which at that time was most specifically a theologically oriented term.

While the conception of shūkyō (religion) as a narrowly based, theologically and doctrinally oriented phenomenon, associated with belief in a specific faith, continues to have some resonance in contemporary Japan (as does the term "religion" in English-speaking cultures), in scholastic terms it has far broader meanings that incorporate ritual, folk customs, and even etiquette. A brief glance at contemporary Japanese scholarship shows this well: in his book Nihon shūkyō no kōzō (The structure of Japanese religion), for example, Miyake Hitoshi discusses this-worldly benefits, rituals, spirit possession, festivals, asceticism, taboos, and the relationship of Buddhism with folk customs. Doctrines and creedal teachings, by contrast, are given little prominence.[12] Numerous studies of folk practices and beliefs are considered to come under the rubric of shūkyō (religion): Shinno Toshikazu's Nihon yugyō shūkyōron, for example, which is concerned with the study of pilgrimage, wandering ascetics, folk legends, and miracle stories, and Miyata Noboru and Tsukamoto Manabu's edited volume Minkan shinkō to minzoku shūkyō, which discusses shamanism, the role of the gods in providing worldly benefits, and the roles of gods of sickness and good fortune.[13] While modern-day Japanese analyses of the influences of "religion" (shūkyō) discuss levels of faith and belief, they are also concerned with observance of calendrical rituals and festivals, ranging from memorial visits to graves to New Year visits to shrines and temples, and with matters such as the purchase of amulets and other lucky charms, visits to diviners, attitudes toward spirits, and the potential incidence of miracles.[14]

Since the terms (and concepts) of religion and shūkyō are imbued with multiple meanings and historical accretions that provoke different interpretations and suggest different and frequently elastic meanings to different people in different contexts, we should state where we stand on this issue. In this book we are using parameters similar to those found in much of contemporary Japanese scholarship: thus we use "religion" as an inclusive term that has elastic frontiers readily intermingled with cultural and social themes in which belief and doctrine can play a part but are not essential. Under the rubric of "religion" we include such things as visits to shrines and temples (locations that cannot be classified other than as religious institutions), participation in festivals that are focused on shrines, temples, and deities, the acquisition of amulets and talismans, and the seeking, through petitioning of deities, of worldly benefits. We treat religion as a matter not only of doctrine and belief but of participation, custom, ritual, action, practice, and belonging. It is as much a matter of social and cultural influences and behavioral patterns located in day-to-day concerns and the ordinary processes of life—as concerned with ameliorating problems in the present, in producing explanations of why things have gone wrong, and in proposing mechanisms that offer the hope of improvement—as it is with ultimate concerns, theological explanations of the nature of the universe, or the destination of the soul. Rather than reject the term "religion" defined in narrow theological terms, we employ the word with expansive meanings drawn from a broad spectrum ranging from theological abstractions to mundane practicalities.

In taking such a perspective on religion, we may sometimes appear to emphasize the popular, customary, pragmatic, and secular more than the doctrinal and theological. We do not seek to privilege one form of inquiry (such as the anthropological concern with practice and ritual) over others (such as theologically or textually oriented studies). Rather, we recognize that fruitful studies of religion can be more readily carried out when different academic perspectives are brought together. As subsequent chapters of this book show, we argue that topics such as praying for worldly benefits must be studied not merely from anthropological and suchlike perspectives but have to be seen in relation to the wider picture of religion in Japan—that is, in terms of the doctrinal sources and meanings associated with such practices and the textual sources that affirm them.

A similar point has been made recently by Robert Sharf in an article which critiques the methodological disjunctions that have hampered the study of Japanese religious phenomena. Sharf argues that these schisms have resulted from a basic division of labor between sociologists and anthropologists, on the one hand, who are concerned with synchronic analyses and tend to neglect historical and doctrinal matters, and Buddhologists, on the other, who focus on text, philology, and doctrine. The Buddhologists, he notes, "tend to dismiss the new religious movements as degenerate popularizations utterly devoid of doctrinal sophistication or subtlety."[15] The results of this division of labor, according to Sharf, include a lack of studies of new religions that are sensitive to their scriptural precedents and a lack of ethnographically textured studies of older Buddhist schools in the modern period.[16]

Although there is a growing convergence between these two approaches in the study of Japanese religion,[17] there remains a tendency in academic writing to differentiate between "true religion" and superstitious practice. In a recent edition of their volume on the Japanese in the present day, Edwin Reischauer and Marius Jansen conclude that "religion in contemporary Japan is not central to society and culture."[18] It is not just the new religions, but all the other traditions as well, that either fail the test of being a real religion or, if they qualify, as Christianity does, have only a small number of adherents. Reischauer and Jansen admit the prevalence of superstitious folk beliefs and the popularity of a wide variety of visible institutions and rituals, but they count little of this for true religion, since 70 or 80 percent of Japanese do not profess to believe in any religion. Most of the elements of real religion are seen to be missing: there is no faithful affirmation of teachings that provide guidance in life.

The view of Reischauer and Jansen, that "religion in Japan offers a confused and indistinct picture,"[19] results, however, from their expectations of what is real religion rather than from any understanding of the actualities of Japanese religion. As we have noted, there are many other valid elements in Japanese religion besides those considered by Reischauer and Jansen. Indeed, Japanese religion is less a matter of belief than it is of activity, ritual, and custom.[20] The vast majority may not assert religious belief but—a point demonstrated in numerous studies and surveys of behavior in religious contexts—that same majority participates in religious activities and rituals.[21] Even Reischauer and Jansen, despite their view of a society in which religion does not play a central role, admit that Japanese life is "intertwined with religious observances."[22] Indeed, understood as active participation, religion is hardly a peripheral phenomenon in Japan.

The picture on the front cover of Reischauer and Jansen's book makes exactly this point: the Japanese are very much involved with religion—in particular, with ritual behavior and practice involving the pursuit of practical benefits through religious situations and means.[23] The photograph, which shows a family catching the holy water of Otowa no Taki (Otowa Falls) with long-handled ladles at the famous Kiyomizu Temple in Kyoto, is representative not only of Japanese religion but of contemporary Japan. Otowa no Taki, the first of the so-called ten famous springs in Japan, is visited by throngs of people seeking to drink its water in order to cure illnesses, prolong life, and fulfill wishes. A sign at the premises advises people to drink the water, make tea with it, or mix it with powdered milk; supplicants are told they can take home a bottle for 500 yen. Taking home the water, which can produce the benefits cited here because it comes from the sacred location of the temple and is therefore associated with its main figure of worship, the bodhisattva Kannon, is one of a number of actions open to the visitor seeking benefits on offer at the temple. As we shall see in subsequent chapters, temples, shrines, and other religious institutions provide—for a fee, as with the water at Kiyomizu—a whole range of means whereby people can take home with them the signs and representations of the sacred power of the location. Among the objects we shall encounter in this book are numerous and often generic forms of amulets, talismans, and votive tablets, to say nothing of assorted lucky objects and charms, as well as more specialized representations of good fortune, benefits, and spiritual power such as the water of Kiyomizu.

Nor do the religious institutions that provide these services, materials, and access to the various forms of *genze riyaku* discriminate. Anyone may purchase an amulet, request a special ritual prayer, or make a personal supplication to the gods or buddhas. There is no need, and no demand, for special affiliation or specific denominational involvement before one can approach a deity or utilize a temple for such services. Kiyomizu Temple, for example, has the reputation of being everyone's temple since it does not cater in any specialized way to a particular group of people. It is for everyone. No one is barred from searching for good fortune, seeking the providence of Kannon, imbibing the holy powers, and receiving the benefits there. Reischauer and Jansen's picture of the emblematic activity of taking water at a temple and thereby receiving benefits is most appropriate for a book entitled *The Japanese Today*.

Buddhism and This-Worldly Benefits

The assumption that searching for this-worldly benefits and using practices linked to magic and materialism are characteristic of false religions not only gives a pejorative reading of the new religions but misrepresents the nature of Buddhism and other religious traditions. As we shall see, the promise of this-worldly benefits is an intrinsic element within Japanese religion in general. To a great extent the materialism and economics of worldly benefits are in fact typical of Japanese religion, including Buddhism, and, if the matter were to be pursued further, of religion in general. Buddhist temples have long been as active as the new religions in promoting the practical benefits that can be acquired through venerating their figures of worship and through prayers, petitions, and the purchase of talismans and amulets. Such temples are by no means the exceptions; indeed, they are often located right at the heart of supposedly normative Buddhism. Many head temples of Buddhist sects are renowned as centers of this-worldly benefits: Ikegami Honmonji, one of the four head temples of the Nichiren Buddhist sect, is renowned for its role as a protector of children;[24] Sensōji, otherwise known as Asakusa Kannon, the head temple of the Shō Kannon sect, is renowned for protection from danger (*yaku yoke*).[25]

Many guidebooks available in bookstores throughout Japan denote, outline, and discuss this-worldly benefits in terms of the places where they may be sought. Such guidebooks, which we shall focus on particularly in Chapter 7, generally center not on the new religions but on Shinto shrines and Buddhist temples—that is, on the religious institutions of the established religions of Japan.[26] In such accounts of the benefits that can be sought, and the places where one may petition for them, one is liable to find numerous well-known Buddhist temples most commonly associated with austere religious practice and behavior. Thus an entry for the renowned head temple of the Sōtō Zen sect, Eiheiji in Fukui prefecture, which is famed for its austerities and for the monastic training of its monks, can be found in a popular guidebook of this-worldly benefits. There it is lauded as an efficacious place to pray for career advancement—efficacious in part because of the severe practice of its monks, which endows the temple with spiritual power and thus makes prayers said there especially potent.[27] The Sōtō sect itself represents a good example of how deeply rooted praying for this-worldly benefits is, how closely associated it is with other core Buddhist practices such as meditation, and how inseparable it is from the monastic aspects of Buddhist training. Sōtō Zen Buddhism expanded in Japan during the Muromachi period and its doctrines penetrated into Japanese society in general; it achieved this penetration through the use of prayer formulas that promised this-worldly benefits, at times even using prayers supposedly addressed to its founder Dōgen.[28]

Several important Sōtō Zen temples have become famed as prayer temples (*kitōdera*), auspicious locations at which to petition for worldly benefits. In particular the sect has three major prayer temples (*sandai kigansho*),[29] usually cited as Saijōji in Kanagawa prefecture, Myōgonji, also known as Toyokawa Inari, in Aichi prefecture, and Kasuisai in Shizuoka. Saijōji is one of the largest and most dominant temples in the sect, head of its second largest temple lineage with over four thousand affiliated temples, and famed, because of its association with the ascetic mountain hermit Dōryō, as a center for all manner of benefits including (at least in recent years) increasing one's monetary wealth, for which the temple sells lucky talismans.[30] Myōgonji is one of the most famous centers for the veneration of Inari, the deity most commonly associated with Shinto but also venerated in certain forms in Buddhist temples.[31] Among the benefits it is known for are the opening up of good fortune (*kaiun*) and business prosperity (*shōbai hanjō*). Kasuisai is renowned for providing protection against fires (*kanan yoke*).[32] Occasionally another Sōtō temple, Zenpōji at Tsuruoka in Yamagata prefecture, is also counted (instead of either Myōgonji or Kasuisai) as one of the three great Sōtō prayer temples.

What characterizes all four of these temples is that they are among the small number (less than thirty in all) of temples classed as special monastic training centers (*senmon sōdō*) where monks undergo training to become priests and practice meditation and other spiritual austerities.[33] Like the guidebook mentioned earlier, which considered Sōtō's most famous monastic training center, Eiheiji, to be a good place to pray for worldly benefits because of its focus on austerities, the publications of these other monastic training centers see no contradiction between worldly prayers and spiritual training.

Thus the commemorative volume produced by Saijōji on the six-hundredth anniversary of its founding focuses on the temple as a training center for monks and as a famed place of prayer whose protective guardian is the spirit of the fourteenth-century ascetic monk Dōryō. Dōryō continues to guard the temple and provide petitioners with worldly benefits, showing his presence "with mysterious occurrences and by his responsiveness to prayer."[34] The two predominant aspects of the temple—its focus as a center of Zen Buddhist meditation designed to achieve enlightenment and its role as a prayer temple where people come to seek this-worldly benefits—are complementary, not contradictory, as a senior monk at the temple told one of us during a visit in April 1996.[35] Whether performing Zen meditation or praying to the gods and buddhas for help, one is "throwing away" one's self, affirming one's faith, and achieving rewards for behaving well. In this monk's interpretation, this-worldly benefits come as a reward for prayer and faith: they do not reflect self-seeking and immoral activities so much as ethical and highly religious ones.

We shall return to these issues in later chapters. Here we have drawn attention to the incidence of this-worldly benefits in one particular Buddhist organization, Sōtō Zen Buddhism, to indicate the centrality of this topic to Buddhism in Japan and to show that monasticism and seeking this-worldly benefits occur within the same location and are not contradictory so much as complementary. Indeed, commentators from the Buddhist tradition who criticize the new religions are perhaps being disingenuous, for the term "*riyaku*" itself is originally a Buddhist word relating to the benefits granted through the grace of buddhas and the merits of the law of Buddhism. The concept of *riyaku* and Buddhism's power to bring benefits is integral to the Buddhist tradition, particularly as it has developed in Japan, and, as Chapter 2 demonstrates, can be found amply in the scriptures and practices that attend the passage of Buddhism from the Asian continent to Japan. The suggestion that Buddhism is neither practical nor beneficial is anathema to its central claim of being an effective remedy for the pains of existence. It is therefore not surprising that *genze riyaku* should be held in great esteem even at the highest levels of understanding. The promise of practical benefits has had a wide appeal to all classes of people and has served as a common ground giving rise to abstruse philosophies as well as folk stories telling of the powers of this religion and its deities. The stories and tales that have developed within the Buddhist tradition in Japan resonate well with the account of Michiko given earlier and establish in dramatically clear ways the tangible rewards for those who commit themselves to belief and exert themselves in practice. All of this is consonant with classical Buddhist ideas such as karma and causality, which make it nearly impossible to affirm that things happen by chance. Practical benefits are not accidental but, as we shall see in Chapter 3, result from deliberate, ethical, and correct action.

Buddhism, after all, was introduced to the Japanese in precisely such terms: as a religion that rewarded commitment with material benefits. When the Korean king of Paekche in the sixth century sought to interest the Japanese court in Buddhism, he did not assert its philosophical richness or claim that it could provide an otherworldly path of transcendence. He did not even speak of enlightenment, nirvana, emptiness, or any of the other philosophical explanations of Buddhism that he admits can hardly be understood. Nor, indeed, did he speak of the potential for this new religion to pacify the souls of the dead or help them in their passage to other realms (roles that became central to Buddhism in Japan in later ages). Rather, he introduced Buddhism as a means of attaining benefits and even affirmed the goodness of desire, which had been denounced by other doctrinal formulations such as the Four Noble Truths:

> This doctrine is amongst all doctrines the most excellent. But it is hard to explain, and hard to comprehend. Even the Duke of Chou and Confucius had not attained to a knowledge of it. This doctrine can create religious merit and retribution without measure and without bounds, and so lead on to a full appreciation of the highest wisdom. Imagine a man in possession of treasures to his heart's content, so that he might satisfy all his wishes in proportion as he used them. Thus it is with the treasure of this wonderful doctrine. Every prayer is fulfilled and naught is wanting.[36]

It could be said, however, that kings are not always endowed with philosophical skills and the king's interest in practical benefits might be excused as resulting from the limited understanding of a pragmatic politician. The king's compromised understanding might be explained in a more respectable way, perhaps, by resorting to the expedient idea of skillful means. This doctrinal tenet can be cited to

explain the king's lack of a higher understanding and thereby to preserve what otherwise would have to be regarded as a degenerate
interpretation.

The importance of the concept of skillful means in Mahāyāna Buddhism is widely recognized. Explained in texts such as the *Lotus Sutra,*
the concept asserts that Buddhism, in its drive toward universal truth
and the establishment of the unchanging Buddhist law that can bring
full enlightenment to all beings, has had to avert its gaze from the
higher standards—not in order to lower its expectations but to bring
people closer to its ultimate aims—and must utilize various means at
its disposal, including the assimilation of ideas and rituals seemingly
incompatible with its ultimate ends, in order to create a more fertile
ground. The stories in the *Lotus Sutra* that show the Buddha using
various tricks to get his message across are widely cited cases of skillful means in action. Likewise Buddhism's accommodating stance toward the ancestors and Confucian family ideals is occasionally cited
as an example of the expediency of a religion whose primary focus
was on monastic celibacy, withdrawal from the world, and the affirmation of impermanence—in marked contrast to the notion of ances-
torhood and its belief in a permanent soul that retains some connection with this world after death. Buddhism in such terms is seen as
using skillful means in order to come to terms with local religious and
social mores, thereby enabling it to establish roots in the culture and
spread its message. The promise of practical benefits can thus be
justified as one of these expedient tricks used to lead people to the
higher objective of renunciation and transcendental wisdom: by affirming the powers of Buddhism, and of the buddhas, to grant practical benefits, those who promote the creed of Buddhism are effectively making belief. They are seeking to develop faith in those who
have received benefits or believe that they might do so.

Although skillful means as a concept affirms the role of Buddhism
in pointing toward an absolute truth (and in such contexts Buddhism
itself may be seen as a skillful means carrying out this role of mediating between conventional truth and the absolute), it is often utilized
by scholars and Buddhist priests alike to draw distinctions within the
realms of Buddhist practice and activity—between, for example, supposedly pure Buddhist practices, such as meditation, and others that
somehow look more appropriately classified as the accretions of
popular folk religion assumed by Buddhism through its desire to
bring all beings closer to the truth. Japanese Buddhist priests who
perform memorial services for ancestors or sell amulets for good fortune and personal benefit at their temples, for example, may (as
many have done in conversation with the authors) readily turn to a
discussion of skillful means to explain why they do so. The concept

also allows academics who are disturbed by Japanese Buddhism's apparent focus on worldly concerns to explain it in terms that imply that these are not parts of true Buddhism but accretions gleaned from the folk tradition through Buddhism's desire to expand its influence and reach greater numbers of people.

Whatever the intent of the concept, it has provided a means through which those who wish to do so can legitimize the apparent accretions and assimilations from the folk tradition and therefore reaffirm many of the notions about high religion as opposed to popular and folk religion, notions advanced in the critiques of true versus false religion to which we alluded earlier. But such a perspective merely reinforces what we consider to be an untenable differentiation between religion as doctrine and religion as practice. Thus the concept of skillful means—helpful though it has been to scholars and priests in giving expedient answers to questions about how and why a religious tradition such as Buddhism has developed from its roots in monastic enlightenment beneath the bodhi tree to its role of provider of good fortune, business prosperity, and ancestor veneration in modern Japan—has in a way problematized more than it has clarified our general understanding of Buddhism. By providing a plausible "answer" to why such things happen, it has facilitated the continuing image of Buddhism as a religion engaged in mundane and material pursuits only as a device and stratagem, rather than as matters of proper religious concern. Within the context of Japanese religion and Buddhism in general, as we shall see, Buddhist activities of providing magical efficacy are central to its dynamic rather than ephemeral or expedient. The doctrine of skillful means, rather than being a truly central dynamic that leads people to, and legitimates, the practice of seeking practical benefits, is actually closer to being an afterword: it is the centrality of practical benefits to Buddhism that creates the need for the doctrine of skillful means for those who invoke it rather than the doctrine creating the need to promote practical benefits.

Shinto and Practical Benefits

If Buddhism is intimately associated with the pursuit of benefits, so too is Shinto. One of the major differences is that Shinto priests as well as academics studying Shinto have had little problem in accepting the idea that religion may be concerned with worldly benefits as normative.[37] Indeed, this is its raison d'être: Shinto deities are constantly invoked for the benefits they are believed to provide, while the whole thrust of Shinto mythology and legends, as set out in texts such as the *Kojiki*, speaks of the role of Shinto deities (*kami*) in providing the good things that contribute to fruitful human life. Shinto shrines dedicated to deities such as Hachiman, Tenjin, and Inari draw large crowds of petitioners seeking blessings, good luck, and protection from misfortune. Deities such as Inari are called upon to support a good harvest, bless new business ventures, or assist in their particular spheres of influence. Tenjin, the god of education, is prayed to by Japanese students seeking help in passing examinations or entering a college of their choice.

Shinto in general terms has provided ready affirmation of the availability of this-worldly benefits through faith and veneration at its shrines, while numerous religious groups registered as Shinto organizations in Japan stress the importance of this-worldly benefits in their doctrinal structures and teachings. This is usually done within the context of emphasizing the importance of worshiping the particular *kami* venerated within the particular Shinto organization and hence affirming the close relationship between faith and the acquisition of practical benefits.[38] The Shintō Kotohirakyō (a sect or *kyōha Shintō* organization based on Kotohira Shrine in Shikoku), for instance, affirms that through reverence for its *kami,* and through prayer at their shrines, one can attain such benefits as being blessed with children, business prosperity, and family safety.[39] Shinto has never renounced the desirability of the good things in life. It has been a comfortable advocate of the powers of its deities to help people secure practical benefits and thus has provided a ready ally to the buddhas and bodhisattvas who could do the same.

Genze riyaku in Japanese Religion

As the preceding comments illustrate, the promise and pursuit of this-worldly benefits are not limited to the new religions. Thus critiques accusing new religions of being focused on this-worldly benefits are themselves unreasonable: while new religions are, in general, centered on issues related to *genze riyaku,* this is because they tend to follow a normative path within Japanese religion, not because they are in any way a perversion or aberration of Japanese religious traditions.

This book is centered on the role, meaning, and nature of *genze riyaku* in Japanese religion. Our basic argument is that *genze riyaku* is a normative and central theme in the structure and framework of religion in Japan—sought through numerous ritual practices, symbolized by various religious objects such as talismans and amulets, and affirmed in doctrinal terms in various religious organizations as well through textual traditions. It is, as we shall see, vigorously proselytized not just by the new religions but by established ones as well. And in this proselytization the established religions and their institutions proclaim a similar underlying meaning as that of the religion the office lady Michiko joined: a religion that is true because it accomplishes things.

The range of complexities and themes related to the seemingly simple notion of a benefit (*riyaku*) that is attained, enjoyed, and experienced in this life (*genze*) will become more evident as the book continues. Here, however, we note that when we talk of *genze riyaku* (and the various English translations, such as "practical benefits," that we introduced earlier) we are, in effect, using a shorthand for the interlocking framework of themes, concepts, practices, and meanings that are associated with the seemingly simple act of asking a deity to provide one with something of practical use in one's life. In framing this book around the nature, role, and position of *genze riyaku* in Japanese religion, we see *genze riyaku* both as a descriptive term, referring to a particular phenomenon and practice, and as a means through which, by examining the various elements that are associated with it, we can begin to understand the nature and dynamics of religion in Japan.

There are two primary points we wish to introduce here that will provide both the framework for the chapters that follow and the definitional focus to the wider subject we are discussing. The first is that, in affirming the centrality of *genze riyaku,* we are arguing that Japanese religion in general is governed by a world-affirming religious viewpoint. This does not mean that we are disregarding the importance of various ideas and practices relating to salvation and death and what happens afterwards: funeral customs, concepts about the spirit after death, views about postdeath salvation, and such concerns are extremely important. Indeed, in terms of engagement in religious activities, few practices are as important in Japan as activities related to the ancestors and to rituals and practices centered on the deceased and their graves, and few concepts have been more powerful or so hopefully held than the promise of salvation and entry into the Pure Land after death.[40] While one can argue that such practices themselves contain a this-worldly orientation (by venerating and ritualizing ancestors, the living are seeking their protection and favor in this life, and ancestors are regarded as a potential source of benefits, while faith in postdeath salvation is an important element in the development of this-worldly peace of mind), one must also consider the importance of these issues in the wider understanding of religion in Japan as well as Japanese religious practices. Since these issues have been the subject of far greater study than the topic of *genze riyaku,*[41] we would suggest they have led to a more otherworldly nuance being placed on many aspects of Japanese religion—and a disproportionate sense of the weight of otherworldly as opposed to this-worldly views—than the situation demands.

The second point is that the practice of seeking this-worldly benefits should not be seen as simply or even primarily materialistic. As we shall see, a number of other qualities and spiritual states, including peace of mind and salvation, are closely related to these practices and the meanings upon which they are based. If we understand materialism to imply that it is through material advances alone that happiness is achieved, and that materialism is a way of thinking which emphasizes above all the acquisition of material wealth and goods, it is not parallel to the concept of *genze riyaku*. As we shall discover in Chapter 3, there is a strong moral underpinning to the concept and practice, which relates most directly to living a good, happy, and positive life in the present—a concept that is perhaps most clearly articulated in new religions such as Tenrikyō, which sees it as a moral injunction to live a *yokigurashi*, a bright and happy life,[42] but which permeates much of the Japanese religious spectrum.

Riyaku (also *goriyaku*) are material and this-worldly in that they improve the living circumstances of the petitioner in a direct and immediate way by offering educational success, happy marriage, safe childbirth, traffic safety, business prosperity, and so on. They also reflect the understanding that happiness itself requires freedom from anxiety (hence the prayers for safety as a means of reassurance) and a certain level of material support. This is different from saying that the concept and pursuit of *riyaku* are synonymous with materialism. While the pursuit of *riyaku* suggests the acquisition of material benefits, it is rarely framed in terms of suggesting that material advance alone is good.

A number of prayers seek benefits that are intangible (health, safety) or seek to protect the supplicant from misfortune. Nevertheless, they will clearly improve the seeker's quality of life. They are externalizations of inner wishes that manifest the realities of what people see as important in life. Such inner wishes, reflected in prayers for success, amelioration, good health, safety, and so on, express what are commonly accepted as essential human needs and essential aspects of living a satisfied life, one with meaning and value.

The concept and practices related to the pursuit of this-worldly benefits demonstrate a worldview in which psychic causation is considered to play a major part in the actualization of events. Just as spirits or ancestors, when not treated properly, may be seen as causes of illness (a view that affirms the psychic worldview in which spiritual causes are manifest as physical events, a dominant theme in Japanese religious culture that is strongly articulated in the present day by many of the new religions),[43] so does the expression of inner thoughts reflect an important part of the process of actualization. Praying for benefits also reflects an implicit recognition that human beings are unable to accomplish everything by themselves: they need some support, or at least a feeling that they are being supported, in their endeavors. Implicit, too, in such prayers is the notion of cooperation: in praying for a god or buddha's aid, one is effectively pledging one's willingness to act in accordance with the deity or buddha one prays to, thus committing oneself to a particular course of action based on faith and ethical duty.

In connection with these spiritual and material questions, we should mention here three terms that are linked to the concept and practices surrounding *genze riyaku*. These terms are "peace of mind" (*anshin*), "faith" (*shinkō*), and "salvation" (*kyūsai*), all of which would no doubt be considered germane to "spiritual" questions. As we shall see throughout this book, however, all of these terms are so closely related to the concept and practices surrounding *genze riyaku* that at times they are virtually inseparable from it. This is especially so regarding *anshin* (peace of mind) and *shinkō* (faith). Both terms have occurred frequently during the interviews with priests. One of the first discussions with a Buddhist priest on the topic of *genze riyaku* was less a formal interview than a relaxed conversation with the head priest after the New Year's celebrations at a Sōtō Zen temple in northern Japan.[44] Questions were based on relative inexperience, for this was the interviewer's first visit to Japan and he was still attempting to comprehend the seeming contradictions between what he had read about Buddhism as a religion emphasizing nonmaterialism and the prayers and rituals for worldly advancement and success that were being made by the priest on behalf of visitors who paid him for this service.

The gist of his response was quite straightforward: by praying to the buddhas, displaying faith, and acquiring their benevolent grace, one attains peace of mind. He did not dispute that praying to the Buddhist figures of worship would lead to the acquisition of their grace and benevolence: as befits his position as a Buddhist priest and guardian of a number of sacred images, a priest whose role at the temple was to perform such rituals of supplication, he naturally had deep faith in the power of the buddhas and in the efficacy and benevolence of their response. The peace of mind that results from having prayed and acquired a sign (an amulet or some other tangible object) of the grace of the buddhas has the effect, he stated, of enabling one to focus one's mind on the task at hand, such as studying for an examination or driving carefully. This recognition that one can operate more efficaciously when one is in a good mental state is simple enough, but it shows how closely *anshin* and *genze riyaku* are related.

Peace of mind, in such terms, leads to practical benefits. It also leads
to deeper faith: in making supplications to a buddha, or indeed any
deity, one is expressing some form of faith, at the very least in the ability of the deity to "hear" that prayer and act on it. As the priest put it,
the acquisition of the benefits sought will deepen the supplicant's
faith. *Shinkō* is thus deepened and extended through the process of
seeking and receiving benefits. Again, one should note that the priest
did not question that benefits would result from praying to the buddhas he served at his temple.

In this explanation, then, we see that *anshin* and *shinkō* are related
to, are components of, and are also to some degree products of *genze
riyaku*. As the conversation with the priest was neither sophisticated
nor especially deep, it may be suggested that the linkage between
these issues, *anshin, shinkō,* and *genze riyaku,* is rather simplistic. However, there are times when the simple and straightforward explanation is not just the most direct but also the most reasonable. This, we
would suggest, is the case here. It is an explanation that has emerged,
in some form or other, in many subsequent conversations and interviews with other priests. While there are many layers and themes in-
terwoven into the question of practical benefits and their relationship
to peace of mind, faith, and the like, we want to affirm here that it is
important to pay attention to the simple and direct and not always
seek deeper and more complex meanings and "answers" to questions
that are, like Japanese religion itself, direct and readily understandable without recourse to abstruse speculations that make things more
indistinct than they actually are and often lead to the erosion of clear
arguments and to the privileging of theory over reality.

In suggesting that peace of mind was the immediate product of
prayers to the buddhas and was thus the precursor of *genze riyaku*, it
might be considered that the priest was in effect stating that peace of
mind, rather than practical benefits, was the real goal of prayer. This,
indeed, is a response we have heard from other Buddhist priests
many times in the course of discussions. Practical benefits, in such a
perspective, are side products of a search for the spiritual state of *anshin* rather than goals. Indeed, the notion of *anshin* itself presents pit-
falls for the researcher. Like the skillful means argument discussed
earlier, it provides a convenient argument, if not excuse, for priests of
all religious traditions, particularly Buddhism, to explain (or explain
away) the issue of *genze riyaku*.

To explain *genze riyaku* primarily in terms of *anshin* (that is, to treat
pleasant material benefits as side effects of "true" spiritual goals) provides another useful means of explaining why temples say prayers for
practical benefits and why they sell objects (the amulets and so on)
that are purchased in this practice. But this is a form of explanation

not dissimilar to the skillful means argument: plausible, useful, and yet, we would contend, ultimately incomplete. If peace of mind were the real goal of supplicants, it would be what they prayed for—yet as a rule they do not. As we shall see in Chapter 1, people do not make oblique requests: they pray for direct, often tangible, but always practical things, normally for themselves or their social group. It is normal to make blunt requests and demands of the gods, ranging from petitions for protection and safety to petitions for wealth and entry into good schools. Is it not disingenuous, looking at these overt prayers, to assume that the "real" intention of the petitioners was peace of mind? After all, there is nothing to prevent someone asking directly for peace of mind in a prayer. Yet requests (*onegai*) to the gods and buddhas usually focus on a particular benefit. When requests are directed toward peace of mind, they often do so via a specific and materially oriented request. Consider the following message on a votive tablet seen at the temple Kokawa-dera in Wakayama prefecture (in June 1988). In this case the supplicant sought spiritual solace in connection with a practical aim: "May I pay back the money I have borrowed quickly so as to become spiritually at ease (*shakkin o hayaku kaeshite seishinteki ni ochitsukemasu yō ni*)." The person appended a second wish, as well, asking that she might be cured of an illness.[45]

Were *anshin* the primary goal of petitioners, it would be more clearly expressed as such in their petitions. To "explain" the practice of seeking benefits as really centered on peace of mind is to downplay the crucial importance of practical circumstances as essential elements, for most people, in the attainment of happiness. Certainly peace of mind may be a major desire of those who pray at shrines and temples, but it is rarely a direct and pragmatic goal. It is, instead, one that is intertwined with other needs and concerns which may be material and may be more urgent. Peace of mind is a goal that is most readily expressed within the context of attainment: I will (or might) be happy and attain peace of mind when I have passed my examination and got into a good college, when my business prospers enough for me to afford a better house and car, and so on.

Anshin cannot properly exist in normal terms without material substance. It rests, for the vast majority, on one's day-to-day conditions, one's work, the success of one's business, good health, one's children's health and (most certainly in Japan) their academic success, and so on. One person we talked to regularly used traffic safety amulets but had had a number of traffic accidents. To some eyes this series of accidents might suggest that the amulets were ineffective. Her interpretation was very different: she had not been injured in any of the accidents, and this was proof of the amulets' effectiveness. The accidents, rather than eroding her faith in the merits of amulets, actually increased it: each accident without injury was a reaffirmation of the amulet's efficacy and the religious power it signified. Thus she was constantly reassured by the amulets in her car, and this contributed to her peace of mind when driving. The practical benefit, the *riyaku*, of traffic safety was also a spiritual benefit, manifested as peace of mind and deepening faith.

This woman's faith in the amulets reflects the other aspect of the priest's comment—that the acquisition of a sought-after benefit would intensify faith—and demonstrates the close relationship between faith and benefits. While some degree of faith is often a precursor of the search for benefits (in that one might need at least the inklings of faith to engage in the process of praying for benefits), the attainment of benefits is sometimes equated with the possession of faith. In his introduction to a popular guidebook to shrines and temples in the Kansai region of Japan famed for their provision of worldly benefits, the priest Imai Shōmyō has written that in visiting such places and having one's wishes realized, "the mind of the believer becomes peaceful and at ease, sufferings are swept away, and one penetrates into the spirit of the law."[46] Arai Ken, writing about the new religions, has argued in this context that benefits are the products of faith, not its aim.[47] The Honmon Butsuryūshū, a Nichiren-based group that claims to teach the true Buddhism of Shakyamuni, speaks of "practical benefits as the actual proof" (*genshō goriyaku*) of faith.[48]

This view was expressed by a priest at the temple Ichibata Yakushi in Shimane prefecture in outlining the temple's foundation legend (*engi*), which affirms the importance of faith as a producer of benefits. The temple's foundation story, which dates the origins of the temple to 894 C.E., centers on the miraculous healing of the blind mother of a poor fisherman who lived on the Japan Sea coast. The fisherman, named Yuichi, who was devoted to his mother and a model of filial piety, found a statue of the Buddha of Healing, Yakushi, in the sea, enshrined it in his home, and prayed earnestly to it. His faith was rewarded with a number of wonderful events, the most dramatic being the restoration of his mother's sight.[49] The temple that developed around this statue and legend has become widely known for the benefit of healing eye problems and has been at various times in the past affiliated with different Buddhist sects—first the Tendai sect and then the Myōshinji branch of the Rinzai Zen Buddhist sect. In the modern era it separated itself from the Rinzai Myōshinji sect and became the main temple of an independent Buddhist sect, the Ichibata Yakushi Kyōdan, although still classified under the Rinzai lineage. Despite these changes of sectarian affiliation, its central focus has remained constant: belief in the healing powers of Yakushi and the ability of that buddha, in that location, to provide benefits, especially in relation to eye problems, to petitioners. This in itself is an indication of the central role the concept of benefits plays in Japanese religion: it is the concept of benefits, based on faith in the power of a Buddhist deity, that has been the primary factor in the history of the temple and has withstood changes of sectarian affiliation. Tendai or Rinzai sectarian affiliation would thus appear to be less important, in terms of the temple's function, than faith in the provision of practical benefits.

Ichibata Yakushi is by no means the only temple with such a history of experiencing sectarian change while retaining a fundamental faith in the provision of practical benefits. This process can be seen also in the history of Saijō Inari in Okayama prefecture. Once a Tendai temple, it became a temple in the Ikegami branch of the Nichiren sect in the sixteenth century and in 1954 became head temple of an independent sect of Nichiren Buddhism, known as Saijō Inarikyō. The temple is famous as a center for praying for worldly benefits, and this has been a constant factor in its history despite sectarian changes.[50]

Such changes of sectarian affirmation are quite common in Japan. Yet as we shall see in the discussion of temples, shrines, and guidebooks in Chapter 7 these changes do not appear to affect the central place played by practical benefits in their histories. Ichibata Yakushi and Saijō Inari, both of which have emerged as head temples of their own Buddhist organizations, demonstrate that *genze riyaku* is not just a vital element that survives such transitions but a core organizing principle around which temples function and develop. It is also a principle that can provide doctrinal focus and definitions of faith. Ichibata Yakushi today receives hundreds of thousands of visitors from all over Japan and is the center of a small sect focused on the benefits provided by its main image of worship. The Ichibata Yakushi Kyōdan as an independent Buddhist sect affirms the importance of *genze riyaku* as a central point of its doctrines (*kyōgi*):[51] benefits are, as the priest affirmed, the result of faith, and the sect's doctrine thus links faith and benefits together. The doctrines of Ichibata Yakushi Kyōdan as set out in the organization's registration as a religious corporation under the Religious Corporations Law (*shūkyō hōjin hō*) affirm that practical benefits, such as the healing of eye problems, can be acquired through ritual practices carried out at the temple and through faith in Yakushi.[52] Faith and benefits, therefore, are intimately linked: the former produces the latter; the latter reinforces the former and is central to the doctrines that one has faith in.

We shall return in subsequent chapters to the question of faith. Here we want to emphasize that the concept of seeking practical benefits is closely linked not only to questions of peace of mind but also to issues of faith, its development, and its intensification. It is also in many respects associated with notions of salvation (*kyūsai*), which may contain a this-worldly dimension. Shimazono Susumu has demonstrated for the new religions that salvation is related to the attainment of happiness in this world and can therefore be considered in this-worldly terms: indeed, as he shows, new religions are very often religions of this-worldly salvation.[53] The promise of this-worldly salvation is not a prerogative of the new religions alone, however, for it can be framed also in Buddhist terms. The cult of faith in the bodhisattva Kannon (Kannon *shinkō*) in the Nara and early Heian era was strengthened by notions of this-worldly salvation in Kannon's Pure Land (Fudaraku), which was believed to be located within the terrestrial domain of Japan, in the mountains of Kumano. Pilgrims were certainly motivated by the promises in texts and stories associated with Kannon that they could attain this-worldly salvation through journeying to the region of Fudaraku.[54]

Faith in Kannon is based on her ability to confer this-worldly benefits and to intercede in the form of miraculous interventions that save people from danger or even death.[55] At the temple Honkakuji on the island of Shōdoshima, there is a votive tablet depicting a car crashing over a cliff and a "hair's breadth Kannon" (Ippatsu Kannon) protecting the driver from injury. According to the inscription and to the story related at the temple, Kannon had saved the driver when the car went over the precipice. As a result of emerging wholly unscathed and for his salvation, he offered a votive tablet of thanks.[56]

Salvation may be immediate rather than transcendent, therefore, and such salvific interventions are quite clearly practical benefits. Salvation may be of a more clearly spiritual kind, as indeed the experiences of people like Michiko, cited at the beginning of the chapter, show. Her reprieve from losing her job, which was so important to her life and continued happiness, represents a form of salvation in this world—a salvation brought about, she and her religious mentors would argue, because of her religious devotion and the religious practices she performed. Thus practical benefits can contribute to, and be closely associated with, the notion of salvation in this world, a point clearly emphasized in the new religions but present in Buddhism as well.

Indeed, Buddhist priests who deal on a day-to-day basis with the requests of people who visit their temples recognize that salvation—and religion in general—must have a this-worldly dimension that is not at all inconsistent with true religion. Matsumoto Jitsudō, the head priest of Hōzanji, a well-known temple near Osaka specializing in the provision of this-worldly benefits, linked these issues together in a booklet published by the temple and entitled *Kankiten shinkō e no michi* (Toward faith in Kankiten), Kankiten being the main figure of worship at the temple. Matsumoto writes as follows:

> One thing I would like to state here is that there are some people who say that praying for this-worldly benefits such as the healing of illness and business prosperity is not true religion (*tadashii shūkyō de wa nai*), but in fact religion absolutely has to be something for living human beings. Religion itself, along with showing us the existence of the gods and buddhas, provides the spiritual foundations for human life, releases us from its sufferings and pains, gives rise to a joyful life, and teaches us an awareness of the way toward respecting the true nature of human beings. In the end, seeking the Pure Land and praying for its realization are nothing if not a this-worldly activity: after all, if there are no this-worldly benefits there can be no salvation. Is not, after all, seeking entry into the Pure Land a request for an extension of this-worldly benefits? Since present and future are inseparable, to disregard the present is in effect to disregard the future as indeed Shinran himself recognized when he wrote that "desire itself is the spirit of future rebirth."[57]

Matsumoto, who subsequently links worldly benefits to the expression of true faith,[58] not only refutes the view that true religion has nothing to do with this-worldly benefits but firmly emphasizes that they are in fact central to its endeavors. By linking salvation to benefits he affirms the points we are making here—that the "materialistic" practice of seeking this-worldly benefits cannot be separated from "spiritual" elements of the religious enterprise. There is, in reality, no conflict between seemingly "spiritual" notions such as peace of mind, faith, and salvation, on the one hand, and apparently "material" ideas such as the pursuit and attainment of practical this-worldly benefits on the other. The latter are essential aspects of, at times even prerequisites for, the former. Any attempts to draw definitional lines between them in terms of "true" versus "false" religion, or materialism versus spirituality, are extremely problematic since they do not account for what people actually believe and practice.

A Common Religion

There is one more point we wish to emphasize in this Introduction: within the pursuit of this-worldly practical benefits there is a worldview that is so much part of the common ground—indeed, the bedrock—of Japanese religion that it operates as perhaps the most vital common religious denominator in Japan. In light of this religious common denominator many of the categories that have been used as conceptual tools in the study of religion—including the notion that there are high and low, or true and corrupted, religions—can be seen to fall apart. We have already stressed the invalidity of such divisions, and it is now widely recognized in academic studies that categorical divisions do not always work in practice.

In his comprehensive study of medieval English Catholicism, for example, Eamon Duffy has noted that "no substantial gulf existed between the religion of the clergy and the educated elite on the one hand and that of the people on the other."[59] In stating that "the liturgy was the principal reservoir from which the religious paradigms and beliefs of the people were drawn,"[60] Duffy argues that the divisions between "elite" and "popular" religion, which have been assumed by scholars in discussing medieval religion, did not exist in reality. Not only scholars focusing on "elite" religion have made this assumption: those studying the "popular" traditions have done the same. Duffy's critique of Keith Thomas's *Religion and the Decline of Magic*,[61] for example, is that Thomas pays virtually no attention to the liturgy's role in forming the religious worldview of medieval people.

Duffy's arguments are pertinent to our own study. For as we have indicated, there is much in Buddhist and other liturgy and scripture that provides source materials for popular religious pursuits and encourages these practices. Moreover, as we shall see in later chapters, Buddhist sutras, the supposed repository of doctrine and philosophical meaning, often serve as magical spells or incantations used to call for spiritual grace and to petition for benefits. And Buddhist temples, statues, and figures of worship that have been closely associated with so-called high or elite culture (and have subsequently been designated as National Treasures (*kokuhō*) or Important Cultural Properties (*jūyō bunkazai*) have often been regarded as among the most efficacious providers of benefits.

Within Japanese religion in general, there is no substantial gulf between what the clergy said and did, what the elites wanted and experienced in their religion, and what the people did, wanted, and experienced. The goal of many formal ritual practices conducted at Buddhist temples in Japan is to achieve this-worldly benefits, and the ritual implements include recitations of prayers and Buddhist sutras offered by priests as part of the process of sanctifying amulets and talismans and petitioning for worldly benefits. To illustrate this lack of a gulf between elites and the common people, let us briefly look at pilgrimage, a topic we shall explore further in Chapter 5.

Pilgrimages developed as a lay religious activity during the Heian era, at which time the practice was especially associated with the upper echelons of society: many of the pilgrims were aristocrats and (especially in the pilgrimages to Kumano) retired emperors. Yet they did not make these pilgrimages in a different guise or with different intentions from those from the lower strata of society from the late Heian era onward. Although there was a class division in the modes of travel (the ordinary people walked, the aristocrats as a rule went by horseback accompanied by retinues of servants), the desire for acquiring practical benefits from their pilgrimages was shared by all. The aristocrats set out on their pilgrimages with the intention of getting practical benefits just as did the artisans.[62] At times, perhaps, those with different stations in life would seek different types of benefit: the retired emperor or leading aristocrat involved in court intrigues would, for instance, be more likely to petition the gods and buddhas for benefits related to temporal power than would a simple artisan; the artisan would be more likely to pray for developing his work skills or for his business to prosper.

The requests were not always all that different, however. As Barbara Ambros points out in her study of female pilgrims to Kumano in the Heian period, seeking wealth and success was a common thread among rich and poor. While aristocratic women did not have the same financial needs as poor women, they wished to make successful marriages and advance in society and sought such benefits through their pilgrimages. Other needs, such as the wish to bear children and the desire to avoid or be cured of illnesses, were benefits commonly sought by aristocratic women, but of course were important to women at all levels of society.[63] Social circumstances produce different manifestations of the need for benefits and divine support: they do not produce different *types* of religion. Despite the differing requests of the rich and poor, the elite and the common, the pursuit of benefits unites all. The elite pray for benefits just as do the ordinary people. To insert concepts of differentiation based on elite versus ordinary categories of people (in social and economic terms) is spurious.

Pilgrimages were also egalitarian in that every pilgrim—no matter how he or she made the pilgrimage—became equal at the temple gates. At the gateway to pilgrimage temples one often finds stones with the ideograms "*geba*" (dismount from your horse). Such markers can be seen, for example, at the gate of Matsunoodera in northern Kyoto prefecture, the twenty-ninth temple on the Saikoku pilgrimage, and on one of the paths leading to Shiromineji, the eighty-first site on the Shikoku pilgrimage. The ideology of convergence (that all pilgrims were the same, all equal, when wearing their common pilgrims' robes) is prevalent in Japanese pilgrimage even if there remain important distinctions between them in practice. Pilgrimage thus serves as a good example of the unifying dynamics of the religion of practical benefits: it provides a means through which all can seek the benefits pertinent to their situation in a common setting.

Duffy, in arguing for the unity between "elite" and "popular" religious forms, is critical of the term "popular religion" because, as he notes, it is a "term laden with questionable assumptions about the nature of *non-popular* religion and the gap between the two."[64] We concur with such a critique. The term "popular religion," referring to the religion of ordinary people, implies that somehow there is religion that is unpopular—and that what is unpopular is the religion that elites belong to. Thus it appears to affirm a division between what elites think and do and what ordinary people think and do. It also suggests that elites are focused on doctrine and adherence to the philosophical niceties of scripture, immune to what is often termed "superstition," while the ordinary people are ignorant of doctrines, unaware of what is said in religious scriptures or performed in religious rituals, and almost entirely bound up with superstition and magical practices. As we shall see in subsequent chapters, such divisions are themselves inadequate and fictitious. We have already indicated that "popular" practices related to *genze riyaku* may be doctrines in Buddhist sects. The "elite" monks who read their Buddhist sutras were quite clearly aware, because the texts reiterate it so often, that their religion specifically promises practical benefits and offers rituals and other practices through which they may be obtained. The aristocratic elite who patronized Buddhist temples and other religious institutions may have affected an interest in spiritual disciplines such as meditation, but they were more commonly concerned with the benefits their religious patronage gave them whether through access to direct benefits or artistic accomplishments.[65] Such religious practices as sutra copying, a highly popular religious activity among the elite in the Heian period, were accessible to the elite because they were literate, knew how to copy the ideograms of the texts, and were wealthy enough to have access to the brushes, ink, paper, and texts required for the practice. Yet the intention of sutra copying was little different from the practices of ordinary peasants standing before their gods: the aristocrats wanted their children to be born safely, their wives to conceive, their cattle to thrive, and their lands to be safe and prosperous. In our own time, when nearly everyone is literate in Japan, sutra copying is practiced by people in all walks of life.

There is little need here to emphasize further the lack of significant differentiation between the religions of the elite and the folk—or, to put it in other terms, the continuities between textual religion and religion in practice. We should, however, clarify our terminology. Many scholars have argued that there is a substratum of common ideas, practices, customs, beliefs, and ritual and festive activities that shapes religious consciousness in Japan. This substratum has been termed "folk religion"[66] (in Japanese either *minkan shinkō* or *minzoku shūkyō*).[67] There are problems, however, in attempting to use "folk religion" as a suitable term to describe this common religious stratum. Folk religion as a category still implies the divisions mentioned earlier, between the elite and the ordinary people, divisions that are not real but imagined. The problem with the definitional term "folk religion" is that it implies a folk/elite division and implicitly denies doctrine, text, and scriptural tradition. The criticisms that Duffy levels against Thomas's work on religion and magic can just as well be applied to Japanese studies of folk religion: text and sutra are barely mentioned and little attention is given to the role of liturgy in shaping the religious worldview of the people.[68] The term implies, as does "popular religion," that the "folk," the ordinary people, did not know what was contained in elite traditions and scriptures and that their religious actions and beliefs were thus conditioned solely by (for want of a better word) superstitions. There is perhaps an implicit association between the words "folk" and "ignorance" that is too close for comfort. The term "folk religion," in our view, is too problematic for what we are describing.

There are similar difficulties with "primal religion," a term recently used by Michael Pye to denote what he terms the "wide, general pattern of religious activity with which all Japanese are more or less familiar."[69] Although the purpose is clear and important—to illustrate common religious characteristics that, Pye argues,[70] have been the matrix of all postwar religious activity in Japan—and although Pye rightly notes that this religion is life-affirming, the nomenclature and indeed the scope of Pye's "primal religion" are problematic. The term "primal," indicating the primitive, is fraught with pejorative meanings. In anthropological studies of religion it is closely associated with preliterate societies and notions of mystical awareness as they have existed in such societies.[71] It is questionable whether concepts, rituals, and practices added to Japanese religion by Buddhism among other faiths could be seen, in strict anthropological terms, as "primal." The focus on activity mentioned by Pye suggests a similar problem to that criticized by Duffy: the problem of overlooking the role of liturgies and so-called elite religious influences.

To avoid the problems raised by such words as "popular religion," Duffy has suggested a replacement: "traditional religion," a term that "does more justice to the shared and inherited character of the religious beliefs and practices of the people" than the term "popular religion."[72] By "traditional" he does not mean unchanging or static: he is quite aware of the ways in which new saints, devotions, and practices emerged and replaced older ones in medieval religion. Medieval religion as he portrays it is dynamic and vibrant—perhaps more so than his espousal of the term "traditional religion" might suggest. Duffy, however, is also aware that underlying this process of change and the replacement of old with new practices was a religious culture that had certain general characteristics "rooted in a repertoire of inherited and shared beliefs and symbols, while remaining capable of enormous flexibility and variety."[73]

In terms of its notions of shared beliefs and symbols subject to manipulation and change, Duffy's concept of traditional religion is, despite his contention to the contrary, too close to notions of stasis. As such it fails to convey the flavor of dynamism that he otherwise portrays. In the Japanese context the word "traditional" is perhaps more problematic still, associated as it is with the status and support structures of the "traditional" established religions (*kisei shūkyō*). This is especially true given that the primary focus of the academic study of religion in the modern age has been on the new religions; thus the term and concept of "traditional religion" have acquired negative values and images of stagnation and the like.[74] Moreover, the extent to which the image of the "traditional" has been used in contemporary cultural polemics and in advertising contexts in Japan—where so much emphasis is placed, in public rhetoric, on the image of tradition as a counterbalance to modernity—imparts a static nuance to the term "traditional." It also suggests a cultural, ideological, and even ethnic orientation that is perhaps inappropriate here. In Japanese cultural polemics, as in advertising imagery, although "tradition" implies a sense of identity and belonging, it also signifies the unchanging and that which has been lost to modernity. It is redolent with a sense of nostalgia and speaks of the past rather than of the present, of the untouched and the pristine, of stasis rather than the dynamism that, as Duffy recognizes, is at the heart of the religious world he portrays.[75] Thus, because of the images it evokes in Japanese contexts, it would be wrong to utilize the term "traditional."

We recognize that any term used in this context to describe a shared and common set of religious ideas, values, practices, beliefs, and behavior is bound to provoke objections: it is easier, certainly, to show why terms are inappropriate than it is to agree on whether a term is useful. Nevertheless, we must use terms if we are to define the frameworks within which we are operating. Two words in particular, when linked to the noun "religion," come close to the mark of what we are talking about. These terms are "shared" and "common," as in "shared and common religious stratum." Of the two we consider the term "common religion" to be the most appropriate for our purposes. Although "shared religion" conveys some of the ideas we are talking about, the word "shared" implies possession and ownership and therefore exclusion of those who have no share. Things that are shared are different from things held in common, and what we are talking about are religious ideas and practices upon which no single group, person, or institution can lay any claims of proprietorial rights. Although they may be shared, they are in fact held in common. In the old English legalistic meaning of the term as it related to the common grazing ground and public space, no one held any proprietorial rights: the common was something "belonging to, open to, or affecting the whole community."[76]

In such a sense we propose that "common religion" is the best term to use in this case. We do not mean "common" in the negative sense of being ordinary, hackneyed, or low: "common" is not a term limited to the "low," the "folk," or even the "ordinary" people. By "common" we mean something that belongs to the whole community and can be used by anyone in the community, refined or coarse. It refers to a set of sentiments, behavior, practices, beliefs, customs, and the like that is shared by the vast number of people and is common to all classes and groups in society, including the elites (aristocratic, economic, religious) and ordinary people. While recognizing that any term used to label something has its drawbacks, we think it conveys the general meanings considered in this volume.

"Common religion" involves the customs, beliefs, and practices that are broadly accepted within a culture—including the scriptural influences and liturgical traditions, as well as the artistic and iconographic ones, that have shaped these customs, beliefs, and practices. In utilizing the term "common religion" and affirming that it includes popular customs and beliefs and scriptural influences and traditions, we are not asserting the preeminence of the "little" tradition (of customs and local beliefs) over the "great" tradition (of organized, historical, and textually based doctrinal systems). It is not a case of one triumphing over the other, but an interaction between different religious strands, some of which are frequently attributed to the "great" tradition of historical religions and others to the "little" tradition of folk religion.

In the Japanese case, this common religion involves common acceptance of various spiritual entities, such as gods (*kami*) and buddhas, as well as ancestral spirits and spirits of powerful humans who have become deities after death. It also includes the idea that such spirits can confer protection and success on the living and that petitioning for such benefits is a fundamental and highly ethical religious value. It also incorporates the various teachings expressed in the major scriptural traditions that have shaped Japanese religious history—notably Buddhism, its textual traditions, and the doctrinal formulations they have imparted but also Shinto and the mythic structures and ideas it has propagated. It comprises also the liturgical systems and ritual practices that have in many cases been formulated at the elite level of the temples and shrines by the ordained priesthoods but have themselves played a major role in producing the patterns of worship and practice expressed among ordinary and not-so-ordinary people.

To take but one example: people petitioning the buddhas for grace and favors frequently use Buddhist scriptures and liturgies in this process. Common Buddhist texts such as the *Hannya shingyō,* the shorter *Heart Sutra,* themselves pregnant with doctrinal meaning, are chanted as part of the ritual of supplication and may be used as ritual devices designed to bring about the intercession of the buddhas thereby petitioned. Mantras and other such liturgical devices may also be intoned to gain the attention and powerful support of the buddhas invoked. It may be argued that the ordinary people who do these things do not realize the textual complexities and subtleties of a sutra such as the *Hannya shingyō*—that what they chant are "mere" ritual formulas, just sounds without meaning. We take note, however, of two things here. First, there is no guarantee that the so-called elite religious specialists are much different: Buddhist priests are more likely to be trained as ritual specialists capable of carrying out ritual performances and services than they are to be trained in the intellectual analysis of scriptures. This is hardly surprising. After all, it is the ritual efficacy of the text that is important in creating the correct environment in which efficacious religious results may occur.

Second, one should not assume that just because sutras are intoned as ritual formulas the people reciting them do not comprehend their meaning. There are many configurations within the *Hannya shingyō* whose meanings are well known to many of those who chant them, such as the famous sequence *shikizokuzekū, kūzokuzeshiki* (form is no other than emptiness, emptiness no other than form).[77] Moreover, there are plentiful opportunities for people to gain knowledge of the sutras they chant as ritual invocations and to understand why these sutras are both doctrinal propositions and ritual tools. Countless volumes, including *manga* (cartoon) books, are produced in Japan to explain the sutras (and indeed virtually every aspect of religion) at a variety of levels from the highly intellectual to the simple. Such popular explanatory books—and the *Hannya shingyō* is one of the most popular texts in this genre—often sell in large numbers.[78] Priests lecture on scriptures such as the *Hannya shingyō* (or sections of it) regularly: one of us, for example, has heard a number of explanations of different parts of this text during priests' sermons at pilgrimage temples in Shikoku. It would perhaps be more appropriate to suggest that, rather than not knowing the content of the text they are chanting, most Japanese who know it as a ritual formula are aware of some of its inner content and meaning and know that its efficacy as a spell is related to its meaning as a text. In other words, the apparent division between the textual religion of priests and the practical religion of people is true in such a limited sense that it borders on being false: the two rest on common ground and complement each other.

At the heart of this common religion is the practice of seeking this-worldly benefits. This common religion provides an open-access, total-care system for its members. This statement requires three stages of definition. By "its members" we mean Japanese people in general without, however, excluding foreigners. While there are some Japanese who do not join in any of the numerous practices, from calendrical rituals to individual prayers and petitions, and who either eschew religious behavior entirely or belong to exclusivist religious groups,[79] most Japanese do participate in a variety of religious practices—ranging from the customary first shrine visit of the year (*hatsumōde*), to festivals, to touristic visits to temples and shrines as part of their leisure activities—in which prayers for benefits are made.

The term "open access" relates to this broad conceptualization of the common religion's accessibility to virtually all Japanese. By this term we refer to the fact that there is a fluidity to religious practice in Japan in which no prior commitment or affiliation is required: anyone who wishes to seek the aid of a deity for any purpose may go to a shrine or temple to make a supplication without ever having had a previous commitment to that place. Furthermore, the system is "open access" in that the level at which the supplicant relates to it is determined by his or her own needs and inclinations. As we shall see in Chapter 5, for example, practitioners determine at what level they wish to interact with the deity or buddha being petitioned.

The meanings surrounding the term "total-care system" have to do with the provision for every individual need and requirement in spiritual and material terms throughout one's life, from birth to death and even the afterlife. The baby who is blessed and placed under the protection of the local gods may grow into a child needing help at examination times throughout his or her academic career; into an adult seeking a good spouse, suitable job, and healthy children; and into a senior citizen wanting, perhaps, to beseech one of the Buddhist figures of worship, such as Kannon, for help in avoiding senility and getting a swift, painless, and merciful death. Besides such life-cycle activities, there are also calendrical festivals and ritual occasions that provide scope and structure for petitions and prayers, as well as facilities for individuals to visit and petition deities in relation to their needs at the time. It is a program that covers one from cradle to grave.

Although the term "system" might appear to imply a formalized structure with a single framework, this is not the case here. The "system" is not so much constructed by a hierarchy or set of officials who determine its parameters unilaterally; it is determined by each of its participants on a personal basis conditioned by place of residence and local custom. By "system" we are referring to a vast array of places and practices that offer the individual as well as the community avenues for dealing with their every need, concern, worry, and aspiration, as well as the underlying principles, ethics, and dynamics inherent within the pursuit of practical benefits. By calling it a "system" we also indicate that although it is broad, flexible, and innovative, the common religion of this-worldly benefits is not amorphous and ill-defined but takes shape in distinct and fascinating ways that make it possible, fortunately for us, to describe it with precision.

Overview of the Book

Since these points are developed in greater detail in subsequent chapters, we leave them now and turn to a brief overview of the shape and structure of this book. Chapter 1 provides a general description of the types, scope, and nature of benefits that are commonly sought, along with an outline of the ritual settings in which these are expressed, including various rites connected to the calendar, community, and individual life cycle. We show also that sacred places such as shrines and temples have their own specialties and traditions, forming a geography of benefits that provides a localized framework for this common religion and conveys a sense of local identity and belonging. Chapter 2 examines some of the scriptures from the Buddhist and other religious traditions to demonstrate that, not only is *genze riyaku* legitimated and affirmed by such sources of "high religion," but it is repeatedly emphasized as a vital religious value, not just as an expedient device or skillful means or a compromise with folk or popular practices.

Nor, indeed, can the pursuit of benefits be considered the simple manifestation of a materialism that is contrary to the genuine nature of religion. Michiko's success was not achieved without some effort on her part: As we shall see in Chapter 3, rarely are benefits merely portioned out. Supplicants, even those who simply buy an amulet for good luck at a shrine or temple, have to *do* something, to take part in a practice. There is a basically ethical nature to the practice and an affirmation, too, that the fulfillment of desires is not a matter deserving condemnation. The stories, tales, and histories told to promote the efficacy of specific religious centers, statues, deities, and saints contain an intrinsically moral dimension that asserts correct and incorrect modes of behavior and, frequently, demonstrates the negative side of benefits lost or punishments suffered through failing to pursue the correct patterns of behavior. At this point it becomes apparent that the Weberian assessment of the relationship between ethical and magical aspects of religion—which suggests that as ethical considerations increase within a religious culture its magical orientations diminish—is inaccurate. Rather, magical and ethical means work together to form one whole, which illustrates the morality implicit in magical performance. Morality and magic, furthermore, join forces in this common religion to control the anarchy of their common foe called chance or luck. It is not surprising that we should find the ubiquity of charms and talismans for good luck. On one level these objects can be seen as superficial, but they represent at the same time an attempt to address a moral problem that may not be as serious as that of evil but is bedeviling nonetheless: happenings beyond our control.

The magic and morality that make gods, saints, temples, shrines, and participants work together in what might be called a system are effectively explained by the language of commerce. Indeed, the term for "profit" in Japanese (*rieki*) is written with the same characters as "benefits" (*riyaku* is the Buddhist pronunciation), so the overlap of meaning can hardly be disregarded. The transactional nature of Japanese religious behavior is evident in the system of benefits and lends itself to explanation by exchange theories. In his modified version of exchange theory, Winston Davis notes that while conventional exchange theory explains transactions in the context of cultural values, it does not pay enough attention to obligatory expectations such as duty, devotion, and loyalty to family and social institutions. Building on the work of Albert Schutz, Davis devises his own paradigm for transactions in two parts: motivated action—giving or doing something "in order to" solicit a response—and obligated activity arising "because of" the need to return the favor of things received.[80] Although Davis explains the practice of seeking material benefits in terms of motivated action in order to get something, this part of his paradigm, in our view, does not adequately account for obligatory behavior and—since obligation is only one kind of moral action—for morality in general in the context of seeking benefits. In Chapter 3 we propose that goods and benefits are not so much exchanged as they are bought. The model of commercial transactions, or what might be called purchase theory, accounts for a dynamic of paying and receiving that includes the crucial function of morality that is lacking in exchange theory and Davis's "in order to" paradigm. In making a purchase, the buyer pays a material and a moral price to try to ensure that the good things in life can be guaranteed, and the bad kept at a distance, rather than being left to chance.

The pursuit of practical benefits by contracting with the gods to eliminate chance is an ambitious undertaking filled with imaginative, sometimes complex, details. In Chapter 4 we explore the providers of practical benefits—the vast host of gods and deities, buddhas, bodhisattvas, saints,[81] and other spiritual figures, each with their own specialties, powers, rituals, and requirements. No distinction is made between Buddhist and Shinto deities, all of whom can be petitioned by anyone regardless of religious, social, or sectarian identification. This phenomenon, however, is not explained by the much-discussed notion that Buddhism and Shinto have converged to produce a syncretism in Japan, since it is difficult to see the vaunted assimilation of the gods and the buddhas in shrines that are decidedly for *kami* and temples that are mostly reserved for buddhas and bodhisattvas. The Buddhist and Shinto religions, while they count each other as close friends, are still largely segregated and normally allow only their own deities on their main altars. To account for the convergence of the *kami* and the buddhas we need a larger rubric that encompasses them both. And that greater category, we propose, is the conceptual and ritual framework of this-worldly benefits that holds them—and them it—in common. Saints and founders are called upon in this process, as well, especially since they are immediately accessible in human terms of respect and intimacy. In Chapter 4 we shall look in some detail at Kōbō Daishi, the Buddhist holy figure and founder of the Shingon Buddhist sect who is in certain ways the paragon of benefactors.

In Chapter 5 we turn our attention to practice and the ways in which people petition for benefits. Besides considering the forms such actions take, we look at some of the locations where they occur. Like real people, real places are important in a system that leaves little to pure abstraction, even in its symbols and metaphors, all of which feeds effort and performance. As has been widely recognized, action and ritual are intrinsic to Asian religion in general and to Japanese religion in particular. The pursuit of benefits is a basic religious activity expressed through the performance of rituals and actions most often, though not exclusively, in the formal religious settings of shrines and temples. Sometimes the pursuit of benefits may be closely associated with ludic activities (such as visiting religious places at holiday times or attending festivals), and in Chapter 5 we draw attention to the close relationship between entertainment and religious practice.

The culture of practical benefits, both in its means and its ends, is decidedly material. A wide array of objects is used, some bizarre, others mundane. Amulets, talismans, bumper stickers, trinkets, food, and more are part of the currency used to purchase benefits. Amulets alone can be found as pieces of paper, carvings, brocade, bells, pencils, dried reeds, porcelain, and a wide variety of other materials and forms. Although we introduce the subject of amulets and suchlike in Chapter 5, in Chapter 6 we expand on this theme by looking at how these objects are marketed and how new forms of amulets relating to changing needs may be developed. In this chapter we examine the whole process of selling benefits and its interrelated theme of promoting temples and shrines and, indeed, spreading religious teachings. As has been widely noted, the practical benefits and miraculous deeds provided by the spiritual powers enshrined at temples and shrines, according to legend and repute, caused these places to become popular, to attract clienteles, and to become centers of faith.[82] Thus we look at the role of practical benefits in the development of religious institutions. How have temples and shrines promoted practical benefits, and how have they sought to create faith and, simultaneously, to thereby ensure their own survival and stimulate their economic development? We also look at how, in so doing, religious centers have adapted to the times. Finding a need and filling it is good advice for temples and shrines as well as entrepreneurs, and resourceful priests have often repackaged old benefits (fertility, for instance) and related them to new concerns (such as sexually transmitted diseases, especially AIDS). And if the need does not exist, it can be manufactured. We also consider how much of what is sold can be seen to be responding to social needs, and how much can be seen as creating uncertainty, a process that some Japanese scholars call *fuan sangyō*, the manufacturing of anxiety.[83] In discussing the trading of benefits—the buying and the selling—we also consider how people experience benefits and how, through making claims about the efficacy of the benefits they can provide, religious institutions and movements are effectively making truth claims that mark them out from their rivals.

In Chapter 7 we develop this focus on the selling of religion by examining a popular genre of literature that provides immense amounts of information on, and insights into, the dynamics of *genze riyaku* as well as the stories, legends, and places associated with it. This chapter looks at the various guidebooks that furnish information on shrines and temples that have developed reputations for providing *genze riyaku*. In essence, the chapter presents a mini-guide to some of the many temples and shrines in Japan that deal with this topic, while introducing some of the fascinating amulets and talismans that demonstrate the underlying humor and themes of entertainment that pervade the topic. In Chapters 6 and 7 we also examine the question of reputation—how certain places have acquired reputations for particular benefits, how these places and benefits are described in guidebooks and the like, and how, indeed, a whole genre of religious

literature has developed to inform people about the different benefits and the religious institutions that can be visited for such purposes.

The pursuit of benefits, we contend, is intrinsic to Japanese religion and constitutes a core theme of all the religious customs, traditions, and doctrines (whether Shinto, Buddhist, folk religion, or new
religion) that are active—visible and invisible. That benefits are so
central to Japanese religion informs us that the primary aims of religion in Japan are focused (not surprisingly) on the pursuit of a happy
and positive life in which ultimate meaning is to be found in this
world. Although the new religions have emphasized this point more
clearly than have the formal teachings of Buddhism, we demonstrate
that the practices of Buddhism place an equal emphasis upon the
good things in this world. In Chapter 8, "Conclusions," we discuss
these points more fully and show how closely religious success in
Japan is related to the question of *genze riyaku*. The chapter returns us
to our starting point by affirming that there is a core set of values, a
common religion centered on worldly benefits, and a this-worldly
affirmative stance that is central to the worldview of Japanese religion.
This, indeed, is the *form* of religion that visitors to Japan are most
likely to see, not just through festivals and other famed rituals, but
through their visits to shrines and temples. Temples such as Asakusa
Kannon and shrines such as Meiji Shrine in Tokyo receive large numbers of tourists for whom the visible surface of Japanese religion displays amulets, votive tablets, and prayers and practices that are focused on the pursuit of worldly benefits. Thus far, however, this topic
has been given far less attention in academic studies than it de-
serves.[84] The aim of this volume is to bring the topic center stage in
the study of Japanese religion and give it the prominence it merits.

1

Benefits in the Religious System
Settings and Dynamics

Hōzanji is a Buddhist temple situated on the upper slopes of the Ikoma Hills that separate the city of Osaka from the plains around the ancient Japanese capital of Nara. It is famed as a center of worship of Kankiten, a deity of Hindu origins and one of those many figures of worship that have been assimilated into Buddhism through its encounters with other religious traditions. Depictions of practices associated with the deity and aimed at preventing misfortunes and acquiring the support of Kankiten through ritual worship can be found in a number of Buddhist texts, such as the *Daishō-ten Kangi-shōshin binayaka hō,* which, as Alexander Kabanoff notes, describes ritual procedures to be followed in order to "expel all disasters."[1] Kabanoff, in providing details of other textual references to Kankiten, shows how this deity came to be transmitted from India to China (and hence to Japan) as a deity of the Esoteric Tantric tradition. He notes, moreover, that the Chinese found Tantrism attractive "not for its philosophic doctrines," but rather for practical aspects such as the promise of worldly benefits. Kabanoff's list of such worldly benefits includes defeating enemies, becoming wealthy, attaining longevity, dispelling diseases, securing high positions, and winning someone's love.[2] Although the veneration of Kankiten flourished in Japanese Esoteric Buddhism (*mikkyō*) from around the ninth century, Kabanoff notes that Kankiten was regarded with a certain ambiguity. The deity contained potentially dark sides as a ferocious and demanding deity associated inter alia with angry spirits and capable of divine wrath. Kankiten thus required special veneration and offerings, as well as pledges of faith and commitment, in order to harness its powers for the benefit of the petitioner.[3]

Kankiten is known by a variety of other names as well. The most common is Shōten,[4] and it is this name, linked to the temple's geographical location, that gives Hōzanji the name by which it is popularly known: Ikoma Shōten. Hōzanji developed as a center of Kankiten worship from the seventeenth century onward: its founder, the monk Hōzan Tankai, was a worshiper of the deity and hence enshrined Kankiten at the temple he founded. Kankiten is not, however, the *honzon,* or main image of worship, enshrined at the temple. (The official *honzon* at Hōzanji is Fudō.)[5] And, like Japanese temples and shrines in general, Hōzanji is not a location with a single focus of worship or indeed a single purpose in the benefits it provides. Rather, it consists of a number of halls of worship and figures of worship that are scattered through its precincts and enshrine various buddhas and other deities. Besides Kankiten the temple enshrines Monju (the Buddha of Wisdom), Kannon (the bodhisattva of compassion), Jizō (the protective bodhisattva), and many others, and its courtyard contains numerous subtemples housing these and other figures of worship.

Hōzanji features prominently in an extended series of studies of the religious culture of the Ikoma Hills carried out by a group of Japanese sociologists of religion during the 1980s and early 1990s.[6] Iida Takafumi, one of the participants in that research project, has described the Ikoma Hills as a "marketplace for this-worldly benefits" (*genze riyaku ichiba*) and Hōzanji specifically as a "mecca for faith in this-worldly benefits" (*genze riyaku shinkō no mekka*).[7] Hōzanji is but one, however, of the vast number of shrines and temples of all sizes that are scattered throughout the Ikoma Hills and cater to the needs of the people of Osaka and the surrounding region. These include most notably Ishikiri Shrine, whose deities of worship are famed for healing and assisting in recovery from surgery, and Chōgosonshiji, better known as Shigisan, whose main figure of worship, Bishamonten, is one of the Seven Gods of Good Fortune (*shichifukujin*), a popular group of deities who are commonly depicted as riding together across the seas in a treasure boat (*takarabune*) with treasures and benefits they will distribute to those who seek them. The benefits Bishamonten offers at Shigisan are diverse, but he is especially active and efficacious, according to the temple's literature, for business prosperity, family safety, and the development of good luck.[8] The reputation of these three places in terms of providing this-worldly benefits is such that each receives several million visitors per year: in all it has been estimated that around 10 million people visit the shrines and temples of Ikoma each year, the majority visiting the three major centers of Hōzanji, Ishikiri, and Shigisan.[9] All three have developed networks of religious associations and groups of worshipers centered on faith in the efficacy of these places in terms of this-worldly benefits. Besides these major institutions, the Ikoma Hills are home to hundreds of other shrines and temples of varying sizes that also attract visitors and adherents.

Hōzanji is well known in the region for, among other benefits, those of *shōbai hanjō* (business prosperity) and *tachimono* (giving up something or abstaining from something that is not good for one).[10] Kankiten is, as noted, a potent deity but one that needs to be properly appeased. In seeking Kankiten's assistance one is not just harnessing the deity's powers of moral support in the struggle for abstention but opening oneself to its wrath if, after pledging abstinence and asking for its help, one reneges on this commitment.[11] Hōzanji's *ema* (votive tablets) symbolize this benefit and the commitment it involves: they depict a padlock and are inscribed with the Japanese ideogram "*kokoro*" (spirit/mind) to signify mental determination and the locking of the mind against temptation. On these tablets people write their wishes and pleas before hanging them up at the temple; among the petitions, vows, and requests that have been noted by observers of the Hōzanji votive tablets are those for giving up alcohol, stopping illicit relations with a member of the opposite sex, giving up tobacco, and, reflecting the ways in which prayers and petitions manifest changing social situations and patterns, giving up drugs.[12]

According to temple lore, Shōten (Kankiten) will respond to requests that have failed to be realized through petitions at other shrines and temples:[13] in short, this is a deity that is powerful and responsive especially to those in great need. The power of Kankiten to grant wishes and benefits is affirmed by the temple's numerous publications outlining cases of miraculous events experienced by petitioners and worshipers, whose passing on of such stories and rumors of benefits has played a large part in the development of the temple's reputation.[14] Such indeed is the gratitude of successful petitioners that grateful worshipers often donate large sums of money to the temple. According to Murata Jūhachi, it is not uncommon for believers to give as much as 1 or 2 million yen when their prayers have been realized.[15]

Hōzanji is a thriving temple, and its steady flow of clients support a number of commercial enterprises that constitute its *monzenmachi,* "the town before the temple gate," which refers to commercial settlements that have grown around shrines and temples. On the steep steps leading up to it from the nearest local train station there are a number of inns as well as shops and food stalls. The numbers of customers also help support a cable car railway that runs close by, and although it also leads to the summit of the Ikoma Hills and a large funfair there, many of its passengers are headed for the temple. On

Sundays, when most people do not have to work, the temple receives large numbers of visitors who, seeking benefits from Kankiten, perform various practices ranging from simple acts of veneration—lighting a stick of incense, making a small offering of a few coins, purchasing a talisman or amulet, praying briefly—to ritual austerities designed to facilitate this transaction, such as the *hyakudo mairi*. This practice, meaning "one hundred times around," involves walking around a designated area, usually two stone markers set within a shrine or temple courtyard, one hundred times to demonstrate one's sincerity to a deity when making a request. At Hōzanji the *hyakudo mairi* is generally performed around one of the halls of worship within the courtyard and is often done barefoot.[16]

Figures given by the temple and by Japanese scholars estimate that it receives around 3 million visitors per year.[17] While this figure may well be somewhat speculative—given that people may access the temple from a number of different entrances and there is no check at any of them to assess the flow of visitors—it nonetheless indicates a general feeling by those who have studied the temple and those who work there that Hōzanji receives a fairly large number of visitors.[18] The figures themselves imply that an average of 57,000 visitors go to Hōzanji every week. In reality the flow of visitors is a little more uneven, for there are a number of festive occasions that draw extremely large crowds, while the normal weekly traffic is rather less, although still, certainly on Sundays, busy. Hōzanji draws its biggest crowds on special occasions in the temple's ritual calendar: like most shrines and temples Hōzanji has a series of yearly events and rituals (*nenjū gyōji*) that punctuate the yearly cycle, provide the basic framework for the temple's general activities, and demarcate its holy days and main religious observances.

At Hōzanji, for example, the first and sixteenth days of each month are regarded as particularly efficacious days for praying there. These days are *ennichi,* a term with multiple but related meanings. Each deity and figure of worship has (like saints in the Catholic tradition) its own special holy day or days that are pregnant with religious meaning, days on which the deity is especially accessible to petitions and prayers and when visits to its centers of worship are considered to have greatest merit. An *ennichi* is thus the holy day of a deity, the day (*nichi*) when the opportunity to develop karmic fortunes, affinities, and connections (*en*) with the deity is at its highest. Because it is a special day in this respect, it may also be a festival day (another related meaning of *ennichi*) or a day when a fair or market (also an *ennichi*) may be held at the shrine or temple. The multiple meanings of *ennichi*—encompassing issues of increased sanctity, enhanced karmic connections, the significance of certain phases in the calendrical cycle as special religious occasions, and the importance of festivity, commerce, and economic activity—are by no means random. Indeed, as we shall see throughout this book, all these themes are intertwined and form a whole, in which there is little contradiction between the economic and the spiritual. The economic dimensions of temple and shrine activity, signified by the *ennichi* as a commercial market, do not conflict with the notion that such days are specially holy days when the deity may be especially responsive to petitioners. Rather, they reinforce each other: the economic lure of the market that draws people to the place can increase the numbers who will, in the course of their visit, pray to the deity; the attraction of a special receptiveness to petitions on that day will not only bring increased numbers to the religious center but boost the size of the crowds at the market and increase its economic potential. Religious events such as *ennichi*, occasions of festivity, prayer, and veneration, are equally occasions for economic barter and activity and an opportunity for the religious institutions themselves to acquire and increase the economic support they need to function.

The interplay of festivity, economic activity, sanctity, prayer, and worship permeates Hōzanji's yearly calender. Besides its two monthly *ennichi* the temple has a number of other special religious festivals: the *setsubun* festival in early February in which rituals are enacted to drive away evil and beckon the coming of spring and warm weather; a grand *goma* (Esoteric Buddhist fire ritual) on April 1; the celebration of the Buddha's birthday on May 8; and several other events throughout the year.[19] But the occasion when the greatest crowds visit the temple are the first three days of the year—the occasion of the *hatsumōde* or first shrine or temple visit of the year. This event is part of a wider cycle of social and religious rituals covering the ending of the old year and the beginning of the new year, rituals full of the symbolism of eradicating the misfortunes and hindrances of the past and ushering in renewal.[20] At New Year it is customary to pay a visit (or indeed a series of visits, since many people visit not one but many places at this time) to a shrine or temple to make a first greeting of the year to the gods and buddhas. In the process of greeting the gods, it is the general practice to make wishes and ask favors for the coming year and acquire various talismans, amulets, and other lucky objects that are taken home as signs of the spiritual benevolence and protection of the gods or buddhas.

The number of people who perform *hatsumōde* visits has grown steadily in Japan in the 1980s and 1990s. According to the figures released each year by the Japanese police, the numbers of those who have taken part in this practice have exceeded 80 million (approximately two-thirds of the entire population) each year.[21] Participation can be affected slightly by the weather: in 1989, for example, a small decline in numbers from the previous year was blamed on inclement weather, while the rise in numbers between 1992 and 1993 was partly attributed to good weather. But the economic climate is also considered to influence the turnout. The economic troubles of the 1990s are seen as closely linked to the increase in the numbers of participants in *hatsumōde*. According to interpretations widely circulated in the media, the uncertainties caused by Japan's economic crisis—and people's need to "turn to the gods" for reassurance and seek increased help, support, and benefits as a result of that crisis—account for this growth.[22] The 1994 figures (coming at a time when the economic recession had already gone on longer than many had expected it to) showed the largest number ever of people performing this rite: 85,440,000, over half a million higher than the year before.[23]

Every year newspapers publish a list of the most visited religious centers. The list is usually topped by major shrines and temples such as Meiji Shrine in Tokyo (which in 1993 received 3.5 million *hatsumōde* visitors); Kawasaki Daishi, a temple in Kawasaki, southwest of Tokyo; and Shinshōji, at Narita, a temple popularly known as Naritasan and famed as a place to obtain traffic safety amulets and to have one's car blessed and placed under divine protection. In the Kansai (western Japan) region, the most widely visited centers tend to be Fushimi Inari (widely regarded as the country's most important shrine to the deity Inari) in southern Kyoto and Sumiyoshi Shrine in Osaka. Such religious centers are certainly national in that they attract visitors from across Japan and are usually featured on national television each New Year to show the size of the crowds taking part in this annual ritual.

Hōzanji, although it is one of the most important temples dedicated to Kankiten in Japan, is not as widely known as the places just cited. Unlike the famed temples and shrines of Kyoto, it is not regarded as a tourist attraction or a special example of Japanese cultural or artistic achievement and hence worthy of a visit to admire its architectural splendor or cultural treasures. Moreover, it never makes it to the "Top Ten" list of the most visited shrincs and temples published by the newspapers at *hatsumōde*. Nonetheless, it receives around half a million visitors on average during the first three days of the year, approximately one-sixth of its annual visitors.[24] Along with businesspeople and merchants who are attracted by Kankiten's reputation as a source of benefits related to business prosperity, the temple is especially popular with those who work in Osaka's "water trade" (*mizu shōbai*), the vast nightlife industry in Japan centered around drinking, bars, nightclubs, and sexual entertainment: praying at Ikoma for Kankiten's protection and support is seen as a rite of passage necessary for those wishing to enter this business.[25]

Hōzanji is not what is commonly termed in Japan a *bodaiji*—that is, a Buddhist temple with a parish that includes a number of households (*danka*) affiliated with it and for whom the temple conducts ritual services relating largely to ancestor and mortuary rites. This *danka* relationship, and the fees from the temple's services in these contexts, form the primary economic underpinning for the large majority of Buddhist temples in Japan. Hōzanji has no *danka* and hence it occupies no fixed place in the social structure of community religion. Economically it depends on attracting visitors who will make donations, purchase amulets, pay for their prayers and petitions to be offered to Kankiten, and so on. This dependence (which is not limited to Hōzanji but affects any temple in Japan that has no affiliated parishioners or households) is a motivating factor in the development and promotion of *genze riyaku* activities at Hōzanji and elsewhere.

The importance of this point, in the present context, is that Hōzanji receives visitors not because of its formal position in Japanese social structure but because of voluntary associations related to seasonal events, occupational factors, personal needs, and even through casual circumstances—accompanying a friend or family member who wishes to make a petition, for example, or while visiting other places in the area. As noted earlier, there is a large funfair nearby, a little further up the hillside, and people may visit both places during the course of a day out. Although Hōzanji has a sectarian affiliation (it is in fact a *daihonzan,* or head temple, of the Shingon Risshū Buddhist sect) its visitors, like those of other popular institutions dealing with *genze riyaku,* are not limited to that sect alone. Shingon Risshū has 105,000 affiliated members, according to 1994 figures,[26] considerably less than the number of people who visit Hōzanji at New Year. This nonsectarian nature of shrine and temple visiting and praying for this-worldly benefits indicates Hōzanji's accessibility as a center of the common religion.

We shall encounter Hōzanji again in a number of chapters. Here we have focused on it to emphasize a series of vital points. Hōzanji tells us of a religion that, as noted in the Introduction, is *practiced*—a religion that is pragmatic and related to daily real-life concerns, to occupational and locational identities (attracting as it does people from the Osaka water trade), and to seasonal and temporal changes. The pragmatic nature of religion is demonstrated through Hōzanji's primary claims to fame and its predominant functions. The temple deals with the pertinent needs and worries that concern people in all walks of life, handling all manner of issues from business prosperity to painful addictions. This pragmatism relates to the ways in which people may visit the temple, as well, and to the flexible nature of religious veneration in Japan: while some visitors may be driven by urgent personal crises, such as addiction to drugs or alcohol, others may be far more casual, dropping in on their way to the funfair or during a hike in the surrounding hills. There is, for example, a pleasant hike that can be made from Ishikiri Shrine across the hills to Hōzanji (or vice versa). Temple officiants do not discriminate among the different types of visitor: all may be accommodated, none is left out. And in operating as a protective temple related to a particular industry, Hōzanji tells us also of the extent to which occupation and social circumstance may exert a religious influence on people and, indeed, frame their religious culture and activities.

In praying and asking for favors, however, people incur moral obligations and become involved in a series of ethical considerations relating to what they should do to thank Kankiten and the duties they take on when making requests. Given the demanding nature of its deity, Hōzanji informs us of the moral obligations incurred by petitioners and the ethical dimension of their activities. Praying for benefits implies an obligation to express gratitude for the rewards that come from prayer. While this obligation need not involve the large financial donations mentioned earlier, it does necessitate returning the favors granted by expressing gratitude—themes we discuss more fully in Chapter 3, where we encounter stories of what may happen when these procedures are not correctly followed and the debts of obligation incurred through prayer and supplication are not fulfilled. Hōzanji's dependence on the provision of this-worldly benefits to sustain itself economically informs us also of the necessity for temples and shrines to publicize such issues in order to gain and maintain customers. Hence the importance of publicizing cases where benefits have been acquired and affirming the truth claims (the miracles and efficacious provisions of benefits) that these imply.

From Hōzanji we can also discern something of the extent of prayers for this-worldly benefits and the extent of such pragmatic religious activity in Japan in general. Hōzanji, as pointed out earlier, is a flourishing temple specializing in this-worldly benefits: it receives large numbers of petitioners not just at special occasions such as *hatsumōde* but throughout the year. Yet it is only one of a number of religious centers in the Kansai region around Osaka and Kyoto and is by no means the most famous of them. It is only one of many centers catering to various forms of this-worldly benefits even within the Ikoma region. Nonetheless it can still count its visitors in the millions. Although the extent of praying for practical benefits is infinitely difficult to discern in statistical terms, the indicators suggest it is extremely widespread. The *hatsumōde* figures alone would suggest so, and while one cannot—given its special nature as a social and cultural occasion—claim that this particular occasion is *representative* of Japanese religious practice, it does show the popularity of seasonal and calendrical occasions with religious themes. High levels of participation in religious occasions and events are a recognized characteristic of Japanese religion in general, as is its concern with seeking this-worldly benefits.[27] The extent of this practice is indicated in various major surveys of religious attitudes such as those carried out by the Japanese Broadcasting Network (NHK). The responses to the 1983 NHK survey, to cite but one example, show a high level of activity related to the acquisition and use of amulets and talismans, objects that are closely associated with the pursuit of practical benefits: the numbers using such charms either often or sometimes were around 75 percent of all respondents, with a high point of 80 percent for those in their twenties and thirties.[28] The extent of such prayers may be more discernible when one looks at specific needs, occupations, and situations. As has often been observed, for example, many students follow the common practice of praying for success before their school or university entrance examinations.

In introducing Hōzanji we are in effect rejecting the notion that religion is irrelevant in Japanese society and culture, an impression suggested by Reischauer and Jansen and gleaned by artificial questions about belief and "true religion." Such an impression falls apart when we look at what happens on a day-to-day basis at such religious centers. Hōzanji tells us of a genuine and *practiced* religious culture, concerned with ordinary needs, deeply embedded in Japanese society.

Comprehensive Responses: Types and Extent of Practical Benefits

The benefits offered at Hōzanji, such as business prosperity and assistance in giving up harmful addictions, are just a sample of the many and varying forms of benefits that may be had at shrines and temples in Japan. Their scope and extent are enormous, relating to every conceivable need, aspiration, and circumstance of individuals and social groups. Nor are they static. New forms and variations may appear at any time in line with changing social and individual needs, the demands of petitioners, and the inventiveness of religious officiants. Here we outline their general scope and extent while indicating how new forms of benefit may emerge.

It is possible to discern two main divisions in the forms of benefits that are proffered at shrines and temples: benefits that relate to protection from external dangers—in other words, benefits acquired through warding off negative forces to avoid bad luck—and benefits that are directly beckoned through actions designed to induce good fortune. In Japanese terms these categories can best be described by two broad and generic labels (which themselves are categories of *riyaku* widely prayed for in their own right): *yakuyoke* (the prevention of danger) and *kaiun* (the opening up of good fortune).

Yakuyoke is preventative. Its mechanics are perhaps best illustrated by referring to one of the most commonly used religious objects connected to this-worldly benefits. *Omamori* are amulets that represent manifestations of a spiritual entity such as a god or buddha: the Japanese verb *"mamoru"* means "to defend, to protect." Although *omamori* may also have beckoning functions to induce good fortune, they are widely used in this preventative sense to guard against misfortune and defend against bad luck. These amulets normally consist of a prayer or some form of religious inscription, invocation, or sacred text placed in a brocade bag or similar container and carried on the person. Sacralized by religious rituals that transform them into *bunshin* (spiritual offshoots) or *kesshin* (manifestations) of the deity, they are physical objects that contain the spiritual essence and powers of a deity or buddha. One of the more common forms of *omamori* is the *migawari omamori*. *Migawari,* meaning "changing or substituting one's body," refers to the notion that a particular buddha, bodhisattva, deity, or other figure of spiritual power can offer itself in place of the person it protects and thus absorb any negative forces that might otherwise afflict the person. A *migawari Jizō omamori,* therefore, is an amulet that represents the bodhisattva Jizō and, by force of religious ritual, has become transformed into the body of Jizō. Such an amulet is worn or carried by the person seeking protection. If the person is threatened by ill fortune, the spiritual force of Jizō is thought to act as a *migawari,* or substitute, absorbing or deflecting any bad luck or negative forces to hand, leaving the person unharmed, and thus opening the way for the enjoyment of good fortune.

Amulets and benefits, however, are not only prophylactic. As noted earlier, they may also be concerned with beckoning good fortune—as typified by the term *"kaiun."* Besides warding off bad luck, one also seeks to attract good luck, to beckon blessings and benefits, often through the use of a variety of lucky objects (*engimono*) that represent the presence of a *kami,* buddha, or some other spiritual entity who, it is believed, will help the possessor attract benefits. Thus the intent of an amulet for success in education (*gōkaku omamori*) is to beckon good fortune for its owner. The most commonly petitioned deity for educational issues in Japan is Tenjin, a Shinto *kami* whose main shrines are the Dazaifu Tenmangū Shrine (at Dazaifu near Fukuoka in Kyushu) and the Kitano Tenmangū Shrine in Kyoto: a Tenjin *gōkaku omamori* would thus be utilizing Tenjin's spiritual powers as a deity of education to bring good fortune to the petitioner. Among the lucky objects commonly used is a set of pencils especially blessed for writing successful exams.

Although it is possible to differentiate benefits into these two primary categories—protecting against misfortune and bringing good fortune—the two overlap and may be found in many diversified forms. To give some insight into this complexity of forms and indicate the scope, extent, and nature of the benefits people seek, we turn now to a popular guidebook to practical benefits. (We focus specifically on guidebooks in Chapter 7, but our intention here is to illustrate this wide variety of benefits and their availability within a given geographical area.) Naitō Masatoshi and Shimokawa Akihito's *Tōkyō no jisha* (The shrines and temples of Tokyo) is basically a guidebook to shrines and temples providing this-worldly benefits in the Tokyo area.[29] Its focus on a particular region is not unique, for many similar guidebooks have a specific geographical focus such as Tokyo, Osaka, or the Kansai. In their table of contents, Naitō and Shimokawa divide the world of benefits into a number of categories within a geographical framework that deals with each ward and section of the Tokyo area in turn. Such is the scope of the book that its table of contents, which merely lists categories of benefits and the temples and shrines covered in the book, takes up twelve pages. The book divides benefits into five broad types: prosperity in daily life (*seikatsu no han'ei*); male/female relations (*danjo kankei*); human life issues connected with childbirth and childrearing (*hito no issei*); the prevention of accidents and misfortune (*sainan yoke*); and recovery or healing from illness (*byōki no kaifuku*). Each of these five major categories is divided more narrowly into specified forms of benefit with entries for the various shrines and temples that can be visited in connection with each of them. In all there are forty-six types of benefits listed under these five main headings (as well as several subdivisions within these types).

Under prosperity in daily life, for example, seven major benefits are categorized: *kin'un* (increasing one's money); *shōbai hanjō* (business prosperity); *shōbu un* (winning); *kaiun* and *shōfuku* (beckoning or opening up of good fortune); *sarariman kankei* (matters of concern to office workers); *gakugyō jōju* and *juken kigan* (educational advancement and success in examinations); and *gigei jōtatsu* (progress in the arts). Several of these have their own subcategories. Under business prosperity, for example, we find not just entries for shrines and temples that cater to this benefit in general but also specific entries that deal with particular occupations and forms of business activity, including noodle shops (*sobaya*), seaweed merchants (*noriya*), pharmacies (*kusuriya*), tofu makers (*tōfuya*), fish sellers (*uoya*), drapers (*orimonoya*), seal makers (*hankoya*), silk dealers (*kingyō*), and jockeys (*kishu*). The occupations given in this section might be described as "traditional" occupations rather than those associated with the modern urban economic environment. Such "newer" occupations associated with the modern business world are, however, dealt with under such headings as *sarariiman kankei*. In the section on winning there are references to shrines and temples where one can pray for success in winning lawsuits, achieving victory at sports, and being successful at gambling.[30] (The latter two wishes are dealt with by the shrine Kanda Myōjin in Chiyoda ward.) One should note here that the system of practical benefits, being pragmatic and situational, is not without its internal contradictions. Kankiten may, as we have seen with the votive tablets at Ikoma Shōten, be prayed to in order to help the petitioner stop addictive vices such as gambling; but elsewhere deities can be found who support one's gambling endeavors and hence act as an encouragement.

Categories such as male/female relations (*danjo kankei*) include various forms of benefit that cater to every eventuality in human relations and wishes—from linking two people together in a relationship (*enmusubi*) to severing bonds between them (*engiri*) when their love wanes or one of them realizes the detrimental effects of their relationship. Human life (*hito no isshō*) benefits range from being blessed with children (*kodakara*) to giving birth safely (*anzan*). (Under this heading there is, somewhat contradictorily, a reference to *mizuko kuyō*, the performance of memorial services for fetuses that die, most commonly because of abortion, in the womb.) Thus there are religious centers where one can pray for producing adequate mother's milk for babies (*chichi no de o yokusuru*), for help in child-rearing, and for the prevention of various children's problems (such as prevention of worms, a common medical problem for children). Following on from childrearing, the benefits under this category of human life issues include safety from illnesses and disasters as well as longevity and a happy rebirth in paradise (*gokuraku ōjō*). The inclusion of rebirth in a volume that is clearly focused on this-worldly benefits demonstrates the extent to which even after-death benefits such as entry into paradise can have a this-worldly dimension. By assuring recipients of their ultimate fates, they grant them confidence and thus contribute to their happiness and sense of salvation in this world.

Although these categories have focused largely on achieving or beckoning certain types of good fortune and benefit, the table of contents deals with two major categories relating to prophylactic action: the prevention of accidents and misfortune (*sainan yoke*) and the recovery from (and prevention of) illness (*byōki no kaifuku*). The category of *sainan yoke* includes protection against theft (*tōnan yoke*), traffic safety (*kōtsū anzen*), protection against fires (*kanan yoke*), and various other general forms of protection ranging from the ubiquitous *yaku yoke* (prevention of danger) to the specific, such as protection against being struck by lightning (*kaminari yoke*) and prevention of bad dreams (*akumu tsuihō*). Traffic safety may be general or specific: there are subcategories of places where one can pray for the protection of one's children as they go to and from school (*gakudō tōkō anzen*), for safe air travel (*kōkū anzen*), and for safety at sea (*kōkai anzen*).

The general category of recovery from illness and protection against disease is broken down, in the guidebook, into specific parts of the body (shrines and temples good for problems with the head, ears, eyes, and so on) and specific complaints. There are temples and shrines that provide protection against (or healing of) one or more of the following: colds, measles, coughs, whooping cough, toothaches, rheumatism, nervous diseases, intestinal and stomach disorders, skin complaints (from warts and corns to boils and ringworms), sexual diseases, "women's medical problems" (*fujinbyō*) (such as irregular menstruation), fevers, hemorrhoids, and complaints of the feet or hands. Besides these (some of which may be dealt with by the same temple or shrine) there are places that offer general help in repelling diseases. Included under the general rubric of prevention and protection against disease are a number of institutions that offer help in resisting the temptation to drink or smoke (*kinshu, kin'en*).

We cite this particular guidebook not because it is somehow special but because it represents an important genre of religious literature related to the widespread practice of this-worldly benefits and illustrates the broad varieties of benefits that may be found within one geographical area. Nor is it comprehensive: while Naitō and Shimokawa introduce several hundred institutions within the Tokyo area alone with religious specializations relating to various forms of worldly benefit, their book does not cover every type of benefit that one could find on offer somewhere in the region and they do not detail every institution in Tokyo that has some renown connected with this-worldly benefits. One could easily find additional examples of general and specific benefits mentioned in other guidebooks or advertised at religious centers.

The Social Geography of Benefits:
Benefits and Religious Identity

Naitō and Shimokawa's guidebook, then, is but a sign, rather than a complete compendium, of the comprehensive and ubiquitous provision of this-worldly benefits in Japan. Although the table of contents divides its material by different types of benefit, the organization of the book itself is regional, dealing with all the various parts of Tokyo in turn, thus enabling the reader to readily determine what benefits are on offer in any particular area.

To take one example: the book outlines some forty-six different types of benefits offered within the boundaries of Taitō ward alone at a number of different institutions and ranging from air travel safety to the healing of ear diseases.[31] Several institutions provide a multiplicity of benefits. Sensōji, the temple popularly known as Asakusa Kannon, is a major center for this-worldly benefits: the main temple and its various subshrines between them take up some fourteen pages of the book and offer a total of twenty-five different forms of benefit. Residents of Taitō ward, given this range of benefits, could thus deal with virtually all of their worldly religious needs within the boundaries of the district in which they live. Members of one family in the ward, for example, said they normally visit a local shrine, a block from their house, to pay their first respects to the gods at New Year and to acquire a talisman, but they also visit Asakusa Kannon, the largest, most encompassing, and powerful institution in the area, during the New Year period and at other times depending on their needs.

Given the efficiency of modern urban transportation, access to other religious centers may be equally easy. Thus the network of locations providing benefits within reach of the Taitō ward dweller is enormous. Yet there is also a sense of local religious identity relating to this-worldly needs—an issue we hinted at earlier when we noted the role of Hōzanji in dealing with the needs of certain local occupations and trades, as well as the network of temples and shrines around Osaka that offer this-worldly benefits. The point is that these networks of temples and shrines constitute a form of social religious geography and a sense of religious identity that relates to location.

This issue was emphasized in an interview with a couple in their sixties who were on a pilgrimage on the island of Shikoku.[32] They were "Osakans" (*Osakajin*), they said, and their religious activities centered around important shrines and temples in the Osaka region and were not limited to the Tendai Buddhist sect to which they belonged. Thus Shitennōji, the major Buddhist temple in southern Osaka, was where they went to pray for their ancestors and seek

benefits on occasions such as the temple's monthly *ennichi* related to
Kōbō Daishi, while Sumiyoshi Shrine, a focal point for businesses and
merchants, was their place of choice for the New Year's *hatsumōde*. As
retired proprietors of a small shop, they had a high regard for
Ebisu—one of the Seven Gods of Good Fortune and a deity especially
important for small businesses and merchants. Hence they always
participated in the *hatsu Ebisu* festival (the first holy day of the year
for Ebisu) in January at the Nishinomiya Ebisu Shrine halfway between Osaka and Kobe.[33] Among other points of reference on their
religious and social compass were Kōyasan, the religious center
founded by Kōbō Daishi, to whom they felt a special reverence (reflected in the fact that they were then engaged in the Shikoku pilgrimage), and Sefukuji (also known as Makinoodera) outside of
Osaka, which is one of the Saikoku pilgrimage temples but has especially close associations with Kōbō Daishi as well.

Such regional patterns take precedence over sectarian affiliation
even for members of the Jōdo Shin sect, which officially rejects the
pursuit of benefits as superstition. A college student—a Jōdo Shin
member well versed in the teachings of her sect—described in an interview her religious activities, which included a *hatsumōde* to the
local shrine in her neighborhood and visits to nearby shrines and
temples to acquire *omamori* for traffic safety, academic success, and a
good marriage partner. When asked if her religious conduct
conflicted with the teachings of her sect, she acknowledged the discrepancy but then defended her actions by saying, "But I am only being a good Japanese."[34]

For this student and the couple mentioned earlier, regional religious affiliations related to calendrical cycles and the seeking of benefits defined their religious identity and activities far more than did their
official sectarian affiliation. The patterns they displayed were little
different from the inhabitants of Edo (seventeenth- and eighteenth-
century Tokyo) studied through their journals by Miyata Noboru.
Miyata draws a picture of socially oriented religious behavior in which
the prime coordinates are occasions (especially seasonal and calendrical events and festivals) and needs. Citing the journal of the Edo
inhabitant Saitō Gesshin as an example, Miyata notes that Saitō's life
had a structure related to the changing of the seasons, which was
reflected in his visits to different shrines and temples and attendance
at different religious rituals.[35] Saitō's journal thus informs us that a
person from Edo (*Edojin*) such as himself lived within a sociocultural
and religious framework in which certain places and times fitted together as parts of the social calendar of ritual-religious behavior.

The social geography of benefits therefore provides a nexus of
religious behavior and a sense of religious identity that transcends

sectarian affiliations. To the outline of Osakan religion touched on by the couple on pilgrimage, one could add various other religious centers within the region that are frequently visited by people from that city and its environs. Ishikiri Shrine is a widely visited religious institution for people in the Osaka area before they (or a relative or friend) undergo surgery; Nakayama-dera, at Takarazuka just northeast of Osaka, is generally considered to be *the* religious center for dealing with pregnancies and safe childbirth.[36] One could extend such lists to institutions like Kiyoshi Kōjin (to give it its popular name),[37] which enshrines the protective deity of the cooking cauldron. Given that the kitchen (at least in the days when cooking was done over open fires) is the most likely place for a house fire to start, Kiyoshi Kōjin has come to be seen as a protector against fires (*hinan yoke*). For Osakans wanting this benefit, Kiyoshi Kōjin is *the* place, or one of the places, to go in this respect.[38]

The social geography of benefits helps to frame the religious culture and identity of the region. Visits to specific religious centers at particular times throughout the year become part of the area's identity structure, and certain temples and shrines are seen as symbols of local and regional culture and belonging. This does not, of course, mean that people are limited to a specific region in the pursuit of benefits, but it does suggest that journeys further afield are more likely to be undertaken in order to make use of a specifically powerful provider of benefit or in times of great need. Thus a priest at Kawasaki Daishi—one of Japan's most famed locations for the benefit of *yakuyoke*, though it caters to numerous other benefits besides— noted that visitors from outside the temple's immediate catchment area were more likely to come in order to pray for *yakuyoke* than anything else. He said that the temple received quite a few visitors from the Chiba prefecture district that is on the opposite side of Tokyo from Kawasaki Daishi. People from Chiba who had prayer rituals (*kitō*) said at Kawasaki Daishi, according to this priest, usually focused on *yakuyoke* but did not as a rule petition for traffic safety (*kōtsū anzen*), although this was a recent specialty of the temple. They did not need to travel to Kawasaki Daishi for this request because in their immediate area was the temple Shinshōji, one of the most prominent centers in the whole of Japan for *kōtsū anzen*.[39]

Thus people may travel further afield for important needs and visit the deities and buddhas most widely famed for a specific benefit, but in general terms they tend to seek help within their local geographical sphere, which offers a network of benefits and locations of worship relevant to their local needs and identities. To this extent we suggest a slight modification of the comments made in the Introduction, where we implied that rather than being (say) "Buddhist" or "Shinto,"

Japanese people really are members of a common Japanese religion centered on practical benefits. Although the vast numbers of benefits available, covering every aspect of life, do justify this notion, we should note that this common religion is closely linked to questions of identity and belonging and generally has a regional focus. Thus common religion is linked not just to general customs, beliefs, and practices but to a series of relationships and visits to set locations in a specific region. And this location itself is therefore part and parcel of the common conceptual framework and ritual structure. In describing her visits to local shrines and temples as the activities of a "good Japanese," the Jodō Shin college student exemplifies the way in which the pursuit of this-worldly benefits partakes of the commonalties within a local area as well as the common religion of the nation as a whole.

Changing Times and New Benefits

Although many of the benefits cited in Naitō and Shimokawa's book relate to traditional aspects of Japan, we also note the occurrence of institutions catering to new professions and new concerns. Within the benefits market, as it were, there is a constantly modernizing dynamic, and new forms of benefits related to contemporary needs appear with regularity and often with great speed. Travel safety is one such area where new developments occur regularly because of the expanding and changing nature of travel. In this area, for example, we have seen the appearance of rituals of purification of automobiles in order to ward off potential accidents—a form of activity that emerged in the early 1960s but has grown rapidly in line with the growth in car ownership since that era—and the appearance of seat belt amulets when new laws made wearing seat belts compulsory in the 1980s.[40]

Air traffic safety is another new form of benefit that has flourished in recent years, as increasing numbers of Japanese have begun to travel regularly by air. In the early 1980s it was quite rare to come across talismans, amulets, deities, or institutions that catered specifically to this form of protective benefit, which tended to be subsumed within the wider category of kōtsū anzen (traffic safety). Through the 1980s, however, the growth of air travel—coupled, at least according to some priests, to a number of air crashes involving Japanese, most particularly the 1985 crash of a jumbo jet in Gumma prefecture which killed over five hundred people—created an anxiety that developed into the specific benefit of air travel safety, the production of amulets for this purpose, and the evolution of certain deities and figures of worship into protectors of air travelers. Increased air travel and increased awareness of its dangers have thus created unease. As a priest at Saidaiji, a popular prayer temple outside Okayama, remarked, the rapid increase in the numbers of Japanese who travel overseas for holidays and the like has heightened fears about the perils of traveling overseas, becoming ill in another country, losing their money, and all the other apparent dangers of stepping outside the familiar into the unfamiliar.[41] Overseas travel safety (*kaigai anzen*) is developing as a new variation on the travel safety theme as a result.

Many temples and shrines that have become active in air traffic safety had already acquired a reputation for travel safety in general. Given their roles as protectors of travelers, it was quite natural for temples such as Kawasaki Daishi and Shinshōji to extend their services to this newly popular form of travel. Other institutions not necessarily associated with travel safety also began to develop a reputation in this area for reasons connected with the deity they enshrined. The temple Shōbōin in Tokyo, for instance, was established in 1530 as a prayer temple (*kitōdera*) connected to the Tendai lineage of the ascetic mountain religious sect Shugendō. This temple is popularly known as Tobi Fudō (Flying Fudō) because of its main image of worship. According to temple legend, the image acquired this epithet in the Tokugawa era when the head priest took it with him to the Mount Omine region, where he intended to participate in Shugendō austerities. The statue, however, flew miraculously back to the temple in Edo (Tokyo), clearly indicating its wish to remain there and serve local petitioners (thereby, one might comment, displaying its loyalty to its regional following and the social locale) and subsequently provided numerous benefits for them.[42]

While the main benefits provided by this Fudō were family safety, business prosperity, and the prevention of danger and the opening of good fortune, travel safety had not been considered one of its specific capabilities. But given the analogy between its name and image—a temple related to flying—it began to receive petitioners seeking Fudō's grace in connection with air travel safety as the era of mass air transport evolved. Many such travelers wanted a talisman or amulet specifically related to air travel. As a result the temple responded to popular demand and developed its own prayers, rituals, and benefits connected to air safety and created an *omamori* focused on the benefit of *ochinai* (not falling) in this respect.[43] The temple's courtyard is filled with votive tablets (*ema*), on the back of which are prayers for safety complete with itineraries and flight numbers. The front of the *ema* depicts a traditional-looking Fudō holding his sword of wisdom. Across his chest flies, level and steady, a Boeing 747.

The generic benefit of travel safety has diversified further still in recent years. Today there are amulets for overseas safety and, more

飛不動尊

奉納

Tobi Fudō *ema*

recently, an advance into the final frontier of space. The Kotohira
Shrine in Shikoku and its main deity Konpira are famed as the
guardians of sailors and ships: to petition the gods for their protection, shipbuilders and shipping firms regularly place large votive
tablets at the shrine depicting the vessels they have built or commissioned. In February 1991 a new votive tablet appeared there, put up
by one of the country's broadcasting corporations, Tōkyō Hōsō
(Tokyo Broadcasting Company), to give thanks to the gods in connection with the flight of Japan's first spaceman, Akiyama Toyokiro.
Akiyama was a journalist working for Tōkyō Hōsō, which paid for a
place on a Russian spacecraft in December 1990 in order to boost its
ratings by having Akiyama broadcast from space. The votive tablet
placed at the shrine after his safe return depicts him in a spacesuit; to
the side is a space rocket blasting off. Not only does this demonstrate
the flexibility of the deity of seafaring ships to extend its influence to
spacecraft. It also exemplifies the underlying recognition—even
among modern media organizations and in relation to the most advanced technological enterprises—that the gods have a role to play
and even a tightly controlled scientific enterprise may have a religious angle necessitating the observation of religious proprieties.[44]

Such examples of new benefits connected to travel safety demonstrate the ability of Japanese religious institutions to retain a contemporary relevance and keep abreast of the prevailing needs and trends
in society. Sometimes the responses of shrines and temples can be

Astronaut *ema* of Akiyama Toyokiro

extremely rapid and extremely topical. On September 26, 1996, the Japanese government announced that both houses of the Diet would be dissolved and a joint general election held on October 20. Less than a week later, the Tamō Hachiman Shrine in Ehime prefecture began to advertise on the Internet prayers for the victory (*hisshō kigan*) of one's preferred candidate or party. Emphasizing that its main deity Hachiman is a god of victory—and that this election would be crucial in the effort to resolve the uncertainties that had afflicted Japan's political system in the 1990s—it enjoined people to express their aspirations relating to the election through prayers at the shrine.[45] That this new benefit was announced on the Internet is just an example of the ways in which new technologies continue to shape the world in which religious institutions operate. Later we shall return to this point and the availability of benefits via the Internet.

This benefit is perhaps remarkable in its speed of appearance, but it reflects the close and direct relationship between contemporary social issues and the manifestation of new forms of benefits. Often there is only a brief lapse of time between an event and the appearance of religious responses to it. Indeed, one can often get an idea of what issues are troubling people at large by observing what kind of this-worldly benefits are being offered. Although AIDS, for example, first manifested itself in Japan in the latter 1980s, the response of public and health authorities was not always immediate, and it was not until the early 1990s that it came to be regarded as a disease to which ordinary Japanese (rather than foreigners and homosexuals) might succumb. Yet some realization of the dangers and potential transferability of AIDS was to be found at religious institutions earlier than this. By 1987, for example, at least one shrine had begun to take up the issue by producing amulets relating to AIDS and harnessing its deities to confront the disease. This was the case with the Kanamara Shrine in Kawasaki (located within a short walk of Kawasaki Daishi Temple), an institution that has long been associated with fertility and helping those suffering from sexual diseases. As the shrine's own literature puts it: "What could be more natural, then, that the shrine should embrace those who are concerned with the spread of the acquired immune-deficiency syndrome—AIDS?"[46]

The shrine began to note the spread of AIDS in Japan from 1987 onward, and commissioned a well-known artist to design a votive tablet that would draw attention to the importance of safe-sex practices. The votive tablet utilizes the popular "see no evil, hear no evil, speak no evil" (*mizaru, kikazaru, iwazaru*) three-monkey motif found in Japanese folklore—but adds two more monkeys, the monkey that transmits no evil (*sezaru*) and the one that receives no evil (*sasezaru*). The former is covering its genitals, the latter its backside, and the message is clear: the importance of the moral commitment to safe sex, specifically in the form of abstinence. The votive tablet also bears the inscriptions "*kanai enman*" (fulfillment in the home) and "*shison han'ei*" (prosperity for one's children). The mention of these benefits—the latter is related in particular to heterosexual activity—demonstrates an underlying recognition that AIDS is a disease that

Monkey *ema* with moral advice for prevention of AIDS at Kanamara Shrine

affects not just one form of sexual orientation or one segment of the population but everyone. The accompanying leaflet instructs people to place the votive tablet with a prayer on it at the shrine or to hang it in one's home: either way the tablet should "serve as a demonstration of your commitment to safe sex and a manifestation of your prayers for the protection from the scourge of AIDS."[47] Such benefits are not only related to contemporary issues but assume an ethical and indeed educational nature, a theme that we take up in Chapter 3 dealing with the moral meanings of prayers for this-worldly benefits. The example of Kanamara Shrine's rapid response to AIDS illustrates the ways in which new forms of benefits—and, indeed, of talismans and amulets—may be manufactured in line with new personal and social concerns.

Another benefit that has developed in response to a contemporary social problem is that for the prevention of, or protection against, senility (*boke fūji*), a function commonly carried out by the bodhisattva Kannon. Although the prevention of senility is closely linked to prayers for a swift and painless death (*pokkuri*), which has a long history in Japan,[48] *boke fūji* has especially grown since the latter 1980s as public awareness of the problems of aging has spread. This benefit is not the product of the religious world alone, nor indeed just of anxious petitioners asking their priests for something to relieve this growing worry. Part of the stimulus has come from the world of commerce—in particular from a Buddhist statue manufacturer in Kyoto whose creation of the original *boke fūji Kannon* statue has been welcomed enthusiastically by a number of Buddhist priests around the country, aware of the concerns of elderly people and eager to ease their anxieties. Many of these priests recognize too that as a focus of current concern it is likely to bring people to temples and therefore provide a new means of activity, custom, and support for their institutions.[49]

All these cases, whether of election victory, air travel safety, AIDS, or the prevention of senility, demonstrate that the appearance of new benefits appropriate to new needs and situations is a recurrent feature of Japanese religion and, moreover, inform us of its reflexive and pragmatic nature. To return to the comments made by the priest at Saidaiji cited earlier, new situations create new forms of unease and hence new needs in the field of practical benefits. Modernity, rather than eradicating unease, has simply shifted its locus. People may be less worried now, for example, about the dangers of diseases such as smallpox that have more or less been eliminated by modern science; hence the deities that once coped with this disease are no longer needed and can be pensioned off. But new diseases such as AIDS provoke new fears, while changing patterns of life can present new dangers—whether on aircraft, in the streets of foreign cities, or in terms of the perils of aging. There are times, of course, when these fears may be manipulated by religious specialists who, in so doing, increase the prospects of people coming to their temples and shrines seeking protection and help.

Concerns about dangerous activities do not, of course, prevent their development. Although the various traffic safety amulets appear to have evolved in response to people's growing awareness of the potential dangers of travel, such forms of travel (whether by car or more recently by air) have continued to spread. People do not as a rule refuse to travel by car because they fear an accident or, like the woman cited in the Introduction, cease to drive because they have had accidents in the past. Rather, the religious response allows people to express their fears, reassure themselves about a proposed activity or course of action, and do what they wish to do: travel. The provision of overseas and air travel safety amulets enables people to go beyond the confines of Japan in the company of the gods, under their protection, and thus plays a part in the legitimation of such travel.

Although the expansive lists given in popular guidebooks indicate the general scope covered by the practice of seeking this-worldly benefits, they do not and perhaps cannot manifest the entirety of the practice, which has the potential to cover any and every human need, desire, and situation. The reflexive nature manifested at Tobi Fudō—where the temple responded to requests from petitioners and pro-

duced a service and charm that addressed their needs—is comple-
mented by an inventiveness and occasionally an opportunism, the
impetus for which frequently comes from priests and religious specialists who are adept at discerning trends, recognizing new areas of
need, and creating new benefits in line with them. This is an important dimension of practical benefits because it pertains to the ways in
which the promises of benefits are made and how they—and hence
the religious institutions and figures—are proselytized, disseminated, and even manipulated. In Chapter 6 we discuss the marketing
and promotion of benefits and return to the creation of new benefits
in response to changing needs.

Practical Benefits, Religious Institutions, and Ritual Processes: The Case of Kawasaki Daishi

Religious institutions need not cater only to one category of
worldly benefits but may provide an extensive year-round service
dealing with all manner of needs, ritual services, and religious objects
that relate to benefits. Earlier we gained some insights into this theme
in our discussion of Hōzanji. Here we examine in some depth a
temple we have already mentioned: Kawasaki Daishi. What underpins
the sacred nature and reputations of religious centers? What is the
calendrical cycle of praying for benefits? In what ways can benefits be
sought? What ritual processes and religious objects are associated
with them? While these topics are discussed in later chapters, it is important to offer some introductory remarks here.

Kawasaki Daishi is the name by which the temple Heikenji is
known throughout Japan. Like many other religious centers, it has
become famed under its popular rather than official name: "Daishi"
refers to its main figure of worship, Kōbō Daishi, the posthumous
name of Kūkai, the Buddhist monk active in Japan at the end of the
eighth and beginning of the ninth centuries. The founder of Shingon
Buddhism in Japan as well as important religious centers such as the
temple Tōji in Kyoto and Kōyasan south of Osaka, Kūkai has a huge
reputation as a religious teacher, practitioner, and Japanese cultural
hero. After his death—or, as his later followers would have it, after
his entry into eternal meditation in his mausoleum at Kōyasan—he
was eventually granted the posthumous title Kōbō Daishi by the imperial court in the year 921. By then legends affirming that he was still
alive and capable of performing miracles, interceding to help the
faithful and punish the wicked, had begun to develop, promoted in
great part by priests and wandering ascetics connected with the Shingon Buddhist sect and with Kōyasan.

Kōbō Daishi is one of the most important and frequently petitioned providers of benefits in Japanese religion: prominent as a

figure of worship in numerous pilgrimages, he is also venerated at numerous temples such as Kawasaki Daishi in Japan, and many other temples have acquired special sanctity by claiming him (usually with a degree of poetic license) as their founder.[50] Although Kūkai, as the founder of a particular sect of Buddhism in Japan (Shingon), has specific sectarian associations, in his subsequent guise as Kōbō Daishi he has transcended these boundaries and, through his reputation as a provider of benefits and performer of miraculous intercessions, has become venerated not only at Shingon temples but across the spectrum and is prayed to by people regardless of their sectarian affiliation or orientation.[51]

Kawasaki Daishi is one of the most visited religious institutions in Japan: it is the most frequently visited Buddhist temple at *hatsumōde;* the only shrine in Japan that receives more visitors at this time of year is Meiji Shrine in the heart of Tokyo. Although it is of the Shingon sect, those who visit come from all walks of Japanese religious life and their main concerns are in the powers of the temple and of Kōbō Daishi to grant benefits to them.[52] The temple's fame comes from the reputation of Kōbō Daishi and its foundation story (*engi*), which sacralizes the temple and allots immense sacred power to its main image of worship, a statue of Kōbō Daishi.

Foundation legends (*engi*) affirm the sacrality of a location and play an important role in constructing an image of power. In the Introduction we encountered the foundation legend of Ichibata Yakushi, in which a pious fisherman found a miraculous statue of Yakushi, who restored his blind mother's sight; as a result of this miracle and his faith, a temple centered on this statue was founded and became known for healing eye problems. Such legends may well have been invented by priests in order to provide religious institutions or sacred images with a reputation for efficacy (or indeed as a post hoc legitimation for the existence of a religious institution and as an affirmation of its power) and are widely publicized as a means of creating faith and encouraging the faithful to visit religious institutions. Although they often have no historical veracity, *engi* represent a living religious tradition—an exposition of what has in other contexts been described as "mythistory,"[53] the mythic construction of a tradition that speaks of religious truth and validity and provides a form of historical origin. As such, *engi* are potent tools in the proselytization of religion and religious efficacy, and their use in affirming the powers of specific locations and images has been seminal in the formation of Japanese religious culture and the development of networks of popular religious centers and pilgrimage routes.[54]

In the case of Kawasaki Daishi its *engi* connects the temple to its main figure of worship, Kōbō Daishi, who although he never visited the site is nonetheless considered to be present and active there. According to various versions of the *engi*, Kūkai (Kōbō Daishi) carved a statue of himself in his forty-second year. In common Japanese religious belief (derived from Taoist influences) the forty-second year is the *yakudoshi*, or dangerous year, for men—a year when they are especially open to misfortune and should take steps to protect themselves by calling on the gods and buddhas. Praying for the eradication of dangers—*yakuyoke*—is a major category of benefit seeking, and *yakudoshi*-related prayers and actions are one of the most prevalent occasions when this occurs.

Kōbō Daishi is a prominent source of protection in Japanese religion with regard to the *yakudoshi*. Because Kūkai was a historical figure, it has been possible to attribute to him numerous actions that (so legend avers) he performed in order to avoid the spiritual dangers of his age and possible, too, to construct various legends that relate to actual things linked to Kōbō Daishi, such as pilgrimages he is said to have created or statues he is said to have carved. In 815 (Kūkai's forty-second year), for example, legends state that he walked around Shikoku, the island of his birth, founding the island's eighty-eight-stage pilgrimage route, which is focused on Kōbō Daishi.[55] Although this pilgrimage story is historically inaccurate (the pilgrimage did not come into existence until centuries later, and as far as is historically known Kūkai was not in Shikoku in 815), it provides a legendary impetus and foundation myth to the pilgrimage by associating it with the sacred figure at its heart. It also affirms the value of the pilgrimage as a religious action designed to safeguard one against dangers such as the *yakudoshi*. Many pilgrims do indeed perform it in their dangerous years.[56]

Among the other activities attributed to Kūkai/Kōbō Daishi in connection with his own forty-second year was the carving of various statues and images of worship. The statue at Heikenji (Kawasaki Daishi) is one of these and, according to the temple's *engi*, after carving a statue of himself he cast it into the sea. The subsequent whereabouts of the statue were revealed in the twelfth century to Hirama Akinori, a retainer of the powerful Minamoto clan, to whom Kōbō Daishi appeared in a dream. Using the services of a priest from Kōyasan, Hirama founded a temple enshrining this statue: the temple took its official name from the *on*, or Chinese readings, of the two ideograms of his name (*hei* and *ken*). Since Hirama had founded the temple in his forty-second year, there are strong associations with various forms of *yakuyoke* and the temple has become, in the words of one of its priests, a center for *yakuyoke shinkō* (faith in preventing danger).[57] The temple's fame derives from its dual associations with Kōbō Daishi—both as carver and original sacralizer of the main image and as the main image itself. Thus the statue is a spiritual manifestation of

Kōbō Daishi and the intercessionary and protective powers he is believed to possess. This sanctity is further reinforced by the miraculous founding legend that brought the statue to Kawasaki (and implies it was Kōbō Daishi's specific will and intention that his protective aura should be manifested there) and is closely linked to the questions of *yakudoshi* and *yakuyoke*.

The legends of founding and the image of power and sanctity so constructed have fueled numerous other legends, stories, and reports of benefits received at the temple throughout subsequent centuries, and these too have contributed to its fame and increased the numbers of people who have come to the temple to seek help. In the modern era perhaps the most widely circulated of such stories relates to the air raids that devastated Kawasaki on April 15, 1945, in the closing months of World War II. The area around the temple was severely damaged and many of its buildings were razed to the ground. A few days earlier, however, the head priest had had a premonition that the statue was in danger and moved it away from the temple. Thus the statue was saved—miraculously, as temple officiants put it. Given that the statue is the key to the temple's power as a religious site, the priest's premonition saved the temple, while the story of the premonition itself (which may be read as suggesting that the statue's miraculous powers were behind this warning) added to the temple's fame and the numbers of people who subsequently came to seek its assistance.[58]

Kawasaki Daishi has had a major impact on the geography of its region. Located in the industrial city of Kawasaki just south of Tokyo, the temple is surrounded by public utilities that bear its name and indicate how important a local landmark it is: by car one reaches the temple by coming off the capital's expressway Route One at the Daishi exit; by bus by alighting at Kawasaki Daishi bus stop; by train by alighting at the Keihin Railway's Kawasaki Daishi station. Between the station and temple one passes through an arcade of shops and stalls similar to those found before other temples and shrines: besides shops selling ordinary goods, there is a preponderance of stores selling souvenirs connected to the temple and other lucky objects (*engimono*) such as *maneki neko* (the beckoning cat, a traditional Japanese symbol of good luck) and Daruma dolls (also signs of good fortune), shops specializing in incense and other articles associated with religious practices and institutions, restaurants catering to the visitors, and the like. Even inside the temple precincts one finds stalls selling lucky objects and foodstuffs during festival times such as New Year.

The stations and shops are highly profitable for those that run them, for the temple receives millions of visitors every year. Kawasaki Daishi's visitors regularly top 3 million during the first three days of the year—in 1993 it received 3.15 million visitors in this period and even a week after New Year's day the temple was crowded and bustling.[59] Besides New Year, the temple has a whole series of yearly events (*nenjū gyōji*) that are occasions of special rituals and can draw people. The temple's cycle of calendrical rituals and festive events form a temporal framework that organizes its year: in all, Kawasaki Daishi's list of *nenjū gyōji* details forty-one separate events throughout the year—commencing with the opening fire ritual on New Year's morning (*ganchō daigomaku*) to summon good fortune in the coming year and ending with a ritual on the evening of December 31 to sweep away the old year and the ills that went with it (*joya hōraku*). This ritual calendar encompasses the two major forms of benefits we discussed earlier: from the summoning of good fortune at the beginning of the new year to the banishing of bad fortune in the last rite of the year. Its most recurrent feature is a ritual celebration of Kōbō Daishi's holy day (*ennichi*) on the twenty-first day of each month.

Not all the calendrical events relate directly to *genze riyaku*. Some relate to caring for the ancestors—as do the *higan* festivals of spring and autumn in which families pray for the safety of their ancestors— or to commemorations of important events in the (legendary) life of the Buddha (such as *hana matsuri*, the Japanese commemoration of the birth of Buddha (held on April 8) and *nehan-e*, the commemoration of his passing from this life into paranirvana (February 15). This does not mean that those who attend these services cannot say their own private prayers for benefits, purchase amulets, or offer votive tablets. The system is, as noted earlier, open and accessible at all times. Particularly auspicious, however, are the numerous special occasions and festive times when praying for this-worldly benefits is especially efficacious and encouraged, such as the monthly festive *ennichi* when there is a market held at the temple.

Visitors need not limit their prayers to these special occasions in the ritual calendar, however, or to their own private supplications whenever they happen to be at the temple. They can seek special prayer rituals from the priests in accordance with their own wishes and needs. To cater to their needs, for example, there are regular performances of the *goma* (fire) ritual—one of the most important rituals conducted in the Shingon sect of Buddhism and the primary ritual held at the temple connected to petitions for this-worldly benefits. On normal weekdays, such *goma* rituals are held usually eight times per day, the first at 6:00 A.M., the last at 7:00 P.M., while there are normally nine performances on Sunday, which as elsewhere tends to be the busiest day of the week for the temple. In the *goma* ritual sacred sticks of wood (*gomagi*) bearing religious inscriptions and petitioners' specific requests are immolated in a sacred fire. The *goma*

ritual is found in a variety of forms in Japan—from the rituals of Esoteric Buddhist sects such as Shingon and Tendai, to new religious
movements such as Bentenshū and Agonshū, to Shinto shrines.[60]
Kawasaki Daishi is by affiliation a Shingon Buddhist temple and hence
uses the special objects, incantations, gestures, and ritual actions laid
down in the Esoteric Buddhist manuals and texts of the Shingon sect.

The list of benefits that may be petitioned for at Kawasaki Daishi
through the *goma* ritual is extensive and impressive: according to
temple literature, such benefits include:

> *saiyaku shōjo* (eradication of calamities)
> *kanai anzen* (family safety)
> *kōtsū anzen* (traffic safety)
> *shōbai hanjō* (business prosperity)
> *shinjō anzen* (physical safety)
> *byōki heiyu* (recovery from illness)
> *shingan jōju* (accomplishment of all one's heart's wishes)
> *kaiun manzoku* (successful opening of fortune)
> *nyūgaku jōju* (successful entry into school or college)
> *ryōen jōju* (making a good marriage)
> *anzan manzoku* (safe childbirth)
> *kaijō anzen* (safety at sea)
> *kaigai ryokō anzen* (safe overseas travel)
> *jigyō hanei* (business success)
> *kōji anzen* (safety when undertaking building and construction
>   work)
> *hōjo* (protection from unlucky directions)
> *mushi fūji* (protection against roundworm)
> *sono ta: shogan jōju, o-fuda* (also: fulfillment of all vows, talismans)

The final category represents a catchall that in effect means the ritual
can be utilized for whatever purpose the petitioner wants.

In outlining the meanings and processes of the *goma* ritual, the
temple affirms both its deep connection to Esoteric Buddhist thought
and practice and its efficacy as a means of providing the petitioner
with this-worldly benefits—which are, it is affirmed, produced
through the grace of Kōbō Daishi allied to the spiritual purity and endeavor of the priests acting as the ritual officiants mediating and re-
laying the requests of the ordinary visitors to the figure of worship.
While petitioners may approach the holy figure directly in prayer, it
is generally considered more efficacious and ritually correct, in matters of great concern, to do this through the services of a trained religious officiant who is versed in the temple's specific practices and
occupies a powerful position as priest and guardian of the sacred
statue. The ritual itself involves the burning of *goma* sticks to immo-

late symbolically the evil passions that hinder happiness. By removing bad luck and danger, the ritual opens the way for good fortune and happiness.

The temple describes the "beneficial merits of the *goma* ritual" (*o-goma no kudoku*) as follows:

> The religious practice of the *goma* is a powerful rite that is under-pinned by profound and highly significant philosophical meanings and by the true doctrinal principles of Esoteric Buddhism as fol-lowed in the Shingon sect. The word *"goma"* comes from the San-skrit *homa*, which means "to burn" or "set fire to," and expresses the meaning of immolating the evil passions (*bonnō*—the root of all suffering) through the fire of Buddhist wisdom.
>
> The *goma* ritual is a strictly Esoteric rite in which a priest (an as-cetic practitioner) who has cleared his body and spirit of impedi-ments through ritual purification makes offerings of various things such as five varieties of grains, incense, and flowers at the *goma* al-tar situated before the main image of worship. In burning the *goma* sticks in the central hearth of the altar the priest begins the service of offering to the main image of worship: the Danger-Preventing Daishi (Yakuyoke Daishi).
>
> The beneficial merits of the Daishi, as well as the prayers of the spiritually pure priest, unite completely with the meritorious faith of all the worshipers. At the end of the rite, a *goma* talisman (*o-goma fuda*), which is the crystallization of the spiritual power produced by the performance of this austere ritual, is given to all who participate.
>
> Please make a sign of prayer and recite the sacred mantra of Kōbō Daishi (*namu Daishi henjō kongō*). Through this *goma* ritual all one's evil passions are burnt and purified, and all dangers are erad-icated. Thus all one's wishes concerning gaining good fortune— family safety, business prosperity, healing of illness, the achieve-ment of all wishes, and so on—begin to be realized.[61]

This text thus affirms the point made in the Introduction about the role and indeed the efficacy of Buddhism in providing good fortune and protecting against misfortune. It is a high Buddhist ritual ex-pressing core Buddhist values (such as the destruction of evil pas-sions), underpinned by Buddhist thought and conducted by Bud-dhist priests, which is able to produce this-worldly benefits. The text also makes clear that *yakuyoke* is closely associated with—and, in terms of the ritual process, is an integral part of—the acquisition of good fortune. Thus the unity of different forms of benefit is affirmed: at bottom *yakuyoke* and *kaiun* signify two sides of the same coin. *Genze riyaku*, as manifested through the ritual, is produced as a result of the interaction of the priest fortified through observations of ritual purity, the ritual texts, ritual formulas, true faith, doctrinal correctness in the performance of the ritual, and the commitment of the petitioner. Practice and the acquisition of benefits are thus inextricably tied together.

As a result of participating in the ritual, the petitioner receives a talisman (*fuda*) that, as the temple states, represents the spiritual power created by the ritual and may be taken home to provide protection. *Fuda* are similar to *omamori* in that they too are regarded as manifestations (*bunshin, kesshin*) of the sacred entity enshrined at the temple or shrine. Usually made of flat strips of shaped wood or paper with religious inscriptions (at Buddhist temples these are generally Buddhist prayers or mantras) as well as the name of the shrine, temple, and deity, these *fuda* are given to petitioners as a result of their participation in the ritual services. They can also be purchased, however, without the necessity of participating in such rituals. The terms "*fuda*" and "*omamori*" are normally translated as "talismans" or "amulets," but each of them can span the theoretical functions differentiated with these English words (the amulet as protective device, the talisman as beckoner of good fortune): one can have protective and fortune-beckoning *fuda* and similarly *omamori*. The prime difference between the two objects is that *fuda* are generally considered to protect or bring fortune to an area (such as a house or building and its occupants) or social group (a family, a company), while *omamori* are normally considered to relate to a particular individual who wears or carries it on his or her person. Such objects, as the description of Kawasaki Daishi's *goma*-related *fuda* illustrates, are usually considered to represent the spiritual powers of a specific religious institution, deity, and ritual performance and, as in the example of the *migawari* Jizō amulet mentioned earlier, manifests the spiritual force of a particular deity or figure of worship.

Besides *fuda* and *omamori*, petitioners at Kawasaki Daishi, as at other religious institutions, whether Shinto, Buddhist, or some of the new religions, can also avail themselves of numerous other protective objects and amulets as well as lucky charms and talismans and other "fortune-beckoning" objects (*engimono*). Petitioners can write their requests on the *gomagi*, the wooden sticks that are immolated in the *goma* ritual, to convey their messages to the buddhas and deities. At virtually all religious institutions, whether Shinto or Buddhist, they can also avail themselves of such devices as votive tablets (*ema*) on which they write their prayers and wishes and address themselves directly to the gods. Such votive tablets are thus "letters to the gods" through which people can externalize, publicly express, and put into concrete form an inner desire.[62]

Many other such objects are available at shrines and temples. Like the Kawasaki Daishi *goma fuda,* they represent the idea of *genze riyaku* and constitute a means of expressing one's desire for good fortune and spiritual protection from bad luck. Such religious paraphernalia, the most tangible aspect of the ritual process of seeking this-worldly benefits, are virtually inseparable from the wider theme of the practices relating to *genze riyaku*—and to commercial issues, as well, since they are sold at religious institutions and thus represent the economically profitable side of the pursuit of this-worldly benefits. Although we discuss them in greater detail in Chapters 5 and 6, we mention them here to show that institutions like Kawasaki Daishi provide their petitioners with a variety of services related to this-worldly benefits, not just in terms of formally organized prayer rituals such as the regular *goma* services, but also in more privatized ways.[63]

The extensive list of benefits offered, combined with the temple's reputation, draws large numbers of petitioners. Their ranks have been augmented in the past two decades by those who visit the temple seeking the protective benefit of traffic safety, which has become, since the 1960s, one of the temple's specialties. Such is the popularity of this function that Kawasaki Daishi has had to establish a prayer hall just for this purpose, complete with parking lot to accommodate cars, motorbikes, and even wheelchairs. Prayer services occur in the parking lot on a regular basis, almost hourly, and the lot is often full. The temple's services are sought out not just by individuals but by organizations as well: in 1993 a number of taxis belonging to taxi firms in the area were seen being blessed in the lot, as well as buses and other commercial vehicles. Temple records show that services have been held from the 1960s onward for major commercial organizations such as the Seibu Department Store in Ikebukuro—which had services for traffic safety for its automobiles—as well as regular services for traffic safety on behalf of the Kanagawa prefectural police force, which has its police cars and motorbikes blessed at the temple.[64]

Individual Wishes and Social Requests

As we have seen in this chapter, the occasions when people seek benefits touch on every form of potential need: from calendrical events related to the seasons to life-cycle events related to growing up and developing into an adult. They deal not only with issues related to individual success and prosperity but with matters for social groups (such as family safety) or organizations (such as company prosperity). Shrines and temples provide a comprehensive range of practices, rituals, and sacred objects that can be utilized to express wishes and ac-

Kawasaki Daishi car blessing lot

quire benefits. And where existing services or forms of benefits are unable to cater to particular needs, there is always the possibility of creating new ones. We can see, then, that this-worldly benefits are widely sought and comprehensively available for total life care, and the institutions that deal with them, such as Kawasaki Daishi and Hōzanji, frame the religious map of Japan and structure its religious environment.

That the seeking of benefits is not specifically or even primarily a personal affair is demonstrated by the fact that organizations ranging from commercial companies to the police force take part in group prayers and petition for benefits at temples such as Kawasaki Daishi. We shall return to this topic in Chapter 5 where, besides looking at individual behavior associated with this-worldly benefits, we touch on some of the social religious organizations (kō) whose raison d'être is linked with the pursuit of this-worldly benefits, as well as some of the commercial enterprises that invoke the gods and patronize shrines and temples in the pursuit of practical benefits.

Our discussion of Kawasaki Daishi shows also that benefits are closely related to actions and ideas formally prescribed in texts and maintained by tradition. That pursuit of this-worldly benefits finds its validation in textual sources, most notably Buddhist texts, has raised interesting questions for Japanese Buddhist scholars, many of whom would prefer to see the pursuit of benefits as an expedient or folk practice that is not fully in accord with Buddhism proper. What do the scriptures say, and how do Japanese Buddhist scholars, particularly when looking through the prisms of their own sectarian perspectives, deal with the topic of *genze riyaku*? It is to such questions that we turn next.

2

Scripture and Benefits

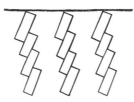

THE TODOROKI FUDŌ TEMPLE, the oldest Buddhist institution in Tokyo's Setagaya ward, is surrounded by a large grove of trees bordering a shallow ravine with a clear stream running through it. Because of recent efforts to eliminate its many polluting sources along the banks, the stream is clean enough for fish to thrive, and the path through the ravine makes for a walk that has the feel of mountain country rather than one of the world's largest cities. The path quickly takes one away from the busy Todoroki train station and leads to an old wooden temple, a subsidiary of the modern Shingon complex called Manganji, Temple for the Fulfillment of Wishes.

Manganji carries the designation of *jōhō danrin*—center for the continual study of the teachings. The head priest is highly educated, as are his two sons, one of whom is his successor, the other a university professor. The temple's main deity is Dainichi Nyorai (Mahāvairocana), the statue of which is said to have been carved by Kōbō Daishi himself. Much more open to the public than Dainichi, and visible at all times from the open courtyard, is the Hitokoto Jizō, the Jizō of One Word. This Jizō is known for its power to fulfill wishes, but it asks that the supplicants be selective and reduce their requests to the economy of one word (*hitokoto*). Jizō, in turn, will be equally efficient in granting those wishes. Both the classical Mahāvairocana, sitting serenely in the back of the altar in the main hall, and the popular Jizō of One Word, accessible to all visitors crunching their way over the gravel in the expansive courtyard, exist in the same compound in complete harmony with each other. For the priests as well as the parishioners, there is no tension between the two, just as the modern steel-reinforced concrete of Manganji complements the ancient wood of Todoroki Fudō Temple.

71

The Todoroki Fudō Temple bears a tradition of past and contemporary popularity. It is said to have been established by Kakuban (1095–1143), the medieval reviver of Kōyasan and founder of the Shingi (New Meaning) branch of the Shingon school. The statue of Fudō was supposedly made by En no Gyōja, the legendary founder of Shugendō mountain asceticism, and a figure of the Gyōja in a small rock niche is a popular stopping place along the path that winds up from the ravine to the temple. The temple's foundation story, its *engi*, tells how Kōbō Daishi, who now sits as a young child (*chigo Daishi*) in a shrine at the bottom of the ravine, had a dream in which he was told that the En no Gyōja Fudō, which at that time was in the Yamato (present-day Nara) area, had a strong connection with a place in Musashino (present-day Tokyo). Taking the statue to Musashino, he found a ravine marked by auspicious clouds and there dug a cave from which burst a stream of water that formed a waterfall with a roaring (*todoroki*) sound. Today the waterfall is but a clear trickle under which laypeople, increasingly young women, still stand in all seasons to purify themselves through this Shugendō ascetic practice. The Todoroki Waterfall, also called the Waterfall of Fudō, is popularly known as the Waterfall of the Sharp Sword. The sharp sword, or *riken*, is carried by Fudō to cut off bad karma and is also associated with Amida's ability to do the same. "*Ri*," the character for "sharp," is the same ideogram as used in "*riyaku*" and it too means "benefits."

The Todoroki Fudō is still a popular place for individuals as well as groups of pilgrims. They seek readings of their fortunes and, if good, tie their divination slips (*omikuji*) to trees and racks to ensure that the predictions will come true. They purchase *omamori* and *ema*, too, one version of which is a particularly beautiful rendition of the Seven Gods of Good Fortune. On certain designated Saturdays the head priest from Manganji, true to his temple's designation as a study center, conducts a seminar at the Todoroki Temple. A recent session, attended by about forty people, only seven of whom were men, featured a lecture on the *Lotus Sutra*.[1] The participants were all given xeroxed passages from the sutra, and the priest lectured on the text line by line, explaining its meaning and adding little homilies to illustrate its points. The lesson that day included the famous parable of the burning house, as well as passages describing the virtues of building stupas of sand. Kōbō Daishi, the priest reminded his audience, lived out the prescriptions of the *Lotus Sutra* by building sand stupas as a child. The participants sat on small cushions used also for meditation, for this was not just study but practice as well, and a short session of quiet sitting followed the lecture in which term after technical term had been explained. Outside the pilgrims jangled the bell, tossed their coins noisily into the offertory box, and silently recited their prayers for health, wealth, and the other important benefits of life. Like the peaceful coexistence between the classical Mahāvairocana and the popular Jizō of One Word, there was no incongruity between the doctrinal study going on inside the temple and the prayers and purchases for benefits being uttered by the dozens of noisy pilgrims on the other side of the paper-thin shōji doors.

This-Worldly Promises: The *Lotus Sutra*

If sutra study and prayers for practical benefits go hand in hand, it is because the sutras themselves teach about the power of Buddhism to fulfill the wishes and desires of the people. It is not a matter of expedient means or syncretic assimilation of folk practices that allow Buddhist priests to promote the practices for practical benefits; it is the explicit doctrines of the sutras that speak directly to the virtue of acquiring material as well as spiritual boons. In speaking of the universal applicability of his teachings, Shakyamuni in the *Lotus Sutra* explains how he preaches appropriately to the clever and the dull, the diligent and the lazy, "so that all of them are delighted and are able to gain excellent benefits therefrom."[2] The sutra continues: "Once these living beings have heard the Law, they will enjoy peace and security in their present existence [*genze an'non*] and good circumstances in future existences [*goshō zensho*]."[3] So that no one mistakes Buddhism for an impractical religion, Shakyamuni reiterates the point:

> I appear in the world
> like a great cloud . . .
> so that all are able to escape suffering,
> gain the joy of peace and security,
> the joys of this world
> and the joy of nirvana.[4]

The good things of the present world, *genze*, are clearly affirmed, not denied. And this understanding of what the Buddha taught was seldom seen, at least before the rise of modern Buddhist studies, as being anything other than an authoritative doctrine prescribed by the scriptures themselves. This particular section of the *Lotus Sutra* was well remembered and reiterated almost as a catch phrase. The Japanese monk Mujū (1226–1312), author of *Shasekishū* (Collection of sand and pebbles), tells the story of a monk delivering a sermon on how Buddhism gives "peace and security in this present existence and good circumstances in future existences." This is particularly true for dealing with the travails of life: "Problems from an ordinary point of view cause grief, but through the teachings of the Buddha become pleasures."[5]

In *Eiga monogatari* (Tale of flowering fortunes), a group of ladies serving the empress made a gorgeous copy of the *Lotus Sutra* and arranged with the help of Fujiwara no Michinaga (966–1027) to dedicate the sutra in a ceremony conducted by a monk who gave a lecture, much like that by the head priest of Todoroki Temple, to explain the "general meaning, titles, and text of the sutra" to the mostly female audience.[6] Praising the women for their understanding of the sutra and their concerns for the well-being of those around them, the monk affirmed that through their "intercession every sentient being may also achieve peace in the present life and rebirth in paradise."[7] A few days before Michinaga died, a courtier dreamed that a little monk emerged from the side of an image of Amida and announced that through his faith in the *Lotus Sutra* Michinaga had achieved "tranquility in the present life and a good place in the next."[8] This passage from the *Lotus Sutra* was a popular phrase intoned in modified versions, often without reference to its scriptural origins. Even in the Nara period it was invoked to affirm the power of Buddhism to provide benefits not only in this life but the next life as well.[9] In modern Japan the passage continues to be prominent in the religious landscape. It can be seen inscribed, for example, on a foot-square, ten-foot-high stone column at the entrance to the Ima Kumano Temple in Kyoto, where the buses park to unload large numbers of pilgrims—a reminder, literally carved in stone, that scripture promises practical benefits to the people of this world.

Although the lecturer in the *Eiga monogatari* praises the women for their understanding of the *Lotus Sutra,* he also repeats the sutra's own characterization of itself as being "impossible to comprehend, impossible to penetrate."[10] Tao-sheng (ca. 360–434), one of several Chinese commentators of the *Lotus Sutra,* described the "subtle words" of the sutra as being "profound and abstruse, mysteriously separated from hearing and seeing."[11] This is the reputation of Buddhist sutras and doctrines in general: they are hardly understandable or understood. When the king of Paekche recommended Buddhism as an effective means for fulfilling desires, he too noted the impenetrability of the teachings. Yet this repeated admission of the incomprehensible nature of the sutras and the doctrines is not a complaint but a boast—ineffability is what makes Buddhism so profound and so effective. The late scholar Tamura Yoshirō, himself a believer in the *Lotus Sutra,* once remarked in a roundtable discussion of Buddhist,

Lotus Sutra passage on practical benefits carved in stone at Ima Kumano

Christian, Shinto, and new religion representatives that "it is sometimes said that the more difficult it is to understand, the more valuable a sutra is when a Buddhist priest chants it."[12] Jiko Kohno, a
Tendai nun who is the chief priest of Jikoji in Osaka, founder of a
branch in Los Angeles, and president of Kohno Pharmaceuticals,
cites Yamada Etai, the late chief abbot of the entire Tendai sect, as
approving of her practice of never touching on the meaning of the
scriptures so as not to confuse her followers, who should only be encouraged to chant and pray wholeheartedly.[13]

The value of the sutra is not just in the discursive meaning of the
text, but in the ritual invocation that activates its mysterious powers.
Kanaoka Shūyū, commenting on the shorter *Heart Sutra (Hannya
shingyō)*, which is widely used as an incantation in rituals and ceremonies and whose final mantra is often regarded as a particularly potent magical spell, notes that wisdom (*hannya*) itself is a spell or
charm (*majinai*) that dissolves all suffering.[14] Satō Taishun, the former head priest of the Sōtō sect and its head temple Eiheiji, affirms
this point in his commentary on the *Hannya shingyō*. Wisdom (as
shown in the sutra) has, according to Satō, the power to dissolve all
obstructions and to guard against evil spirits, and through it all suffering and all danger will be eradicated.[15] The mantra which ends the
sutra is a repository of power that not only accomplishes such magical purposes but offers a means for realizing the highest ideals of
Buddhism; thus the magical spell that ends the sutra is the final link
uniting the meanings and workings of the text.[16] Satō's commentary,
in recognizing and discussing the meanings behind the "highest wisdom" of the sutra, focuses on its magical qualities, viewing the sutra's
mantric ending as the powerful force that activates its meanings. Far
from being a misuse of the sutras, the ritual and magical use of them
(which does not require understanding of the text) has long been
recognized as proper. Ritual incantation of the sutras, in other words,
is efficacious, practical, and in accord with the true principles of Buddhism. If this were not the case, sutra copying and chanting would be
for nothing.

This is not to say that sutras have no discursive meaning or that
they are effectively meaningless. The idea of impenetrability is a concept discursively described without confusion; it is articulated over
and over in the sutras' own words, which are, for the most part, not so
much sublime as hyperbolic and at times lacking in subtlety. Scriptural virtue, here understood as the power of a sutra to bring about
good effects, is clearly articulated in the text and easily understood
without much intellectual trouble. If we are to understand the scriptural orthodoxy of practical benefits, we must at least briefly note
some of the many times the texts assert and affirm the power of Bud-

dhism to produce the good things of life. The scriptural conviction of the practical efficacy of Buddhism is not an East Asian invention but goes back to normative Indian Buddhist teachings.

Benefits in Early Buddhist Teachings

"All India is an empty thing; it is verily like chaff! There is no one, either recluse or Brahman, capable of discussing things with me, and dispelling my doubts."[17] Thus lamented King Milinda as he went from sage to sage, besting them in argumentation, silencing them with questions they could not answer, searching for but not finding a capable teacher. King Milinda did not win his arguments because he had a superior point of view; in fact, he had no position except that of an intelligent seeker looking for answers to his tough questions. Befitting a king, his questions were pragmatic, centering primarily on the weighty matters of right and wrong, good and evil. He was well known for his hard questions and even more for his severe critique of all answers. The Buddhists, like all others from the various religious and philosophical schools, knew him as "that King Milinda [who] is in the habit of harassing the brethren by knotty questions and by argumentations this way and that."[18] Seeking once again to find a worthy teacher, King Milinda visited the Elder Ayupāla to ask about Buddhism and, as he expected, received an answer he skillfully demonstrated as making little sense, thus causing him to lament once again: "All India is an empty thing; it is verily like chaff!"[19] The stage was now set for his meeting with Nāgasena.

"Endowed with instantaneous and varied power of repartee, and wealth of language, and beauty of eloquence,"[20] Nāgasena would finally satisfy the king. While their extensive discussions sometimes ranged into abstruse metaphysics, the king's initial question, the one that Ayupāla could not answer, was simple enough. "Of what use," he had asked Ayupāla, "is the renunciation of the world carried out by members of your Order?"[21] The key term here is "use." In the Chinese translation of this eminently pragmatic question, the word is rendered with the character "*li*," the same term that for Fudō's sword means sharp, but which also means profit, gain, advantage, benefit, interest, privilege, or usefulness. Ayupāla was driven to silence, not because he was unable to specify the benefits of Buddhism, but because he could not demonstrate that renunciation was required for the acquisition of the benefits in question—namely, righteousness and spiritual calm. Laypersons, Ayupāla admitted, were able to acquire spiritual calm, and the king therefore concluded that renunciation was necessary only for those who were in need of atoning for their past evil deeds.[22] Not being satisfied with Ayupāla, the king re-

peated his question to Nāgasena: what is the point of renunciation?
Nāgasena replied that the great benefit of severing oneself from the
world is that sorrow is thereby destroyed. That, recognized the king,
is the "high reason" for joining the order, but are there others? Of
course, replied Nāgasena, who then specified a remarkably frank list
of other benefits for becoming a Buddhist renunciant: freedom from
the tyranny of kings, safety from robbers, immunity from creditors,
and the gaining of a livelihood.[23] Different as King Milinda might
have found Ayupāla's and Nāgasena's answers to have been, there was
common agreement on the point that Buddhism had benefits to offer laypersons and clerics. If there were not practical benefits, why
would anyone become a Buddhist?

What is interesting about Nāgasena's answer is that it asserts a positive relationship between renunciation and worldly benefits—two
categories that in other doctrinal treatments are seen in an antago-
nistic relationship whereby renunciation is precisely the rejection of
worldly benefits, not the cause of them. Confirming the fruits of renunciation to spiritual benefits is a major theme in Buddhist writings,
and in taking note of Nāgasena's different formulation we are not
suggesting that worldly denial is unimportant or is somehow refuted
in the texts. In focusing on writings that affirm the world and the
good things of it, we seek to balance our understanding of Buddhism
by showing that worldly affirmation is just as important as worldly denial, even when both stand in contrast to each other. Both exist side
by side, equally important, though they have different roles to play,
different audiences to address, and different configurations of how
they stand in relationship to one another.

The one-sided view that Buddhism is primarily a philosophy of
truth that transcends any concern for the mundane matters of profit
and gain has been produced by academic traditions of the study of
Buddhism extending back through many centuries of interpretation
by scholar-monks in the past and academicians in our own time. The
resulting high-toned rejection of worldly benefits (which has manifested itself also in the critiques of the new religions mentioned earlier) was particularly strident because one of the very foundations of
monastic Buddhism was the rejection of all desire. Benefits are fulfill-
ments of desire and therefore represent the fruition of the most fundamentally wrong emotion or thought one could ever have, at least
in this understanding of the teaching of the Buddha. The dilemma,
of course, was that the rejection of desire had to be desired. And such
a desire could not be rejected since it promised in a profoundly self-
contradictory way that it would lead to the cessation of suffering, a
benefit much desired even by the strictest of monks. Though it is the
root cause of suffering and therefore deserving of renunciation, de-

sire could not be totally destroyed, even for the renunciant, and from that inevitable condition it was not difficult to affirm that renunciation produced desired results, and that affirmation of the world was also possible. Both strands coexist and produced a religion that supported clerical monasticism and lay worldliness.

Buddhist scriptures and their commentaries, both of which might be considered to comprise the highest level of Buddhist literary expression and authority, are filled with accounts of the practical benefits of the dharma. The concern for benefits is a major theme running throughout Buddhist writings from the earliest scriptures to the most contemporary tracts. In the *Book of the Gradual Sayings* (*Anguttara Nikāya*), for instance, Sumanā, a ruler's daughter, is told by the Buddha that those who give alms will surpass the nongivers in lifespan, beauty, happiness, honor, and power.[24] Upon being asked by Cundī, another ruler's daughter, about the best religion to follow, the Buddha replied that "whosoever put their trust in the Buddha, put their trust in the best, and unto them is the best reward."[25] Sīha, the general, as might be expected of a military man, wanted to know what "visible result" would accrue from giving alms. The Buddha replied that the man who gives alms will have good and wise followers, confidence in being with nobles or recluses, fame, honor, joy, and rebirth in heaven.[26]

The virtue of good benefits is pervasive, forming not only the results of a commitment to Buddhism but the cause of it as well. Getting rich, for instance, is not only one of the rewards of Buddhism but is good for its own reasons, five to be exact: wealth lawfully gained allows a householder to make his family and slaves happy; to provide for his friends; to ward off ill luck from fire, robbers, and enemies; to make oblations to relatives, guests, and kings; and to make offerings to the Buddhist order and thereby receive spiritual peace. These are the "reasons for getting rich," and they are the same reasons, received as results, for pledging oneself to the support of the dharma.[27] There is an appropriate mutual dependence between benefits and Buddhism, a kind of self-sustaining, ever improving, system: give so that you may receive, so that you may give again and receive even more. Longevity, beauty, happiness, honor, power, rewards, fame, joy, rebirth in heaven, and wealth: these are but a few of the myriad benefits of Buddhism. If the later Mahāyāna sutras speak freely of practical benefits, it is not because they acquired such a crass idea from non-Buddhist sources. They were repeating what was already in the early canonical writings, at least in those sections addressing the interests of laypersons.

The recommendations of the spiritual utilitarianism of the dharma are so ubiquitous in the Mahāyāna sutras that they are easily glossed over as typical hyperbole. The *Flower Garland Sutra* (Ch. *Hua-yen ching;* Jp. *Kegon-gyō*), for instance, lists at length the virtues of the aspiration or determination for enlightenment:

> The aspiration of enlightenment is like good medicine since it can cure all illnesses and afflictions; . . . it can sever one from all poverty; . . . it is like the wish-fulfilling gem, since it drives away all poverty; it is like a vase of virtue, fulfilling the desires of all sentient beings; it is like sweet dew since it can take you to the peaceful realm of immortality; . . . it is like the Agada elixir of life, since it can immunize one from sickness and bring about eternal comfort (*an'non*); . . . it is like a marketplace, since it is the place for enlightened businessmen and traders; it is like a great benevolent society, since it fulfills the desires of all sentient beings.[28]

The list includes the protection of logical thinking, motivation of people toward their goals, the rejection of the useless, and on and on with a host of other good things. The language is reminiscent of the familiar promise of comfort and benefits in the *Lotus Sutra:* "The aspiration for enlightenment is like a home since it gives comfort (*an'non*) to all sentient beings. The aspiration for enlightenment is to be relied upon, for it confers benefits (*riyaku*) on the entire world."[29]

One could perhaps argue that this language is hyperbolic, metaphorical, not to be taken literally. The text, however, does not differentiate between promises of mundane benefits to be taken metaphorically and the loftier virtues of emptiness, nonduality, noncognition, enlightenment, and the like to be understood literally. And if the utilitarian pleasures of Buddhism are not real, then neither can the higher wisdom be real. Both are but hyperbole—pure fictions or "magical sermons" as Tominaga Nakamoto (1715–1746) came to see the content of the sutras.[30] This interpretation is a privilege for critics like Tominaga, but not for the sutra writers or believers, who at some level, if not all levels, regard these claims to be literal truths. Both are tied together: to understand one in a certain way is to understand the other in exactly the same way. The sutra speaks equally of mundane benefits and supramundane enlightenment.

Benefits as Divine Blessings: The *Flower Garland Sutra*

So, too, do the sutras speak equally of the cessation of desire. As ubiquitous as the promises of good things are the condemnations of passion and selfishness that give Buddhism its reputation for worldly denial. The affirmation and rejection of desire most often stand as unresolved contradictions that force interpreters, as we shall see, to cite external exigencies to justify the internal inconsistencies between the rejection and acceptance of desire. But sometimes there is an inner logic to it all, at least in one section of the *Flower Garland Sutra* in which the young aspirant Sudhana makes his famous pilgrimage to seek wisdom from a wide variety of people. When he visits the Night Goddess, she tells him about the time when the Buddha Vairocana (Dainichi) took pity on the miserable human condition caused by craving and she thereby promises vast improvements:

> [Vairocana] saw all living beings entangled in themselves and their belongings, existing in the dark room of ignorance, entering the dense forest of all opinions, bound by greed and love, corrupted by anger. . . .
>
> So he gave rise to a mind of great compassion to provide practical benefits (*riyaku*) to all living beings. He made a vow that they should obtain all kinds of marvelous treasures and material resources. He embraced the minds of living beings and promised to provide all of them with all the material assets for living so that they would not feel destitute, be free of attachment to all things, and be without craving in all spheres. He showered upon them a mind for material treasures in accord with what they desired.[31]

Desire, greed, love, and the many other passions are clearly the root of much suffering, and the sutra does not hesitate to condemn such emotions. The solution proposed here, however, lies not in renunciation but in the fulfillment of these desires. What makes this fulfillment of desires acceptable is the wish-granting agent. Vairocana displays a utilitarian compassion: accepting human desires as an unavoidable fact, he takes it upon himself to fulfill these desires, thus sparing people the selfish task of having to pursue their own passions by themselves. To satisfy one's own desire is greed; to have a buddha satisfy one's own desire is a blessing. The great benevolence and compassion of the buddhas lie in their willingness to grant us our desires, to intercede on our behalf, legitimately fulfilling for us what we can fulfill for ourselves only under the condemnation of greed. Herein lies an important aspect of the conceptual and ritual framework of this-worldly benefits: *riyaku* are divine rewards granted by compassionate divinities who affirm the immorality of selfishness but allow for the morality of petitioning the gods, who themselves fulfill wishes. Divine altruism makes it possible for there to be personal fulfillment without persons having to personally fulfill their wishes. It would be a way of having our cake and eating it too—except for the fact that the benefits are not free, since the morality of reliance upon the gods exacts a price. Only by first *purchasing* the cake can we then eat it.

Eating the cake with a clear conscience is important because requesting and receiving practical benefits could so easily be seen as improper acts. The widespread and deeply rooted practice of acquiring benefits, however, makes it clear that very few people in fact feel there is anything wrong here. Although their easy acceptance of these practices could easily be explained in terms of superstition and ignorance, they are also carrying out, consciously or not, the provisions in the sutras that call for devotion and effort in asking the gods to fulfill their wishes. We have suggested that there is a logic by which divine altruism not only legitimates the fulfillment of desires but is also consistent with moral discipline and the restraint of desire. Those who fail to see this scriptural logic have difficulty accepting the contradiction between restraint and fulfillment. They can only see the latter as improper human expression and not as a divine act of grace. For them, practical benefits fall unavoidably into the category of superstition and bad religion. This condemnation would be easy to sustain except for the problematic fact, which they too recognize, that the recommendations for benefits are to be found incontrovertibly in the sutras. The challenge for those who find it difficult to accept praying for this-worldly benefits as a normative component of Buddhism is one of justifying the scriptural affirmations of these practices without compromising their sense of what constitutes true religion. As we shall see in the following sections, where we discuss how a number of Japanese scholars have attempted to deal with the question of *genze riyaku* in relation to Buddhism, this leads to all manner of methodological problems but rarely succeeds in squaring the circle. Part of the problem is due to the fact that many Buddhist scholars in Japan are also priests who work at Buddhist universities, and as a result practice a form of scholarship that is close to confessional theology.

Benefits as Windfall: Fujii Masao

True religion, according to Fujii Masao, a Japanese scholar who has written widely on the topic of *genze riyaku*, can legitimately contain provisions for practical benefits, but the precise conditions under which such pleasures are to be enjoyed must be clearly understood if one is to avoid falling into the false religion of practical benefits (*goriyaku shinkō*). Writing primarily about Buddhism, Fujii has analyzed the *Sutra of Golden Light* (*Konkō-kyō*), the *Sutra of the Benevolent Kings* (*Ninnō-kyō*), and the *Lotus Sutra* (*Hoke-kyō*) and specified the conditions under which practical benefits can be affirmed. It is important to note, he says, that the practical benefits are all explained in these sutras in the sections that follow the explanations of the main principles and doctrines. Benefits therefore must not be divorced from correct practices and the true teachings, and, furthermore, are provided for in the latter sections for the sake of propagating the sutra. Practitioners do not gain these benefits by themselves but are granted them (as we noted earlier) by the buddhas. Citing Chi-tsang's commentary to the *Lotus Sutra,* Fujii points out that benefits require moral action as well as true religious understanding and practice. The most important condition to understand, however, is a psychological one: the mind of the practitioner must be free of all desire for, and expectation of, benefits; then and only then will benefits naturally and spontaneously result from correct understanding and practice. Practitioners, in other words, must never be supplicants. There must be an absolute purity of intention, an absence of desire, as one practices without expectation of any gain. If benefits result— and Fujii recognizes that the sutras conceive of the power of Buddhism to include unequivocally the capacity to produce benefits— they are but a windfall, understood here as unexpected gains. Repeatedly Fujii insists that this-worldly benefits are "not sought but naturally acquired (*fugu jitoku*)."[32]

Fujii's points are well taken, especially his insistence that benefits are divinely granted and result from proper moral and religious effort. The problem with his analysis, however, lies in his understanding of what constitutes proper religious practice, particularly the matter of prayer. Since his main point is that practitioners must not seek benefits as objectives of their practice, "religious prayer is only a matter of throwing oneself before the gods and buddhas with devotion; it is the antithesis of the arrogance by which human beings claim to have the power to manipulate the deities and magically control them."[33] Fujii clearly insists on the impropriety of *expecting* benefits, since such an expectation assumes that one can manipulate the deities. Benefits must be unexpected rewards—a recognition of good works performed only for the sake of good works. Prayer is not supplication, or petition, but pure devotion with no thought of having the gods do something for us. Without expectation—and only without expectation—will we be blessed enough to receive. The difference, then, between true and false religion can be detected on the basis of whether or not there is expectation. Those who expect are fallen; those who do not expect are pure. While the psychology of intent may differ, the mechanism is the same: good works and correct practice will be attended naturally by appropriate benefits, whether they are sought as objectives or not. If Fujii is correct in holding that prayer can only be for devotional purposes free of expectation of divine boons, then prayer cannot be petitionary. Prayer as petition would be, in his logic, a shameless asking for divine benefits as the objectives of prayer. Benefits petitioned for in prayer are not the natural, unexpected windfall that Fujii insists must result from true devotion; they are, rather, deliberately sought effects. Fujii's rejection of the false religion of practical benefits is also the rejection of prayer as petition and supplication.

This understanding of prayer, as we shall see, cannot be supported by scriptural teaching or traditional practice. Fujii's own analysis at times betrays his insistence on the need for zero expectations. In his treatment of the *Ninnō-kyō* (Sutra of the benevolent kings), for instance, he says that the sutra has the Buddha teaching kings about the highest wisdom "for the sake of securing peace in the country"[34] and "in order to avoid the Seven Calamities and obtain the Seven Blessings."[35] In his discussion of the theoretical structure and psychology of *genze riyaku,* he agrees with other scholars who understand the religion of practical benefits as a means of dealing with frustration and failure and regard religious ritual as a means to reestablish existential coordinates and bearings when all other measures fail.[36] These are all petitionary strategies with clearly desired objectives: securing peace, avoiding calamities, obtaining blessings, dealing with frustration, and reestablishing directions in life. These are not the natural consequences of religious practice that takes pure devotion as its sole objective; they are the deliberate purposes for which devotion is a means of acquisition. Fujii does not indicate that he recognizes the existence of these deliberate expectations. For him the placement of passages on this-worldly benefits in the later sections of the sutra gives them the subordinate role of being expedient means for the propagation of the philosophical and moral teachings that are prior in the text and therefore have priority. For him the psychology of practical benefits is rooted in pure motives devoid of any expectation of getting something in return for right understanding and practice. Benefits just happen, as if they have no relationship to actions. Certainly undeserved, they come close to being uncaused results.

Benefits as Objectives: Iijima Yoshiharu

Fujii's idea of benefits as windfall raises questions about causality and deliberation, topics we shall explore in the next chapter. Here it is sufficient to note that the very notion of morality depends on these questions—for if actions do not have consequences or cannot be planned, then goodness is left to whim and chance. We suggest, however, that the conceptual and ritual framework of practical benefits clearly involves, even on the theoretical level, a moral deliberation that establishes causes for gaining specific results that are profits earned and not just rewards fallen from the wind of divine generosity. Fujii, of course, recognizes that while they cannot be justified in theory, practical benefits are deliberately sought in fact. Except to speak of practical benefits as expedient means for propagation purposes, however, Fujii does not entertain much in the way of explaining the actual practice of seeking benefits.

Building on Fujii's windfall theory, Iijima Yoshiharu ventures forward to provide a historical explanation of how the understanding of benefits shifted from windfall to earnings. Like Fujii, he starts with the usual citation of the *Lotus Sutra* passage on peace and security in this life and reiterates Fujii's analysis that benefits are "not sought but naturally acquired" (*fugu jitoku*).[37] These unsought benefits were initially limited to spiritual benefits but gradually came to be material boons deliberately sought through an inversion of the windfall idea—a shift that Iijima locates as having begun in the Muromachi period with the rise of the *machishū*, the urban class with commercial interests. This secularization process blossomed in the Edo period with the greater development of *chōnin* (merchant) culture, and it was during that time of increasing urbanization, commerce, self-sufficiency, and prosperity that an earlier Buddhism of purer spirituality succumbed to the Japanese worldview that insists on economic returns on any investment of effort and resources. Buddhism itself had changed.

In 1688 the Bakufu made an official distinction between "old trace" (*koseki*) temples built before 1631, when a ban on new temples had been instituted, and the "new ground" (*shinchi*) temples that were allowed to be built after that. Under the temple registration system (*terauke*), the older temples had their own members who looked upon their temples as *ekōdera*, family temples for the transfer of merit to the ancestors. The new temples became *kitōdera*, prayer temples that did not have a fixed congregation but served any worshiper or supplicant wanting rituals and prayers to be offered for desired ends. The popularity of the prayer temples was enhanced by the official ban on religious itinerants such as holy men (*hijiri*), shamans (*miko*), and ritualists (*gyōnin*), all of whom were barred from taking their services to the people. The people therefore went to the prayer temples, the new centers for the religion of practical benefits. Without a fixed congregation, the prayer temples sought to increase their clients through stories of miracles and divine powers creditable to the resident deity or priest. Auspicious days (*ennichi*) were established in which visits to the temples would be rewarded with benefits far greater than those available on ordinary days. Special times for "lifting the curtain" (*kaichō*) to expose deities otherwise hidden from public view also attracted people to the temples. In 1692, temples that had been built as new ground temples were reclassified as old trace temples, and new construction was again forbidden. Orders banning new temples had to be issued two or three times later—an indication of the difficulty of controlling the rise of new prayer temples and their offers of prac-

tical benefits.[38] Political restrictions had the effect of raising the value
of the controlled substances.

In addition to the political reasons for the increased numbers and
value of the prayer temples, Iijima locates the driving force behind
this transformation of Buddhism into a religion for practical benefits
in the social and economic conditions of the time. Urbanization
brought increased tension in social relations, and people turned to
the temples and shrines that offered prayers and rituals for better
marital relations, harmony in the family, smooth dealings with friends
and business associates, and the like. Commercialization and con-
sumerism fueled materialistic appetites that motivated people to seek
the help of the deities for increasing their wealth, ensuring business
success, and avoiding disaster. All of this secularization placed greater
emphasis on this-worldliness, *genze,* and religious institutions thrived
in response to this new market demand. Like other economic enterprises that did not enjoy guaranteed customers, the prayer temples
vied with each other to promote their virtues and attract clients.
Buddhism, now commercialized, lost its original understanding of
benefits as unsought spontaneous returns and became a spiritual
means for deliberately gaining secular ends.[39] Buddhism, in short,
degenerated, and that is how it became a religion of practical
benefits.

The problem here is that Iijima is striving to offer reasons why Buddhism "became" like this: focused, as he sees it, on the deliberate gain
of secular ends. In so doing the reasons he has devised for this de-
generative development are located in the political, social, and economic arenas: in other words, the reasons for Buddhism's involvement in such activities come from without, not from within, and as a
result he creates an image of a Buddhism that was once pure but is
now defiled. Thus Iijima, through this explanation of why Buddhism
is involved in proselytizing this-worldly benefits in Japan, appears to
be articulating the type of differentiation between "true" and "false"
(or degenerate) religions that we have already argued is erroneous.

We have already seen how the sutras defined and affirmed the deliberate seeking of benefits long before the Muromachi and Edo periods—indeed, well before Buddhism ever arrived in Japan. The economic and social changes Iijima describes were certainly fuel for the
fires of this-worldly benefits in those eras, but they were not the
sparks that started the blaze. No shift was required for a religion that
had long affirmed spiritual means to gain secular and practical ends
and had long boasted of its powers to bring about such effects. Commercialization provided the conditions that were perfect for Buddhism's growth on its own scriptural terms, not as a result of an in-
fection by external agents breeding a wildly spreading cancer of
mutant and defective cells.

Iijima's portrait of Buddhism as a degenerating religion includes another mutation of religious behavior—namely, the shift from a consciousness of people being under the control of the deities to an awareness that it is humans who control the gods. Like Fujii, Iijima assumes that asking for benefits presupposes that we can control the gods or at least influence them to fulfill our requests.[40] We demand; they obey and supply. Iijima's focus on the dynamics of the relationship between people and the gods is suggestive, certainly, but control is not the issue. To ask someone for something is not to control the person but, almost to the contrary, to be obligated to that person, especially if the request is granted. What is at stake here is not control but obligation and gratitude. As we noted earlier in our discussion of the *Flower Garland Sutra,* to have the gods give us what we want is to be spared the vice of selfishness and to obligate ourselves morally to earn our rewards. This is a favor but it is not a free gift. To pray for practical benefits means to study diligently, to keep going to the doctor, to work hard at the job, and all of the other kinds of right conduct that prayers do not obviate but invoke instead. Commercialization does not require control of the gods; what it demands is the obligation to pay for what one gets.

Benefits as Concession and Mystery: Ōchō Enichi

Like Fujii and Iijima, Ōchō Enichi, a respected scholar of the *Lotus Sutra,* faced the dilemma of justifying practical benefits in terms of what he regarded to be true religion. Recognizing that the passage on "peace and security in their present existence (*genze an'non*) and good circumstances in future existences (*goshō zensho*)" is the locus classicus for the belief in practical benefits, Ōchō noted the contradiction between the monastic and antimonastic trains of thought in the sutra. Rather than affirm the contradiction as a safeguard against an overemphasis on antimonasticism, much as Sueki Fumihiko credits the contradiction between the antinominism of affirming the world as it is and the discipline required for enlightenment through verbal identity as having "saved *hongaku* teachings from becoming completely corrupted,"[41] Ōchō attempted to bring about conceptual order by insisting on the primacy of "this life" (*genshō*) over "this-worldly" (*genze*). It is legitimate, he argued, for there to be good things in this life, but these good things are not to be understood as this-worldly benefits, which are secular and therefore have nothing to do with religion. Furthermore, these good things are the result of meritorious acts (*kudoku riyaku*) requiring primarily genuine faith. Ōchō notes that while the Buddhist technical term "*riyaku*" is pronounced "*rieki*" in ordinary Japanese, in a religious context it must always be spoken of as "*riyaku*" to distinguish it from "*rieki*" and its meaning of interest and returns on financial investments, which religion most certainly is not about. The benefits in this life promised by the *Lotus Sutra* are not this-worldly boons but otherworldly ones—namely, the promise and prediction of buddhahood in the next life. This-worldly benefits are based on desires that are soundly condemned in the parable of the burning house, and it is clear that only religious faith matters in this world. Any worldly joy affirmed by the sutra, even the benefits promised in the "Medicinal Herbs" chapter, results from cessation of the desires that cause suffering, and there is therefore no affirmation of this-worldly benefits (*genze riyaku*).[42]

Ōchō's interpretation is significantly forced. It is possible only by overlooking the passages in the "Medicinal Herbs" chapter, for instance, in which the Buddha does not make the same distinction that he makes between right and wrong religious practices and, in fact, promises to rain benefits impartially on all, the "eminent and lowly, superior and inferior, observers of precepts, violators of precepts."[43] Ōchō continually wrestles with the sutra to make it support his interpretation that the benefits it so freely promises are not to be understood literally and, moreover, all serve higher spiritual purposes. When the Never-Despising Bodhisattva was about to die, he heard the *Lotus Sutra* and gained two hundred and ten thousand million nayutas more years of his life,[44] and this, notes Ōchō, does not mean longevity in the ordinary sense but a prolongation of life for the sake of preaching the sutra. Ōchō cautions against any interpretation that would twist this passage to make it promise the this-worldly benefit of simply living longer.[45] Yet it is only by twisting the text that we can escape what is a straightforward promise of longer life:

> This sutra can save all living beings. This sutra can cause all living beings to free themselves from suffering and anguish. This sutra can bring great benefits to all living beings and fulfill their desires, as a clear cool pond can satisfy all those who are thirsty. . . .
>
> If a person who has an illness is able to hear this sutra, then his illness will be wiped out and he will know neither old age or death.[46]

The text can be twisted to make it not say what it does say, and the clearly promised longevity and immortality can thus be construed as not being promised.

Ōchō's solution to his dilemma of making the sutra fit his modern understanding of right religion comes by claiming that concessions to external factors had to be made in order to propagate the sutras. The message of the sutra, however, persists. And as Ōchō continues to note the places, especially in the latter chapters of the sutra, that promise a host of this-worldly benefits, he has no choice but to criti-

cize the scripture itself. Citing the passages that promise the fulfillment of desires through the granting of this-worldly (*genze*) food and
clothing to those who recite the sutra, Ōchō exclaims: "What kind of
brazen passage is this? Religious people should not crave such material benefits of this world."[47] And yet the promise clearly exists in
the sutra. Ōchō finally resorts to the common way of dealing with
troublesome scripture: by explaining that the promises were made as
a concession to common people in order to attract them to the faith.
Without such crass promises, the sutra could not be propagated. If
the scripture held only to the high road of strict discipline and faith,
the road to enlightenment would be blocked. The fulfillment of desires had to be promised in order to keep the road open and invite
people to travel on it, but Ōchō is still critical: the sutra goes too far
in affirming desire. Realizing, perhaps, the dangers of criticizing the
sacred writings, Ōchō takes refuge in the *Lotus Sutra*'s reputation for
being incomprehensible. The sutra clearly promotes this-worldly
benefits, he concedes, and his final justification is that the rationale
for such a brazen message is to be relegated to the profound mystery
of the sutra that surpasses human understanding.[48]

It is an interesting hermeneutic tactic to reject a disagreeable part
of scripture by claiming an inability to understand it. Ōchō arrived at
this point by passing through three stages: exegesis of terms (*genshō*
is not *genze*); concession theory (the sutra must appeal to practical interests); and cognitive defeat (ultimately the promises of benefits are
a mystery). Exegesis has clear limitations—after all, there are only so
many ways a text can be made to mean something other than what it
says, although a rejection of literal meanings opens up a very wide variety of alternatives. Defeat is the least acceptable though easiest way
out since the interpreter withdraws from the struggle to make the text
mean what it does not say. The most respectable approach is to invoke
some form of concession theory, which is closely related to the use of
the idea of skillful means as a way of justifying what otherwise would
remain unacceptable. Concession theory allows the interpreter to let
a disagreeable teaching stand, explaining it as a less than right but
more than necessary concession to human limitations or practical exigencies that must be addressed if the sutra is to gain a following. It is,
as we have seen, the most common way of explaining away the disturbing affirmation of the magic and superstition of this-worldly
benefits at the highest levels of scripture and doctrine.

Benefits as Folk Syncretism: Tsuruoka Shizuo

While the concession argument is widely used to explain the acceptance and development of practical benefits at the higher levels of

Buddhist thought, the idea of syncretism follows closely behind it in trying to justify the open acceptance of what is less than right but more than necessary. The difference between the two lies in the degree to which the process is deliberately carried out. Concession implies deliberation, which is required in any act of writing, and it is therefore an appropriate category to use in the study of sutras and their affirmation of practical benefits. When we look at actual practices and beliefs in real communities, however, as opposed to the deliberations of written texts, we need a concept for explaining a less conscious process, one in which people adopt and adapt without really planning for it or even being aware that some kind of compromise or concession is taking place. The idea of syncretism tolerates such a lack of awareness of the difference between what is right and what is necessary and allows for a naïveté that contrasts with the condescension of concession. It is problematic, however, as a means of analyzing or explaining the interactions between Buddhism and Shinto or the worship and functionings of buddhas and Shinto deities, as we shall see in Chapter 4.

Syncretism is the primary conceptual device used by the Association for the Study of Japanese Buddhism (Nihon Bukkyōkenkyū kai) to explain the development of practical benefits in Japan. Their collection of studies set out in the volume *Nihon shūkyō no genze riyaku* (This-worldly benefits in Japanese religion), originally published in 1970 and reissued in 1991, is still the most comprehensive examination of this topic,[49] and they too faced the task of squaring practical benefits with true religion. Taking the case of beliefs and practices surrounding Yakushi, the Medicine Buddha or Buddha of Healing, in early Japan, Tsuruoka Shizuo reserves for scholar-monks and sectarian founders the ability to understand the doctrines of Buddhism. Laypersons, however, be they aristocrats or commoners, did not understand doctrinal religion and used religious means only to seek practical benefits. Tsuruoka views the existence of practical benefits as a later accretion to Shakyamuni's religion, which originally did not include practical benefits or petitionary prayer, and he sees one of the earliest examples of this kind of syncretism in the cult of Yakushi. The case of Yakushi exemplifies the manner in which a wide variety of beliefs about practical benefits were absorbed into an originally pure form of Buddhism that was seldom understood correctly in terms of its profound doctrines. Because of this syncretism, people thought of practical benefits as being a part of Buddhism, but in fact it was an external system picked up along the way. Specifically Yakushi came to be associated with healing when it was assimilated with an indigenous mountain *kami* in Japan known for its healing powers.[50] The important point of Tsuruoka's study—and it is a widely held viewpoint reminiscent of Iijima's analysis—is that practical benefits entered into Buddhism as it absorbed native beliefs and practices.

We would not deny that numerous interactions between Buddhist and Shinto deities took place. But as we shall see in Chapter 4, to explain this simply as "syncretism" does not work. What facilitated the interaction was that both religions spoke something of the same language in terms of the ability of their deities to provide practical benefits. Just as Iijima's analysis attributes the "corruption" of Buddhism to forces outside its "real self"—to political, social, and economic factors in Tokugawa Japan—so does Tsuruoka shift the "blame" for the appearance of this-worldly benefits away from Buddhism and onto another external force, in this case the absorption of native tendencies, beliefs, and practices. Tsuruoka's analysis does not work any better than Iijima's, however. As we have seen, the portrait of an original Buddhism free from the notion of practical benefits cannot be maintained. In the case of Yakushi, the healing powers of this buddha were not acquired from Shinto *kami* but were already well defined in the sutras long before they were brought to Japan. In his preface to the *Sutra on the Merits of the Fundamental Vows of the Master of Healing Tathāgata (Yakushi-kyō)*, the Sui-period scholar-monk Hui-chü wrote that

> those who recall, concentrate on, and call out the Buddha's name will be freed from all suffering. Those who make requests of the Buddha and worship him with *pūja* offerings will have all their wishes fulfilled. This even extends to the case of a sick person whom one seeks to save. Though that person ought to die, he will live again.[51]

The cult of Yakushi, as Raoul Birnbaum notes, originated in India and Central Asia, and the *Sutra on the Merits of the Fundamental Vows of the Master of Healing, the Lapis Lazuli Radiance Tathāgata* makes it very clear that the Yakushi who came to Japan in this sutra was already fully equipped with powers to heal and grant other boons. Among Yakushi's twelve vows are promises "to cause all beings to obtain all that they need" and to cure the "ugly, stupid, deaf, blind, mute, bent and lame, hunchbacked, leprous, convulsive, insane," and others so that they shall "have neither sickness nor suffering."[52]

The list of benefits is similar to what can be found in the *Lotus Sutra* and other Mahāyāna scriptures: food, clothing, prosperity, longevity, peace, kindness, knowledge, and enlightenment. Once again we note the easy juxtaposition of material gains with spiritual virtues. The analysis of the causes of misfortune and sickness is typically Buddhist, and all blame is affixed to one's bad karmic record. The cure therefore requires, besides ritual chanting and offerings, improved moral behavior—and this ethical requirement, as we have suggested, is an important part of the conceptual and ritual framework of practical benefits. We note here that the sutra has its own sense of true and false religion and clearly condemns what it considers to be superstition. The first of nine "untimely deaths" befalls those who believe the "masters of black magic" and ask "divinatory questions," calling upon the "spirits of the waters" to lengthen their lives. "Stupid and confused, believing in false and inverted views—it follows that such a person is led to an untimely death and enters into a hell with no definite time of release."[53] Yakushi the Buddha has powers that are real and true, and one should shun the local spirits and masters of magic and false views. The sutra in fact boasts of Buddhism's sufficient and superior power to provide all good things desired in life, and to understand this is to have an unquestionably correct doctrinal understanding that warns against any syncretism with the wrong religion of the local spirits.

The issue of right religion is a matter of constant concern in the sutras. There is always the fear of heresy—the fear that readers of the teachings will not get the message right. In the *Sutra on the Merits of the Fundamental Vows of the Master of Healing, the Lapis Lazuli Radiance Tathāgata,* heresy consists, not in believing in Yakushi Buddha's power to heal and fulfill desires, but in seeking those benefits from non-Buddhist deities. Even worse than unfaithfulness is slandering the buddhas by believing that they cannot heal. Taking our cues from scripture, we suggest that the easy working relationship between Shinto *kami* and the buddhas occurred not because the *kami* could do things the buddhas could not, but because it was easy to add a complement to what was already there in self-sufficient force. It was the acceptance of minor allies rather than the hiring of a mercenary army to do the dirty work of satisfying people's base demands.

The *Sutra on the Merits of the Fundamental Vows of the Seven Buddhas of Lapis Lazuli Radiance, the Masters of Healing* puts forth a typical pattern of the condition that makes possible the practice of practical benefits. The condition is the vows made by the the buddhas, vows that give efficacy to the practice of chanting and hearing the names of the buddhas. The fourth vow of the Buddha Auspicious King, for example, is representative:

> I vow that when I attain enlightenment in the future age, if there are any sentient beings who lack clothing, food, necklaces, bedding, property, precious things, fragrant flowers, or music—if such beings are able to call out my name with perfect sincerity, due to my

spiritual force whatever was lacking in their lives will be obtained in ample quantity, and they will reach enlightenment.[54]

The pattern of divine vows fulfillable by the hearing of the name is a common one that has been made popular particularly in the Pure Land (Jōdo) and True Pure Land (Jōdo Shin) sects. The famous vows of Amida that form the basis of Pure Land belief promise, among many other benefits, immunity from rebirth in hell, mastery of extraordinary faculties, knowledge of other people's minds, the divine eye and ear, immeasurable life, analytic understanding, homage from the world, noble robes, rebirth in the Buddha's country, sweet perfumes, jewels, and other boons and bounties.[55] Jōdo Shin scholars and priests are particularly insistent—it is their interpretive right to do so—that the religion of practical benefits is unacceptable superstition, but this argument is possible only by ignoring what their own sutras say.

The idea that such benefits can be realized just through the hearing of the divine name is truly fabulous, and the author of the *Sutra on the Merits of the Fundamental Vows of the Seven Buddhas of Lapis Lazuli Radiance, the Masters of Healing* was well aware that some would read this and doubt it was right religion. He thus addresses this issue with an explicit treatment of the problem of wrong belief. The doubters are the demigods who wonder, "How can it be that by fleetingly hearing the names of the present Tathāgatas of Buddha realms far distant beyond calculation, one can be granted protection without bounds and rare blessings?" No less a buddha than Shakyamuni himself responded to their doubts. He replied by entering into deep meditation, causing the three thousand myriad realms to shake in six ways, and making the heavens rain down celestial flowers and incense powders. The Seven Tathāgatas, the subjects of the sutra, gathered around and took their seats on lion thrones, and around them gathered all classes of beings, human and nonhuman. When the demigods saw this spectacle of the Seven Tathāgatas lecturing on the teachings to the multitude, their doubts were dispelled: "Excellent, excellent, Shakyamuni. You have benefitted us. To remove our thoughts of doubt, you have caused the Tathāgatas to come and visit this place."[56] With this display of a miraculous scene, Shakyamuni answered the question of how hearing names can miraculously create rare blessings. There is no discursive explanation, no rational discourse; the matter is not subject to conceptualization, as Ōchō Enichi finally came to admit. But it is incontrovertibly there, clear and understandable: the buddhas have the power to grant blessings. The granting of blessings is thus real religion, and those who deny that the buddhas have that magical power are heretics.

Postmodern Jōdo Shin Catholicism: Sasaki Shōten

Despite the teachings of the many sutras that affirm practical benefits and other aspects of what some modern scholars refer pejoratively to as "folk religion," these practices and beliefs still find themselves in the camp of heresy, at least in the light of sectarian doctrine. Placed under the diagnostic lamps of Shinran and Dōgen, for instance, folk religion appears to stand in direct opposition to the Jōdo Shin (also referred to as Shinshū) and Sōtō doctrinal systems, especially as forged in the Edo, Meiji, and modern periods. The doctrinal formulations that reject the superstitions of folk religion have worked well for those who understand that an essential ingredient of modernity is a rationality that has no place for magic. It is on this basis that Jōdo Shin, Zen, and Buddhism in general have been promoted as religions compatible with science. By limiting analysis to sectarian doctrine and only a very selective slice of sutra literature, the proponents of sectarian doctrine can claim to have ousted folk practices from the safe territory of true religion.

Since the mid-1980s, however, the confidence of scholars and sectarian leaders has been seriously shaken by studies that show how members of these supposedly folk-free religions are rather rampant in their acceptance and use of heretical magic. It is not that the magic they practice is particularly black. Even the innocuous customs of funerals and memorial services are proscribed by doctrines narrowed severely enough to exclude everything except forms of salvation and enlightenment attainable by rarefied and nearly abstract notions of pure faith and meditative insight. The sociological findings that affirm the prevalence of folk religion (or common religion, as we would term it) cannot be the incipient cause of the current crisis, however. For as anyone—and this includes most parish priests—familiar with the actual conditions of parish life would know, folk practices centered on funerals, memorial services, and practical benefits have always been at the core of Japanese Buddhism. So long as the antimagic doctrines are disregarded, there is little problem. But once the choice is made to take those doctrines seriously again, the crisis will arise as it always has done in times of doctrinal remembrance. The recent sociological studies have given opportunity once again for invoking doctrine, and thus the current crisis exists.

There have been a number of sociological studies conducted in recent decades by Japanese Buddhist sects, most notably by the Sōtō and Jōdo Shin sects, that have demonstrated the prevalence of "folk" practices among their members. The study published by the Sōtō sect in 1984 showed that many members had a very limited knowledge of facts relating to their sectarian affiliation but were often aware of folk religious services—such as the presence of spiritual healers and diviners—in their localities.[57] For more than ten years Kaneko Satoru of Osaka Municipal University carried out surveys of priests and laypersons belonging to the Nishi Honganji branch of Jōdo Shin Buddhism. His findings repeatedly confirmed that members practiced a "this-worldly-benefit-oriented folk religiosity" instead of the sect's doctrine of pure faith that eschews such superstitions.[58] Admitting that these "data shook us terribly," a team of Jōdo Shin scholars led by Sasaki Shōten investigated this problem and devised what they called a "postmodern theology" that would account for rather than reject folk practices.[59] This theology is postmodern, explains Sasaki, because it is time to get past the modern formulations that reject the actual practices of Jōdo Shin members.

Accepting that folk religion "forms the basic religiosity of the Japanese people and is not likely to disappear merely because scholars in their theories condemn and reject it"[60] and that "in the face of the 100 million Japanese who indulge in superstition, we should rather reflect on our lamentable failure as guides of the people and come to the conviction that it is high time we made folk practice and popular belief a topic of our theology,"[61] Sasaki is highly critical of the elite scholars and priests who formulate and propagate in the name of modernity an orthodoxy that he calls "Shinshū P," a sectarian puritanism intolerant of anything but the official doctrines of truth. Sasaki makes a plea for replacing Shinshū P with "Shinshū C," a model based on Catholicism and its willingness to accommodate local beliefs. There is also the model of Zonkaku (1290–1373), who accepted the funeral practices that his father Kakunyo (1270–1325), one of the patriarchs of Shinshū P, rejected. For his heresy, Zonkaku was disowned and excommunicated by his father. This stern and unsympathetic stance is no longer acceptable, says Sasaki, especially in a time when empirical data show that Jōdo Shin members often predominate among those seeking the services of temples and shrines offering magical rituals and practical benefits. Instead of seeing popular religion as silly superstition, Shinshū P must realize that people resort to these methods in times of real pain and trouble and, furthermore, that spirit belief, as opposed to belief in a saving deity, offers a mechanism for manipulating the forces which affect our lives—and that kind of control "perfectly matches the way of thinking and the manipulative attitude of modern" technology.[62] Sasaki, in referring to this issue, cites the argument made by Shimazono Susumu about the modern compatibility with spirit belief,[63] and Sasaki accepts this "shocking idea" as one that must be taken into account.

While Sasaki's call for an affirmation of folk magic is aimed primarily at his Jōdo Shin colleagues, he notes that his position is applicable to all forms of Japanese Buddhism.

Sasaki and his team have been soundly criticized in the Jōdo Shin sect for departing from the orthodox line founded by Shinran himself and for their advocacy of a movement to modernize Jōdo Shin to keep it in harmony with contemporary science. Like all reformers, Sasaki defends himself by saying that his call for revision aims at nothing other than a true return to Shinran that takes into account modern realities of actual practice. The standoff between folk religion and orthodox doctrine, however, represents a fundamental difference and raises the question of whether there can be any compatibility between the two. Is it possible to weave the heresy of magic into the orthodoxy of modernity? Claiming to have been misunderstood by his critics, Sasaki seems to be arguing that accommodation of the one by the other is possible in Shinshū C. Using the sword as a metaphor, he suggests how this might be done:

> Contrary to theology P, which cuts down superstition by logic and rejects it forthwith, one does not directly negate it here [in Shinshū C] but looks for salvation by way of empathy. One spares and embraces the popular practices to turn them into something Shinshū-like; one gives in to them in order to take them back to one's own side. Rather than drawing one's sword against the sword of the enemy, one grasps the other's sword to remold it into the shape of the *nembutsu* and give it back as a *nembutsu* sword that *cuts through all superstition*. This is ultra-C supreme swordsmanship![64]

If accommodation means acceptance, then it is not what Sasaki is speaking of in this passage. Embracing popular practices is for the purpose of gaining possession of them so that they can be reworked and ultimately done away with. This is not real empathy but false sympathy used to gain entry into the room of the enemy where, by gaining their confidence, their swords can be taken, refashioned, and given back to practitioners of popular practices to slay their own superstitions. Under the guise of Shinshū C, Sasaki is really a Shinshū P agent working to supply the enemy with their own reworked weapons to destroy themselves.

On the thorny matter of funerals, Sasaki describes the P and C positions and their respective differences:

> On the point of pure doctrine, P theology is clear-cut; but from the viewpoint of the field with its C practice, there must be found a way to realize a community of *nembutsu* practitioners as envisaged by Shinran, in trying to *liberate the people from their animist-shamanist*

complex and to transform this into true Shinshū belief by observing the funeral rites with heart and soul. That is certainly what we are looking for and, therefore, our endeavor to establish a theology that articulates Shinshū C must not evoke the fear that we would be going away from Shinran.[65]

Here again we see the essential role of subterfuge. Sincere observation of the funeral ritual is for the sake of liberating people from the animist-shamanist complex and transforming it into true Jōdo Shin belief, which cannot include the folk practices from which people must be liberated. Sasaki is correct in saying that there should be no fear of Shinshū C defecting from Shinran. For what he is proposing is a subversive C agent who will adopt the pose of the superstitious people in order to infiltrate, transform, and ultimately liberate them from their delusions. Acceptance of folk religion is only a means to destroy it so that "true Shinshū belief" and the Shinran of Shinshū P can prevail.

Sasaki's approach is reminiscent of the skillful means argument by which something wrong can be temporarily adopted in order to do something right. It differs, however, in that the seeming wrong is not just a method for doing what is right: it is the object that must be destroyed. When, for instance, the father in the *Lotus Sutra* story of the burning house lies to his children with promises of nonexistent presents to get them to leave the house, he never has to condemn or destroy his lies. They stand as lies. In fact that is the beauty of skillful means: lying is good so long as it aims at doing good. While at times Sasaki seems to be affirming folk practices for what they are without calling for their eventual rejection, his final position is that superstition must be cut off by the *nembutsu* sword and people must be liberated from the animist-shamanist complex. Folk religion is not a means to an end, but a means to put an end to the means itself.

Enculturation through Coexistence: Nara Yasuaki

Inspired in part by postmodern Jōdo Shin theologians, Nara Yasuaki, the Sōtō Zen scholar and president of Komazawa University, examines the problematic relationship between folk beliefs and the orthodoxy of his own Sōtō Zen tradition. Like Sasaki, Nara seeks a view by which both sides can be seen to be more compatible than exclusive. Recognizing that the Jōdo Shin theologians defined the problem well but failed to solve it, he develops an approach that we might call the "Enculturation through coexistence" theory. He describes two levels of religion in Japan, the elite and the popular, that are fundamentally opposed to each other—an opposition that is defined by "orthodox" Buddhism. The essential characteristic of "orthodox" Buddhism is that it is transcendental (Skt. *lokottara*) and opposed to the secular (Skt. *laukika*). Prayers for practical benefits, funerals, and ancestor worship are this-worldly (*genze*) and therefore part of the the secular level that is "cultural" and "not Buddhist," as opposed to the "doctrinal" level of transcendental enlightenment, the "only authoritative norm of conduct." Both levels in Japan, however, have undergone a process of enculturation by which they can coexist, and Buddhists therefore accept and engage in popular practices. This does not mean they are fully integrated, only that Buddhists are allowed to enter the popular sphere without condemnation by the orthodox.[66] In outdated political terms, Nara's position might be characterized as describing a kind of spiritual cold war in which two implacable foes agree to a peaceful coexistence that affirms and preserves an iron curtain representing a fundamental difference that should nevertheless not lead to open warfare.

The tensions between both sides are always there, and Nara describes specific examples of this conflict in Jōdo Shin and Sōtō Zen. There is a "puritanical" aspect to leaders such as Shinran, Kakunyo, and Dōgen, who did not accept a more "Catholic" kind of flexibility, but others in their own traditions, out of concern for the common people, did make concessions. Keizan allowed for the first time officially in the Sōtō sect the performance of funerals for the laity, while Zonkaku, Kakunyo's son, explained the *nembutsu* as the best means for obtaining practical benefits in this world.[67] For his heresy, Zonkaku was disowned by his father, who apparently could not bring himself to coexist peacefully with his own son. In religion as well as politics there are hawks and doves.

The heresy of the doves, however, did not consist of a peaceful coexistence by which they passed respectfully through the gate in the wall that separated both sides; it consisted of a total peace that tore down the wall itself. Their crime was full integration. Zonkaku did not say that seeking practical benefits was allowable on one side of the gate but not on the other side that was the separate territory of the *nembutsu*. He integrated both—fully accepting the *nembutsu* as the best magic for acquiring benefits. The medieval Sōtō Zen funeral texts that Nara translates in his article show this full integration of the orthodox deities and sutras into the popular funeral. There is no question that there were elite priests who found this integration, or even the peaceful coexistence, egregious in the extreme. There is no question, to put it in other terms, that the doves were traitors in the eyes of the hawks. But there is a question of whether the doves were thereby at odds with the scriptural as opposed to the ecclesiastical or sectarian tradition.

Take the case of the *nembutsu* in the Pure Land sutras. It is true that there are repeated descriptions of how the world is filled with suffering in contrast to the bliss of the transcendental Pure Lands. Even without going the full route of a nondual analysis by which this world in and of itself can be found to be the Pure Land, the *Sutra on the Meditation of Amida,* for example, makes it absolutely clear that the *nembutsu* leads to an expiation of sins in this life and thereby removes the wall that prevents rebirth into the Pure Land. In what by now we recognize as a standard promise of practical benefits, the sutra says that

> those who practice this meditation [on Kannon] will not suffer any calamity; they will utterly remove the obstacle that is raised by karma, and will expiate [their] sins. . . . Even the hearing of the name of this Bodhisattva will enable one to obtain immeasurable happiness.[68]

The sutra allows for recitation of Amida's name if meditation and visualization are too difficult, and "on the strength of (his merit of) uttering [Amida] Buddha's name he will, during every repetition, expiate the sins which involve him in births and deaths during eighty millions of kalpas."[69]

The benefits are immediate, and one need not wait. This instant reward is contrary to the patience one must have in Nara's description about the practice of *laukika* acts of merit that lead to a later— "no one knows when!" Nara states—enlightenment on the transcendental *lokottara* level.[70] The sutra even entertains the nondual possibility of becoming a buddha in meditation: "In fine, it is your mind that becomes Buddha, nay, it is your mind that is indeed Buddha."[71] Shinran himself had his moments of nondual convictions that imply, we assume, a lack of distinction between secular and transcendental, a claim often made by "orthodox" Buddhists. "When we consider," he wrote, "the ocean of the single vehicle of the original vow, [we find that it is] the teaching of perfect interfusion, complete satisfaction, extreme immediacy, nonobstruction, and absolute nonduality."[72] Though the immediate benefits were spiritual and not material, Shinran used the term "*genze riyaku*" to describe what his religion could produce. These were, however, but moments; and we would agree with Nara that Shinran for the most part rejected the expectation of benefits to be acquired in this life. In so doing, if he so did, he stood against much of what the sutras of his own tradition taught. In falling away from the teachings of Shinran and Kakunyo, Zonkaku reaffirmed the scriptural teachings of this-worldly benefits.

Like the postmodern Jōdo Shin theologians, Nara describes a sympathetic attitude toward folk magic but fails to resolve the serious tensions that keep orthodoxy and superstition apart. He in fact affirms the separation and only declares an uneasy truce to prevent open conflict. The problem is always cast as a fundamental incompatibility between folk religion and a Buddhism that can in various ways tolerate but never fully embrace it. The religion of practical benefits is cast as this-worldly and secular, Buddhism as transcendental and spiritual.

Sutra Buddhism as Folk Religion

The conflict that emerges in all of these cases, and in so many other instances as well, is not between sutra Buddhism and folk religion but between sectarian doctrine and sutra Buddhism, which affirms both the transcendent and the secular. If we declare the power of ritual and faith to obtain the less than spiritual objectives of health, success, wealth, and other practical benefits to be a form of magic characteristic of folk religion, then it must be admitted that sutra Buddhism embraces that kind of religion without hesitation. In an essential way sutra Buddhism is folk religion as much as it is a monastic way, and if sectarian orthodoxies find folk beliefs problematic they should also find disturbing the sutras on which their sects are supposedly based. Buddhist scholars, as we have seen, do find the sutras problematic insofar as the sacred texts—from the early Indian writings to the Mahāyāna classics such as the *Lotus Sutra* and the *Flower Garland Sutra*—affirm the power of Buddhism to produce practical benefits. The mundane benefits are recommended as easily and comfortably as are the transcendent goals of enlightenment and liberation.

In order to deal with this scriptural acceptance of worldly benefits, scholars who find this disturbing have had to introduce incompatibilities through clever strategies for making distinctions between primary and secondary meanings. Pure devotion free of any expectation of benefits, according to Fujii, is what is primary; and the benefits are a natural and secondary windfall. Iijima explains the phenomenon of practical benefits as an inversion of what Fujii identified as primary and secondary: the benefits that were not supposed to be sought (in Fujii's view) are deliberately sought as ends in themselves. The fault, according to Iijima, lies not with the sutra but in people's misuse of it. Ōchō attempts to resolve the problem by reading expedient intentions into the sections of the sutras that commend practical benefits. These are concessions to ordinary people and do not represent the primary meaning of the scripture. In Tsuruoka's treatment, the fact that sutras affirm practical benefits is less a matter of deliberate accommodation and more a process of unconscious assimilation of folk practices. This syncretism was not planned but came about almost of its own accord, riding on the willingness of sutra writers to compromise without forcing the issue. In what would seem to be a bold move to accept fully the religion of practical benefits, postmodern Jōdo Shin theologians like Sasaki reject past condemnations of superstition and seem to embrace folk practices. A close reading, however, is not required to see that such an acceptance is but a strategy for rejection, and practical benefits still must be eliminated as being far less than primary. There is little difference between the Shinshū P that rejects by rejecting and the Shinshū C that accepts in order to reject. Nara is perhaps the most realistic in his approach: he does not try to transform folk religion into something that it is not. Clearly he regards it as being at odds with primary Buddhism, but since it exists and will not go away, peace must be made to allow it to coexist in a territory to be clearly demarcated from the realm of authentic Buddhism.

What plagues the Buddhist scholars is the conflict created by the splitting of Japanese religion into orthodox Buddhism and folk beliefs. As an analytical category, the notion of folk or popular religion is, as we have noted in the Introduction, a problematic concept since it is used to distinguish itself from a higher orthodoxy. Still, we would not argue that the idea should be discarded, because it does serve the function of identifying a part in the whole. In making a case for the integrity of sutra Buddhism and folk religion, we not only use the term meaningfully but lay out the necessity for devising a category that encompasses both: this larger framework we call "common religion." Strictly speaking, then, our contention here is not that sutra Buddhism is a folk religion but that it takes its place along with folk religion within the common religion, which is entirely comfortable with and embraces both Buddhist scriptures and the popular practices of this-worldly benefits. The conflict, as noted earlier, is between these popular practices and sectarian orthodox doctrines based on notions of true and false religions. And for the resolution of that tension, we have no conceptual category to suggest.

What we do suggest is that the sutras, in all their quantity and clarity, affirm this-worldly benefits along with many other teachings. As sacred scripture they preach messages at the highest levels of authority; but as texts they can be appropriated only through that complex process called reading, and their meanings can therefore be changed by force of interpretation. What is remarkable about sectarian interpretations is their adamant refusal to accept what the sutras say about practical benefits. The blame cannot be laid solely upon a modern notion of true religion, although in our own times it is far more difficult to justify superstitions than it might have been in the past, for the opposition is an ancient one. It is a long-standing schizophrenia born to a religious tradition that has declared war with the world but cannot quite bring itself to kill it. Like Shiva, who torched Kama to death only to have to revive his foe lest life itself be ended forever, the Buddhist sutras love life and promise the best things in it.

Kubosa: Bourgeois Benefits in Shinto

Unlike Buddhism, Shinto does not suffer from the schizophrenia of loving and yet appearing to hate the good things of life. It consistently affirms the power of the gods to grant blessings and benefits, and it recommends without guilt the propriety of humans to ask for them. The primary purpose of the gods is to grant such provisions, and they require little in the way of renunciation and denial. This is such an obvious and unquestioned part of Shinto that the very idea of benefits does not require a technical term. In some respects all the terms of Shinto speak to the giving and receiving of benefits, as indeed do Shinto doctrinal structures, as we noted in the Introduction.

It would be wrong, however, to suggest that there is no specific word corresponding exactly to the Buddhist term "*riyaku*." "*Kubosa*" (also "*kuhosa*" or "*kaga*") is the Shinto pronunciation given to the character "*ri*," benefits. It is not widely used in Shinto classics such as the *Nihongi*, and when it does appear the word is not related to prayers or supplications to the gods. In the *Nihongi* section on the reign of Empress Suiko (592–628), a Korean immigrant is said to have appeared with a face flecked with white spots, and people wanted to banish him to an offshore island. He persuaded them from doing so, however, by telling them that he had a talent for landscape drawing that could "benefit" the country. The people found his skill useful, especially since he could draw pictures of Sumeru, the mountain that is the center of Buddhist cosmology.[73] This Buddhist element is totally unrelated to the benefit he had to offer, and it certainly had nothing to do with the persuasiveness of his argument. The benefit he had to offer had nothing to do with the gods, Buddhist or Shinto. When governors were appointed to the provinces in the reign of Kōtoku (645–654), they were told to take an inventory of the people and the land and consult the people about the distribution of "profits" derived from the gardens, ponds, water, and land.[74] Emperor Temmu (673–686) issued an edict to his officials asking them to come forth with suggestions for "benefiting" the state and increasing the welfare of the people.[75] In all these cases, benefits refer to secular advantages derived from human skills and, when government officials are involved, responsibilities that might be expected of good Confucian magistrates. In this early period, *kubosa* are not divine dispensations.

Described in other terms, however, the favors of the gods are rife. In battling his enemies, the legendary Emperor Jimmu prayed for specific instructions and was told in a dream to make platters and jars for offering sacrifices to the gods of heaven and earth. Having pleased the gods, Emperor Jimmu easily defeated his enemies and then asked them to help him establish his rule over the land so that he could bring peace.[76] The emperor knew the power of sacred words and gave a "secret device" to Michi no Omi no Mikoto, thereby enabling him to "use incantations and magic formulae so as to dissipate evil influences. The use of magic formulae had its origin from this."[77] *Norito,* or Shinto prayer, is based on *koto-dama,* the mystical power contained in words, and can be understood as "a general term meaning magic by means of words."[78] "It is abundantly clear," writes Donald Philippi, "that the ancient Japanese delighted in pronouncing 'blessings' designed to insure longevity and prosperity."[79] Emperor Sūjin, another legendary ruler, worshiped "eighty myriads of Deities" for whom he alloted shrines; the result, according to the *Nihongi,* was that "the pestilence . . . ceased, the country at length had peace, the five kinds of grains were produced, and the peasantry enjoyed abundance."[80] But Emperor Sūjin did not worship the gods completely or correctly, and his successor understood that Sūjin's early death was due to his ritual shortcomings. "Be watchful," Emperor Suinin was told, "in regard to the ceremonies of worship . . . [and] the life of thine augustness will be long, and moreover the Empire will have peace."[81] The *norito* from the tenth-century *Engi-shiki* collection of official rituals repeat over and over requests for blessings and prosperity from the gods.[82] We recognize, in short, that classical Shinto is consistently and thoroughly a religion of practical benefits.

The *norito* in the *Engi-shiki* are, in the words of Joseph Kitagawa, "a unique form of stylized prayer" that were "fixed" for recitation on various sacred occasions.[83] Modern *norito* are stylized, too, but they are certainly not fixed since each ritual occasion may call for a new prayer to be written specifically for it. While much of the diction and phrasing is characteristically ancient, details pertinent to each circumstance are built into the prayer, which then becomes, like the *Nihongi* itself, as much historical document as religious text. Funeral *norito,* for instance, combine eulogy into the prayer, and collections of *norito* list them by the name of the deceased as well as that of the priest who composed the prayer.[84] As a religion of practical benefits, Shinto and its prayers find easy company with ordinary people and thus reflect their stories and histories. Popular rituals—that is, rituals of the populace—combine fixed forms with circumstances of the moment and, once preserved or remembered, can maintain and later tell something of the particular time of its performance. In describing the "Once-Every-Thirty-Three-Years Kannon Festival" of a Sōtō Zen temple, William Bodiford notes that many of the rituals had very stylized and fixed forms that created an atmosphere of great seriousness and mystery, the understanding of which was totally unnecessary for an emotional and dramatic appreciation of the ceremonies; and yet at the same time the rituals included secular entertainments that were seen as entirely consistent with the spiritual nature of the occasion. In 1993, these entertainments included a comedy act, a magic show, and a well-known singer; the previous festival in 1960 featured a television set turned on at the altar where people sat glued every night for the thirty-three nights of the celebration. The memory of that ritual preserves the historical moment when people watched the magic of television for the first time in their lives.[85] In a similar manner, Shinto *norito* combine the dignity of stylized form with the particularity of the occasion.

Primarily meant to be spoken, *norito* require *furigana* that specify the unusual and archaic pronunciations of the *kanji* characters, but they can also be read silently for meaning by ignoring the *furigana* put in for speaking. Like Buddhism, Shinto has its own traditions of pronunciation: what is *"rieki"* in ordinary Japanese and *"riyaku"* in Buddhist pronunciation becomes *"kubosa"* in Shinto diction. It must be stressed, however, that *"kubosa"* is not the Shinto pronunciation of the characters for *"rieki/riyaku"*; it is the primary and unchanging spoken word that is denoted in writing by the Chinese characters. The written text is the gloss for pronunciation, but this is not to be confused with the ancient *man'yō-gana* system of using Chinese characters purely for pronunciation. Unlike that manner of writing, the written text in modern *norito* can be read for meaning if one chooses to ignore speaking it. *"Kubosa"* means benefits, and it can be written with the characters for *"riyaku"* or, as we shall see, with other characters as well.

Modern *norito* give the word *"kubosa"* the characters for *"riyaku"* and, surely under the influence of the Buddhist usage of *"riyaku,"* likewise understand benefits to be that which is requested and received from the gods as well as from human agents. At the Festival of Watches (*Tokei matsuri*) sponsored in the mid-1950s by the Kinki Region Watch Sellers Association, a Shinto priest named Kawada Haruo composed and offered a prayer for divine blessings to be received by the association and all the people in the area. Calling attention to the splendid offerings being made, the priest asked that the "diligent efforts" of the association members be rewarded, that there be a rise in the volume of business, and that members experience an increase of benefits or profits (*kubosa/riyaku*). The prayer ended with hopes for the protection of "those engaged in this business of dipping into the flow of the water clock established by the Great Deity."[86] On behalf of the Mitsuwa Pearl Production Corporation, the head priest from the Ōkami Jinja in Nara noted in his prayer that the deity of his shrine had been designated recently in 1956 the "protective deity of this company" and asked that the president and employees be blessed in their work. He prayed that there not be storms in the seas where the pearls are grown and that the buyers and wearers of the pearls at home and abroad be free of disasters. The pearls, he said, are exported abroad and should bring an increase in *kubosa* (here indicated with the characters for "benefits of the nation"). Let there not be accidents to hands or legs, he prayed, and let the families and relatives of the employees be protected day and night. The *norito* ended with an interesting apology to the oysters and an explanation of why they had to be "sacrificed for the people of the world":

> Crushing your bodies, we make beautiful jewelry of the pearls, establish your great and meritorious service to the world and its peoples, and increase the great benefits (*kubosa/riyaku*) between our great nation and the countries overseas. The people of the world will know that this is a remarkable contribution made to the great enterprise of rebuilding our imperial country.[87]

Offered sometime around 1956, this *norito* commemorates not only the production of pearls but the rebuilding of postwar Japan as well. It affirms that prosperity is sought, not just for the individuals or companies involved in the pearl trade, but for the whole nation. As popular prayers, *norito* are offered for celebrating almost anything: highways, water pumps, businesses, buildings, factories, crops, seasons, people, watches, pearls, and more. The corpus of *norito* provides a catalog of the ordinary concerns of ordinary people who ask the gods for material and mostly bourgeois comforts in particular times and places.

In a prayer for traffic safety, the head priest of the Ontake Jinja described the increase of traffic in the Kiso Valley and the harm that traffic accidents inflict on drivers, passengers, and residents. In his petition for divine help to augment the efforts of the Kiso Traffic Safety Association to reduce accidents,[88] we see an important element common to all *norito*—namely, that benefits and blessings are always sought in conjunction with activities that in and of themselves, with or without divine blessings, require serious commitment and effort. Shinto prayers are seldom presented apart from responsible actions and do not lessen the need for good conduct. The religious process of seeking practical benefits most certainly employs the magic of words and rituals to accomplish what human effort alone cannot guarantee, but it does not dispense with hard work. Shinto is not as concerned about transcendent salvation as it is about individual happiness in the here-and-now and the life of the community. Thus Shinto priests are called upon to compose prayers for adding blessings to its most important concerns such as selling watches, producing pearls, increasing traffic safety, and serving and enriching the community and nation. As such it is civic (not civil) religion at its best, affirming and augmenting the values of bourgeois society and responsible citizenship. And as its *norito* inform us, it recognizes that benefits are not free but are surrounded by ethical considerations and meanings.

Civil religion, which Winston Davis defines as "a network of moods, values, thoughts, rituals, and symbols that establishes the meaning of nationhood within an overarching hierarchy of significance,"[89] is primarily ideological. Civic religion, however, is centered in moral responsibility. Civil religion through emperor worship, for example, or, more recently, Japan theory (*Nihonjinron*) gives a cultural and ideological sense of national character and identity; civic religion, by contrast, is concerned with the importance of business success, community well-being, and well-adjusted individuals. While the idea of a common religion, which we defined in the Introduction, has some suggestive similarity to the notion of "Nippon-kyō," the unique civil "religion of Japan" defined by Kanzaki Noritake as the combined beliefs in the unity of *kami*, buddhas, and ancestors,[90] we do not regard the common religion we describe to be unique or limited to the Japanese case. Hence it does not function as a civil religion for Japan, prescribing as it does pathways for benefits that are held in high esteem by the community but do not define national identity. While the pursuit of this-worldly benefits can become a selfish obsession—one of the reasons why it has been criticized as inferior to true religion—at its best, that is, as a civic religion, it is rooted in community values that translate into individual responsibility. It is this moral character of this-worldly benefits that we are now ready to examine in the next chapter.

3

Buying Out Chance
Morality, Belief, and Prayer

IT IS A TYPICAL SIGHT in Japan: a red Shinto torii gate marking the entrance, to one side of which is a tree with dozens of folded paper fortunes tied to branches laden with hopes for the auspicious predictions. Once inside, the people go through ritual motions and hold themselves in deep concentration as they make their offerings of coins in the hopes of gaining good returns. There is an air of great solemnity; few people speak, each absorbed in their performance. Located in a shopping area, it is a popular place that is almost never empty during the day and is crowded even well into the night. Several signs outside announce the services and offerings that can be made to the deity of the place. And yet the passersby do not stop and bow in front of the place. Despite its religious trappings, they know that it is not a shrine but a pachinko parlor.

The name of this parlor in downtown Hiroshima is "Lucky," written in English, an appropriate name for an establishment that lures people in with the prospect of making something for nothing. Pachinko is a pinball game of chance played for prizes and money, and many players seem resigned to let their fortunes be determined by luck. Some of them do not even bother to manipulate the knob that determines the force with which the shiny steel balls are catapulted into the maze of pins and holes. They simply jam a piece of cardboard to hold the knob in place while they sit with arms folded, often taking long, slow drags on their cigarettes, languidly watching the balls bounce their way toward their winnings or losings. Luck does not require intervention or effort. Luck, good or bad, is undeserved, and good luck is what the passive people in Lucky hope will fall into their laps without their having to do so much as lift a finger.

The Lucky Pachinko Hall in Hiroshima

Good Luck (*kōun*) and Moral Luck (*kaiun*)

It would be a mistake, however, to think that the gamblers are leaving everything to luck. Many players say that it is not just a game of chance and luck but an art requiring great knowledge and technical skill honed through countless hours of practice that enable one to place the cardboard in just the right spot. Nakamori Kyōko,[1] a veteran player who, unlike most players, regularly wins, can explain in great detail how to read the machines and manipulate them to her advantage. It may be that luck is the only real determinant in pachinko, but Kyōko, even as she hopes to get lucky, does not depend solely on luck: she adds her own skill and technique to take the game out of the hands of fate and bring it under her control. Her friend, an avid player himself, regularly reads pachinko magazines filled with tips and advice on how to improve one's skill. He says that only losing is a matter of luck; winning is due to skillful effort.

The religious decor of Lucky plays on the ambiguities of luck and effort. The Shinto facade is not meant to deceive anyone into thinking that this shop is a shrine, but, as a form of clever advertising, it makes an appeal to an important aspect of gambling as well as the conceptual framework of practical benefits. The signs outside invite people to participate in a "ritual offering of coins" (*tama kuyō*) to the "Great August Deity of Pachinko" (Pachinko Daimyōjin). "Great August Deity" is standard nomenclature for Shinto deities, and while there is no deity named Pachinko in the traditional pantheon, Shinto

is well known for its comprehensive flexibility to deputize or to produce deities to deal with almost any practical situation. The religious
flavor of the appeal allows the pachinko parlor to make a claim that
is more believable than it would be if left in a purely secular form of
advertising: the signs say that players are "certain to win" (*hisshō*).
Everyone knows there are always more losers than winners, but the
religious language suggests to the patrons that they think of playing
the pinball machines as a ritual offering of coins to the Great
Pachinko Deity. Pachinko at this particular place is no longer just a
game of chance or luck randomly dispensed by the blind god Fortune; it is overseen, rather, by the Great August Deity, who, like all
Shinto deities, can tip the scales of chance in one's favor and thereby
promise certain victory, even at gambling. Magical thinking is an important part of gambling and religion: it persuades people that in a
game of chance, be it pachinko or life itself, there are efforts that can
be made to override accident. Pachinko at the Lucky "shrine" is not
just a matter of luck; it also involves rewards earned for right effort expended through knowledgeable skill and "religious" ritual.

The amulets and talismans that can be acquired at real shrines and
temples are often described as good luck charms. But, as it is with
pachinko, religious good luck is also understood to require effort before the desired ends can be realized. If effort were not required and
rewards were solely a matter of luck, people would be helpless victims
living in a kind of existential pachinko machine bouncing about the
posts of life and falling into winnings or losings entirely by chance.
They would not feel the need to perform prayers, make petitions, or
take any of the steps designed to achieve the getting of good fortune
and the preventing of bad. Such actions occur not because people
feel helplessly at the mercy of fate and impersonal chance (situations
that would invalidate the point of petitioning or otherwise seeking to
improve one's chances of good things). They occur, rather, because
people feel that chance can be modified, that it can be made to work
for them, and that it can be explained in a moral context that is fath-
omable to human beings.

If luck is a matter of chance, rather than the result of calculated deliberation, then a good luck charm is not about luck at all, since it
symbolizes two kinds of *causes* that work cooperatively together: human effort and divine help. Whenever charms or amulets are described as things that "bring" good luck, a confidence is being expressed in the ability of those objects to act in some fashion as a causal
agent. Underlying this confidence is a basic understanding that the
causes of events are found not merely on the physical level but have
psychic and spiritual causes as well: the question why one becomes ill
is thus not answered solely in terms of germs and physical causes but

requires an explanation of why those causes have inflicted a particular person. Interpretations of illness and misfortune, which are dominant themes in many Japanese new religions, hinge on moral and ethical issues relating to the sick or afflicted person (and generally his or her family or social group). Consequently the processes of healing and of reinstating good fortune require moral actions and ritual behavior that deal with the spiritual aspects of causation.[2] The conceptual framework and ritual processes of practical benefits speak the same language as the new religions here: they place the individual person (and failure to perform the correct ritual and moral actions appropriate to the situation) at the center of explanations of misfortune and illness while attributing good fortune to right actions and ·the sincere and correct performance of religious activities (as in our story of Michiko in the Introduction).

In the conceptual framework of practical benefits little is said about *kōun*, which is good luck understood as a lucky break that just happens without any cause or deliberate effort. Much, however, is said of *kaiun*, a compound consisting of an active verb and direct object that literally mean "to open up luck" in the sense of bringing or even making good luck. A pamphlet on the Star Ritual (Hoshi kuyō) published by the Kōyasan Shingon Buddhist sect explicitly says that we can be happy only if we "call" or "summon" (*yobikomu*) luck into our lives. This is done by performing the Star Ritual and engaging in religious practice to "get rid of bad luck." The pamphlet concludes: "Once good luck has been summoned, the matter is settled: your life will become a triumph. Someone once said, 'Even luck is a matter of effort.'"[3] In the framework of practical benefits, little is said about *kōun* because good luck has nothing to do with deliberate effort. But *kaiun* is the opposite: luck affected and even created by morality and religious ritual. Luck, then, can be caused by right effort, and therefore earned as *kaiun,* or uncaused and therefore undeserved but still enjoyable as *kōun* so long as one is willing to leave it entirely to chance. *Kōun* can be translated as "good luck," while *kaiun* is best understood as "moral luck."[4]

The problem with good luck is that since it is a matter of chance it may never grace one's path. Moral luck, however, is "a matter of effort," and effort is controlled not by chance but by human deliberation. What the tactics of practical benefits attempt to achieve through ritual and its objects is nothing less than the transformation of chance into destiny—a result ordained by causes that are under our control. *Kōun,* in other words, is to be made into *kaiun.* Like the four women who gathered at the Joy Luck Club in Amy Tan's novel to choose and make their own luck,[5] people do not simply hope for *kōun* but work to create *kaiun.*

In terms of the classical Buddhist idea of causality, there is no chance to eliminate or transform since chance is not subject to causes and conditions. The doctrine of causality, which David Kalupahana calls the "central philosophy of Buddhism,"[6] shares an interest with science in the attempt to arrive at knowledge that can explain what appear to be accidental occurrences, which he calls "multiformities," but are actually events that are caused and therefore predictable: "A belief in events that sometimes happen may be replaced by belief in events that always happen." Strictly speaking, "according to the Buddha's philosophy, there are no accidental occurrences; everything in the world is causally conditioned or produced (*paticcasamuppannam*)."[7] Kalupahana recognizes, however, that the entire medley of causes and conditions is so complex that there seems to be a random character to some of it and therefore our *knowledge* (and morality) must admit of something akin to the vagaries of chance. Our ignorance, however, does not prevent the event itself from being anything other than the strict result of causes and not chance, and in this regard the practical benefits framework, which affirms causation and not accident, is consistent with the doctrine of causality.

The doctrine of karma is also at the heart of Buddhism, and it too can be understood as a teaching of how luck is denied in favor of morality. Put into practice, the idea of karma aims at doing away with chance by making everything that happens to us the result of our actions. While there is no problem with good actions that produce, according to the law of karma, good results, everyone still faces a fundamental flaw in the fact that no one's moral slate is entirely clean. One of the great attractions of Buddhism lies in its offer of a wide variety of humanly available methods for getting rid of bad karma (*metsuzai*) from the past and establishing good karma for the present and future. The teaching of Sōka Gakkai to its members in Britain reflects this point and characterizes what the parent religion in Japan says to its members there:

> Misfortune, temperament, character dispositions—are all laid to the charge of the causes created in the past years or even in earlier incarnations. By chanting *Nam-myōhō-renge-kyō* "the shackles of one's karma are progressively weakened until they are finally severed completely." . . . Although some aspects of karma are mutable, in the sense that they might be moderated by willpower, only *Nam-myōhō-renge-kyō* provides the possibility of total emancipation from negative karma. Members are told, ". . . chanting *Nam-myōhō-renge-kyō*, and taking action based on that chanting, is the greatest good cause we can make to change even the worst karma into good fortune."[8]

The power of the chant overshadows the capacity of nonritual actions based on "willpower" to change bad karma because the record of the past, having been written by the results of actions, is beyond the reach of ordinary action and can only be rewritten effectively by the extraordinary power of ritual. Karma is not a deterministic force producing unalterable retributions, and the present time is an opportunity for shaping future karma through willpower and rewriting the record and results from past karma through ritual power. Buddhist liberation is freedom from the stranglehold of karma—and that freedom, moreover, is attended by tangible as well as intangible rewards. Practitioners can expect "conspicuous benefits" such as better relationships and sounder finances as proofs of their faith.[9]

While we maintain that ritual action falls within the reach of moral action and willpower, we do recognize the common Buddhist distinction that is made between moral virtue and ritual virtue. The English word "virtue" has two meanings that happen to reflect the distinction between *dōtoku* (or *rinri*) and *kudoku*. *Dōtoku* is virtue as moral propriety; *kudoku* is virtue in its other meaning of efficacious power, especially that of ritual. While both work together, ritual power, which accesses the aid of the gods, is more potent than moral virtue and is sometimes regarded as being sufficient to relegate morality to a minor role. The *Longer Sukhāvatīvyūha Sutra* offers hope even to those who are morally inferior and "unable to acquire any merits,"[10] for they too can be reborn in the Pure Land if they are mindful of the Buddha and hear the profound dharma. Moral imperfection is not an insurmountable barrier, and grace is more powerful than works; but this is not an invitation to antinomian freedom, and the sutra ends with an extended and eloquent homily on the nature of evil. Moral and ritual virtues are both important, but they play different roles: ritual virtue (*kudoku*) can accomplish what cannot be achieved by moral virtue (*dōtoku*).

Chance, then, insofar as it is perceived to exist, is to be eliminated by the causal workings of moral effort, which, when it falls short of completing the task, can be augmented by ritual virtue. The magical qualities of ritual as power, however, should not blind us to the intrinsic moral qualities of ritual performance. As William R. LaFleur has argued in his discussion of the Buddhist rituals performed in connection with aborted fetuses in Japan, "ritual . . . can operate with considerable effect and power in the realms of morals."[11] Thus the act of performing a memorial service for a fetus contains moral meanings and ethical statements about right conduct, a point to which we shall return. Ritual magic is more powerful than moral action, but it does not dispense with it.

Despite the moral and ritual confidence in being able to destroy bad karma, there are times when the mighty power of evil deeds cannot be broken. This is not the metaphysical evil embodied in demonic figures like Mara or Satan but, perhaps more frightening, the moral evil that any ordinary person can commit. The limited good of moral deeds can be augmented by ritual virtue, but the force of evil deeds sometimes remains untouched even by the power of ritual. When it comes to evil doings, the law of karma can transcend the reach of ritual, and no appeal is possible once retribution has been rendered. The monthly motto for May 1996 at Hōzanji at Ikoma was a grim "You reap what you sow." On large signs and flyers, and in the temple's monthly newsletter, the message was made clear:

> It is said that your destiny is determined by your own actions. What have you done today? The slightest move of your hands and each footstep create your own destiny. The effects of your good acts and your bad deeds will fall back upon you. This is an important teaching for you to believe. Clearly understand the law of cause and effect.[12]

The message is a standard affirmation of karma, but the first of three testimonials published in the newsletter tells the hard details of how an evil deed remained unredeemable. Related by a woman named Yamamoto Mitsuko, the story tells of her father and how his habit of gambling caused her mother great grief. After repeated pleas from his wife, he and his gambling partner went to Ikoma and made vows to the main deity, Shōten-san (Kankiten), that they would quit. The promise was short-lived, however, and the very next day they went back to betting on cards. A day later, her father was afflicted with a terrible skin disorder on his hand and his friend lost most of his sight. Realizing that he was being punished for breaking his promise to Shōten-san, he went back to the temple and apologized to the deity, dedicating himself to spiritual exercises, but he suffered from his hand condition till the day he died. And his friend, despite visits to the Yanagida Kannon in Kyoto, never regained his sight. "Shōten-san," Yamamoto concluded, "will support good deeds but is frightful when it comes to bad."[13]

The lesson is clear: ritual virtue can supplement the limitations of good acts, but it is powerless to right certain wrongdoings. A similar perspective may also be expressed by Japanese new religions in their discussions of karma and their interpretations of misfortune: despite its general affirmation that its spiritual healing process (*okiyome*) can eradicate misfortune and cure illness, Mahikari does not consider *okiyome* to have any efficacy in treating leprosy, since this affliction is regarded as a punishment sent by Su-god (Mahikari's supreme deity) to the sufferer.[14] What is affirmed in these cases is the primacy of action and the personal responsibility that goes with it. It is a heavy moral burden to bear, but despite the immunity of some forms of evil to the corrective action of morality and ritual, the hopeless cases are the exceptions rather than the rule.

Like *riyaku*, ritual virtue (*kudoku*) is a ubiquitous and immensely important idea that has not received much scholarly attention. Both terms suffer from being associated with the language of ritual magic—which, as we have seen, does not sit well with modern understandings of what Buddhism in particular and religion in general ought to be. The links between the two, however, become immediately apparent when one examines both scholarly and popular writings related to practical benefits. The scholars Yoritomi Motohiro and Shiraki Toshiyuki, for instance, in their introduction to a popular guidebook on practical benefits, state that *kudoku*, in fact, is "very similar to" *riyaku*. Both terms refer to "something that is helpful or beneficial," but whereas *riyaku* is something gained from the outside, *kudoku*, the cause of those benefits, comes from actions motivated from within oneself.[15] Moral action and ritual power combine to produce practical benefits that do not come just by chance—a point affirmed repeatedly in the testimonies of members of new religions. This comment by a twenty-six-year-old Japanese Sōka Gakkai member illustrates his confidence in the Buddhist intolerance of chance: "If I were to die now, there'd be a meaning to it; there are no accidents."[16] The great objective of Buddhism and indeed of many other religions has been achieved here: the destruction of chance through effort and virtue.

Though she is not specifically identified as a Buddhist, Pearl's mother in Amy Tan's novel *The Kitchen God's Wife* lives in a religious world devoid of chance. Pearl, a very modern Chinese-American woman, complains about her mother's superstitions:

> To this day it drives me crazy, listening to her various hypotheses;
> the way religion, medicine, and superstition all merge with her own
> beliefs. She puts no faith in other people's logic—to her, logic is a
> sneaky excuse for tragedies, mistakes, and accidents. And accord-
> ing to my mother, *nothing is an accident*. She's like a Chinese version
> of Freud, or worse. Everything has a reason.[17]

She is also a good Chinese version of the Buddha—or at least is living in a world as it would have been viewed by the Buddha. Pearl's mother could have lived in the world of Jesus, as well, if Wayne Oates is right in saying that "Jesus did not leave anything to chance or luck."[18] The Christian world of providence is stripped of chance, too, since human destiny is held in the inexorable grip of God's causes and reasons, which, when mortals are unable to fathom them, give a mysterious or miraculous cast to events. As miracles divinely caused, the acts of God are not accidents and therefore are not covered by insurance policies. The scientist too has no place for accidents. "Accidents, luck, and all that are just manifestations of your ability," says Taniguchi Tadatsugu, the Japanese molecular biologist who elucidated the genetic structure of beta-interferon. His is a supreme appraisal of human ability, but even his language lapses into theistic tones: "The Goddess of Fortune visits all researchers. The question is whether or not you let her escape. If you see the Goddess in front of you, you've got to hold on to her tightly."[19] Grabbing the goddess is a good part of the religion of practical benefits. As the common religion of Japan, it shares with other systems of knowledge and belief the conviction that the virtue of divine power and human effort can immunize life from the ravages of chance and luck.

Material Spirituality

While this-worldly practical benefits are demonstrative of a world-affirming viewpoint, this does not mean they are simply materialistic. If we understand materialism to imply that it is material things alone that produce happiness and the highest priority is to be given to the acquisition of material wealth and goods, then this is not, as we argued in the Introduction, parallel to the concept of *genze riyaku*. Just as there is a moral price to pay in the purchase of benefits—and a moral role (augmented by ritual) in the efforts to eliminate chance and luck—so is there a moral responsibility tied to the good and happy life of plenitude. Of course there are many cases in which moral responsibility is totally obscured by the self-satisfaction of physical comforts, but this-worldly benefits are not entirely mired in selfishness. In his book about the Togenuki Jizō Temple in Tokyo—which is billed as "the book of unlimited this-worldly benefits" and comes with a paper *omamori* inside the back cover—Hara Mitsuju points out that financial profit is not what this-worldly benefits are about. He castigates new religions, which "pocket prayer fees and swagger about with fraudulent claims made in the name of the Buddha that people can increase their profits several times over through *genze riyaku*."[20] Hara's comment reminds us of the critics of new religions cited in the Introduction. His underlying message, though, once one leaves aside the problematic nature of his value judgments about the new religions, is highly important and relevant to the topic at hand: put to selfish materialistic uses, *genze riyaku* is being misused.

The moral quality of legitimate this-worldly benefits derives from the goodness that is inherent in educational success, happy marriage, safe childbirth, traffic safety, business prosperity, and the other things in life that are good in the moral and material senses of the word. There is nothing intrinsically evil or immoral about a high level of satisfaction and comfort, and an easy argument can be made for the moral depravity of material privation. Shingon Buddhism is particularly forthright on this point. The *Handbook for Believers* of the Kōyasan branch of Shingon Buddhism affirms the natural goodness of this-wordly benefits:

> It is natural for people to want to be blessed with good health or an economic livelihood so that they can live. In this life, which we speak of as one in which all things change, we human beings, who have no idea what might happen next, all want to escape from calamities safely, and to that end we pray for ourselves and others, asking for the protection of the buddhas. It must be said that this mind of prayer is most noble in this world.
>
> The fundamental nature of human life and existence, regardless of the individual or society, lies in what might be called the ideal of wanting to live, the search for happiness, and the desire for human livelihood.
>
> Shingon Buddhism is described as being the main organization among Buddhist groups for petitionary prayers and practical benefits. This is because it affirms as its fundamental point that in and of itself the body should be healthy and there should be the blessings of both material as well as spiritual benefits. All of this is a natural matter of course, and we have no trouble in saying that those who think that prayers for blessings and practical benefits are superstitious are people who do not know the true conditions of life. The reason for this is that our religion of truth asks that this body become a buddha, and seeks to know this earthly world as none other than the pure land of quiescent radiance.[21]

And yet the discomfort with materialism persists—especially since spiritual means, which should be free of selfish satisfactions, are used to acquire comforts that please the self. Ichirō Hori voices a representative concern of how true spirituality excludes base superstition and magic, which persist "like weeds" among the common people:

> Therefore, all religious leaders who have a sense of vocation to enlighten the common people, regardless of their religious affiliation, share an urgent responsibility. They should lead people from folk beliefs into a high level of religious experience, or from popular superstitions into right faith, as well as from magic to metaphysics, if we may borrow Max Weber's term.[22]

Such "modern" understandings make it difficult for some scholars to embrace the magical simplicity of primitive religions that promise concrete rewards, like candy for children. It may be all right for ancient Incas to believe that "if spirituality did not help you grow corn, it was pointless,"[23] but Japan is a technologically advanced nation and such crude notions grate against college-educated minds. It is not, as we saw in the Introduction, just scholars who have tried to push the topic of this-worldly benefits out of the ambit of "true religion" and are embarrassed by the very presence of this-worldly benefits in Japanese religion. Many priests themselves have been sufficiently discomfited by the topic to resort to explaining benefits away through the language of peace of mind or skillful means. Despite all their stratagems, the fact remains that such "primitive simplicities" not only thrive in the advanced civilization of Japan but, as we saw in Chapter 1, Japanese civilization is continually inventing and adapting new forms of them to deal with the vicissitudes of modern life and devising new religious practices and talismans that can carry out the functional equivalents of growing corn.

It is not, of course, the "primitive simplicities" of this-worldly benefits or the magical processes involved with them (the techniques, rituals, and objects that are utilized to acquire benefits) that are the problem. The problem is the putative conflict between magic and morality and the notion that right faith involves a distancing from magic and folk beliefs. Insofar as amulets, talismans, prayers, and promises related to worldly benefits all involve the utilization of spiritual forces such as the power and grace of buddhas and gods and ritual processes to achieve material and physical ends, they are indeed associated with magic. At the same time, as we have seen, such practices are shot through with moral injunctions and ethical advice that reinforce the point made in the Introduction—that the separation of the spiritual and the material is wholly problematic.

These moral injunctions are amply illustrated by the amulets that are used to deal with chance and bring practical benefits. The sign written in Japanized "English" at the Narita-san Temple, famed for traffic safety amulets, states: "With Buddha mind praying at the steering wheel, your driving is free of accidents." The material benefit of safety is also a spiritual benefit (since the message implies that through the amulet one may attain the Buddha mind). But it can also be read as a moral one: one should have the Buddha mind at the wheel and drive with a pure and focused mentality. The amulet is a reminder signifying an ethical teaching and a moral obligation to be attentive and exercise caution for the sake of oneself and others— just as the amulets and talismans for educational success are reminders to students of their ethical duties prior to examinations and the need to study hard in order to acquire their heart's desires and, indeed, to fulfill their obligations to their families who have supported them, linked their aspirations to the student's success, and invested time and money in those aspirations.[24]

At times the teachings embedded in the practices of this-worldly benefits may appear to be more oriented toward ethical injunctions—as with the "receive and give no evil" AIDS amulet of Kanamara Shrine—but they rarely eschew an affirmation of the magical force that accompanies them. The transport companies and the police forces that use Kawasaki Daishi's traffic safety services (Chapter 1) are making moral statements and ethical commitments in their espousal of the importance of traffic safety, but they do it not through pious public statements of intent but through adopting the magical force of the temple's powerful fire rituals and through the amulets sacralized at the temple and used to guard their cars and buses. Similarly, the railway companies that place traffic safety amulets in their trains to reassure the public of their commitment to their customers are making use of religious objects that represent the magical powers of Buddhist figures of worship.[25]

In such terms, the separation of the spiritual from the material, like the separation of the ethical from the magical, is problematic. It is comparatively easy, of course, to see a conflict between spirituality and materialism in the broad context of a contrast between value systems. The materialism of contemporary society—which measures progress solely in terms of material goals such as economic growth and reckons its signs of success solely in material acquisitions—can stimulate people to search for happiness in other ways (hence the search for religious values and "spiritual" goals). This is exactly how numerous priests and scholars in the present day explain the popularity of practical benefits: in extolling the virtues of Shinto, Ueda Kenji argues that the present "scientific age" (*kagaku jidai*) has produced new tensions, new problems for humanity both at micro- and macro-levels, and hence has increased the need for religions such as Shinto that are able to deal with the this-worldly needs of the Japanese people.[26] Similarly Yoritomi Motohiro affirms the religious values of practical benefits, which he sees as a spiritual path made necessary by modern materialism. Scientific, technological, and medical advances have "enriched our material life" but have at the same time ushered in serious new problems such as AIDS and social alienation. In terms of human relations and the persistence of chance and accidents, modern life, he claims, is no different from life a hundred or a thousand years ago, and this is why *kudoku* and *riyaku* are still so widely practiced and pursued.[27] If the spirituality of *genze riyaku* aims at a better materialism, materialism can be said to breed a persistent spirituality. Though distinguishable by their different color and texture, the threads of both are woven in a common cloth.

A talisman sold at the Sōtō Zen monastic training center of Saijōji, which we encountered in the Introduction, makes this point rather well. This talisman is for making one's money grow—a worldly benefit that appears to speak of a very basic materialism. Described as a "tree that becomes money" (*kane no naru ki*), the talisman is made of plastic and metal. The plastic part is shaped like a small pine tree around five centimeters high with green leaves and a short brown trunk attached to a key ring. Interspersed in the greenery of the tree are five small brass bells that can be shaken to produce a ringing sound. There are multiple puns implied and intended here: the word "*kane*" is a homonym that can mean either bell or money depending on the ideogram with which it is written; the word "*naru*" (to become) can also mean, with a different ideogram, to cry or sing. Hence the tree that becomes money can also be the tree that rings the bell. On the tree are written the name of the temple and the words "*kaiun*" and "*shōfuku*" (opening up luck and beckoning good fortune). Attached to the talisman is a card that sets out, under the heading "*okane no tamaru hō*" (the way to collect money), ten actions that are necessary:

1. Maintain the mind that venerates the gods and buddhas (*shin-butsu*).
2. Maintain the mind that respects the ancestors.
3. Maintain good relations with your family members.
4. Strive to be healthy.
5. Take great care with your food and possessions.
6. Live within your means.
7. Make your work your hobby.
8. Always attain your objective.
9. Never put your faith solely in money.
10. Live a life of gratitude.

In small print underneath, words enjoin one to place this card in one's wallet or purse and keep these instructions in mind every day. While the talisman is vended as a lucky charm aimed at bringing money to the purchaser—and thus would appear to suggest material self-seeking and to apply the magical powers of Dōryō, the temple's famed guardian, to this end—it underpins these material ends and the magical nuances of similitude and word power (which link the bell and money through the homonym "*kane*") with ethical teachings and exhortations to correct behavior in religious and social terms.

The intertwining of spirituality, materialism, and morality is evident, too, in the time after benefits have been acquired. The Saijōji talisman affirms the importance of gratitude—an important quality and, indeed, a moral imperative that is part of the process of seeking and receiving benefits. Seeking benefits does not end, the talisman reminds us, with having one's prayers answered. If it ends at all, it is with expressions of gratitude. The dozens of Jizō figures lining the walkway up a hillside at Hōzanji at Ikoma include "Kansha Jizō," the Jizō of Gratitude. At the Temple of the Flying Fudō (Tobi Fudō) in Tokyo, travelers write their prayers for a safe flight on *ema* showing a Boeing 747 flying across Fudō's chest and hang them up with dozens of other *ema,* some of which contain messages of sincere thanks from those who have returned safely from their trips. Many businessmen go to pray for success at the Kurumazaki Shrine in Kyoto and, if things go well, return to thank the gods for their successful closing of a deal, the monetary value of which is written on rocks along with words of thanks. At the front of the Hechima Yakushi Temple in Nagoya, there are stacks of gourds on which are pasted slips of paper saying, "In gratitude for the fulfillment of my wishes." When people first make their requests, they take home a small gourd amulet, rub it on an ailing spot on their bodies, place it on their home altars, plant a gourd seed, raise the plant, and, if their wish is fulfilled, pluck a gourd for writing their words of thanks. The gourds literally represent fruition and the importance of thanksgiving after the harvest. Oda Ryūkō, founder of Yotsuya Reibyō, a multistory temple/mausoleum complex in central Tokyo, tells the story of a fisherman whose luck was changed through prayer but failed to express his gratitude after his good fortune. Since the fisherman failed to follow up on his petitionary prayer (*kisei,* "to pray and promise") with the completion of his vow (*kisei,* "to carry out a promise"), he died suddenly. And that, says Oda, was the "punishment of the Buddha because he forgot his debt to the Buddha and thought it a waste to make offerings."[28] Like the breaking of a promise to the deity at Hōzanji by Yamamoto Mitsuko's gambling father, failure to say thank you can incur irreversible negative karma and its dreadful consequences.

Social Welfare and Repayment of Gratitude

Gratitude is part of the moral character of seeking practical benefits and an important element in the practice of visiting shrines and temples. As the research of shrines and temples of Ikoma by the Society for the Sociology of Religion (Shūkyō shakaigaku no kai) has demonstrated, many of those who regularly visit these institutions are making visits of gratitude in return for favors granted.[29] While visits of gratitude are mostly carried out on an individual basis, there is also a social and institutional aspect to the morality of *genze riyaku.*

Religious institutions that profit from selling benefits to people have an obligation themselves to give back something in return for the benefits they have received from their customers. This obligation is frequently discharged in terms of social welfare services. Narita-san, for instance, "lives up to the principle that 'votive money should be spent on community needs'" and therefore supports several K–12 schools, a library, a museum, and an orphanage.[30] Immediately after World War II, Hōzanji at Ikoma established a home for orphans and later built a children's hospital, a home for the elderly, and a care facility for mentally impaired children. In 1981 Hōzanji's social welfare institutions were staffed by over two hundred people and had a total budget of 682 million yen (a sum in excess, at present prices, of $6 million), an amount that "ordinary temples cannot afford."[31] Minami Hokkeji in Nara prefecture, popularly known as Tsubosaka-dera and the seventh temple on the Saikoku pilgrimage route, is known for its Kannon who cures eye ailments: its votive tablets, which bear the word "*me*" (eye) written in the cursive hiragana script, contain numerous wishes from supplicants asking Kannon to care for their eyes or heal eye disorders. The temple is rich as a result of the income from such votive tablets and other prayer services, as well as from the sums spent by the thousands of Saikoku pilgrims who visit every year. The income has enabled the temple to establish a home for elderly blind people, the first of its kind in Japan, as well as a Garden of Fragrances and a Library of Sounds for use by the visually handicapped.[32] In the Sugamo section of Tokyo, Kōganji, better known as Togenuki Jizō (the Jizō Who Extracts Thorns), is immensely popular for its practical benefits—especially the drawing out or removing of painful problems—but also for the social services it offers at an adjacent office building of its own. Counseling is provided for those who seek advice on legal, personal, academic, marital, or religious problems. Counselors hired by the temple include lawyers, college professors, and social workers, and all this is provided free of charge to supplicants. Sensōji (Asakusa Kannon) in Tokyo spends part of its considerable proceeds on a modern hospital located behind the main hall.

We could go on giving examples of temples (and shrines) that disseminate some of their wealth in such ways, for the list is quite extensive. The point is that although Japanese religions in general, and the Japanese Buddhist establishment in particular, have been repeatedly and sometimes justifiably criticized for their relative lack of social ethics, the picture is not as bleak as is sometimes made out. While Western Buddhists agonize over this failure and set about to construct what they call "Engaged Buddhism," social responsiveness is not totally lacking and can be found most prominently in Japan hand-in-hand with the provision of this-worldly benefits. Temples famed for *genze riyaku* continue to do what they have long been doing in the use of their *genze riyaku* profits to be socially engaged.

This-worldly benefits are thus closely linked at institutional levels to the processes of social service, welfare, and engagement. Social service as an expression of gratitude and responsibility can also be thought of as a secular *kuyō*, or offering, to the community. The religious meaning of "*kuyō*" is "offerings" and also refers to the ritual services in which such gifts are made. Specifically *kuyō* are associated with funerals for the dead—the ancestors who should be honored and remembered for the indebtedness the living owe them. People and ancestors are obviously important, but the many material objects used in daily life are significant, too, and when they wear out, a *kuyō* should be held in their honor. The iron ring placed in the cow's nose is an important object for livestock keepers, and worn-out rings deserve the respect of proper burial rather than the disgrace of being thrown away or melted down. On an ancient *kofun* burial site in Kibitsu in Okayama prefecture, some 6,500,000 worn-out nose rings are piled up to form an imposing grave mound topped by a *gorin-no-tō*, a five-tiered gravestone of exactly the same type that is used in graves for people. When a *kuyō* is conducted to add another nose ring to the pile, the offering is made to an appropriate deity: the Horse-Headed (Batō) Kannon, a patron deity of farmers and work animals.[33] Few people sew by hand (or machine) anymore, but in the time when most clothes were sewn at home, needles enjoyed a valued status. When they became rusty, dull, or broken, a *hari kuyō* or needle offering was carried out so that they could be placed properly in a tombstone niche and commemorated for their service.

A few blocks away from the Ryōgoku Sumo wrestling hall in Tokyo is a graveyard for dogs and cats—complete with tombstones, wooden *sotoba* markers with the names of the deceased animals, a columbarium for the ashes of the more privileged creatures, and an incinerator around which living cats lick the remains of cans of cat food. The temple, Ekō-in, was originally established to commemorate the deaths of over 100,000 people in the Great Fire of the Meireki period (1657) and now is famous for its *petto kuyō* (services for pets). A good dog is trustworthy and places itself at its owner's service every day and hence is worthy of remembrance and gratitude. But so do credit cards and telephone cards serve their owners upon demand. And when they expire, they can be properly entombed in a repository at the Ichihime Shrine in Kyoto. The shrine's brochure, which includes a form that can be mailed in with 1,000 yen to request prayers for benefits, sums up the importance of material gratitude:

> Every day we make important use of various cards to certify our personal identification. Are these cards to be crudely thrown away after we are finished using them? At this shrine we give thanks to

Credit card memorial receptacle at Ichihime Shrine

these used cards by purifying them in the grave for cards. Having purified your old cards at the grave for cards, you may step toward your future good fortune with a purified feeling full of new hope in your new card.[34]

Base materialism consigns used things to the junkyard, but the proper protocol for practical benefits calls for ceremonial burial of creatures and things that serve us so well in life and deserve our grateful respect when their usefulness is at an end. In these terms, then, the search for benefits and their enjoyment (whether the benefit of good fortune or the relief of eye problems) are linked to the necessity of repayment in some form or other—the gratitude of supplicants who return to thank the gods for their benefits, the activities of shrines and temples in supporting social welfare causes, or the actions of those who have used material objects for benefit and pleasure and subsequently wish to express their thanks to them.

Materialism, Selfishness, and Prayers for All

Both materialism and spirituality have their crass and refined facets and can combine in the conceptual and ritual framework of practical benefits with effects that range across a broad spectrum. We do not hold, however, to a configuration of the spectrum with materialism on one end and spirituality on the other. Both are intertwined and can be used for crass or refined purposes. If selfishness forms one end of the spectrum with the other end located in a protocol of moral action and ritual power, both materialism and spirituality, alone or in any combination, can be found at any point along this line. Brash materialism is self-centered, socially disengaged, and indebted to none; spiritually informed materialism rejects greed and insists that there is a propriety to acquisition which requires, to put it in the simplest of terms, that one must work hard and say thank you. Proponents of the values of *genze riyaku* such as the Association for the Contemporary Study of the Gods and Buddhas (Gendai shinbutsu kenkyūkai)— which has produced a comprehensive dictionary of the deities that provide benefits, the mechanisms by which, they aver, this is done, and the moral underpinnings of this-worldly benefits—condemn those whom they view as the lazy ingrates produced by the crass materialism of modern society and hold to a socially conservative critique of individualism, feminism, liberal sexual mores, and scientific control of all life processes.[35]

The critics of materialistic culture recognize, as we have indicated earlier, that while it offers many advantages, it produces as many problems as it does solutions and, on balance, little real progress has been made. Materialistic culture therefore magnifies the need for spirituality. But this spirituality is not of an otherworldly kind: it is necessarily limited to the cares and concerns of everyday living. The only way in which it admits of otherworldliness is in its call upon the gods and buddhas to control the "transcendent" forces of chance and accident, but it is all aimed at the fulfillment of ordinary and natural desires through a proper protocol. The moral nature of material spirituality shows itself not only in the ethical demands "in order to" purchase benefits but also in the etiquette of expressing individual gratitude and institutional graciousness "because of" the favors and profits received. Virtue and prosperity are linked here: one works hard, says thank you, and enjoys benefits that have been gained not as windfalls but as a result of spiritual help and personal endeavor.

Yet the question has to be asked: is praying for this-worldly benefits not just a selfish (*wagamama*) act? In some cases (praying for traffic safety, for instance, or for good health), one can quite easily argue that concern for one's own safety naturally means that others too will be safer: if one drives with the Buddha mind as instructed by Naritasan's amulets, then one will make the roads safer for others; if one remains healthy as a result of benefits received, one will not spread germs to others or be a burden on them. Yet there are times when praying for benefits cannot be so readily equated with such socially ameliorative results: students who pray for success, hoping to get into a leading school, are aware that not everyone will be able to succeed in this aspiration. Many more apply to the elite universities than are able to enter. Hence praying for the gods' help in enabling one to enter, say, Tokyo University means de facto (if not in terms of expressed volition) praying for someone else to fail to get in.

In personal terms, of course, individual petitioners can validate their own aspirations for success. Indeed, through the process of placing their petitions before the gods, they may even acquire a sense of legitimation and righteousness about their own success. If they have been chosen it is because they have studied harder and hence been blessed more copiously than someone else. Given that the services are there on offer—the gods and buddhas and their amulets and talismans speaking of success are available—the problem might seem unimportant for individuals. But it remains a constant one for religious organizations, shrines, and temples, who, in attempting to affirm the social and moral aspects of praying for this-worldly benefits, must confront the dilemma of selfishness.

How they do it varies from place to place, but in general terms it tends to be phrased within a rhetoric of criticizing self-centered benefit seeking while affirming the importance of seeking amelioration for all humanity. Purchasers of amulets and talismans at Iwashimizu Hachiman Shrine are given these religious objects in a paper envelope. On the envelope are written the following words: "In praying to the great god Hachiman for the prevention of danger and opening of good fortune, and for the realization of all wishes, let us strive to develop a well-rounded character and a peaceful family, and to build a splendid nation (*rippa na kokka*)." Iwashimizu Hachiman Shrine, in articulating an ideal of Shinto at the national level, thus ties individual benefits to the development of character and the happiness of family and nation. Prayers for benefits may thus be individualized but, from the shrine's perspective, they have as an ulterior and final goal the benefiting of the whole nation.

Kawasaki Daishi does not emphasize the importance of the nation as such (perhaps understandably, given its Buddhist orientation in contrast to Iwashimizu's Shinto outlook and links with the imperial family).[36] But in explaining the inner meanings of its prayers for traffic safety, Kawasaki Daishi articulates similarly broad-ranging social values. In popular pamphlets available at the temple, petitioners are informed of the "prayerful mind" (*inoru kokoro*) that is required to invoke the buddhas. Having this mind means to pray to the buddhas with all one's body and spirit and, in so doing, to develop one's own peaceful mind, which is focused on the correct ways of living and "must nurture the seeds of a mind which does not harm others." The pamphlet continues: "This correct way of praying in itself is connected to the building of a tranquil and secure family, and to the peace of society, and thus is connected to the prosperity of all peoples, which is the sole prayer and wish of all the people of the world."[37]

Similar notions are expressed elsewhere at Buddhist temples: the correct way to express prayers, as a Sōtō Zen Buddhist guidebook to "true belief" (*seishin e no joshō*) informed the sect's members, is to seek for self and others simultaneously. And the best way to do so, the volume states, is to ask for a priest to perform the task of offering up the prayer to the buddhas, because a trained priest not only knows the correct way to do this but is thereby able to transcend the petty self-seeking of individual prayers.[38] This linking of oneself and others is affirmed also by the Sōtō priest Nakajima Ikufū in a sermon published in another of the sect's publications: "Good fortune for one person alone is never possible . . . ; one's own good fortune is the fortune of others."[39] In the same series of sermons, Matsumoto Hideo warns specifically against praying only for oneself as dangerous and liable to lead to folly and spiteful anger.[40] In affirming the impossibility of separating self and other (*jita*), Nakajima's sermon draws on the concept of *jiri rita*—what benefits the self benefits others (and vice versa)—a point underlined by the statements concerning the importance of correctly praying for benefits as outlined by the Iwashimizu Hachiman envelope and the Kawasaki Daishi pamphlet.

It may be argued that what these temples, shrines, and priests are articulating is an ideal that may not be followed in practice. Certainly we need to recognize that benefit-seeking prayers most frequently are directed toward the benefit of the individual and, generally, his or her immediate social group. Nonetheless, in recognizing the moral underpinnings of the process of seeking benefits, one must also be aware that there is an implicit universality to such prayers: they are linked to the broader sense of world affirmation that is central to Japanese religion in general and seeks well-being for all.

All this is to portray practical benefits in moral and mostly rational terms, terms that we would defend, but we do not wish at the same time to overlook the irrational and magical elements involved in making a profit through utterances of prayers, moral actions, and ritual motions. Such issues require investigation, too. In the following section we turn to the vital question of how prayer and ritual performance are considered to make people healthy, wealthy, and wise.

Belief and Disbelief in Magic

As the question of whether belief is a necessary component of religious practice has been discussed elsewhere, we shall merely reaffirm here the primacy of action over belief.[41] This is especially true if belief requires intellectual understanding, and the Buddhist tradition is filled with recognitions of the limits and even unimportance of understanding. To the cases of the king of Paekche and the late Tamura Yoshirō, mentioned in Chapter 2, we add a scriptural example taken from the *Soapberry Seed Sutra* (Ch. *Mu-huan-tzu ching;* Jp. *Mokugen-kyō*), in which an Indian king complains about the difficulty of understanding the teachings and asks the Buddha to teach him something practical that he can use to rule his country. The Buddha responds to his request by showing him how to make and use a rosary, a ritual object that proved to be very effective and made understanding the teachings unnecessary.[42] Human understanding is not a prerequisite for ritual to have power and effect.

Belief as a willingness to accept that rituals can indeed bring about the desired effects, however, is a more complicated matter, and the personal testimonies fall on both sides of the fence. Cognitive acceptance of the claims made about the efficacy of ritual is not always necessary for the ritual to be efficacious. When pressed with the question of whether or not they believe in the ability of an amulet to achieve its stated purpose—curing disease, for instance—many people we interviewed deny any belief in such magic. Honda Sōichirō narrates how a group of space engineers visited Tsukuba Shrine to pray for the successful launching of a Japanese telecommunications satellite: he notes that scientists are the most rational of people in terms of their profession and must have the highest faith in their own abilities. Indeed, the leader of the group expressed no sense that the mission might not succeed. Yet as Honda notes, they also recognized the limits of their (or science's) capacity to explain everything.[43] The scientists certainly did not believe that the magical powers of a god were needed to launch the spacecraft they had so carefully constructed. But like anyone else who has prepared for an event, whether a school examination or a hospital operation, they were faced with the gap between knowledge and certainty, the space between desire and fulfillment, a territory where nothing is certain and the gods may be invoked to answer the emotional needs of the moment.

People who use amulets, prayers, and the like commonly expressed to us not so much an avid belief in their efficacy as a kind of sympathetic skepticism: "it can't hurt," or "maybe it'll work," or "just in case." At Kane Arai Benten (Money-Washing Benten) in Kamakura, there is a cave in which a spring of water gushes forth. A popular notion holds that money washed in the water will double. When asked if they thought this would happen, no one in the mostly young group of people visiting the cave in June 1995 said they believed it would certainly happen, but several people expressed the responses just noted: after all, if rinsing your money in water might cause it to double, why not try?

The "insurance factor" is probably the most commonly articulated sentiment—especially among the students we interviewed who have written prayers for educational success or have used charms for this purpose (and know full well that their fellows will be doing the same). In the case of Kane Arai Benten, it should be noted, some people quite clearly believed in highly endowed insurance policies: while some people washed a few coins, several placed two or more 10,000-yen notes in the water and then carefully dried them before inserting them back in their purses. One could suggest that this action not only expressed an optimistic view of the notion that "it might work" (if it might, then it would be better to hope for more rather than less) but might even have demonstrated a degree of sincerity in the petitioner: if you are going to ask for the benefit of having your money doubled, perhaps you should show the gods your confidence in them by getting a large sum of your money wet.

A Japanese foreign service officer, a well-educated man who holds a Ph.D. from an American university and claims not to be religious, once told of having purchased an *omamori* because his young son was to have major surgery. Asked if he believed in the power of the amulet to affect his son's surgery, he replied emphatically in the negative. After reporting that the surgery was very successful, he was again asked if he believed the amulet had anything to do with it and again he said no. Then why did he buy the amulet? It is, he explained, not a matter of belief but of human emotion—of his great desire for the well-being of his son. The conversation ended there for the moment, but a little while later he volunteered the confession that he could not help thinking that the *omamori* did have some kind of real effect. Asked once more if this meant he believed in the amulet's power, he again said no. Efficacy and meaning, in his way of looking at it, did not require belief.[44] His position is reminiscent of the scene in Amy Tan's *The Kitchen God's Wife* when Pearl asks her mother if she believes in the spirit money and incense that she will burn at Aunty Du's funeral. "What's to believe?" her mother replied. "This is respect."[45] As a priest at Zenkōji in Nagano told an American professor who declared that he did not believe in Buddhism, anyone who chants the *nembutsu* sincerely will be born in the Pure Land even if they do not believe. The American found the claim—that one could practice and receive salvation without requiring belief—in itself unbelievable.[46]

But what does it mean to believe? Does sincerity imply belief? Can one believe without being able to articulate the content of belief? Certainly the terms "*shinkō*" (belief) and "*shinjiru*" (to believe) are widely used in the context of practical benefits.[47] Like other impor-

tant terms, "*shinkō*" has a range of meanings, two of the most important of which are "belief" (or "faith") and "religious custom" (or
"practice"). "Belief," in turn, has two distinct nuances that depend on
the degree to which there is an intellectual content or an affirmation
of a more emotive order. Belief as intellectual understanding,
thought, or knowledge is based on doctrines or teachings—as when
we say, for instance, that the ideas of dependent origination or karma
are Buddhist beliefs. The emphasis here is on some kind of content
that is cognitive in nature and can therefore be explained and discussed in the mode of theology or its secular counterpart philosophy.
This kind of belief we call *cognitive belief*.[48]

The second nuance of belief is expressed in terms like "faith,"
"trust," or "reliance." The content of this *affective belief* can be described and even cognized at a primitive level but not rationally explained since it is mostly of a mythic and magical world of pure lands,
hells, gods, and demons. It is a world apprehended as something
"simple and immediate, framed by myth and magic. A man no longer
subordinated one thought to another with mathematical precision;
instead, he apprehended similarities and balances, types and paradigms, parallels and symbols. . . . It was a world not of thoughts, but
of images."[49] This description by Thomas Cahill is of the European
Dark Ages in which classical Greek and Roman thought had been
eclipsed by this mythical and magical worldview, which can also be
seen in Japan and its version of mythic similarities, magical symbols,
and vivid images. Cahill's use of the word "thought" is narrow and re-
strictive since it does not point out the intricate relationship between
images and thinking, but his comments are still a useful reminder
that cognition and intellectual thought are not the only ways by which
the world can be affirmed and believed in.[50] To his description we
would add that it is also a world of sincerity and feeling. When deities
are the "objects" of faith (such as Kannon *shinkō*), it is affective belief
that is at work, although subsequent explanations of Kannon can be
systematic and rational enough to approach cognitive belief.

The distinction between affective and cognitive, forced and artificial as it may be, does allow for an explanation of the often heard report that people sincerely purchase amulets but do not really believe
in them: they are engaging in a customary practice with affective sincerity but not cognitive belief. The key to all of this perhaps lies in the
interesting notion of sincerity (*makoto, seijitsu* or *shinjitsu*, "to be
true"), which we define here as affective belief. While the disbeliev-
ing American visitor to Zenkōji did not recite the *nembutsu*, he did offer a prayer for his father, who was ill with cancer. He too, like the
Japanese foreign service officer, repeatedly insisted that he did not
believe (cognitively) in the power of the Zenkōji Amida Triad to help

his father, but his prayer was nevertheless totally sincere and, not having been said in jest or mockery, was something he believed in—affectively. It is not necessary to believe cognitively that a ritual utterance can cause a cure in order to be affectively sincere in prayer. The distinction between affective and cognitive is difficult to maintain, since feeling and thought are intertwined. Yet without such a differentiation it would be even more difficult to explain how it is that people use amulets sincerely without believing in them. We state again: they use them affectively but not cognitively.

Unquestioning sincerity is essential, and the word "shinkō" is often explained in terms of this moral and affective virtue. It is not surprising that the Association for the Contemporary Study of the Gods and Buddhas warns against the lack of belief as a *moral* danger: "The gods and the buddhas are not wonder medicines for specific cures, and to offer 10 or 20 yen and pray to be granted practical benefits right then and there can only be thought of as extremely selfish and greedy."[51] As we shall see in Chapter 5, there are various levels at which one can articulate one's prayers, some displaying greater earnestness (and hence implying greater meritoriousness in receiving benefits) than others. Affective belief is being earnest (*nesshin*), which is virtually identical with sincerity. Using the example of what supplicants are told at Hōzanji, the Association for the Contemporary Study of the Gods and Buddhas explains that practical benefits will become manifest if new believers follow the example of experienced believers, do not request or discuss logical explanations (cognitive beliefs), rely upon Shōten-san with a single undisturbed mind, exert themselves in their own efforts, and deepen their mind of faith (affective belief).[52] Herein lies a good definition of *shinkō:* be sincere, do not doubt, work hard, and don't ask for explanations. In a similar vein, the Shingon *Handbook for Believers* stresses the morality of belief as the only protection against the magic of materialism by which people mistakenly think they can get something for nothing.[53] Belief, again, is hard work and sincerity, itself a cardinal value.

Affective belief and hard work are important elements in the second meaning of "shinkō" as religious custom or practice, which is what is primarily meant by terms such as "minkan" or "minzoku shinkō" (folk belief/practices). Customary practices and rituals are often carried out without much thought—that is, without cognitive belief—a point frequently noted about Japanese religious practice.[54] Frits Staal notes this to be a characteristic common to ritual in general and argues that those who expect participants to be able to explain the meaning of their performances will be disappointed.[55] It is a common error on the part of investigators, especially those who think that all religious behavior is rooted in some kind of teaching, to expect that cognitive belief must always attend affective belief and customs. Speaking of those who wish to penetrate the veils of Asian cultures to find wisdom, a longtime observer of Japan, Ian Buruma, recently noted that the problem is not the inscrutability of the East but the confusion of the Western traveler. "Often by peering into apparent mysteries too deeply," he writes, "we miss what is on the surface. Zen, and indeed much of Japanese art and culture, does not pretend to be deep; on the contrary, it celebrates the surface of life, what meets the eye; hence its aesthetic genius."[56]

The spiritual genius of the conceptual and ritual framework of practical benefits is that it works through the embroidered and textured surfaces of feeling and sentiment, beneath which there is often little or no thought, at least in Cahill's narrow sense of the term. *Shinkō* as custom, then, are practices habitually carried out within a worldview of myth and magic affirmed through affective belief but not always through cognitive belief. Lest we overstate our case, however, we hasten to add that of course there is a great deal that is thought and said about this common religion (and hence a book can be written about it). And to the degree that myths, images, metaphors, legends, similitudes, and dreams can be cognized, there is thought; but it is not in the way of precise analysis and consistent presentation. We do not wish to deny cognition too strongly, but we do hold that what can be cognized and therefore articulated is filled with inconsistencies (bad karma can be destroyed but then again sometimes it cannot) and mythic license (Amida's radiance will shine upon you) on the intellectual level. But it is relatively clear, and certainly more evident, on the level of customary conduct and action.

Explanations of *shinkō*, to pursue this point further, seldom deal with cognitive content; they urge practice and action instead. Writing in a popular *goriyaku* ("esteemed benefits") guidebook, Nakao Takashi discusses *shinkō* entirely in terms of action (*kōi*), ritual (*girei*), making a trip (*tabi*) to temples, practice (*shugyō*), pilgrimage (*junrei*), and secluding oneself for prayer (*komori*). The fundamentals of these actions are defined in even simpler actions: put your hands together, talk to the buddhas, meet the buddhas.[57] The buddhas in turn need to act out their part, as divine response is a necessary part of belief as practice. Matsumoto Jitsudō, the head priest of Ikoma Hōzanji in 1985, explained the popularity of his temple in utilitarian terms:

Ultimately it's because Shōten-san of this temple actually answers people's requests. People these days do not pray to and believe in buddhas who do not answer their prayers in fact. Because they believe that their requests will surely be granted, and because they have already had experiences in which their prayers have been heard, they believe sincerely.[58]

Supplicants and the deities must both act, and again Matsumoto explains the relationship between practical benefits and belief in terms of effort: "Through one's own power plus the power of the buddhas, the impossible becomes possible."[59]

The results, if there are results, take the form of miracle, *reigen*, a strange occurrence that cannot be explained intellectually but for which a claim can be made: divine powers, not luck or chance, in answer to moral and ritual efforts are the responsible causes of the event. Yoritomi Motohiro, cited earlier, tells the story of how one of his students carved a statue of Bishamonten for Yoritomi's father, who was dying of cancer. Bishamonten did not have the power to cure his illness but became a valuable icon that represented the student's caring kindness as well as a powerful protective deity. After his father's death, Professor Yoritomi placed the deity to protect his temple's northern side, the traditional direction protected by Bishamonten. One day a lace curtain blew onto a votive candle, a fire broke out, and a good part of the room was damaged. Prominent in the charred section of the room, however, was a paper-covered *fusuma* door that remained untouched by the flames. This small *reigen* or miracle could not be explained—except for the fact that the Bishamonten statue was on the other side of the door. Here, then, was the "explanation": Bishamonten prevented the door from catching fire, and it was, in Professor Yoritomi's own words, definitely "not a matter of having good luck."[60] Personal testimonies of the strange ways in which the gods and buddhas work abound. They are very similar to the *reigen* events that are at the heart of the *engi* stories of the origins of temples and shrines.

Sometimes the occurrences are not so strange, but the credit still goes to the divinities. While Americans are preeminent in giving thanks to God for nonmiracles like scoring a touchdown or winning a country and western music award, Japanese are more likely to do the same in the context of *goriyaku* experiences. In relating with great relief how a major ritual involving thousands of people went off without a single incident, a Tendai priest counted it as part of the miraculous benefits of Kannon, the deity for whom the ritual was held.[61] Oda Ryūkō tells the story of a woman who had become a prostitute in order to help her impoverished family and then was sold by her brothel to another operator for service in Manchuria. She prayed to Kannon that she would not have to go to such a foreign place, shaved her head as part of her commitment to Kannon, and reported to her new owner, who, upon seeing the bald-headed woman standing before him, promptly fired her. "Shaving her head," Oda concluded, "was a divine miracle."[62] Shimizutani Kōshō, who recently became the head priest of Asakusa Temple, relates a story of the editor of a Buddhist magazine, visiting Kannon pilgrimage temples in Chichibu, who dropped a camera lens in the snow. In retracing his steps, however, he found it again—and that result, Shimizutani tells us, was not a matter of mere chance or even of looking in the right place but because of Kannon's help and because wondrous events can happen in the context of pilgrimage.[63] The avoidance of disastrous happenings is the divine gift sought in the amulets and rituals for traffic safety, prevention of calamities, domestic harmony, safety from theft, good personal relations, healthy children, immunity from senility, and all the other situations in which the highest hope is for nothing bad to happen. A high priority is placed on this kind of preventive maintenance, and when everything is going well, the absence of mishap is often (though not always) hailed as a miracle.

The miracle of normalcy, if we may insist on hyperbolically calling it that, did not escape the astute eye of the travel writer Saitō Tsuneharu on his *goriyaku* journey throughout Japan. At Tawara Hot Springs in Nagato (Yamaguchi prefecture), where he visited the Penis Kannon (Mala Kannon), Saitō marveled at the hundreds of stone, wood, and concrete "male symbols" pointing to the sky with their promises of fertility, healthy children, and good relations between husband and wife. The red-and-white bibbed Jizō for aborted children were lined in pitiful contrast, it seemed to him, to the couples strolling among them. Many of them were older in years and appeared happy and content:

> It goes without saying that there are reports of believers experiencing the miracles of marital harmony, pregnancies, and healing of lower body ailments; but at Tawara Hot Springs, there are also many good stories of how older couples who come to bathe in the springs still have flowers of love, which have matured without their notice, still blowing about them; and they return home feeling the good fortune of being together. Are these not stories that tell us how broad is the range of *goriyaku*?[64]

Problems, once they occur, can be solved; but better still is the prevention of their occurrence. The broad range of *goriyaku* covers the workings of the gods even in the absence of belief, but more commonly in an active relationship between believers and their deities. Belief, as the *Kōjien* puts it succinctly, is "the conscious aspect of religious action."

In the theological complexities of Jōdo Shinshū, belief is the conscious aspect *without* religious action. In the landscape of practical benefits, Jōdo Shinshū looms large because of its strident rejection of *genze riyaku,* and once again it is important to examine its interesting position on the subject. Shinran rejected prayer and ritual as means of obtaining the good things in life; in place of religious action and benefits he offered the purity of faith (*shinjin*) in the other power of Amida. While the proponents of *genze riyaku* certainly believe in divine power to help them make the impossible possible, it is Jōdo Shinshū that absolutizes divine power (*zettai tariki*) and faith; but their rewards do not include *genze riyaku.* Kasahara Kazuo describes Shinran's mission in the Kantō area as having to sever ordinary people from their false dependence on the "priestly contractors" who were "dumping practical benefits" by preaching that everyone could profit from prayer and get something for doing nothing but pray, as if "rice cakes were falling freely from shelves."[65] Shinran's teaching required that people give up praying and all other religious actions and simply believe instead with no expectation that belief in Amida will bring practical benefits. It is a bit difficult, we admit, to imagine that common people would replace "action for benefits" with "consciousness without benefits," but Kasahara claims that Shinran was exceedingly successful in the twenty years of his Kantō ministry, having converted over 100,000 people during that time. Why would so many people be so interested in forgoing benefits for faith in Amida?

The answer lies in Kasahara's distinction between the "instant benefits" of *genze riyaku* and the "slow-but-sure benefits" of faith in Amida. Kasahara insists that the benefits promised by Shinran were not to be realized only after one's death and subsequent rebirth in the Pure Land: pure belief yields dividends in this life as well. These include nothing less than transcendence from past karma, becoming a buddha in this body (*sokushin jōbutsu*), equality with all other buddhas, liberation from the rounds of transmigration, deliverance from the fear of death, and, finally, self-confidence, courage, and happiness (*kōfuku*), a term that is very much part of the standard diction of *genze riyaku.* For the most part these represent spiritual boons and general virtues and differ from the usual language of *genze riyaku* in the avoidance of promises of specific material and physical advantages such as health, wealth, jobs, good crops, and the rest. For being so grandly spiritual, the Jōdo Shinshū promises are even more fantastic:

> It is more than just a promise that the *nembutsu* person who has firmly established the mind of faith can become a buddha in this world. It is not through one's own power, but through the other

power of Amida, that just by firmly establishing the mind of faith alone, Amida will make that person become a buddha in that person's body. . . . In living in this world, the person who truly attains the mind of faith will be able from that time to live the same life as that of Amida Nyorai.[66]

This is not the "low" magic of producing material things but the "high" magic of being transformed into a living buddha by the power of a transcendent buddha—just through faith. A practitioner of *genze riyaku* would have no trouble accepting the list of slow-but-sure benefits promised by Jōdo Shin Buddhism, but he might have difficulty believing that no effort is required for these boons—even that power-packed belief, according to Jōdo Shin teaching, is not a product of human assertion but a gift of Amida. Jōdo Shin's purity of faith (*shinjin*) combines both cognitive and affective belief but rules out action; and since the benefits are spiritual and sublime, rather than crass and concrete, they are realizable primarily as doctrinal assertions. The life of faith is as much a hope in the promises of the teachings as it is in the other power of Amida. For until one has a real experience of being a buddha, equality with Amida remains an abstraction, which, like all abstractions, depends on the power of words for whatever reality that assertion may have. Despite the strong insistence on the totality of divine action in the prescribed absence of human effort, there still must be something that people have to do—even if it is to assent to belong to the organization that holds to this teaching. Still, the counsel to do nothing is not satisfying. Even Jōdo Shin believers disregard this teaching and go out to do something to get practical benefits. Studies carried out by Jōdo Shin scholars themselves show that members of their own denomination often outnumber those of other sects who seek practical benefits: 40 percent, for instance, of participants in the hundred-round walking ritual (*hyakudo mairi*) at Ishikiri Shrine are Jōdo Shinshū members.[67]

The assertion about becoming a living buddha may be a claim that is more fantastic than that of becoming healthy and wealthy, but what we wish to emphasize here is the common ground shared by Jōdo Shinshū and the conceptual and ritual framework of practical benefits. Both offer seemingly incredible promises that are redeemable through the credulity of commitment and sincerity. Nothing is beyond human reach so long as humans cooperate with the deities through the wide number of moral, ritual, affective, and cognitive avenues available, including that of giving up action. All agree that this cooperation is critical. And all in their own fashions affirm the common religious conviction that the sacred and the secular do not sit on opposite sides of a great divide. For an observer to say this is not to say much, however, since the statement that the secular is related to the sacred is so general as to be an exercise in what is obvious in all religions. But it is exactly the *saying* of this truism in myriad ways by practitioners that makes up the stuff of what observers find so interesting. These sayings in the specific form of petitionary prayer are particularly intriguing, for they raise, once again, the issue of desire and the propriety of its fulfillment.

Prayer and Purchase

Since the primary function of prayers is to ask for something, prayer smacks of selfishness—an issue we touched on earlier in the chapter and which becomes a problem, as we have seen in Chapter 2, for those who view religion as the rejection of desire. Even the supporters of petitionary prayer agree that there is something called wrongful prayers when they are uttered without sincerity or commitment and are not followed by proper thankfulness. But there is correct prayer, too, and one justification for it is to be found in a Shingon interpretation of nonduality, the philosophical heart of Mahāyāna Buddhism: if everything is one, then the desires of samsara can be fulfilled as the enlightenment of nirvana. For a Shingon priest like Oda Ryūkō, the magic of prayer works by the same cosmology of oneness that governs the making of miracles and healing. Divine wonders can take place in the everyday world as extraordinary or mundane events by virtue of the Mahāyāna truth that the sacred and the secular are one. This cosmological concurrence makes it possible for divine energy to be invoked in human bodies and bring about the healing of disease.[68] Prayer is thus an invocation of the doctrine of nonduality, and its affirmation of physical bodies and their desires, and is the means by which the teaching can be transformed into experience. Prayer, as the eminent Shingon scholar Toganoo Shōun put it,

> is an expression of desires reflected in terms of a religious consciousness. . . . It is the Great Desire that seeks to embrace and influence all sentient beings. . . . The prayers and ritual practices for the satisfaction of our material wants are based on this desire. This desire is nothing other than the demand of the great soul of the universe to live forever through the instrument of the human body.[69]

Sometimes prayer can invoke small desires, as well, as attested to by a twenty-six-year-old Sōka Gakkai member:

In chanting Namu Myōhō Rengekyō, I feel power and energy bub-
bling up inside me. While I chant, I pray in my heart about my
work, that it will go smoothly, and I pray for all the people in my
bank, for their happiness. (Sometimes I think of a woman I want to
talk to. Sometimes an image of a naked woman appears, and I'm
horrified, but that's only natural!) [70]

Small desires are natural and in that state are not separated from the
great desire that animates all of nature.

The communicative function of prayer that binds the secular and
the sacred is clearly expressed in the term "*kaji kitō*" (prayer for the
reception of boons), which is often used pejoratively to criticize petitionary prayer as superstitious and magical speech directed to super-
beings who can make happen what humans cannot. Although *kaji kitō*
is associated with the Esoteric Buddhism of the Shingon and Tendai
schools, the idea and practice are found in different ways in all forms
of Buddhism and indeed all forms of religion. The basic meaning of
kaji refers to divine bestowal (*ka*) and human receiving (*ji*).[71] Here
again we see the interplay between the human and the divine realms
existing in a continuum.

Discussions of prayer, like deliberations about desire, are often
strained along the fault line separating true religion from superstition, high from low. Gorai Shigeru is particularly forthright in criticizing those who reject prayer as low:

Since the relationship between magical incantation and religion is
discussed primarily on the basis of Christianity, magical incantation
is castigated as something that is not religion, fit for uncivilized
barbarians, heretical, diabolical, and bad. Japanese intellectuals,
philosophers, and scholars of religion blindly follow the rear of this
horse, oppose magical incantation, think of it as the leader of
superstition, and detest practitioners and prayer priests.[72]

Gorai goes on to note that the transformation of wine and bread into
the blood and body of Christ in the Christian Eucharist is every bit as
magical as Buddhist chants and prayers. But even Gorai gives a sani-
tized definition of prayer by qualifying the act with a virtue we have
already encountered with the notion of belief: sincerity (*seishin* or
makoto). Prayer is the communication of sincerity to the gods and the
buddhas, and sincerity is much more important than form. The priority of sincerity over form is emphasized in a fable told by Katō
Seiichi about an old woman who recited with sincerity, "*Om aburage
sowaka*" (reverence to fried bean curd), and experienced all sorts of
miracles that attracted to her a good many followers. When a priest

pointed out to the old woman that she was wrongly chanting the mantra—its correct form is "*Om abiraunken sowaka*"—she realized her error and thereafter the miracles stopped. What is interesting about this story, Katō says, is that the miracles she experienced were authentic even when in form her chant was incorrect. "The certain faith," he notes, "that people hold within their hearts indicates that even if their faith is mistaken, it can become powerful for them."[73] Katō uses the term "certain faith" (*kakushin*) and clearly means by this the sincere (affective) *practice* of prayer rather than the cognitive affirmation of a tenet. Like Gorai, Katō must make the distinction between right and wrong prayer—and the critical element is sincerity along with, interestingly enough, great desire. Faith and desire are both sources of power. And if people "cease to make the effort" involved in "pure prayer, great desire, and right faith," they will "surely fall into the worldly beliefs of divination and sorcery."[74] The landscape of prayer is uneven: people can fall from high to low even though, in theory, the different levels are one and the same.

There is an objective nature to prayer in the sense that words are offered, like fish and rice wine, as real things to the deities. Prayer is "placed" (*kakeru*) on the altar, just as food is. To pray is to place a request (*gankake*), just as mirrors, rice, statues, cut pieces of paper, and *ema* are placed in their proper places.[75] A prayer is a material thing and is offered like other goods to be received by the gods. In the making of offerings there is a reversal of *kaji* as it now becomes human giving and divine receiving. This, however, is not a simple give-and-take exchange. And here again the metaphor of purchase is more appropriate than that of exchange. For the transaction involves not just the handing over of objective words—which, like currency, are recognizable by the standard form in which they are presented—but the formal tender must be backed by the standard of sincerity. Prayers can be mistaken for fried bean curd, just as money can be misprinted, but it is sincerity that gives the currency a value as solid as gold. An offer of words in return for benefits without the backing of the standard is but an exchange: a bad prayer.

One does not barter for benefits but *buys* them in a transactional system. (This is a point we emphasize further in Chapter 5, when we examine practices involved in seeking benefits, and in Chapter 6 where we discuss how religious institutions sell benefits.) It is a transactional system featuring prayer as a contract containing purchase order and invoice, *ema* and *omamori* as shares signifying access to the gods, good karma as credit, negative karma as deficit, moral conduct as investment deposit, belief as trust leading to active and repeated patronage, offerings as down payments, sincerity as the value standard backing the currency of offerings, ritual repetition as compounding of interest, gratitude as goodwill, and benefits as final profit. All this is backed by the warranty of scriptures. If the actual practices of the common religion of Japan often look like commerce, it is because—in spiritual and material terms—it is a business of buying out chance, the ever present obstacle blocking access to the divine providers of benefits.

4

The Providers of Benefits
Gods, Saints, and Wizards

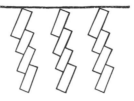

UNLIKE THE RELATIONSHIP between a man and a woman—which, as Sei Shōnagon (b. 965) described it, is "near though distant"—the zigzag path leading to the temple at Kurama is something "distant though near."[1] Located in the mountains about seven miles directly north of the old imperial palace in Kyoto, Kurama Temple is not far in terms of the straight-line distance from the city, but even today, and more so during the Heian period when Sei Shōnagon wrote about lovers and the zigzag path, a trip to Kurama Temple takes one through mountains and forests that make it seem as if one is very far away. Today the train and cable car to Kuramadera make it nearer than it was in earlier times, but the quick change in landscape only emphasizes the sensation of being far away while so near. A few stops before Kurama is the Kibune Shrine, and many passengers get off there to hike the rest of the way to the temple. When the relationship between a man and a woman is threatened by the attractions of another woman, Kibune Shrine becomes a popular destination for women who can stick a pin or nail through the image of the other woman there, thereby driving away with a death curse if necessary a rival who has come too close. In the forests of Kibune and Kurama, evil wishes can be freely acted out and demons, as we shall see, can descend from outer space. So near, Kurama is also distant.

The main gate at Kurama is some distance below the temple itself, and the zigzag path from it passes through Yuki Jinja, a small but exquisite shrine set among the massive pillars of cryptomeria trees. It is a good resting place, where amulets in the shape of cars and books can be purchased for traffic safety and academic success. Nearly all the visitors go up to the main sanctuary, which is designated an Important Cultural Property, and make the usual offerings of coins and prayers. In May 1996 five different people ranging in age from the twenties to the sixties were asked if they knew who the main deity was, but none of them could identify the god to whom they prayed.[2] It seemed not to matter; it was enough to know that the shrine housed a divine presence. A small stream of water trickles alongside the edge of the zigzag path, and at one particular place everyone stops to listen to the sounds of frogs coming from the small crevices in the rocks, but try as they might, no one appears able to find the frogs themselves. The sounds are immediately near, but the frogs are invisibly distant.

According to the legend of Kuramadera, Maō, the Demon King, flew down from the distant but visible planet of Venus and landed at what is now the Oku-no-in at Kurama Temple some 260 million years ago. Though a demon, Maō is a good spirit—an example of how ferocity and warlike powers can be used to subdue evil and thus bring about good. Maō's purpose is to convert devils, protect people, bring peace, and promote righteousness. He is also ruler of a vast underworld metropolis to which there are four entrances: in northern Europe, in the Himalayan Mountains, in South America, and in Japan, specifically at Kurama. Lord of the underworld, Maō is also the creator and destroyer of life who controls all functions of human life, the natural world, and the gods. As the father of humanity, he transcends humanity, but he manifests himself on earth in the form of a sixteen-year-old boy who never grows old. Nevertheless, since Maō is the spirit of the universe, no one can have a direct encounter with him or ever be certain what he looks like. There is only one portrait of Maō. It was done by the painter Kanō Motonobu (1476–1559), who devoted himself to fervent prayer one night at Oku-no-in, received a revelation at dawn, followed a spiderweb hanging from a cryptomeria tree, and reached a spot where he was able to paint a likeness of Maō. The portrait is a hidden image regarded as so sacred it is shown to the public only once every sixty years, 2046 being the next occasion.

On the day of the tiger of the first month in the year 770 C.E., Gantei, a young Chinese priest who had come to Japan with the precepts master Ganjin (688–763), had a dream about a sacred place in the mountains to the the north of Tōshōdaiji, where he was staying. He set out in search of it, but could not find it until a white horse with a jeweled saddle appeared and showed him the way. Finding a level spot just below the summit, he made a fire to spend the night only to be attacked by a female devil spitting poison. After failing to kill the devil even though he stabbed it with his staff, Gantei hid beneath a large dead tree, which, because he recited a mantra with all his might, toppled over onto the devil and killed it. The next day the tree transformed itself into a statue of Bishamonten, guardian of the north and subduer of devils. Gantei built a hut to enshrine it, and this was the beginning of Kuramadera, Temple of the Saddled Horse. An annual festival is still held on the first day of the tiger (*hatsutora*)—a day on which, according to one of the temple's brochures, people have come for ages "to pray for the realization of their deepest wishes, prosperous business, and happiness."[3]

In 796, two years after the capital was moved from Nara to Kyoto, Fujiwara Isendo, the man in charge of building Tōji, had a dream about finding a statue of Kannon in the mountains to the north. Not knowing the exact direction in which to proceed, he saddled his white horse, set it loose, and followed its tracks. The horse led him to the Bishamonten hut on Kurama, but Isendo was puzzled and disappointed since he had still not found Kannon. That night a sixteen-year-old boy (that is, Maō) appeared in his dream and told him that Bishamonten and Kannon were two different names for the same deity. Isendo went back up to the mountain and built a temple in which he enshrined the Bishamonten image and a newly made statue of a thousand-armed Kannon.

The three deities who appear in the legend of Kuramadera—Maō, Bishamonten, and Kannon—are worshiped together as Sonten, the Exalted Divinity comprised of three forms merged into one essence. Bishamonten represents the light of the sun, Kannon the love of the moon, and Maō the power of the earth. As a single triune deity, Sonten is the great spirit and energy of the entire universe and the foundation of the existence of all things.[4] Harmony with the universe is an important teaching of Kuramadera, which broke away from the Tendai school in 1947 and formed its own independent sect, Kurama Kōkyō. In a dimly lit, eerie basement below the main hall, hundreds of people have enshrined in small porcelain jars locks of their hair to symbolize the unity of their bodies with Sonten and the universe. Resembling a columbarium, the room is lined with dozens of shelves holding the jars. At the very back of the room are statues of the three deities, barely visible in the low light. Maō seems to have the face of a wizened old man, but clearly discernible are the wings on his back that made possible his flight from Venus.

Although the cable car was shut down in the spring of 1996 for repairs, thus forcing everyone to walk the zigzag path, the temple was crowded with visitors, many of them clutching rosaries. They offered money, said their prayers, bought their amulets, and hung their *ema*, some of which contained elaborate drawings and lengthy explanations of the circumstances of their petitions. Unique as Kuramadera might be in its own ways, the multiplicity of deities is a common feature seen in other temples. Here one can pray to Shinto gods, classical Buddhist deities, priestly founders, and benevolent demons, all of whom are powerful but work to augment one's own efforts. As the temple brochure states: "We lead our lives by virtue of Sonten. Sonten has bestowed his power on us so that we can lead a good life, casting evil out of our minds with the strength of his power. We make every effort to perfect ourselves."[5]

It is a typical cooperative effort between oneself and a host of deities. Kuramadera and its legends exemplify the ways in which numerous deities may come together and work for the benefit of petitioners. The legends point to the often complex interactions between deities and to the multiplicity of them that may operate within the world of benefits. The pantheon for practical benefits is certainly large. It is also less of a hierarchy than an open conglomerate of equally accessible specialists and generalists—some deities are both at the same time. Near and distant, names known and unknown, the divine providers of practical benefits form an extended family that is multireligious and multicultural, and within it relationships may be long standing or new, emphasized or ignored. The family, which includes its human relatives and offspring, is also modular. Thus different combinations of members may get together according to changing purposes and circumstances.

Personalization and Purchase

The stalwart pillars of the family of deities are venerable and well known. They tend to come more often from the Buddhist side because that side of the family is large, well developed institutionally, and well represented in texts, legends, and collections of miracle stories. Everyone has heard of the various forms of Kannon and Jizō; there are so many of them it is hard to name them all. Were it not for the names inscribed on each of the dozens of Jizōs that line an uphill path at Hōzanji in Ikoma, it would be difficult to identify them since they all look alike. Inscribed beneath their names are the names of the families that sponsor them, and they in turn watch over the members of that family, especially those who have passed away. Each Jizō is thus a personal one with a special relationship to a specific person or group. The particular identities of the Jizōs may at times be enhanced by their own unique clothing, and when they go abroad they sometimes adopt the dress of their new home and can even cross-dress, as the Jizō at a Sōtō Zen temple in Hawai'i has done by wearing a muumuu.

Though pedigreed by scripture and classical by tradition, Jizō is not a remote and formal god with whom intimacy is impossible. On the contrary, Jizō is near at hand, dearly loved, and called by many names and nicknames that allow people to identify with him on a personal basis. In writing of people's personal relations with Inari, Karen Smyers suggests that Inari is free of "the sort of clear historical narrative that would prevent his personalization to fit particular needs."[6] Yet clear historical narratives need not impede personalization. Jizō, for example, has a clear narrative of specific attributes and deeds enunciated in scriptures, commentaries, and stories, but he still remains highly personalized. The narrative, in fact, strengthens rather than impedes people's intimate relations with him. People know a lot about Jizō because much has been said and written about him—and this knowledge makes for detailed familiarity and intimacy. Intimacy can be had with deities who have clear narratives (Jizō) or with those that do not (Inari).

People pray, as we have seen, even to gods whose names they do not know, but the ambiguity does not prevent them from expressing sincere prayers that are deeply personal. The question of which deity commands more personal attention than others is not to be resolved by analyzing what is known or not known about the deity, but by asking petitioners to state their personal preferences. Our interest here is not to conduct a survey to determine which deity enjoys the highest degree of personalization but to analyze the characteristics of this widespread phenomenon as seen in the case of Jizō and other deities. Personalization is a major characteristic of Japanese common religion, and while we would agree with Smyers that Inari is the most personalized in terms of having the largest number of personalized ("my own Inari") forms, the characteristics she describes so well can also be seen in Kannon, Kōbō Daishi, Fudō, the Seven Gods of Good Fortune, and any number of other deities with whom people become intimate.

Like Inari, Jizō has many names, nicknames, and functions. A partial list gleaned from popular religious guidebooks (see Chapter 7) includes the Longevity Jizō, Cough-Curing Jizō, Rice-Planting Jizō, Perspiration Jizō, Bed Wetters' Jizō, Oil-Covered Jizō, Naked Jizō, Buckwheat Noodle Jizō, Bean Curd Jizō, Catfish Jizō, Carp Jizō, Octopus Jizō, Thorn-Extracting Jizō, Wart-Removing Jizō, Face Powder Jizō, and, of course, the well-known Aborted Fetus Jizō (Mizuko Jizō).[7] While Jizō is a classical Buddhist bodhisattva, most of these specialized Jizō are creations made through personal interpretations and local legends that do not always have a formal basis in scripture or commentary. The list goes on and indeed can continue to go on: there is no limit to the number of needs and characteristics that can be related to Jizō. In the form of an amulet or talisman, even a generic Jizō becomes a personal guardian carried in one's wallet, car, or school bag. Jizō is a particular friend of children: he protects them on the roads and saves them if abandoned—as is expressed in the "Sai-no-kawara" song, which tells how children who have died and been abandoned by their parents are saved by Jizō,[8] even before they arc born.[9] Like Kannon with a thousand arms for helping people in all situations, Jizō proliferates as people rename him to answer yet one more prayer. He is always there, ready to be called. The messages written on *ema* to Jizō (or any other deity for that matter) are always personal, and supplicants often identify themselves personally by name, age, and address.

While personal needs are seemingly endless, the personalization process does not allow for total license in practice. Even personal relations demand some degree of formality, and, while it is not prohibited, people do not make up a new Jizō whenever they wish. There is no need for excessive proliferation, since both the generic and the specialized Jizōs can hear prayers for any purpose. Smyers cites Aston's observation that the agricultural Inari has been "enlarged so as to make him a sort of general providence who watches over all human concerns."[10] All the gods and buddhas function as specialists and generalists and can hear the most idiosyncratic of prayers. Thus there is no need to establish a new divine version just for that purpose. Since single deities can hear any number of requests, they have a communal aspect to their personal relations and can therefore serve people from a central place to which petitioners come with their varied needs. The reenshrinement (*kanjō*) described by Smyers is a process for dividing and sharing the deity with another place through the establishment of a branch shrine. As the proliferation increases, Inari worship becomes quite communal whereby "my own Inari" also becomes *our* Inari or *our* Jizō. Personalization has both communal and individual aspects. These multiple features are clearly seen in Smyers' description of how institutions portion out "divided spirits" or "rock altars" to individual believers. In the form of small statues, the divided spirits of Dakiniten from Toyokawa Inari are even taken back to the temple apparently for monthly or yearly ritual renewal.[11] While Smyers notes that the divided spirits in new shrines are "permanently 'alive,'"[12] it seems that the divided spirits, like *ofuda*, given to individuals are taken back periodically for some kind of renewal. These practices are carefully and very formally controlled by the institutions; they are not available for the taking or the making by anyone at will.

The idea of personalization is very broad: examples include any activity involving people who relate to, venerate, or supplicate deities and seek to enter into a relationship with them. Pilgrimage, meditation, sutra copying, and prayer are all very personal actions that seek intimate relations with the divine. In some respects, then, the idea of personalization is too broad to be useful, since most activities involve people. In the institutional practice of personalization, however, one can identify a specific element that gives the idea analytical focus. That element is money. The public display of personalization in the form of individual names posted at large temples and shrines is striking. Hundreds of stone fence posts line the pathways to temples like Hōzanji or shrines like the Iwashimizu Hachimangū, each post carved with the name of a donor and the amount of money given. The long retaining wall behind the main temple at Narita-san is filled with plaques of companies, many with their own distinctive signature styles and logos, that have supported the temple. The patrons of temples and shrines pay money, which earns them the right, if the level of support is high enough, to have their names displayed to show their personal commitment to the institution. While they do not formally purchase partial ownership, they do buy rights to certain social and religious claims. Like stockholders in a nonprivate company, they comprise the public investment base. To this extent, then, personalization is purchased.

Money is prominent, too, in Smyers' discussion of divided spirits (*wakemitama*) and official reenshrinement (*kanjō*). In both practices, the spirit of Inari is not given away free but is sold. When the Meiji government put an end to the practice of *kanjō*, the priests at the Fushimi Inari Shrine successfully objected to the ban by arguing, among other things, that an end to *kanjō* meant a loss of valuable income.[13] In terms of our commercial model, reenshrinement can be understood as franchising: the selling of a license to market the product—the divided spirit in this case—at local centers. While franchisers could pick their own names for their own divided spirit (hence "personalization"), the divided spirit had to come from the headquarters, which insisted that it had sole rights to the establishment of local centers. Unofficial reenshrinement constituted unauthorized distribution: the failure of a proper purchase. The right to set up a new rock altar or take over an old one can similarly be seen as franchising—the average cost of which at Fushimi Inari today is $16,000.[14] The divided spirits sold at Fushimi to individuals are classified into nine separate ranks and cost from $120 to $4,000.[15] Again we note that personalization is not only purchased but systematically marketed as well, and the return on that investment is realized in practical benefits.

Ninomiya's Pill and the Gathering of Gods and Buddhas

That Jizō and Inari share the common ground of personalization raises the question of the relationship between buddhas and *kami*. It is commonplace to say that one of the characteristics of Japanese religion is the lack of strict distinctions between Buddhism, Shinto, and even Confucianism. Representative of this attitude is Ninomiya Sontoku (1787–1856), the peasant sage of Japan, who formulated his teaching on the dignity of labor, the necessity of agricultural planning, mutual help, and frugality into a system he called the "repayment of virtue." He also called it the "pill containing the essence of Shinto, Confucianism, and Buddhism," which was described in the following anecdote:

> Kimigasa Hyōdayō asked the proportions of the prescription in this "pill," and the old man [Ninomiya] replied, "One spoon of Shinto, and a half-spoon each of Confucianism and Buddhism."
>
> Then someone drew a circle, one half of which was marked Shinto and two quarter-segments labeled Confucianism and Buddhism respectively. "Is it like this?" he asked. The old man smiled. "You won't find medicine like that anywhere. In a real pill all the ingredients are thoroughly blended so as to be indistinguishable. Otherwise it would taste bad in the mouth and feel bad in the stomach."[16]

Ninomiya's pill provides an apt image of the highest degree of assimilation in which the different religions can no longer be distinguished one from another. The formerly different parts now exist in a composition in which they are identical and equal in status.

The assimilation of the *kami* and the buddhas (*shimbutsu shūgō*)—based on the *honji suijaku* theory that the Shinto *kami* are manifestations (*suijaku*) of the buddhas who are the original ground (*honji*) from which they emerge—is a widely accepted idea for explaining the syncretism by which Buddhist and Shinto deities find themselves in a relationship of harmony and even identity. It is also used to explain why Japanese practice both Shinto and Buddhism without finding any conflict between them. *Shimbutsu shūgō* is seldom discussed without reference to the doctrine of *honji suijaku,* almost as if both are synonymous concepts. "If we take *honji-suijaku* in its broadest implication," writes Alicia Matsunaga, "it becomes equivalent to *shimbutsu-shūgō.*"[17] The dictionary meaning of "*shūgō*" is syncretism (literally, to practice or learn and conjoin); both *Kojien* and Morohashi's *Dai kanwa jiten* specify that it is a process for harmonizing different philosophical concepts or religious doctrines. There is a strong philosophical character to this syncretism of the *kami* and the buddhas, and in this sense it is more a conceptual theory than a practice. Its theoretical character is brought out even further by its association with *honji suijaku,* which is not just a theory but a heavily polemical one. Formulated by Buddhists, the argument of *honji suijaku* holds that the *kami* are manifestations of the buddhas and, being derivative, are secondary to them. The early exponents of this egregiously anti-Shinto polemic portrayed the *kami* as suffering beings who seek the solace and salvation of the buddhas, cursing, all the while, their misfortune of being born a *kami*. In a collection of biographies of Buddhist priests, the story is told of how a *kami* appeared to a man at the Hie Shrine and said:

> I was born as an evil god so I have had many painful sufferings. I want to convert to the Three Treasures [of Buddhism] to try to escape from my suffering but still I cannot, so will you in my place please build a Buddhist temple here and enshrine the Buddha's image. Thus calamities will not occur and the people will have peace.[18]

Spread primarily by Tendai and Shingon monks, stories like this one might be seen to give Buddhism and Shinto an equal standing that allows both religions to be combined in all sorts of mixed practices and beliefs. Sutras, after all, were read at shrines; Buddhist rituals were also performed there; and Shinto shrines were built within the premises of Buddhist monasteries. These combinations, however, were largely the result of a Buddhist triumphalism based on the *honji suijaku* theory that the *kami* and the buddhas are in some fashion identical but not equal in status—the buddhas being primary and the *kami* secondary—and therefore cannot be the basis for true assimilation. As in Ninomiya's pill, true assimilation requires equality of status, even if the proportion of the parts is not the same. So long as it is tied to *honji suijaku*, the notion of *shimbutsu shūgō* is like the bad-tasting pill whose parts are differentiated by lines that establish what is primary, what secondary.

In the Heian period Shinto priests opposed the assimilation movement and made it clear that the *kami* were most certainly not the manifestations of the buddhas. They wrote works such as the *Kōtai jingū gishiki chō*, in which they spoke disparagingly of Buddhist statues as "inner children" (*nakako*); the sutras as "stained paper" (*shime-kami*); pagodas as *araragi* (a type of garlic bulb); Buddhist priests as "long hairs" (*kaminaga*); and temples as "tile thatch" (*kawara buki*).[19] Nakamaki Hirochika argues in detail how shrine architecture was a conscious protest against Buddhist architectural styles and doctrinal ideas. And to this day, few people would normally mistake a shrine for a temple or vice versa—although we must add the caveat "normally," since there are cases of ambiguity that we examine later in this chapter. The *shimbutsu shūgō* movement was met with the equally important assertion of *shimbutsu kakuri*: the separation of the *kami* from the buddhas. In the medieval period, the Shinto protagonist Yoshida

Kanetomo (1435–1511) retaliated with an anti-Buddhist argument that reversed the relationship to make the buddhas the derivative manifestations of the *kami* (*shimpon hutsujaku*). So far as Shinto priests were concerned, *honji suijaku* was a philosophy of dissimilation that made their *kami* inferior to the buddhas.

If *shimbutsu shūgō* really means, as some scholars and dictionaries define it, that the *kami* and buddhas were "fused" (*yūgō*),[20] or "formed practically an identity,"[21] or "formed the same body" (*shimbutsu dōtai*), or "merged into one body" (*ittaika*),[22] then a full assimilation comparable to Ninomiya's pill cannot be thought of as having taken place in practice. The key factor here is to be found, not in any theoretical assertion of assimilation, but in actual situations in which a *kami* is ritually understood to be a buddha and is treated as one (or a buddha a *kami*).

Assimilation did take place according to several patterns with varying degrees of interrelatedness: combination, transformation, adoption, or correlation. The Sonten at Kurama Temple, for example, is a *combination* of Bishamonten, Kannon, and Maō, all of which retain their individuality and iconography, except when they are thought of in the abstract as Sonten, a composite of the three. *Transformation* is a high level of assimiliation whereby one deity becomes another and, for all practical purposes, loses its original identity though it is never formally forgotten. The Taoist deity Kōshin, for example, was transformed into the Shinto monkey deity Sarutahiko.[23] Buddhists also employed *adoption* as a means of incorporating other deities into their pantheon: Indra was received as Taishakuten, Brahma as Bonten, Sarasvatī as Benzaiten, and Vaisravana as Bishamonten or Tamonten. The *honji suijaku* theory uses *correlation* to pair Buddhist and Shinto deities as identical but unequal partners. This Buddhist theory, however, was seldom put into effect as a Shinto practice; there is little evidence that Shinto priests accepted the theory and worshiped their *kami* as manifestations of buddhas and bodhisattvas.

Whatever pattern is employed to link *kami* and buddhas together, there is one critical test for assimilation: whether or not the combined, transformed, adopted, or correlated deity is given the honor of taking its place as a main object of worship, not just a god who is invited onto the premises but not onto the altar itself. When gods are invited onto the premises but not on the altar, we may see them "assimilated" in the loosest pattern of all, since proximity alone forms the basis of the relationship. That we find Shinto shrines and deities in Buddhist compounds is not an example of full assimilation but simply a presence of one set of deities and institutions within the realms and territory of the other. In this common case, the *kami* and the buddhas represent a *gathering* that can be indicated, if we may suggest a different term, with a homonym for *shūgō* written with characters meaning "getting together and meeting" (*atsumatte au*). The presence of Shinto shrines on Buddhist premises, therefore, amounts to a gathering of the *kami* and the buddhas in a loose association—an association, moreover, of hosts and guests, rather than interfused entities with completely equal status—that does not come close to the intimate relationship of the other patterns of assimilation. Indeed, it could even be said to represent the separation of one from the other: the shrines are like small guest houses for visitors on a large estate. While the *honji suijaku* theory says that *kami* are buddhas, they are rarely the main deities on Buddhist altars; the buddhas and bodhisattvas, moreover, are seldom the central objects of worship at Shinto shrines. If *shimbutsu shūgō* is taken to mean full and complete assimilation—by which there is a clear recognition that a certain *kami* is also a particular buddha (as specified by the *honji suijaku* theory) and can be worshiped as such—then it cannot be found to exist at most shrines or temples, which maintain ecclesiastical, theological, iconographic, and institutional distinctions that prevent the equal exchange of one for the other.

Perhaps *shimbutsu shūgō*, which refers to the phenomenon of assimiliation, should be distinguished and even divorced from the theory of *honji suijaku*. Assimilation took place in many different ways; few, if any, resulted from the theory of *honji suijaku*. Sakurai Tokutarō warned many years ago about the fallacy of understanding *shimbutsu shūgō* in terms of *honji suijaku* without looking at assimilation as a traditional Japanese folk religious phenomenon that took place apart from that Buddhist theory and continues to occur in modern times long after the Meiji abandonment of it.[24] Sakurai examined the relationship of the gods and the buddhas through a careful ethnographic analysis and noted throughout his study that there were objectively discernible differences between a *kami* and a buddha and between a shrine and a temple. Where assimilation did occur he saw it as a result of magic and superstition. (That is, he saw the process as a "folk" religious phenomenon.)

Although Sakurai did not identify *genze riyaku* as a discrete framework within which assimilation could be understood, it is essential to do so if we are to gain a clear understanding of this issue. Of the several factors that account for the assimilation or equal correlation of one with the other, it is the ritual and conceptual framework of practical benefits that is central. People seeking benefits see the equal and interchangeable statuses of the deities: praying to a *kami* at a shrine is as good as praying to a buddha at a temple; the only meaningful difference is their respective reputations for providing certain specialized benefits. If, as is often the case, petitioners do not know the difference between *kami* and buddhas, an even stronger case can be made for the interfusion or confusion of the two in their minds. It is not the spiritual entity (the deity petitioned to) but the objective (the benefit sought) and the common assumption behind that objective (that entities such as *kami* and buddhas can grant benefits) which provide the grounds of assimilation. It is the arena of practical benefits—not the shrines, where only *kami* are enshrined (*saijin*), and not the temples, where only buddhas and bodhisattvas can be the main deities (*honzon*)—that is the place of assimilation.

Kami and buddhas exist in separate systems that are differentiated by architecture, iconography, ritual, names, and priestly dress of those who attend to them. Where they can be found on each other's property, the hosts hold a preeminent position over the subservient guests: shrines on temple grounds are still shrines. Ordinary believers, however, pay no attention to this differentiation. The barriers are torn down by the common objectives they hold equally for and against both kinds of deities: receiving practical benefits. *Kami* and buddhas are fused together with the torch of pious expectation that both are equally capable of providing benefits. The assimilation of the *kami* and the buddhas takes place not in Shinto and its shrines, nor in Buddhism and its temples, but within the conceptual and ritual dynamics of practical benefits that lie at the heart of Japanese common religion. *Shimbutsu shūgō* takes place, not because people think of *honji suijaku,* but because they think of *genze riyaku.* The pamphlets and flyers of shrines and temples are silent about the theories of *shimbutsu shūgō* and *honji suijaku,* but they speak a loud and clear message about obtaining benefits—the ritual and conceptual context of which is the place where the *kami* and the buddhas stand equal to each other and are therefore freely assimilated in the minds and practices of the supplicants for benefits.

Before they were banned during the Meiji period, Buddhist temples built within the precincts of Shinto shrines (*jingūji*) owed their existence in principle to the theory of *honji suijaku* according to which they were supposed to have enshrined the Buddhist deities that were the original ground of the manifest *kami.* Saganoi Takeshi, a Shinto priest and research specialist on *jingūji,* has shown, however, that the main Buddhist deities for these shrine temples seldom corresponded to what they were supposed to be as *honji.* The prescribed *honji* for the three main *kami* at the Iwashimizu Shrine, for instance, were Kannon (or Monjū), Amida, and Seishi (or Fugen), but the buddha actually enshrined was Yakushi, the Buddha of Healing. By far the most popular Buddhist deities at *jingūji* were Yakushi and the Eleven-Headed Kannon, neither of which represented the theoretically correct *honji* of the *kami* at such shrines as Hiyoshi, Usa, and Kasuga. Saganoi's explanation for this is that the Eleven-Headed Kannon's reputation for purification and the extermination of bad karma fit in with Shinto's emphasis on purification, and Yakushi was appropriate because of its powers to heal.[25] More than the theory of *honji suijaku,* it was the concern for purification and practical benefits that determined the identity and meaning of the buddhas that were brought into shrine precincts.

The same point is made by Mihashi Tadashi, who notes that the theory about *shimbutsu shūgō* is to be distinguished from actual Heian-period beliefs and practices, which did not create a fusion of Buddhist and Shinto deities. The distinction between both types of deities was clearly maintained on the formal institutional level, but they were treated in equal fashion by people who prayed to them for' this-worldly benefits. In a manner reminiscent of Sakurai's comments cited earlier, Mihashi argues that *shimbutsu shūgō* must not be understood only as a theory or doctrine but as a characteristic of Japanese religious views which hold that *kami* and buddhas, while different, can supply benefits equally.[26] "As objective forms," Mihashi states, "the *kami* and the buddhas were not assimilated, but in terms of belief about them, people expected common miraculous powers from both and turned to them with the same attitude and same respect."[27] Even after it was said that in theory the *kami* and the buddhas were of a single essence (*ittai*), "the *kami* were always *kami* and were never worshiped as buddhas."[28] What brings the *kami* and buddhas together on equal terms, in short, is not the theory of assimilation but the pursuit of this-worldly benefits. In an analysis suggestive of our argument about the common religion of Japan, Mihashi explains the entire "structure of Japanese belief" as one in which Buddhism, Shinto, and Onmyōdō take their places under the overarching rubric of this-worldly benefits.[29]

In an interesting reversal of the usual approach of understanding theory as the source and justification of practice, Satō Makoto argues that the theory of *honji suijaku* is to be understood in terms of the practice of this-worldly benefits. The theory, he notes, is on dubious grounds doctrinally since, as the medieval text *Shintōshū* points out, the terminology applied specifically to deities is not supported or even presented in Buddhist sutras or commentaries. "Since the foundation of the theory of *honji suijaku* is not found in the Buddhist scriptures," he writes, "it must find its basis in the oracles of the *kami* and miraculous experiences of ordinary people receiving practical benefits."[30] When it can be found, scriptural support is useful to have and is always cited (as we shall see with the case of the *shichi-fukujin*); but if that kind of authority is not available, the force of common practice becomes its own justification. The practice of this-worldly benefits, in this case, vindicates theory, not the other way around.

By providing the arena for the integration and interchangeability of the *kami* and buddhas, common beliefs and practices for this-worldly benefits allow Buddhist deities to take their places on the Shinto altars (*kamidana*) of ordinary households. In a flyer from Narita-san entitled "The Practical Benefits of the Goma Fire Ritual Talisman," suppliants are given the following instructions:

> This Fire Ritual Talisman (*fuda*) has been ritually blessed in an auspicious Goma Fire Ceremony and is the divided body (*bunshin*) of the temple's main deity Fudō Myōō, whose spirit has been placed in it. Since it is the divine spirit transferred, please take it home and place it in a purified place such as the household Shinto altar. Purify your body and mind every day, at morning and in the evening, and make offerings of candles, flowers, incense, tea, and water. Close your eyes, place your hands together, and recite "Namu Fudō Myōō" any number of times. Pray diligently with an undisturbed, focused mind. The deity will inform you without fail that your prayers will surely yield miraculous results, and you must therefore exert yourself wholeheartedly without fail every day. Since you will be protected by the deity, please work at your jobs energetically every day firmly and in good health.[31]

The paper bag in which talismans are handed to petitioners at Kiyomizu Temple in Shimane prefecture contains a similar message: "Since this talisman is the divided body (*bunshin*) of the Eleven-Headed Kannon, our main deity, please place it on a Shinto or Buddhist altar and pray to it." The message on the bag adds that at the end of the year, amulets and talismans should be returned for disposal by ritual burning as an expression of one's gratitude. All the elements required for this-worldly benefits are contained here: sincerity, prayer, ritual, miracles, hard work, gratitude, and the assimilation of Buddhist deities onto Shinto altars.

The interchange is reciprocal: *kami* can be worshiped through Buddhist rituals. Though Inari is technically a Shinto *kami,* only one, Fushimi Inari, of the "three great Inari" (*sandai* Inari) sites is a Shinto shrine. While the Sōtō Zen temple and monastic training complex, Myōgonji, enshrines a thousand-armed Kannon as its main deity, it is famous for its Inari and is known throughout the country as Toyokawa Inari. Inari may not hold the central place of ritual honor that belongs to Kannon, but the temple's popular reputation indicates that for many of the thousands of pilgrims who go there, Inari is the de facto central object of worship: certainly Zen Buddhist priests with shaved heads and clerical robes perform Buddhist rituals and chants to it. Saijō Inari, the third site, is more ambiguous in that the structure is architecturally Shinto with a multitude of torii gates. But here too are banners of the Nichiren sect with "All Praise to the Exquisite Teaching of the *Lotus Sutra*" (*namu myōhō renge-kyō*) printed on them. The priests are Buddhist and perform Buddhist rituals to Inari—who thus becomes, since it is liturgically treated as such, as much a Buddhist deity as it remains a Shinto *kami*. Still, it is not this double identity that makes Inari so popular but its power to fulfill prayers for business success and good fortune wherever it might be worshiped, whether at Shinto shrines or Buddhist temples. Here again is a form of practical assimilation based on equal accessibility to one who is a Shinto and a Buddhist deity.

Assimilation through interchange and crossover has occurred frequently—even to the point of a deity's losing its original identity. It did not require the theory of *honji suijaku*, which is best understood as a prescription not for assimilation but prioritization, for this to happen. This can be seen in the case of a popular deity like Ebisu, whose origins are ambiguous and uncertain because of the multiple identities he has had. Indeed, in a certain sense Ebisu may be said to have no original identity, at least not one that can be clearly discerned. Is Ebisu a transformation or manifestation of Hiruko no Kami—the Leech Child of Japanese folklore—or Kotoshiro no Mikoto, the child of Ōkuninushi no Mikoto (Lord of the Great Country), an important *kami* and main deity of the Izumo Shrine? The identification with the Leech Child is reinforced by a very flexible reading of the characters for "Hiruko" as "Ebisu"; or, to put it the other way around, by writing "Ebisu" with the characters for "Hiruko."[32] Ebisu is also called Saburō-dono—the Third Child—but whether or not Saburō is Kotoshiro no Mikoto is the subject of debate among Japanese scholars.[33] If he is Kotoshiro no Mikoto, then the Japanese dictionary *Kojien* is wrong in saying that Ebisu Saburō is the third child of Izanagi and Izanami, and Abe Masamichi is right in pointing out that Daikoku—the Indian deity Mahākāla, who was adopted into the Buddhist pantheon—and Ebisu have a father and son relationship because Daikoku is often identified with Ōkuninushi no Mikoto on the linguistic grounds that "Ōkuni" can also be read "Daikoku."[34]

These ambiguities, which may be beyond the possibility of resolution, arise because of the way in which Ebisu, whoever he is, has been able to change identities and become associated rather freely with other deities. Ebisu is also said to have taken on the direct identity of Daikoku himself.[35] While some of these associations may have been unconsciously influenced by the theory of *honji suijaku*, these changes and interchanges took place without overt reference to it—and certainly without the polemical need to establish the superiority of the buddhas over the *kami*.

Intensifying Assimilation: The Impact of Meiji Disestablishment

The irrelevance of the theories for assimilation was made dramatically clear during the Meiji period when assimilation continued to take place even as a result of the movement to counter the *honji suijaku* theories with an opposite ideology calling for the separation of the *kami* and the buddhas (*shimbutsu bunri*). In that anti-Buddhist movement, Buddhist temples were removed from Shinto shrine precincts, and, it could reasonably be expected, the deities enshrined within would also go. For the most part the buddhas did leave with their temples, but Buddhist deities known for this-worldly benefits were allowed to remain and even took up residence in the shrines supposedly rid of Buddhism.

The famous nude Benten (also known as Benzaiten) at Enoshima Shrine is one such example that is fairly typical of the complexities of assimilation. Originally the Indian river goddess Sarasvatī, Benten was adopted into the Buddhist pantheon and was described in the *Sutra of the Golden Light* as one who benefited those seeking wisdom, eloquence, longevity, and the elimination of suffering.[36] Benten is also a goddess of music and is often depicted with a lute. As one of Japan's famed Three Benten shrines, Enoshima is associated almost exclusively with Benten. Thus it would seem that the prominence of this Buddhist deity at a Shinto shrine is an excellent example of Buddhist-Shinto syncretism based on *honji suijaku*. In the light of what we have already pointed out, however, about the way in which the theory of *honji suijaku* segregates *kami* and buddhas, it is not surprising that prior to the Meiji period Benten at Enoshima had her own separate temple, Yoganji, belonging to the Shingon Buddhist sect. Benten is not even the main deity of Enoshima Shrine but is associated with it because of the correspondence that was seen between her and Ichikishimahime no Mikoto, one of the three female *kami* enshrined there. Ichikishimahime no Mikoto was one of Susanoo's daughters known for her beauty. When Buddhism was disestablished from Shinto (*shimbutsu bunri*) during the Meiji period, Yoganji Temple was removed, but not Benten. Without the Buddhist temple, an even greater degree of assimilation of Benten into Shinto was possible, and her presence is now described as being a part of "pure Shinto."[37] That a greater degree of assimilation was brought about by the ideological separation of *kami* and buddhas would be ironical only if we fail to remember that assimilation takes place in the context of this-worldly benefits apart from ideology. Itsukushima Shrine, another of the Three Benten sites, repeats this lesson since it too enshrines Ichi-kishimahime no Mikoto with whom Benten was similarly associated. Had the association between buddha and *kami* been made according to the theory of *honji suijaku,* the Buddhist deity should have been Dainichi or Kannon, not Benten. Had the dissociation been carried out according to the strict terms of *shimbutsu bunri,* Benten would not have remained.

Danzan Shrine in Nara prefecture is dedicated to the *kami* spirit of Fujiwara no Kamatari (614–669), the founding patriarch of the Fuji-wara clan. It is architecturally striking since its buildings are all Bud-dhist temples, including a thirteen-story pagoda. It represents a re-versal of the pattern of Benten at Enoshima Shrine insofar as the *kami* here is in a Buddhist structure, but it similarly represents an assimila-tion of Buddhism and Shinto. Here again the integration took place because of the ideological movement to separate Buddhism from Shinto. The Buddhist institution known as Myōrakuji was banned from the precincts, but the temple buildings were not dismantled. The disestablishment of Buddhism from Danzan Shrine made it pos-sible for that Shinto institution to integrate itself completely into Buddhist structures.[38] And while it may be argued that this integra-tion was in physical form only and therefore superficial, there is noth-ing inappropriate to either religion for the spirit of an ancestor to be in a Buddhist structure and at the same time be the *kami* in a shrine known for a this-worldly benefit: peace for the nation.

Contemporary popular literature on practical benefits recognizes this equality of *kami* and buddhas, as well as shrines and temples, in such terms. The guidebooks to places of practical benefits, which we discuss in detail in Chapter 7, are organized not by religious tradi-tions but by geographical location or benefits. Even when a book's title contains the word for *kami* and leaves out the term for buddhas, both types of deities are described.[39] The manner in which the *kami* relate with each other and with the buddhas and bodhisattvas is var-ied and complex and ranges from loose association to full integra-tion. Equality of status, the hallmark of genuine assimilation, is main-tained in the framework of *genze riyaku:* the vessel in which the *kami* and buddhas can share a common passage.

The Seven Gods of Good Fortune

The *takara-bune,* or treasure ship, is the perfect image of the col-lective and common character of this-worldly benefits—especially since it is most often depicted carrying the Seven Gods of Good Fortune (*shichifukujin*), a multicultural, mixed gender, and religiously diverse group of deities who share the common cause of providing benefits to people. We have already introduced Ebisu and Benten, who, despite their mixed identities and uses, are still associated with Shinto and Buddhism respectively. The Seven Gods are well known, dearly loved, and ubiquitous: they make their stylized appearances in many different ways and circumstances that are both religious and secular. As symbols of fortune, they often appear in advertisements for financial institutions. Kōfuku Kurejitto (Good Fortune Credit), for instance, advertises its financial services with the Seven Gods riding in their ship of wealth.

The treasure ship of the Seven Gods was widely seen as a vessel that brought together gods from different traditions, and it is an important element in the origins of the Seven Gods and their early iconographic depictions. The *Baika mujinzō* (Inexhaustible storehouse of plum blossoms) contains a description from the year 1499 of a painting in which Shakyamuni, Kannon, Daruma, Confucius, and Lao Tzu are riding in a small ship. The Buddhist monk Shūgatsu, who lived at the end of the fifteenth century, painted a picture of a boat carrying a group that included Daikoku, Fukurokuju, and Hotei, all of whom are counted among the Seven Gods. Another Buddhist monk named Keishun, working in the year 1491, was inspired by the depictions of the Taoist Seven Sages of the Bamboo Grove and painted a hanging scroll of Ōkuninushi no Mikoto, Ebisu, Uzume no Mikoto, Bishamonten, Fukurokuju, Jurōjin, and Hotei. If Uzume no Mikoto, the female *kami* who danced to lure Amaterasu out of her rock cave, is replaced by Benzaiten, and if Daikoku takes the place of Ōkuninushi no Mikoto, the resulting group comprises the most common configuration of the Seven Gods. Other paintings, literary accounts, and *kyōgen* plays describe what by the end of the Muromachi period (that is, the late sixteenth century) came to be recognized as the Seven Gods of Good Fortune.[40] Their collective character did not prevent them from gaining prominence as individuals: Benzaiten is famous at Chikubushima in Lake Biwa, Itsukushima, and Enoshima; Bishamonten is well known at Kurama Temple and at Shigisan in Ikoma; Ebisu is especially highly venerated at Nishinomiya (where, according to legend, he landed as the Leech Child after being cast adrift by his parents Izanagi and Izanami); Mount Hiei is reputed for, among other things, the Triple-Faced Daikoku. However, the worship of them as a set of seven is far more extensive than reverence given to any one alone. Although there are slight variations in the groupings found in many different sites, as a group they are unmistakably the happy gods dispensing their blessings.

Ebisu wears a floppy, cone-shaped hat and is dressed in field clothes. In one hand he holds a fishing pole; under his other arm he carries a large sea bream (*tai*), a fortunate (*medetai*) catch for anyone. Sometimes Ebisu is shown holding his pole with both hands pulling up a fat sea bream that is still hooked at the end of his line. Ebisu, it is said, "hooks his fish without using a net," and this is seen to represent the importance of taking only what is appropriate and not more. As a god of business prosperity teaching the avoidance of greed, Ebisu is a model for success based on service to customers rather than desire for netting large profits.[41] Here again is a reminder that the pursuit of this-worldly benefits is couched in moral terms. It is little wonder, given this focus on service and intimacy with customers, that Ebisu is especially popular with small shopkeepers and merchants, and those who run small restaurants and the like, people who depend on maintaining a steady clientele and a close relationship to their customers through personalized service.

The name Daikoku, the Great Black Deity, is a direct translation of Mahākalā, the name of the Hindu deity already adopted by Buddhists in India. In the *Commentary to the Mahāvairocana Sutra* he is described as a manifestation of Mahāvairocana who can subdue demons. The *Sutra of the Wisdom of the Benevolent Kings* speaks of Daikoku as a god of war, and in Buddhist iconography he is often portrayed with a fierce and angry countenance. He was also, however, described as a great bodhisattva of good fortune who shares his wealth with the poor, and it is for this characteristic that he is known as one of the Seven Gods. Well fed and smiling, Daikoku carries a sack of good fortune over one shoulder; in his other hand he holds a small mallet for hammering out wealth (*uchide no kozuchi*). He wears a loose cap or headcloth and typically stands on two straw bales of rice. Here, too, a lesson in moderation is to be found in his appearance: the loose headcloth prevents him from looking up and getting too ambitious; the two bales represent an essential sufficiency that should keep him content. There is another agrarian moral about the virtue of labor to be learned from the homonyms for the mallet (*tsuchi*) that hammers out wealth (*takara*). "*Tsuchi*" also means dirt or earth, and "*takara*" can also be read with two words: "*ta kara*," (from the rice field). The straw bales of rice, therefore, do not fall freely from heaven but are produced by "hammering the earth" and working the fields.[42] Again we are reminded that benefits, even if they are given by the gods, are not windfalls but must be earned through hard work and meritorious behavior.

Dressed in armor, wielding a spear, and holding a pagoda in the upturned palm of his left hand, Bishamonten is a Buddhist guardian deity, one of the Four Heavenly Kings (Shitennō). As one who protects Buddhism from natural disasters and human enemies, Bishamonten was described as having many attendants, all of whom could help those who call upon them: troubles will cease, wealth will increase, and all wishes will be fulfilled. In the *Sutra of the Golden Light*, Bishamonten (in the form of Tamonten) rose from his seat and explained to the Buddha his wish-fulfilling mantra, which, when recited, "will cause sentient beings to be free of suffering, obtain happiness, and acquire the two types of commodities for good fortune and wisdom." The Buddha himself recited the mantra several times, and the Four Heavenly Kings as a group lauded the virtue of reciting the sutra, which will enable "sentient beings to realize the wishes they seek."[43] In early Japan this teaching impressed Prince Shōtoku, who, in preparing to go to war against the anti-Buddhist Mononobe clan, knew that "without prayer we cannot succeed." Thus he cut down a tree and fashioned images of the Four Heavenly Kings, which he placed in his topknot. After defeating his enemies, Prince Shōtoku built Shitennōji, Temple of the Four Guardian Kings,[44] now in present-day Osaka. Prince Shōtoku is also credited with building the Shigisan Temple at Ikoma and installing Bishamonten as its main deity. In the famous "Flying Storehouse" scene from the *Shigisan engi* scroll, bales of rice, much like the ones Daikoku stands on, roll forth from the sky to the great delight of the people.[45] Bishamonten, who was sometimes identified with Konpira, the Shinto deity of ships and sailors, displays the protean character of a deity who can assume different forms to protect and bless people in accord with their wishes.

Benzaiten we mentioned earlier, and to that discussion we need only add a few details. The word "*zai*" in her name is written with different homonyms meaning "wealth" and "talent," two of the benefits receivable from her. Like Kannon, Benzaiten can appear iconographically with multiple arms, usually four or eight. Sometimes she holds an upright sword, as Fudō does, and holds a jewel in her other hand. In most popular depictions of her in the group of seven, she holds a lute and can be found sitting or standing.

Fukurokuju and Jurōjin are Taoist deities of longevity. Fukurokuju is identified with the Old Man of the South Pole (Nankyoku Rōjin), who in turn is equated with the star that is closest to the position directly over the south pole. He is short, elderly, white-bearded, has an elongated bald head, and is often attended by cranes and tortoises, themselves symbols of longevity. In another assimilated form, Fukurokuju is said to be Taizan Fukun, the god of Mount T'ai, one of the five sacred mountains in China. Sōtō Zen daily rituals, such as the prayer offered after meals, often refer to paying respects to the deities of the constellations that affect one's life span. Since the south star was regarded in China as the primary heavenly body that controlled the length of life, statues and paintings of Fukurokuju were used by Zen priests and others for the purpose of praying for longevity.[46] While Jurōjin appears as a separate deity in the group of seven, he was also thought of as being the same god as Fukurokuju with a different name. Without the elongated head, Jurōjin appears as a more ordinary old man, often accompanied by deer, the word for which can also be pronounced "*roku,*" a homonym for the middle character in Fukurokuju's name—the entirety of which means good fortune, blessings (especially in the form of a stipend or pension), and longevity. Because of their overlapping and indeed identical characteristics, Jurōjin is sometimes replaced in groups of the Seven Gods by Kisshōten (or Kichijōten, who can also replace Benzaiten) or Shōjō, a mythic animal with a face that is human and a body combining a dog and monkey. Jurōjin and Fukurokuju both can be found holding a rounded fan (*uchiwa*), symbol of the ability to wave away misfortune and death.

Hotei, popularly known in the West as the happy or laughing buddha, holds a similar fan just below his protruding belly. He also carries a cloth sack over his shoulder or at his side, and in it he keeps his bare necessities for daily living. Happy and content, he is always laughing with a round face and bulbous earlobes, but he is not to be mistaken for an easygoing bumpkin. Although he is said to be the only one of the Seven Gods who is based on a historical person—Ch'i Tz'u (d. 916), known more popularly as Master Pu-tai (Hotei)—the stories about him depict his supernormal character, which is reminiscent of the Taoist immortals: he could sleep among the clouds and not get wet, tell people's fortunes without error, and was in tune with his natural rhythms, sleeping when he needed to on a bridge, for instance, head propped on a knee. Clearly a man who had attained the Way, he nevertheless lived an unassuming life among common people whom he understood with sympathy. Paintings show him carrying a staff with which he awakens people from the follies of their passions and loose thoughts, and in this capacity he was much like a wizened Zen master whose mundane actions were profound Buddhist lessons. When a priest walked in front of him, Hotei tapped him on the shoulder and asked for a coin. The priest said he would gladly make such a donation if Hotei could expound the teachings of the Buddha. Without saying a word, Hotei placed his bag on the ground, let go of it, and stood still. The priest then came to realize that he had just witnessed a silent sermon delivered through action on the Buddhist teaching of detachment, a truth that is itself detached from words. Hotei's bag thus represents a dual lesson: it is important to

possess the necessities of life, but one should nevertheless be ready to
let go of them. On his deathbed he wrote the following poem:

> Maitreya as the true Maitreya
> Replicates himself in a thousand million ways,-
> Appearing at times to people of that time,
> But they do not recognize him.[47]

Hotei has thus been associated with Maitreya, and the splendid carving of him sitting in the magnificent repose of that bodhisattva at
Manpukuji, the Uji headquarters of the Ōbaku Zen sect, is worshiped
as Maitreya, the buddha of the future. Hotei thus represents the
classical teachings of Mahāyāna Buddhism, but the moral lesson
of the common religious values is not lost: be unassuming, greet
people with a happy face, and speak with kind words, for "these are
the causes for receiving good fortune and a multitude of practical
benefits."[48]

Ever the source of legitimation, the Buddhist scriptures are found
to be the basis for grouping these gods into a set of seven. In the *Sutra of the Wisdom of the Benevolent Kings,* the Buddha explains to a king
that he is transmitting his wisdom to the kings of all countries and not
to monks, nuns, men of pure faith, or women of pure faith because
"they do not have the power of kings." Furthermore, he says, "I do not
transmit this wisdom to them, but you should receive, hold, read, recite, and understand this doctrine." All the kings of the different
lands suffer from seven kinds of disasters, but "if they recite this wisdom [sutra] the seven disasters will be extinguished, and seven blessings will come to be. All of the people will be at peace and happy, and
the kings will rejoice."[49] Like the passage from the *Lotus Sutra* that is
always cited as the scriptural justification for this-worldly benefits, this
reference to the seven disasters and seven blessings is invoked as the
foundation for the Seven Gods of Good Fortune. Even in the world
of cyberspace, the words of the ancient sutra are not forgotten in the
home page for the *Shichifukujin meguri korekushon* (Collection of
Shichifukujin pilgrimages) on the Internet: "If you visit the Seven
Gods of Good Fortune, you will be able to escape the seven disasters
and will be granted the seven blessings. This is based on the explanation that 'the seven disasters will be extinguished, and seven blessings will come to be' (*shichinan soku metsu shichifuku soku shō*)."[50]

Popular in the Edo period, *shichifukujin* pilgrimages have undergone a renaissance in the last thirty years. From 1975 to 1985 alone,
there were about 130 new routes established throughout the country.[51] Some of the routes have been organized among temples of a
single Buddhist sect. The Kiso pilgrimage, for instance, consists only
of Rinzai Zen temples; established in 1988, it replaces Fukurokuju

with Kisshōten. Said to be the oldest of the *shichifukujin* routes, the Miyako pilgrimage is typical of how different traditions and sects co-operate to form a circuit—in this case, a circuit of a Shinto shrine and temples belonging to the Nichiren, Shingon, Tendai, and Ōbaku Zen sects. The Ōmi circuit is formed by a Shinto shrine, an independent Buddhist organization, and temples belonging to the Rinzai Zen, Tendai, Sōtō Zen, and Shingon sects. The organizing principle is not sectarian tradition or teaching but the social geography by which shrines and temples of a certain area join together to form a circuit that, being geographically confined, does not take long to complete. The organization of *shichifukujin* pilgrimages frequently reflects the close ties between commercial and religious institutions, for many of the recently formed pilgrimages have been developed by shrines and temples in conjunction with commercial organizations, especially private railway companies. The Ōmi *shichifukujin* pilgrimage is promoted and supported by the Ōmi Railway Company, while the Hankyū Ensen Saikoku *shichifukujin* pilgrimage was established and continues to be promoted by the Hankyū Railway Company of Osaka and is organized around that company's Takarazuka line.

Social geography can even override the limitation of the number seven, and more than that number of temples or shrines of an area can band together. In Yokohama, the Seya Hachifukujin pilgrimage adds Daruma to make a total of eight. In 1942, during the midst of World War II, a *shichifukujin* route of seven places was established in the city of Ashikaga for the sake of business prosperity, family well-being, and the promotion of good health; in 1987, as a result of the modern *shichifukujin* boom, it was augmented with the addition of three more places for a total of ten—six Buddhist temples and four Shinto shrines—that includes the usual Seven Gods plus two more Bentens and another Bishamonten. Since Hachiōji City in the Tokyo metropolitan area literally means City of the Children of the Eight Kings, its *shichifukujin* association, which was first organized in the early 1980s, recently added another site to make a total of eight. The well-known route around Asakusa Temple in Tokyo was organized in 1936 and resuscitated in 1977 with the addition of a Fukurokuju and a Jurōjin for a total of nine, an auspicious number. The name of this pilgrimage, Asakusa Nadokoro *shichifukujin*, reflects the importance of geography: "Nadokoro" means "famous place" (and can also be read "*meisho*"), and the additions were made not because of the need for duplicate deities but because of the significance of these famous places in an already famous temple area.[52]

In a certain sense, the Seven Gods of Good Fortune are the epit-ome of the divine providers of practical benefits: they are assimilated with different deities from within and between the religious traditions of Hinduism, Buddhism, Taoism, and Shinto; they are enshrined freely across the boundaries of Buddhist and Shinto institutions; they are accessible as lovable characters; they teach moral lessons of moderation and hard work; they find their legitimation in Buddhist scripture; they converge in pilgrimage routes within socially defined geographical areas; and they dispense benefits desired in everyday life.

The Place of the Gods

The name of a place is a good indication of what is considered important about that location. Often the divine providers of benefits displace the official main deities of a temple or shrine as the source of the place-name. We have already seen this to be the case with Enoshima: its chief fame lies with Benten and it is referred to in terms of Benten, rather than its central *kami*, Tagirihime no Mikoto, Ichikishimahime no Mikoto, and Takitsuhime no Mikoto, and thus is referred to as one of the Three Benten. Even in those places where it is the main deity who provides benefits, it is often the deity's name that is applied to the place and to which the institution may be popularly referred. This is the case with Hōzanji in Ikoma, which, as noted in Chapter 1, is popularly referred to as Shōten-san because of its main deity. Whether or not a main deity is important to a place depends on the reputation of that deity to dispense boons, but the divine providers of benefits are almost always associated with a place and even give their names to it.

Certainly this is widely true of Buddhist temples: Shakusōji in Kyoto is known as Kuginuki Jizō (Nail-Extracting Jizō); Pokkuri-san is the popular name for Anichiji (Nara prefecture), where elderly people pray for a quick and painless death; Tako Jizō, the Octopus Jizō who saved a village from a tidal wave, is the common name for Tenshōji in Osaka. Even *kami* can overshadow the main buddhas at temples if their beneficent virtues are considerable—as are the powers of Toyokawa Inari, the name by which the Sōtō Zen temple Myōgonji is known. Enjuan is a Shingon temple in Osaka where the Kannon it enshrines is overshadowed by Kama Hachiman, the Iron Sickle Hachiman, which is really a hackberry (*enoki*) tree into which the warrior Sanada Yukimura (1567–1615) thrust a sickle and declared it to be Kama Hachiman to whom he prayed for military victory. Today the tree is covered with dozens of sickles plunged into the tree by those who wish to cut off relations with certain people as well as to be free from illness.[53] Like Kama Hachiman, Kikuno-san (Miss Chrysanthemum Field) is a natural object, a stone in this case, and is worshiped for the sake of ending relationships. Though it is located in a small shrine in the precincts of Hōunji, a Kyoto temple belonging to the Jōdo sect, Kikuno Daimyōjin (Great August Deity Chrysanthemum Field) is famous as one of the three great *kami* for severing relationships. The other two are the Motoda Inari in Ashikaga and a hackberry tree in Itabashi ward in Tokyo. The Itabashi *enoki* (hackberry) tree in Tokyo is for cutting relations between man and wife, man and woman, or lovers and for illness, thieves, liquor, gambling, and enemies during war. And for all of these purposes the *ema* showing man and woman standing back to back was offered.[54]

One story is told of the significance of the Kikuno-san stone to a nun who wished to cut all ties with men; another presents the male point of view of a courtier who, rebuffed in his love for the Heian poetess Ono no Komachi, drenched the rock with his bitter tears. Since Hōunji's main image of worship, Amida, is not known for any particular practical benefit, the temple is commonly called Kikuno-san.[55] Widely regarded as the most powerful god of the kitchen is Kiyoshi Kōjin—the name means Pure Kitchen God—located on the grounds of the Shingon temple Seichōji in Takarazuka City. The main deity, Dainichi Nyorai (Mahāvairocana), is almost incidental to Kiyoshi Kōjin, and even the train station for Seichōji is called Kiyoshi Kōjin, so definitive is the *kami* to the place. Indeed, it is not the only deity surpassing Dainichi in popularity at that temple: the bronze statue of Hotei attracts visitors, too, marking as it does one of the sites of the Hankyū Ensen Saikoku *shichifukujin* pilgrimage.[56]

Popular deities give places their names, but the reverse can also happen: the place-name may come to stand for the deity. Even during the weekdays, Ishikiri Jinja in Osaka is a popular destination for worshipers who seek cures for any number of ailments. Few of them know that the central *kami* enshrined there are Amaterukuniteruhoakarikushitamanigihayahi no Mikoto and his son Umashimaji. It is not just that the name of the *kami* is so long and formal, but the identification of the *kami*—and this is true of most *kami*—was seldom indicated by its formal name. Unlike the main deities displaced by subsidiary but more popular gods or buddhas, Amaterukuniteruhoakarikushitamanigihayahi no Mikoto and his son Umashimaji are the undisplaced deities to whom the thousands of worshipers direct their supplications and prayers. But instead of using their names or even contracted forms, people refer to the *kami* as the place: Ishikiri-san. Equally significant is Ishikiri-san's nickname "Denbo no kami-san," the god of tumors, which is based on the *kami*'s reputation for curing inflammations, swellings, and tumors, especially malignant ones.[57] Personalization and impersonalization can thus be found intertwined with each other: the exceedingly lengthy formal name of a *kami* is respectfully left at a distance, and alternate names based on place and practical benefits have developed so that an intimate familiarity can be established with the worshipers who fervently ask them for deeply desired and very personal favors.

Yasaka Shrine in Kyoto has also taken the name of its district, Gion, which itself is derived from another place, the monastery built for Shakyamuni by his disciple Sudatta, a wealthy merchant known for his donations of food to orphans. Sudatta bought the land for the monastery from Prince Jeta and therefore named the place Jetavana, the Garden of Jeta. The essentials of this story were packed into the Chinese characters used to translate the name of this garden: The Garden in Jeta's Grove for Feeding Orphans. In Japanese the characters are pronounced "*Giju gikkodoku on*," which was abbreviated by taking the first and the last characters to form "Gion." Until the Meiji period the Yasaka Shrine—in one of the few instances in which true assimilation allowed a foreign deity to be centrally enshrined—was dedicated to Gozu Tennō (the Indian deity who protected Jetavana) and the native *kami* Susanoo. Both deities were assimilated into each other, but to separate the *kami* from the buddhas (*shimbutsu bunri*) during the early Meiji period, the name Gionsha (Gion Shrine) was changed to Yasaka Shrine. (Yasaka was the name of both the place and family associated with the early history of the shrine.) The association with the place in India could not be so easily eradicated, however, and Yasaka Shrine is still called Gion-san, and Gozu Tennō is still discussed in connection with it.[58] Shrine, deity, district, and a famous festival, first performed to put an end to a plague, are all packed into the place-name Gion.

Places can also give a deity a distinction that sets it apart from similar deities. All Kannons are alike, in principle at least, but their location makes some of them stand apart from the crowd. Places and their names serve a greater function than to identify locale or give an address: they add charisma and spiritual uniqueness. The Yanagidani Kannon in Kyoto, for example, is known for its powers to cure eye diseases—not so much because Kannon is intrinsically good for this kind of ailment but because of the foundation story that explains why this Kannon is in this place. In the year 806, the holy man Enjin, who also founded Kiyomizudera, offered a prayer and request to be able to see a living Kannon with his own eyes. Obeying a Kannon who had appeared to him in a dream and told him to go into the forests at Nishiyama, Enjin entered a valley filled with old willow trees. He looked in the direction of a radiant light and saw a living eleven-headed, thousand-armed Kannon standing on a large boulder and was inspired to carve a statue exactly as he had seen it. The temple built to enshrine it was named Yōkokuji, Temple of the Valley of Willows. Yōkoku can also be read "Yanagidani," and the Kannon of that valley, owing its existence to what Enjin had seen, is still known for its powers to improve eyesight.[59] The Ichiino Kannon (Kannon of the Oak Field) in Kōka district of Shiga prefecture is said to have been carved by Dengyō Daishi (Saichō, 767–822), the founder of the Tendai sect, out of a single oak tree he found growing there. Now designated an Important Cultural Property and admired as one of the finest examples of a Kannon carved in the sitting position, the Ichiino Kannon is believed to have powers to prevent and cure diabetes because of a Meiji-period report of a man whose diabetes was cured by praying to it and drinking a tea made by boiling chips of wood taken from the statue. On November 3 of each year, the statue, which is normally not open for viewing at other times, is publicly displayed through the *kaichō* (lifting the curtain) ritual. People offer their prayers, drink tea made from the wood of the oak trees (*ichii*) that still grow in the area, and can purchase amulets for the prevention of diabetes.[60] The relationship between deity and place is reciprocal: the Kannon, as an important bodhisattva from the classical Buddhist pantheon, gives to the place its generic spiritual presence and legitimacy; in return, by virtue of the local wood from which it is made, it receives from the area its special powers to provide a specific benefit.

The same reciprocity can be seen in the Nakayama Kannon, at Nakayama-dera in Takarazuka, whose power and reputation are based on the legends that locate her in that particular place to which Hideyoshi's wife went to pray successfully for conceiving a child. Pregnant women who go there to pray for safe and easy childbirth receive a set of objects known as the "the bell strings for safe childbirth": a length of cloth to wrap around the stomach, an amulet, a paper talisman, and a candle. In the fifth month of pregnancy, the mother-to-be is to wrap the cloth around her stomach; later, at the first signs of labor, the paper talisman is to be placed in a bowl of water, the candle should be lit, and prayers to the Nakayama Kannon should be offered.[61] Localization thus personalizes an otherwise classical, originally foreign, deity who takes up residence in the area and derives its power and charisma from the place.

The Benefits of a Saint: Kōbō Daishi

The belief in Kōbō Daishi as a provider of benefits, as noted in Chapter 1, is widespread and can be found in many places: temples, pilgrimage routes, and in particular his mausoleum at Kōyasan. Through legends and stories created by priests and the Kōyasan establishment, the human Kūkai was transformed into the divine Daishi (Great Master), who is now worshiped as a living buddha, savior, protector, and provider. Saitō Akitoshi, reporting the results of his survey of 1,375 Shingon sect priests and their temples, has found that although doctrinally the main focus of veneration in Shingon is supposed to be the Buddha Dainichi, in reality it is Kōbō Daishi who is at the center of Shingon worship.[62] While Kōbō Daishi may be the most prominent example of founder worship in Japanese Buddhism, we should remember that most, if not all, of the sectarian founders are highly revered and even divinized to different degrees. In the Nichiren Shō sect, as well as in its erstwhile lay organization Sōka Gakkai, for instance, Nichiren is revered as the eternal buddha. Shinran is the focus of so much Jōdo Shin ritual and piety that this sect elevates him to an exalted status. It is not unusual in Buddhist temples for the founders and promoters of the sect to flank the main buddha or bodhisattva on the altar, and it is commonly understood that they too fall within the wide range of meanings of being divine. In defining the general term "*hotokesama*" (Buddhist deity), an Internet home page put out by a Buddhist ritual supply company explains that it includes buddhas, bodhisattvas, *tathāgata*, heavenly beings, guardian deities, august kings (*myō*), and the sectarian founders: Dengyō Daishi (Saichō), Kōbō Daishi (Kūkai), Hōnen, Nichiren, and Dōgen.[63] Of these founders, though, Kōbō Daishi is most clearly and widely worshiped as a buddha figure who is still alive today.

While the popular beliefs surrounding Kōbō Daishi as described in Chapter 1 might be thought of as originating with ordinary people unschooled in the intricacies of Shingon doctrine, the literary history of the legends that establish his virtues clearly show that priests, many of whom held high ranks in the order, were the authors of these tales.[64] The recent revision of the *Kōyasan Shingonshū danshinto hikkei* (Handbook for Kōyasan Shingon believers), an official publication of the Shingon headquarters at Kōyasan, reaffirms the popular conceptions of Odaishisama, the reverential yet familiar name by which Kūkai/Kōbō Daishi is affectionately called. According to this official source, there are three characteristics that make Odaishisama what he is: he achieved one of the highest ideals of Shingon Buddhism, that of becoming a buddha in his bodily existence (*sokushin jōbutsu*); he was thereby empowered to grant blessings and this-worldly benefits; and he continues to do so from his mausoleum at Kōyasan, where he has entered into the state of eternal meditation (*nyūjō*) free of death. It would be meaningless, the handbook asserts, if becoming a buddha did not include granting benefits to people. In selecting Kōyasan as the site for training his disciples, Odaishisama also chose the place where he would enter into eternal meditation, the Shingon euphemism for Kūkai's death.[65] Kūkai died on the twenty-first day of the third month of 835 at the age of sixty-two, but this entry into eternal meditation was not a simple human death, for the Daishi belonged to a sphere of immortality transcending death. He did not die, but rather attained perfectly the practice of skillful means for helping others and not forsaking the eternal salvation of all beings that is referred to as "the perfection of skillful means" in the *Dainichi-kyō,* the scriptural basis of Shingon Buddhism. On the basis of the passage in the *Kongōchō-kyō* that speaks of "confirming the Diamond Body," which is the establishment of the mind and body of enlightenment, he is also referred to as having "the body that remains in eternal meditation" or as having "entered into the Diamond Meditation."[66]

The handbook thus demonstrates that the belief in Odaishisama as a living savior is firmly supported by sutras and doctrines. While *Daishi shinkō,* belief in the Daishi, originated with the sectarian institution and is supported by it, it would not be a vital element in people's lives if they did not have their own experiences of its efficacy.

It is difficult to capture the fullness of Daishi belief—it is filled with claims of mystery and magic and with legendary stories of healing performed and benefits granted by Kōbō Daishi—but clearly it thrives in modern Japan. Miracle tales focused on Kōbō Daishi are a common and continuing element in the Shikoku pilgrimage and other Kōbō Daishi pilgrimages.[67] They are widely recounted also by priests at Kōyasan and sometimes are of such import that they bring about a complete change in lifestyle for the person who experiences them, as the following story shows. This story was told to us by a priest who had given up his career as a businessman in order to become a Shingon priest because of his encounter with Odaishisama. One day he was standing at home in front of the family *butsudan* containing a small portrait of the Daishi. His teenage sister had become seriously ill, and the young man prayed to Odaishisama with all his might, demanding that the living savior prove himself by saving his sister. When he opened his eyes, he saw Odaishisama's eyes turn red and emit thin beams of light right into his own. At that moment he was transformed. Although his sister did not survive her illness, he became a priest—partly in memory of his sister but mostly to serve people through Odaishisama's teachings and power, which he had witnessed so dramatically. That his prayers for his sister's recovery went unanswered did not mean to him that Odaishisama was powerless, for he came to realize that the beams of light empowered him to deal with his sister's death and defined for him a radically new vocation.[68] None of his fellow priests regard his story as a naive piece of folk superstition. Such stories abound among the priests who train and serve at the Kōyasan headquarters.

Even professors at Kōyasan University recite similar experiences as proofs of Odaishisama's power. One young professor addressing a group of laypeople on a retreat at Kōyasan told them an account of how a man watched in horror as his son was swept into a rain-swollen river. Running frantically along the riverbank, the man knew there was nothing he could do but pray to Odaishisama. Suddenly there appeared an empty oil drum floating close by and the boy reached out to grab it—only to him he saw not an oil drum but, as he explained it later, the shape and visage of Odaishisama. Such experiences, said the professor, are widely reported by people and show that Odaishisama is still a living savior.[69] To cite, once again, the authoritative handbook:

> Odaishisama's mind and body, as explained in the section on the *Kongōchō-kyō* (Sutra of the Diamond Summit), did not die and enter a state of demise, but became the Diamond Body of the Buddha. This is what is called "entering Eternal Meditation." Daishi belief, which places faith in the salvation of Odaishisama, is what mostly sustains present-day Shingon Buddhism.[70]

Whatever differences there may be between the ordinary believer, educated professors, and high-ranking priests, they all share the conviction that Odaishisama is a living god, savior, and provider of practical benefits:

> Odaishisama confers eight practical benefits as the living buddha who continues to live forever: an abundance of the eight grains (the blessings of nature), wealth (economics), respect (honor), family longevity (abundance of descendants), wisdom (right wisdom), love and respect (compassionate love), avoidance of calamities and long life (happiness), and ease of giving birth (blessings of good children in the home).[71]

Shingon Buddhism is noted for its ritual sophistication and doctrinal tenets, and many scholars who write about Shingon focus on these matters without saying much about Kōbō Daishi as living savior.[72] In so doing they miss the central meanings and core dynamics of the sect and fail to recognize where the heart of its ritual sophistication and doctrinal dynamics is located. The handbook, however, reaffirming the point made by Saitō in his survey, makes it very clear where it lies: it is belief in this living savior—a belief supported by rituals and doctrines—that is the core of Shingon Buddhism. All these elements— belief, ritual, doctrine, and living savior—come together in the most common Shingon ritual, the recitation of Odaishisama's sacred name: "Namu Daishi henjō kongō" (All praise to the Daishi, the universally resplendent diamond). Henjō kongō, the consecration name given him by his master Hui-kuo (746–805) in T'ang China, also manifests the main Shingon deity, Mahāvairocana, as well as the Matrix Realm Mandala (*taizōkai*) and the Diamond Realm Mandala (*kongōkai*). The handbook explains how the chant contains all of these meanings:

> Therefore, when Shingon followers chant and meditate on the Sacred Name of Namu Daishi Henjō Kongō, they make a powerful petition for the Daishi's salvation that permeates life and death, they worship at the same time all the buddhas and bodhisattvas in the mandalas, and they receive the profound teachings of Shingon Esoteric Buddhism and bodily protection.
>
> We must pay attention to the matter of making Odaishisama's vow come alive in this world. This is his vow to save the world and benefit people, and in the life of faith in which we chant the Sacred Name as a vow to create the Buddha's country of equality and benefits, both priests and lay members must take the internal mind of faith and turn it outward to carry out acts of social salvation, no matter how small they may be.[73]

Chanting the sacred name is quite inclusive and epitomizes the transmission of the dharma, the presence of Mahāvairocana, the symbolism and teaching of the mandalas, the human Kūkai, the divine Daishi, receiving and giving benefits, and the moral acts of social service.

The divinization of Kūkai is based on the legend of how he entered into eternal meditation, which claims that his human life never really came to an end. The making of Kūkai into a god employs this affirmation of his eternal humanity, and in this sense we may speak of a humanization process that allows Odaishisama to be divine in an importantly ambiguous way. He is a living god who still, at his mausoleum at Kōyasan, needs his clothes changed by priests who report that he even needs a shave. Reminiscent of Jesus the Christ of the Chalcedonian affirmation, Kūkai the Odaishisama is a personal savior who is both fully human and fully divine. Powerful and close at hand, he is a prime example of the concern in Japanese religion for figures of worship who, because of their proximity to the human realms, are more readily venerated than remote figures such as Dainichi.[74]

Wizards

While Kōbō Daishi may be human and divine, there is another class of beings—who are clearly human and not divine at all—who by virtue of their extraordinary intelligence and skill find themselves placed next to real gods. While they may not be as widely venerated as the gods and buddhas, or attributed with the same degree of powers, they still may be found as focuses of worship in religious institutions and as symbols representing the acquisition of benefits or, indeed, as providers in their own right. This class of beings, which we refer to here as wizards, are people who have performed extraordinary feats of scientific invention and who, as such, have been seen to harness the powers of nature and enable human mortals to fly through the sky and light up the night with controlled incandescence. For their genius in such areas such great inventors may be regarded in terms that approach the divine.

The main object of popular worship at the Iwafune Shrine in Osaka is a large boulder in the shape of a boat representing the Heavenly Rock Boat (Ama no Iwafune) in which the *kami* Nigihaya no Mikoto flew down from heaven to the ancient province of Kawachi and from there to the province of Yamato. It was the spirit of Iwafune Nigihaya no Mikoto that was taken to a shrine established in 1926 in Yawata at the foot of the hill on which stands the famous Iwashimizu Hachiman Shrine on the southern outskirts of Kyoto. Nigihaya no Mikoto, the flying deity, is the appropriate object of worship at this particular shrine—the Hikō Jinja, literally the Shrine of Flight.

The Shrine of Flight was founded by Ninomiya Chūhachi (1866–1935), the self-taught aviation pioneer who developed principles and techniques of powered flight. With a propeller driven by thick rubber bands, Ninomiya's unmanned airplane flew successfully on April 29, 1891—twelve years, the shrine literature points out repeatedly, before the Wright brothers took to the air. Two years later, Ninomiya drew up plans for a manned airplane powered by a combination of springs and footpower, but the outbreak of the Sino-Japanese conflict in 1894 prevented further development of his plans. While the Wright brothers were the first to succeed in manned flight, the Shrine of Flight commemorates Ninomiya Chūhachi for his remarkable ideas that found their way into the development of aircraft: wheels instead of tracks for takeoffs, movable wings for flight control and maneuvering, the use of screw propellers, and a wired structure for light weight. He was a technological wizard who—like Thomas Edison, the Wizard of Menlo Park and tamer of lightning—mastered the principles that in his case would allow humans to fly through the skies like Nigihaya no Mikoto.

Ninomiya, who was a trained Shinto priest, selected Nigihaya no Mikoto for its association with flight. But insofar as modern aviation is the shrine's primary concern, the *kami* is almost incidental. Just inside the fence that separates the shrine from a busy roadway is a glass-encased jet engine taken from a fighter plane donated by a unit of the Self-Defense Forces. The torii is made of shiny aluminum, and the

Pedestal shrine and propellers next to the Shrine of Flight

pathway leads directly to a modern glazed tile building that houses the Ninomiya Chūhachi museum and the priest's second-story residence. Off to one side of the pathway is the small shrine with its propellers and radial engines mounted on pedestals. Although Ninomiya's interest in establishing the shrine was to commemorate the aviation pioneers who lost their lives in airplane crashes, the shrine's main focus of interest is Ninomiya. The wizard of flight is the real object of reverence, and he is celebrated for his technological mastery over nature, a feat as good as rainmaking or any other skill that places natural functions at our bidding. The architecture, the literature, and the priest's conversation all keep in mind Ninomiya, not Nigihaya.[75]

Ninomiya is not the only *kami* revered in addition to Nigihaya. The enshrined *kami* (*saijin*) include the souls of all the pioneers and "martyrs" of aviation throughout the world. Declaring that the "sky is one," Ninomiya's second son rededicated the shrine in 1950 to the principle that aviation brings all people together. The practical benefit of aviation is universal and reaches everyone in common, a theme that was celebrated also with the advent of electrical power.

Like Ninomiya, Thomas Edison was looked upon as a genius who tapped the power of nature, seemingly to defy the natural order in enabling people to do what had never been done. And like Ninomiya he too is venerated in the city of Yawata—not at the foot of the Iwashimizu Hachiman Shrine's hill, but at the top, at the shrine itself.

The incandescent light bulb, taken so much for granted these days, made possible the seemingly supernatural wonder of a controlled burning that produced light without smoke. The first uses of electric light caused widespread wonder:

> When the city of Wabash installed arc lights on the dome of the courthouse, ten thousand visitors and reporters from forty newspapers were there to witness the lighting. When the flood of light burst forth, there was no shouting in what otherwise would have been deep darkness. The *Wabash Plain Dealer* reported: "People stood overwhelmed with awe, as if in the presence of the supernatural. The strange weird light, exceeded in power only by that of the sun, rendered the square as light as midday. . . . Men fell on their knees, groans were uttered at the sight, and many were dumb with amazement." It was a religious miracle.[76]

Edison was not the first to invent an incandescent light bulb, but he was the first to make a practical device that burned for some length of time and could be produced in numbers. Production and dissemination gave rise to a whole industry that was seen as a leveling force that would hold people together in common. In 1899, Elbert Hubbard formed a society of technicians and businessmen dedicated to build a classless brotherhood. The group, called the Jovians, enlisted thousands of ordinary laborers as well as leaders like Edison and Westinghouse, all of whom heard Hubbard's standard welcome: "The idea of electricity binding the world together in a body of brotherhood is something we did not look for a few years ago. Electricity occupies the twilight zone between the world of spirit and the world of matter. Electricians are all proud of their business. They should be. God is the Great Electrician."[77]

Electricity was the divine power and practical benefit of this new common religion. It too could heal. Indeed, application of electricity to different parts of the body became a popular therapy, one still practiced in Japan today, usually in shops that also offer acupuncture and moxa burnings. For $18 in 1901, one could purchase the "Giant Power Heidelberg Electric Belt"—a device to which were wired electrodes in a sack that fitted around the male organ to deliver a current that resulted in "liveliness imparted, a vigor induced, a tone returned, a joy restored." Not only did it get rid of impotence, but it could also cure any kind of disease and fortify the body.[78]

The electric light bulb, however, was not the stuff of wild claims, and by 1880 the Edison Light Company was producing commercial bulbs. The first bulbs used carbonized bristol board for the all-important filament, which still did not last as long as Edison wanted. He experimented through trial-and-error with a wide variety of ma-

Thomas Edison *ema* at Iwashimizu Hachimangū Shrine

terials but could find nothing better than bristol board until he picked up a bamboo fan one day, took a sliver from it, carbonized it, and found that it burned longer than the bristol board filaments. He sent expeditions to South America, India, and Japan to search for the best bamboo, and in Yokohama his representative was told that the finest bamboo in Japan grew in Yawata. The sticky, flexible Yawata bamboo did indeed prove to be the best, and Edison imported large amounts for use as the standard filament in his commercially produced bulbs until 1894.[79]

The Yawata bamboo came from the environs of the Iwashimizu Hachiman Shrine—a connection between bamboo and the light bulb that is commemorated at Yawata train station with a large sculpture of a bamboo stalk cut at cross section to reveal a light bulb within it. At the shrine itself a stone memorial is dedicated to the memory of Edison, and a sign to one side describes Yawata's connection with electric bulb production at Menlo Park. One of several *ema* available at the shrine is made of a flat piece of bamboo with an autographed portrait of the wizard himself. On the back of the *ema,* where one writes one's wishes, is printed a translation of Edison's famous dictum: Genius is one percent inspiration and ninety-nine percent perspiration. The message is clear: ask the wizard for the fulfillment of your wishes and remember that the wizard himself succeeded through the hard work of trial-and-error.

The Edison-Hertz stupa at Hōrinji, Kyoto

Nestled on a hillside in the lovely Arashiyama district of Kyoto, the Buddhist temple Hōrinji has a commanding view of the city. It is spared the rush of students and tourists who flock to this popular area by the river, however, because of the steep climb up to it. The path leading back to the river passes the Denden-gū—literally, the "Shrine of Electricity and Wavelength." The sign posted in front explains that the deities of this shrine protect Hōrinji, and that their names are the Patriarch of Electricity (*denki soshin*) and the Patriarch of Wavelength (*denpa soshin*). Here, as at many shrines, it is impossible to see the inner altar and therefore the represented forms of these patriarchs. Halfway down the hillside from the shrine, however, is the Dendentō—The "Stupa of Electricity and Wavelength"—a small structure about six feet high in the shape of a Buddhist stupa, the traditional form for a mausoleum enshrining the relics of a saint or buddha or, as is the case here, the remains or memory of a prominent person. On a masonry wall behind it are two bronze plaques featuring head portraits of Thomas Edison and Heinrich Hertz (1857–1894), the German physicist whose name is still used as the counting unit of electrical and radio frequency (*denpa*). The sign explains that the patriarch *kami* enshrined in the Denden-gū are Edison and Hertz, both of whom laid the groundwork for the development of electricity that made progess everywhere possible, and that the "souls" (*tama*) of these two pioneers are laid to rest in this stupa. Since gravestones of the human dead can take the form of a small stupa, this edifice emphasizes the humanity of the wizards, while the shrine suggests something of the divine. Shrine and stupa preserve this ambiguity of status. But the themes surrounding the wizards are still clear: they mastered the power of nature, provided benefits for all people, and are appropriately commemorated at religious sites rather than in the public squares, which are suitable for statues and plaques of more clearly secular heroes.

The Diverse Gathering

If wizards and saints find themselves in an ambiguous spectrum ranging from the human to the divine, so too are the *kami* and buddhas themselves surrounded by ambiguity—entwined in mechanisms of separation and assimilation, divinization and personalization, generalization and localization, all of which function variously to elevate and bring them down to earth, often at the same time. Their common bond is to provide benefits, and the understanding by which this happens does not require much in the way of sharp distinctions between Buddhism and Shinto, philosophy and practice, the human and the divine. Taken out of the framework of practical benefits, for example, Buddhism clearly distinguishes itself from Shinto. The details of this framework and practice are very Japanese. But the appeal is universal, and prayers to the gods from foreign visitors can be seen on *ema* at many shrines and temples.

So too does the pantheon of providers include figures from the religions of Hinduism, Buddhism, Taoism, Shinto, and Confucianism. While we have not dealt with Confucianism as such, we should mention here that at Yushima Seidō, the Confucian hall of worship in Tokyo, there stands a larger-than-life statue of Confucius before which have been placed *ema* written by students seeking better grades if not learning. A notice informs visitors that success in the acquisition of knowledge is a matter of personal endeavor. Hence it appears to repudiate the notion that Confucius or any other being could grant divine help in this matter. Yet the vending of *ema* by Yushima Seidō clearly encourages students to offer petitions, and the Japanese students who have purchased the *ema* have certainly not taken notice of what the authorities have said: their inscriptions seek divine help for educational success in words no different from those used to *kami* and buddhas at shrines and temples. In the eyes of the supplicants, then, Confucius, the wizard of learning, is clearly treated as a potential provider of benefits and is addressed in the same way as *kami* and buddhas.

The international pantheon that has developed in Japan remains fluid and accommodating, able to incorporate new members whenever they may appear capable of providing assistance. This pantheon has, as we have seen, been augmented by the contributions of wizards such as Edison and Hertz, from America and Germany respectively, and doubtless one could find examples of other figures from other countries that are revered somewhere in Japan. In this pantheon we see a diverse gathering of the gods with general as well as special powers to accommodate any request or prayer. They are equally accessible to all at institutions that do not require membership or even belief as a prerequisite to participation. The shrines and temples of practical benefits offer an open system that anyone can put into practice, and it is to the dynamics of practice that we now turn.

5

The Dynamics of Practice

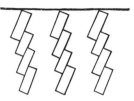

SOME YEARS AGO a Japanese friend of one of the authors made a visit to a famous Shinto shrine with her parents. She was unmarried and in her mid-twenties: in Japanese terms she was close to becoming a "Christmas cake"—a popular epithet used to describe unmarried women over the age of twenty-five. Just as Japanese Christmas cakes pass their sell-by dates and are far less in demand after December 25, so too, according to this phraseology, are women past their optimum age and in danger of being left on the shelf once they are past their twenty-fifth year. Although the trend these days is for women to marry later, the imagery of the Christmas cake remains potent and worries many young Japanese women and, perhaps even more strongly, their parents. The young woman and her parents were concerned that although they had pursued some of the common social processes and formats (enlisting the help of matchmakers and undergoing the process of *miai,* or meeting prospective suitors),[1] nothing they had done so far had brought her a suitable candidate.

In their concern they decided to turn to the gods, and the place they chose to visit was Izumo Taisha (Shrine) in Shimane prefecture, one of the most ancient of all Shinto shrines and famed for love and marriage. Izumo is where, according to Shinto legend, all the gods of Japan gather during the month of October to discuss matters of love and marriage. At Izumo this month is known as *kamiari tsuki,* the month when the gods are present; elsewhere it is *kanna zuki,* the month when the gods are absent. The main deity at Izumo, Ōkuninushi no Mikoto, is regarded as the source of numerous forms of benefits, but the most prominent of these—as the endeavors of the gods during their sojourn at Izumo in the *kamiari tsuki* show—is for love and joining together people in marriage: the benefit of *en musubi.* It was Izumo's national reputation that caused the woman

178

and her parents to select it as the goal of their prayers—even though it was located at some distance from their home and other places closer at hand offered the benefit of *en musubi*.

Because they were asking for something of great importance and wished to demonstrate to the gods their sincerity and worthiness of being granted this benefit, they decided their visit should have an ascetic dimension that would enable them to approach the gods in the purest state possible. From the city of Kobe where they lived, the journey to Izumo takes several hours by car. They decided they would make the round trip in one day, however, eschewing any hint of ludic activities in their visit. Izumo, like most towns centered around major shrines or temples in Japan, is both a religious and a tourist center offering overnight accommodation, souvenir shops, restaurants, bars, nightclubs and other such attractions to allow visitors to enjoy themselves and spend some of their money. The family did not wish to avail themselves of such diversions, however, feeling that any gesture toward tourist behavior would demean the seriousness of their purpose. Instead, they arose very early in the morning and drove directly to Izumo without first having breakfast. By fasting they felt they would be approaching the shrine in a pure state. Arriving early at the shrine, they made their obeisances and had a ritual prayer service conducted by a priest there, paying the appropriate sum for this and receiving in return an *ofuda* for *en musubi*. When they had completed their devotions, they left the shrine area, carrying the talisman they had received, and did not stop to eat until they were well away from the Izumo area and the realms of its gods.

The family's way of dealing with this matter is highly instructive: in their efforts to secure a husband for their daughter they had followed the normal social processes without success and had thus, through pressing need, decided to utilize the services of the religious domain. In so doing they made a number of linked decisions: to visit a place at some remove from their home that had a major reputation related to the benefit they sought; thus to travel afar; and to make their journey and present their petition in such a way as to show the gods their sincerity and worthiness of receiving the desired benefit. In seeking their goal they were therefore aware of the value of the service they sought and the price—in terms of effort as well as money—they needed to pay for it. Although they did not assume their request would be granted without fail, they left contented. They had done their best to secure the success of their venture and could continue to follow the normal procedures for finding a husband—but now with the gods supporting them favorably, so they felt, in this venture.[2]

Benefit seeking is not always viewed in such ways. Not everyone wishes to frame their prayers in such an ascetic mode or feels the need to display their sincerity in this fashion. Casual and spontaneous

activity—recall the visitors to Hōzanji who drop in during a visit to
the Ikoma funfair or hiking in the hills—is also common in the
search for benefits. At times the process of seeking benefits demonstrates not a casual approach to the gods but a sharp sense of the economic commitments involved and the fact that money is being paid
out and results therefore ought to be received. This pragmatic attitude may be seen in an example cited by Robert J. Smith: a woman
who had placed an *ema* at a temple in Kamakura, asking for her
boyfriend's interest in her to increase, had added the words (in Japanese): "After all, I've laid out 500 yen for this thing so it had better
work."[3]

Her attitude—that the gods had a duty to act, owing to her expenditure, and that an object so purchased should produce the results demanded—differs in some ways from that of the family who
hoped for a particular result but did not assume its automatic realization. Yet it does share certain similarities. She had, like the family,
engaged in a process of actions and expenditures designed to harness
the aid of the gods—in her case by going to the temple, purchasing
an *ema,* writing a message on it, and then hanging it there. Like them
she had prayed, and she had paid, for seeking benefits from the gods
involves paying them for their services: praying and paying are linked
together, the latter an essential aspect of the ritual process involved
in the former.[4] Paying does not always mean expending money, although as a rule some financial offering is customary. Paying also involves the expenditure of effort, an intrinsic part of the process of
prayer and supplication. Such expenditure might include visiting
places designated as locations of spiritual power—places where gods,
buddhas, or other spiritual entities are deemed to be present and
where they are represented either graphically (as with statues of buddhas) or symbolically—and engaging in actions and transactions in
which one makes an outlay of time and effort as well as money, just as
the girl and the family did in their different ways, in the hope of gaining some return in the form of the grace of the gods and the benefits
one asks from them.

Hope is closely aligned to expectation: without some form of expectation that their prayers might be answered, people would be unlikely to participate in such activities or spend time and money on
them. Such expectations are created, inter alia, by the reputations of
religious centers and the stories of benefits granted and received at
temples and shrines—issues we examine in Chapter 6. Expectations
are developed, too, by the general assumption that gods and buddhas
provide help when asked: certainly both the family visiting Izumo
Shrine and the girl addressing the gods rather bluntly in her *ema* not
only hoped, but expected, that their prayers would be heard.

The Open Display of Desire

The display of hope and expectation, and the desire for benefits, is not simply an expression of ritualized optimism but also an overt and public one.[5] Both the performances we have cited were publicly visible: the *ema* displayed on a rack at the temple and the petitioners at Izumo having their prayer request ritual performed in the public domain of the shrine. Seeking benefits normally involves such a public display. While writing requests on *ema* and placing them on display at a shrine or temple may be the most readily visible of all benefit-related practices, others, whether through participating in a public event such as the *goma* ritual or simply carrying an amulet on one's person or hanging it up in one's car, are also open to public view. In the *goma* ritual, for example, it is common for the priests to read out, during their supplication to the deities, the names of the petitioners and the request they are making. Desire and ambition are not just affirmed as good in the sutras of Buddhism and the canons of Shinto; they may quite legitimately and openly be expressed in such socially accepted and sanctioned ways.

Desire and ambition are also expressions of intent. Such public display—whether through participating in rituals or exhibiting the signs, symbols, and objects related to benefits on one's person, in one's home, or in one's car—functions as an avenue through which

Traffic safety amulet

one's intent is externalized. The intent, desire, and commitment to drive safely are thus publicly expressed in the *ofuda* hanging in a railway compartment or the traffic safety stickers attached to a car. Such objects also serve the complementary function of advertising the shrine or temple from which they derive and making that site visible in the world beyond the shrine or temple gates.

Praying for benefits often involves placing one's inner desires and feelings, as well as one's private pains and turmoils, out in the open for all to see. Personal ambitions, sufferings, and shortcomings that are written up on *ema* are on public display. In writing out their ambitions, asking for entry into a leading university, exposing their weaknesses, asking for help in overcoming their addiction to alcohol or drugs, or seeking a god's help in attracting the attention of a particularly desired partner, petitioners are effectively opening up their inner feelings to a public audience.[6] Even painful or embarrassing physical problems—such as being afflicted by sexual diseases, hemorrhoids, or ringworm or being unable to produce adequate breast milk, conditions that in many societies might be confined to the privacy of the doctor's office—may be brought out into the open, metaphorically speaking, in the public space and rituals of the shrine or temple.

If praying for benefits involves a ritual display of optimism, it also contains a recognition that one should express that which in other circumstances would be kept hidden from public view. It is understood, in such terms, that in seeking to make real one's inner desires—whether in achieving success and realizing one's wishes or in removing one's pain and suffering—one should give them shape through the process of externalization and public articulation. And the public space of the shrine or temple, and the practices that may be conducted there, form the appropriate vehicle for this end.

Purchase, Practice, and the Price of Benefits

Purchase and practice are inseparable. The religious practices that the family and the *ema* writer engaged in were not just public affairs with symbolic meaning. They were backed with real currency and real effort and invested with a genuine sense of hope and expectation about their worth and projected returns. To seek benefits, therefore, requires a sense of the appropriate level of expenditure (whether money or effort) that should be made in relation to the needs at hand. In visiting a distant religious center famed for a particular benefit that is carried out in a particularly austere way involving a formal ritual petition conducted by a priest, the family cited earlier placed a certain value on the benefit they sought and showed what they were willing to expend in terms of time, effort, and money in its pursuit. It was the price they were ready to pay to purchase the benefit at hand and achieve their aims. The cryptic message on the *ema* reported by Smith not only tells us what that petitioner had paid for her request; it also lets us know what she felt she was entitled for her expenditure.

Financial transactions, then, are an integral part of the process of seeking benefits. Whether purchasing an amulet, talisman, or votive tablet or paying for a ritual service to be conducted by a priest, the petitioner normally has to use money. Shrines and temples and their officiants set the general parameters—through the fees they charge for the performance of rituals and the sale of religious objects—that determine the financial framework of the purchase of benefits. Although the prices of various services (the cost of a ritual, the price of a talisman) are frequently similar from place to place, there is no standard pricing structure that goes across the board.

In theory, at least, as we have repeatedly been told when discussing the costs of amulets and talismans with priests at shrines and temples, one does not buy them by giving money in exchange for the object. This is not a normal financial transaction such as purchasing goods in a store. Rather, one makes a donation to enter into a spiritual contract with a deity and receives in return a manifestation of that deity in the form of a talisman or amulet. What one donates depends on one's feelings (*kimochi*) about the shrine, temple, or deity.

This explanation of donation—and the bestowal of religious objects as a gesture of gratitude for the donor's piety—is a plausible interpretation of the process from the perspective of shrines and temples. It is, however, a rather misleading explanation that camouflages the undoubtedly commercial aspects of the process beneath an aura of sanctity. In reality, the purchase of talismans and ritual services, although shot through with religious symbolism and meanings, is a matter of commercial exchange: it involves the tendering of the appropriate sum of money (normally accompanied, when seeking a special prayer service, by a special order form) by the petitioner/customer and the handing over of goods or the rendering of ritual services by the priests/providers as agents of the gods. Where appropriate, change will be given back to the petitioner. This action itself exposes the fiction that people are making a donation, rather than paying a fixed price, for these services. A woman wishing for a talisman priced at 3,000 yen and finding she has only a 5,000-yen note is not asked by the priest what level of donation she intends to make: 2,000 yen is automatically handed back as change. We have never heard such a question put to a supposed "donor"; nor have we ever heard a "donor" asked how much change he wants. Whatever

Amulet sales counter and price list

rhetoric may be used in respect of the exchange of money and religious objects and services, the process is a matter of purchase. Religious goods are sold in a commercial way: they have a price that customers pay in return for the item or service they ordered.

The sums of money involved may be quite considerable, and temples and shrines often provide their worshipers/customers with a wide choice of different types and sizes of amulets and talismans with different prices. *Omamori,* charms carried on the person, tend to cost less than *ofuda,* which protect an area or a social group rather than just an individual and as a result, in popular perception, are assumed to be more powerful. In 1996, most *omamori* cost under 1,000 yen and often around 500 yen; the price for *ofuda* is generally somewhat higher. *Ofuda* come in a variety of sizes: the more one pays, the larger *ofuda* one receives. At the Naritasan temples, for example, *ofuda* for travel safety may cost anything from 1,000 yen (for small ones) to tens of thousands of yen for *ofuda* that stand a yard or more in height. The latter are commonly purchased by companies with a big fleet of vehicles and hence appear to reflect a sense of scale, but there is nothing—apart from one's sense of what is appropriate—to prevent an individual from purchasing such an expensive item. Similarly the prices of ritual services may vary depending on the level of ritual required or the *ofuda* that is sacralized. Kawasaki Daishi's ordinary *goma* ritual, for example, costs anything from 3,000 to 10,000 yen, depending on one's wishes and the type and size of *ofuda* one seeks. A large *goma (daigoma)* ritual and appropriate *ofuda* cost 20,000 yen, while one can commission a special large *goma* ritual (*tokubetsu daigoma*) and receive a special *ofuda* for 30,000 yen "or more" (*ijō*).

At the Kitano Tenmangū Shrine in Kyoto, petitioners seeking the benefit of academic success are offered two choices: A course and B course. Although each asks for the same form of benefit (success in education including passing examinations and entering a desired institution), they have different costs: A requires 5,000 yen and B costs 4,000 yen. At both levels, students receive an *omamori* and an ink writing brush. The shrine does not, at least overtly, state that one has a greater chance of success with the more expensive A course than with the B course. That judgment is left up to the petitioner. What one gets for paying higher prices is a higher level of service: for the higher A course fee, the student is given the privilege of entering the main altar area to receive his or her prayer blessing. At Kawasaki Daishi, the greater the expenditure the greater the size of *ofuda* one receives or the more extensive the *goma* ritual. It is the prerogative of the petitioners themselves to determine the full extent of their expenditure—not just in terms of energy and effort expended but also in terms of the money they will pay and the levels of service they wish to receive—and to calculate their expenditure in line with what they hope to achieve.

Given the variety of different prices and services that may be offered, the question has to be asked whether paying more means receiving better benefits. In other words: is there a direct correlation between price and benefit? Here there is some divergence between the implications of the services offered (which would appear to encourage the standard market notion that paying more means getting better quality) and the theoretical meaning of the goods and services themselves. Since *ofuda* and *omamori* are held to be manifestations (*bunshin*) of a deity, they (and the religious services through which they are acquired) should all be of equal value: if one receives a *bunshin* of the Naritasan Fudō or the Kitano Tenmangū's Tenjin, one is in theory receiving the presence not of a limited fiscal amount of that deity but its totality. Manifestations of deities are just that: manifestations of the deity's totality, not just a minute sliver portioned out according to the price one has paid for it. In numerous interviews with priests at shrines and temples in Japan this point has been made to us repeatedly—namely, that the divine powers of grace are not limited, conditioned, or restricted by the amount of money that has been paid out. In the purchase of an amulet or talisman that has been made, through ritual sacralization, into a manifestation of Fudō, for example, one receives Fudō as a totality rather than a 500-yen portion of Fudō's grace. Though the purchase of Fudō may be calculated in financial terms, the returns from such outlays cannot be determined as such. One does not get 500 yen's worth of benefits, or 500 yen's worth of Fudō's protection, through paying out 500 yen in the process of purchase.

One can see, in such terms, that although the process of procuring benefits is a matter of purchase, it is not strictly limited by the ordinary rules of the marketplace, where one might be inclined to seek the cheapest available commodity or service or expect a specific level of return for one's investment. When asked in a popular Japanese magazine whether a bigger cash offering meant a higher return in benefits, the folklorist, Shinto priest, and scholar Honda Sōichirō responded negatively. Monetary offerings, he said, are tokens of appreciation and there is no link between them and future returns.[7] When questioned whether it is more beneficial to pay a larger sum for a prayer or talisman at their temple—rather than making do with the cheapest forms on offer—none of the priests we talked to affirmed that the more expensive a talisman is, the more effective it must be. Yet neither Honda's response nor the reply of these priests should be seen as an indication that one might just as well buy the cheapest form of talismans and ritual, since all are of equal value. Alongside the theory of the equality of all purchases is an underlying and not always subtle encouragement to spend more rather than less.

In dealing with questions of the relationship between cost and efficacy, priests are operating in a problematic area. They have a vested interest in the issue of purchase (their institutions benefit financially from this process and may depend wholly on such income) and hence in wanting people to choose the more costly courses. However, in their need to affirm the symbolic value of prayers and talismans and the powers and compassionate nature of the deities they serve—compassion that is presumably not diminished because a petitioner is unable to afford more—priests cannot openly insist there are variations in the efficacies of differently priced talismans. They can, however, imply this in more subtle ways, and if priests may not openly assert that paying more gets better benefits, they rarely deny it either. While we have not met any priests who specifically advised people to buy the cheapest because they are all, after all, the same in terms of efficacy and meaning, we have heard them promote the virtues of the amulets and *ofuda* at their shrines and temples with sales talk that encourages the purchase of the more expensive forms.

Indeed, the affirmation that what one pays depends on one's feelings, or *kimochi*, and the ways in which amulets and talismans are offered in a variety of forms and sizes, seem to amount to skillful sales devices to convince petitioners, without ever stating so overtly, that they would do better to pay more for their prayers. The variations in price and size of talismans implicitly suggest differences in the levels of efficacy between them and hence encourage people to spend more rather than less. It is easy for petitioners to infer that a more costly ritual course of action brings not only better levels of service but a greater potential for results. Certainly the ethical dynamics underlying *genze riyaku,* as we showed in Chapter 3, emphasize how earnestness produces greater merit and hence enhances the worthiness of petitioners to receive benefits. When faced with the choice between paying one thousand or several thousand yen for a talisman, petitioners might well feel inclined, or obliged, to pay the higher fee to demonstrate a greater degree of sincerity and thus make their request appear more worthy of approval. Through financial outlay and personal effort petitioners are thus encouraged to create the merit that makes them worthy recipients of the graces the gods may be able to bestow.

Ethical considerations encourage greater expenditure in other ways as well. Meanness is not seen as a commendable virtue and indeed is quite often portrayed as a sin in religious contexts—a sin, moreover, that may result in the loss of benefits. Among the numerous legends (*Kōbō densetsu*) relating to Kōbō Daishi as a miracle-working figure who dispenses benefits to supplicants for good behavior, there are many that warn against meanness. One of the commonest of these legends depicts an old woman who refuses to give a traveling pilgrim (in retrospect seen as Kōbō Daishi) a drink of water although she has access to an abundant spring. In punishment for this meanness, she is cursed and the spring dries up: the benefit of pure and abundant water is lost through her stingy behavior.[8] The subtle and occasionally not so subtle hints are that generosity serves one better than caution in the presence of the gods and in the use of money when seeking benefits.

One cannot discount, either, the potential value of "brand names" in this respect. Famous shrines and temples can command high fees because of their reputation, which has often been skillfully constructed through the use of stories of efficacy and miracle aligned to intensive proselytizing and advertising. Kawasaki Daishi can readily attract high fees for its services because, as a top brand name in the market of preventing accidents, it has the cachet of name recognition and an established reputation for quality in the public's mind.

The vending of benefits is shot through with commercial and subtly exploitative themes that help shrines and temples to increase the financial expenditures of petitioners. Yet if there are underlying pressures to spend more to avoid the perils of meanness, this does not mean that people will simply throw their money around with great abandon. One can draw a parallel here with the dilemmas faced by Japanese people when determining how much money to give as a wedding present or how much to give a priest for conducting a memorial service for the ancestors. In such cases the dilemma is to avoid being mean and giving too little while not exceeding the standard market prices for such services by giving too much—or indeed falling into follies of excess and extravagance by paying more than is warranted by one's status, a social error that may be seen as virtually parallel to the sin of meanness. Such family dilemmas may be resolved, not just by noting what others do in similar circumstances, but by consulting guidebooks that prescribe the socially correct rates. Thus people develop an understanding of the correct amount to spend in such circumstances and learn how to balance their wish not to appear tightfisted with their wish not to overdo things or pay more than they should.

Indeed, petitioners may develop a fairly sharp sense of the real value of their money—not just, like the female *ema* writer, a clear sense of what they ought to get but in terms of religious bargains. One of us was traveling once with a party of pilgrims in Shikoku, many of whom had memorial services done for their ancestors at a temple where they had stopped overnight. When questioned whether ancestor memorialization was therefore central to their pilgrimage, however, some responded negatively. They explained that the temple in question charged less for these services than they would have had to pay in Osaka, and hence—since doing memorial services for one's ancestors was a socially obligatory action they ought to do on occasion—they were taking advantage of this "bargain."[9] Generosity and sacrifice may demonstrate worthiness and merit, but as in all commercial processes, an attractive price may encourage those who would otherwise hold onto their money to part with it. An expensive *ofuda* might well attract the attention of a petitioner because its price appears to suggest enhanced efficacy; but a cheaply priced one can catch the attention of visitors, too, and persuade them to buy it because it appears to be of good value. The expenditure of money in religious circumstances is not so much a symbolic gesture as a highly pragmatic one that reflects people's sense of value and their knowledge of what they seek to purchase.

The Importance of Plurality

The practices of petitioning and purchasing benefits are, like all activities at shrines and temples in Japan, as varied as the petitioners themselves, and the two examples of the family and the *ema* writer are merely illustrations of this diversity. It is not our intention here to discuss all the various activities that occur at shrines and temples, for such accounts are available elsewhere.[10] Since our main focus here is on the dynamics of purchase in relation to practice, we will simply outline some of the forms and means through which petitions are made and some of the media through which the desire for the attainment of practical benefits is articulated.

In Chapter 1 we noted the peripatetic behavior that is often associated with seeking benefits. This behavior is based on the notion that seeking benefits in one place does not preclude one from doing so elsewhere: no single place or deity ever has a monopoly over a category of benefits. Hence one may encounter cases where people engage in a multiplicity of activities, acquire a collection of charms and amulets, or make a series of visits to different institutions all for the same purpose. Temples and shrines recognize the importance of plurality and hence of reinforcing the power of prayers for practical benefits by utilizing more than one deity or shrine, especially in times of great need. They may even capitalize on this tendency by presenting themselves accordingly to the benefit-seeking public as a source of backup prayers. The Azumamaro Shrine in the precincts of Fushimi Inari Shrine in Kyoto enshrines Kada no Azumamaro, a noted Tokugawa-era scholar of the Kokugaku school, and has built for itself a reputation for academic benefits based on his fame as a scholar. Located at the nationally famed Inari Shrine, which gets several million visitors a year, it benefits from the crowds that are drawn there. It does not compete directly with Fushimi Inari—whose main benefits are for business prosperity and beckoning good fortune—but adds a complementary service. Quite probably, many people visiting Fushimi Inari for its special benefits may be enticed into praying at Azumamaro as well.

The Azumamaro Shrine is noted as a place to make, on the day of one's school or university entrance examination, a follow-up prayer for scholastic success.[11] It is assumed that students will, prior to their examinations, already have prayed for academic success—and that there is nothing wrong with supplementing this prayer with a second one or placing one's faith in more than one deity or institution. Azumamaro Shrine's role in providing a backup prayer on the very day of one's examinations has a distinct pragmatic dimension, since it is located near one of Kyoto's larger universities, Ryūkoku University, and hence is conveniently placed to capture the attention of worried students on their way to examinations.

Bolstering one's fortunes by using a number of sites and amulets is quite common. This religious plurality can at times be quite striking, in fact, as was demonstrated by a young man who was about to take some important school entrance examinations in the mid-1980s. He and his family were so concerned about getting into the school of his choice (a prestigious institution with a reputation for getting its pupils into Tokyo University) that he had acquired five amulets from different locations—all given to him by family members and friends for academic success—as well as other lucky charms for the same purpose. Thus he had an amulet from one of the most famous shrines in Japan for education, Dazaifu Tenmangū, in northern Kyūshū: this amulet had been acquired for him by his eldest brother during a school trip. He also had an amulet from a branch shrine of Dazaifu Tenmangū in Kobe, as well as amulets from two other major shrines to Tenjin in the Kansai region, Kitano Tenmangū in Kyoto and Osaka Tenmangū in Osaka, as well as one from the Rokkō Hachiman Shrine near his home. Besides these five amulets, he also had the following: a lucky headband, purchased for him by his elder sister from a shrine in Okayama during her school trip there, that he wore when studying; an "academic success" rubber eraser purchased from a department store in his home town; and a lucky charm given to him by a Catholic nun who was teaching at his current school. The amulets were either worn or placed on items connected with his studies, such as his school bag and desk. In gathering this array of charms he was encouraged and assisted by his siblings who, through their gifts of amulets, displayed their affection for him, demonstrated their wishes for his success, and also reminded him of his ethical obligations to his family to work hard and succeed.[12] Through his phalanx of amulets, also, the boy demonstrated that in the pursuit of his goals he need not limit himself to one form of practice, charm, or even religious institution: he was not going to place all his eggs in one basket, as it were, by depending on just one source of religious aid but was prepared to harness whatever sources he could.

Rituals, Intimacy, and the Role of Priests

Seeking benefits is normally conducted through ritual activities concerned with the use of objects that represent the providers of benefits and serve as a medium of communication with them. These objects—the talismans, the amulets, the votive tablets, the offerings (money, food, and so on) that people place before the gods—signify the transactional aspects of seeking benefits. The transactions that occur and the objects that are acquired build empathetic links between humans as seekers and deities as providers of benefits: the former purchase empathy, intimacy, and familiarity with the latter to facilitate the transmission and reception of benefits. The talismans taken home and the votive tablets left behind further this intimacy between person, place, and deity: manifestations of the deity are taken home or worn by petitioners; reminders of the petitioner are left at the shrine or temple through the votive tablets, the copied sutras, and so on.

The creation of intimacy does not only concern the deity and the petitioner, however, for the services of religious specialists, such as the ordained priests of the Shinto and Buddhist traditions, are often required in this process. Priests facilitate this interaction in many ways. They care for the environment, the temples and shrines, where the gods and buddhas are venerated and petitioned; they look after the statues; they make the offerings and perform the rituals that honor and care for the deities. Priests serve as mediators and inter-locutors between worshipers and deities, opening up channels between them to promote the transmission of benefits. Operating in this way and receiving fees for their services, priests are in many respects the servants of those who pay them and as such have obligations to them. When priests say they cannot refuse requests or petitions for benefit and have created certain benefits because of public demand, they are speaking of this sense of obligation and the priest's role as servant and respondent to public need. This, of course, is only a partial truth. Priests are not just followers of trends but may actively promote the virtues of their deities and advertise the benefits they can provide, thus stimulating the demand for benefits. Rather than simply reacting to public demand, they may create it and manipulate it—a point we touched on earlier when we noted the skillful ways in which petitioners may be persuaded to purchase the more expensive forms of talisman.

Priests conduct formal rituals that ask for benefits and present petitions to the deities. These rites are frequently accompanied by the incantation of appropriate prayers—customarily prayers of *norito* in the Shinto context and sutras and mantras in the Buddhist setting. Among such forms of ritual are the *goma* fire ritual mentioned in Chapter 1, Shinto purification ceremonies (*oharai*) that seek to banish bad luck, and performances of *kagura* (sacred dances performed by a shrine maiden, with a Shinto priest overseeing the ritual, or sometimes by *yamabushi* or mountain ascetics) in which the deity to be petitioned is summoned and entertained through the sacred dance. The public's notion of such rituals commonly focuses on their perceived aim of gaining results. As Irit Averbuch's survey of public perceptions of *kagura* rituals in northern Japan has shown, "most people . . . thought that *kagura* is danced in order to gain results." These results, they thought, were to prevent calamities (according to 46.3 percent of her respondents) and to bring a good harvest (41.3 percent): some 29 percent of the respondents thought both results were sought in the ritual.[13]

Not all petitions to deities and purchases of benefits are formally routed through priestly intermediaries: petitioners may also pray on their own, purchase the talismans they think fit, write the messages they wish on *ema,* and so on. However, even in such apparently informal and individualized processes, priests play a role as conductors of the rituals that sacralize the media (the talismans and so on) that are used in the pursuit of benefits and transform them into manifestations of the gods and buddhas.[14]

Actions, Amulets, and Obligations

Besides commissioning formal rituals focused on attaining benefits, shrine and temple visitors engage in numerous personal activities to gain the support and grace of deities—usually acts of prayer but also actions designed to demonstrate one's virtue, such as the *hyakudo mairi* practice, mentioned in Chapter 1, and its variants. (At the Monju hall of worship at Hōzanji, for example, petitioners are instructed to circumambulate the hall ten times in order to facilitate their requests for academic success.) There is sutra copying, too, in which people carefully copy out Buddhist texts and offer them at a temple, usually accompanied by a request for a particular benefit. Other common actions may display the petitioner's affection for certain figures of worship. In this category we include such actions as rubbing the heads of statues of Buddhist figures of worship, adorning them with clothes, chanting prayers especially related to them (certain mantras are specific to particular buddhas), and making offerings of coins, food, and drink to them. Other standard actions include acquiring the various sacred objects for sale—talismans and so on that are taken away from the shrine or temple—and making use of the various forms, such as *ema,* that allow the petitioner to place a message or request before the deity.

In Chapter 1 we described the standard forms of these material representations of sacred power, such as *omamori* and *ofuda,* but many different types of such objects are sold at shrines and temples. Here we outline some of the interesting objects that may be acquired, along with the practices that may be involved with them and some of the underlying meanings they espouse. Sometimes the very soil of a temple or shrine operates as a sacred object that, taken away from the location, transmits its spiritual power elsewhere. At Kiyotakisan, a mountain temple on the island of Shōdoshima, for instance, one can purchase sachets of soil taken from the temple's courtyard. According to the words printed on the sachet, the soil has been sacralized by Esoteric Shingon Buddhist prayer rituals and hence is capable of providing great benefits: if one sprinkles it on one's fields it will assist in the production of abundant crops; if spread around one's home, the household will "without doubt" (*utagai nashi*) prosper.

Sometimes the benefit-offering object may have a practical use: temples specializing in the prevention of senility (*boke fūji*) such as Ima Kumano Temple in Kyoto vend pillowcases that may be used as protective amulets while one is sleeping. The temple Nishinotaki Ryūsuiji on Shōdoshima has, as one of its sacred amulets, a lucky hand towel (*mamori tenugui*) that serves many purposes, bringing its owner, according to its wrapper, these "wonderful benefits":

> Traffic safety for people who drive cars
> Prevention of danger for those with dangerous occupations
> Acquisition of wisdom for those going through the education system

It also promises relief from various pains and illnesses, instructing those with such problems to do the following:

> For those with headaches or unable to sleep: please place this under your pillow, and rest.
> For the sick: please place the towel on the spot that hurts, and rest.
> For those who are injured: immediately wrap the wound with the towel.

In all these actions one should also repeat the mantra of the temple (*"on meigyasha niei sowaka"*) twenty-one times and recite the invocation of praise to Kōbō Daishi (*"namu Daishi henjō kongō"*) also twenty-one times.

Lucky charms may also make use of the associations of sympathetic magic in order to symbolize the benefit beckoned or the role they are meant to play. A lucky object frequently found at shrines to the deity Ebisu—who is especially popular among small shopkeepers and is associated with business prosperity and wealth—is the *kumade,* a small bamboo rake. Symbolizing the raking in of money, the *kumade* makes it very clear what the purchasers would like to do in their business dealings. Talismans associated with Fudō (usually depicted carrying a sword) may be in the shape of a sword to illustrate his power to cut through evil and strike to the heart of things. We have already noted, in Chapter 2, that the character for "sharp" (*ri*) is the same as that used in "*riyaku,*" benefits, and hence the links between the sharpness of Fudō's sword and his benefits are evident. Thus petitioners at the Fukakawa Fudō temple in Tokyo purchase a sword-shaped talisman for academic success—the sword symbolizing the power to cut through all obstacles and attain one's goal and reminding petitioners that they need a similar mind-set. At Izumo Shrine one of the charms for attracting a partner (*en musubi*) consists of two intertwined strands of thread—one red, one white—symbolizing the uniting of female and male: this charm should be tied to one's clothing and worn next to the body, according to shrine instructions.

Benefits associated with sex and fertility are among the most colorfully illustrated and suggestive of all in terms of their charms and amulets. Gourds (*hyōtan*) and aubergines are folkloric symbols of fertility, and hence one finds numerous talismans shaped like small gourds or aubergines vended in connection with the benefit of fertility and the production of children. Often the suggestion is more graphic: phallic objects and charms are readily found at famed fertility shrines such as Tagata Shrine near Nagoya (whose votive tablet depicts a penis).[15]

No matter what form the talisman or amulet comes in, the practices involve more than just taking it home or (as in the case of the towels and pillowcases) using it around the house. The act of purchase is not the end point in a religious practice that begins with a visit to a shrine or temple. It is one step in an ongoing process. The instructions given to petitioners when they acquire talismans and amulets inform them that they should treat the object, which is a representation of the deity, with proper respect and continuing reverence. After a *goma* ritual at Kawasaki Daishi in January 1993 (a ritual that is carried out several times every day), priests handed out the sacralized *ofuda* to petitioners and instructed them to care for the talismans, place them in a safe and, if possible, holy place such as a household altar, and treat them as objects of worship. We have frequently heard similar instructions given by priests of both the Shinto and the Buddhist traditions to recipients of talismans after ritual services.[16]

On the paper bag in which *ofuda* are presented to purchasers at Kiyomizu Temple in Shimane prefecture is the injunction to place it in one's household Buddhist altar (*butsudan*) where the family ancestors are venerated or in the Shinto altar (*kamidana*) where the protective deities of the houshold are enshrined. The instructions assume that worshipers will have one of these altars in their homes—a reasonable assumption given that surveys of religious activity in Japan have shown that only 24 percent of households do not have one or the other.[17] Although they come from a Buddhist temple and concern an *ofuda* representing a Buddhist figure of worship (Kannon), the instructions do not insist that it has to be placed in a Buddhist altar. This again is testimony to the cohesion of the two traditions and their figures of worship in the arena of *genze riyaku:* Kannon as represented by the talisman from Kiyomizu Temple transcends Buddhist boundaries and becomes a deity of the common religion, equally capable of being placed in a Shinto or Buddhist altar.

One must treat amulets and talismans as holy: on the paper bag in which the Tsurugaoka Hachiman Shrine in Kamakura places its talismans is a set of instructions on correct usage. One should place the talisman in a Shinto household altar and worship it there.[18] Before praying one should purify oneself. Then one should perform the same form of prayers (clapping one's hands in supplication) as one would do at the shrine itself. Similar instructions are given in a book on the deity Tenjin and its role in the field of education—a book produced in cooperation with various Tenjin shrines such as Kitano Tenmangū in Kyoto, whose head priest has written the foreword.[19] The correct way to venerate the talismans from Tenjin shrines is to place them in the Shinto altar and make offerings of water and freshly cooked rice before them every morning while praying by clapping one's hands twice in the normal manner of obeisance. The book notes that people who have no Shinto altars—for example, those who live in modern apartment dwellings with no space for such things—should place their talismans in a pure place in the room where they do their studies. Amulets (*omamori*) should always be kept on the person, even when entering the examination room, for they will enable one to remain calm and perform well.[20]

Talismans and amulets, therefore, are not just objects purchased in a one-time activity at a shrine or temple. They are, or should be, the focus of continuing faith and practice—an integral part of that process of continuing faith and endeavor. They are equally reminders of the obligation to maintain religious awareness and practice, a point made clearly by the travel safety amulet bags from Kawasaki Daishi which inform the possessor that, before driving, he or she should make a gesture of prayer (*gasshō*) to the amulet and assume a "worshipful mind" (*ogamu kokoro*).

Return and Renewal: The Cycle of Purchase and Gratitude

The instructions to treat amulets and talismans with care and reverence are often accompanied by reminders of the importance of returning to the shrine or temple to express one's gratitude to the deity for help received in accomplishing a task or avoiding a peril. The importance of returning gratitude for favors granted is stressed, for example, in the aforementioned volume on Tenjin, which comments with great pleasure that the number of young people who have passed their examinations and afterwards return to give thanks to Tenjin is on the increase and that votive tablets giving thanks for this benefit may be found at various Tenjin shrines.[21]

Besides the obligation to make return visits of gratitude, shrines and temples encourage further engagement between person and institution through the injunction that amulets and talismans should be returned to the shrine or temple after they have been used for a year.

This injunction is included, for example, in the instructions that come with the Tsurugaoka Hachiman Shrine's talisman mentioned earlier. It is also given on the paper bags in which the various sacred objects sold at the Iwashimizu Hachiman Shrine, such as *hamaya, omamori,* and *ofuda,* come wrapped. Besides informing purchasers to place them in a Shinto altar or some other pure place, the Iwashimizu Shrine tells them to return the objects with a spirit of gratitude to the shrine when they get old and to acquire new talismans and amulets every year.[22] Gratitude for the benefits provided by the old amulets and talismans is thus linked to renewal and the purchase of new ones.

The use of amulets and talismans thus involves an extended and cyclic process of action: when they have served their task—generally it is considered that they should be used only for one year—they should be returned to the place where they were acquired or, if this is not possible, to another religious institution. Although one might consider amulets and talismans, as "deities," not to be limited by such temporal considerations, the popular perception is that after this time they have absorbed bad luck or have beckoned as much good luck as they can and hence need to be replaced. This attitude is widely encouraged by the institutions themselves. After all, their economies depend to some degree on the sale of these objects. Moreover, the process of returning talismans and amulets to the institution and replacing them encourages repeated visits and hence the extension of a relationship between customer and institution.

Most institutions have a designated place in their precincts to which old amulets and talismans may be returned—a practice that is most widely followed at the New Year, when the returned objects may mount up into large heaps. Indeed, the return of old amulets and talismans forms part of the *hatsumōde* process and the cyclic patterns of renewal it symbolizes: the old objects are returned before new ones are acquired. The discarded objects are then usually disposed of through ritual immolation, during which process the impurities and bad luck they are believed to have absorbed are purified and eradicated. Many shrines and temples hold a large-scale ritual at some point in the middle of January for this purpose.[23]

The exchange of amulets and talismans, therefore, can create and extend interactions between person and institution. The amulets and talismans themselves are tangible symbols and reminders of the necessity, in the pursuit of benefits, for continuing reverence and religious action and the continuing association between person, shrine, and deity. Returning to give thanks for benefits received is another element in this continuing process; for gratitude, as we have seen in earlier chapters, is a crucial aspect of religious practice and behavior. Gratitude, as the injunctions to return and give thanks remind us,

Amulets and talismans returned for ritual disposal

means purchasing anew and thus continuing the cycle of purchase and practice.

Leaving Messages: The Use of Votive Tablets

Not all the objects that relate to *genze riyaku* are taken away from the institutions: people may also place their requests before the gods in written form, for example, by writing them on votive tablets that are left at shrines and temples. The act of writing a request on an *ema* and leaving it at the shrine or temple not only conveys the person's desire to the deity but also externalizes a request and thus, by making it public and putting form (in the shape of words) to that inner desire, makes it appear more concrete and realizable. It also creates a link between person, place, and deity, leaving a sign or trace of the person at the religious institution and in the presence of the deity. *Ema,* like other religious objects, come in numerous shapes and forms—from representations of the deity enshrined at the institution to colorful designs intended to catch the eye and attract customers. Again, as with amulets and talismans, their designs may signify the qualities they hope to produce: a common *ema* motif shows an arrow hitting the center of a target, while pentagonal votive tablets are often used for academic success, playing on the fact that the word for pentagon (*gokaku*) sounds almost the same as that for scholastic success (*gōkaku*). The padlock on the Hōzanji *ema* (Chapter 1), which is

Artistic *ema* at Kurama Temple

used to ask Kankiten for help in resolving to give something up, is another example of how *ema* design reflects the benefit sought.[24]

While the designs on *ema* are determined by the vendors (the shrines and temples), what is written on them is a matter for the petitioners themselves. Thus the contents—the messages—can be extraordinarily fluid and expressive. Studies of such messages have shown that, in general, they are commonly the province of younger people, especially those in their teenage years or early twenties, and most particularly those concerned with academic success. Other common categories of petition include good health, family safety, and the prevention of misfortune.[25]

Ema may also be used to seek benefits for others—benefits that in turn could be seen to enrich the lives of the petitioners. Thus students petitioning for help in entering a university may also ask that a close friend succeed in this endeavor, too, or a child may ask a deity that his or her parent may recover from illness. Fans may seek benefits for a favorite sports team or music group—no doubt under the premise that their own sense of happiness and self-worth will increase by association or, at the very least, their good feelings. Messages on *ema* asking for the success of one's favorite baseball team can be seen quite frequently. In the eyes of these observers who have been reading *ema* messages for many years, requests for the success of pop groups appear to be growing. Thus an *ema* seen in April 1996 at Roten Shrine in Osaka was written by a young girl who was a fan of the pop group

SMAP. The message asked that the group might become an even bigger success and as a result do more concerts. The girl's desire to bask in the reflected glory of her favorite group was clearly tinged with a pragmatic motive: as they grew more famous, their public visibility would increase, giving her more opportunities to see and hear them.

Pilgrimage and the Pursuit of Benefits

Pilgrimage, which may be followed in diverse ways from the austere to the ludic, represents in any of these forms a major expenditure of time, energy, and money: it is also a practice in which the pursuit of this-worldly benefits features prominently.[26] Although pilgrimage is suffused with other motifs and motivations—tourism, the search for cultural identity, the practice of austerities, and the veneration and memorialization of the ancestors,[27] on whose behalf many pilgrimages are carried out—the seeking of practical benefits has always been a primary, if not predominant, motivation behind the practice. Ambros's study of the Kumano pilgrimage in Heian Japan, cited in the Introduction, tells of women from the Heian court who sought such benefits as successful marriage, worldly advance, and freedom from sickness through their pilgrimages. This-worldly benefits are equally a dominant feature in many of the pilgrimage routes that have flourished in modern Japan, such as the Seven Gods of Good Fortune pilgrimages (*shichifukujin meguri*) that can be found throughout the country. While *shichifukujin meguri* have been popular at least since the Tokugawa era, they have experienced particular popularity in the past two decades or so, especially since the formation in 1973 of one such route on the island of Awaji. Highly publicized and developed by a local Buddhist priest in conjunction with the island's transport companies and tourist board, this pilgrimage now receives, according to island priests, as many as 200,000 pilgrims per year. One of the attractions of the pilgrimage is that it can be done in one day by organized bus tour: participants can make a tour of the whole island and see its scenic spots in a package arrangement that combines tourism and religious pilgrimage. While sightseeing and tourism are important motives in the Awaji route—and are clearly recognized as such by the priest who helped to develop the pilgrimage, Iwatsubo Shinkō, head priest of the temple Hachijōji on the island—the role of the *shichifukujin* as providers of this-worldly benefits has also, according to Iwatsubo, been highly influential in making this pilgrimage attractive. The pilgrimage itself, he says, is wholly centered on the pursuit of this-worldly benefits.[28]

The centrality of this-worldly benefits is highly visible even in pilgrimages that are widely associated with motifs of death and the memorialization of the ancestors. The Shikoku *henro*, the eighty-

eight-temple pilgrimage route around the island of Shikoku centered on the sacred figure of Kōbō Daishi, for example, is suffused
with images related to death: even the clothing of the pilgrims symbolizes death to the mundane world, a popular conception suggesting that completing the pilgrimage enables the pilgrim to enter the
Pure Land at death. One motive for doing the pilgrimage is to memo-
rialize the ancestors and transfer merit to the recently dead, thereby
aiding them in the other world.[29] However, according to a recent survey of pilgrims' requests (onegaigoto) at one of the Shikoku pilgrimage
temples, the overwhelming motivation of its participants indicates
that concern for genze riyaku in all its forms far outweighed concerns
related to death and the ancestors. The survey involved a study of several thousand osamefuda—the slips of paper that pilgrims carry with
them. On these osamefuda pilgrims may write their names and prayer
requests and leave them at each pilgrimage site to inform the deities
of their visit and transmit requests to them. Osamefuda bear the figure
of Kōbō Daishi and customarily carry a printed invocation for some
form of worldly benefit, usually good crops and family safety. That the
pilgrimage temples, which sell the osamefuda, print a formalized request for this-worldly benefits on them indicates their recognition
that seeking genze riyaku is a central and normative practice within the
pilgrimage.

Pilgrims may also write in their own requests and desires. The study
in question found that approximately 15 percent of the osamefuda did
have written requests on them: a total of 1,073 out of 6,961 osamefuda
deposited at the temple were in this category.[30] Given that the osamefuda already contained a printed genze riyaku wish, it is possible that
many pilgrims did not feel the need to write an additional request
of their own. In any event, the number of osamefuda on which requests were written provides a reasonable insight into the wishes of
the pilgrims.

These requests are largely concerned with this-worldly benefits, as
the following table indicates:

Good health (shintai-kenko)	377
For the ancestors (senzo)	139
Family safety (kanai anzen)	124
Healing (byōki heiyu / naoshi)	116
Education (gōkaku)	83
Traffic safety (kōtsū anzen)	77
Good marriage/children (ryōen/kouke/anzan/yome)	52
Success in vows, opening of fortune (shogan/shingan jōjū, kaiun)	38
Prevention of danger (yaku yoke)	22

For the spirits of dead fetuses	
(*mizuko*)	13
Others	32
TOTAL	1,073

The final category, "others," included gratitude, penitence, absolution of sins, prevention of senility (*boke fūji*), and realization of buddhahood in the present body (*sokushin jōbutsu*). The latter two requests were made once each.

Only 13 percent of the written requests (and only around 2 percent of the total number of *osamefuda*) were on behalf of the ancestors. Given that ancestor veneration and memorialization play a major part in the overall structure of Japanese religion, and that many of the pilgrims in Shikoku are elderly (the age group that according to surveys is the most involved in ancestrally related practices),[31] one might perhaps be surprised at the overwhelming prevalence of this-worldly benefits in the expressed wishes of Shikoku pilgrims. The ancestors certainly are not overlooked by these pilgrims. (Indeed, we saw earlier how a group of pilgrims took advantage of a "bargain" chance to have memorial prayers read for their ancestors.) They are, however, generally less central to pilgrims' motivations for doing the pilgrimage than are practical, this-worldly issues. One of the couples (in their mid-sixties) who had paid for the memorial services demonstrated this point quite strikingly: although they prayed for their ancestors as they made the pilgrimage, their primary focus was on seeking benefits for their family—and especially for their grand-children, who were struggling with Japan's notoriously stressful education system. At every temple they visited, they made an offering of a Buddhist sutra they had copied and then prayed that their grand-children would succeed on their path through the Japanese education system.

Social Organizations and the Pursuit of Benefits: *Kō* and *Kaisha*

Pilgrims in Japan often travel in groups, on organized bus tours—often as members of a religious association (*kō*) that exists to promote certain forms of religious activity. The pilgrimage around the island of Shōdoshima in Kagawa prefecture, for example, is an eighty-eight-stage Kōbō Daishi pilgrimage like that of Shikoku. It gets a large number of its pilgrims from the neighboring prefectures of Okayama, Hyōgo, Osaka, and Kyoto, and many of these pilgrims travel in organized groups or *kō,* usually centered on the area in which they live.[32] While such religious associations may share an affinity in terms of residence, on pilgrimages they also express an affinity in terms of a particular benefit or set of benefits that forms the focus of the pilgrimage. This can be discerned by the banners and lists of names of the *kō* that are left at the pilgrimage sites they visit: besides giving the name of the association and the names of the members of the party, they also cite the mutual benefits that are sought. Thus the Tajima Kongōkai (Tajima Diamond Society) from northern Hyōgo prefecture, consisting in all of 350 pilgrims, did the pilgrimage in 1987 (as they do most years). At the temples they visited they put up a poster giving the name of the group and its leaders, the number of pilgrims, the date, and a list of eleven practical benefits they sought, including good crops, travel safety, family safety, family prosperity, business prosperity, and good health.[33]

Although we have concentrated largely on the individual pursuit of benefits, we should stress that it can also be a group or communal activity, as the banners of pilgrimage associations such as the Tajima Kongōkai inform us. The organization of voluntary religious associations (*kō*) is generally focused on the veneration of a particular deity and often a particular site of worship, but the pursuit of practical benefits is frequently an important element in this process.[34] Thus the Fujikō, a religious association organized around the veneration and ascent of Mount Fuji that was active from the late sixteenth century until well into the Tokugawa period, had as its basic aim "the securing of material benefits in this life."[35]

It is not only through voluntary associations that communal prayers for benefits occur. Such prayers have been an intrinsic element of shrine festivals (*matsuri*) in which communities petition local deities for all manner of benefits important to the health of the community at large.[36] Besides the communal festivals and group prayers that still occur in many parts of Japan, modern Japanese may find themselves engaged in communal pursuit of benefits in the workplace. Company workers in the same unit might, for example, express the desire for practical benefits on behalf of their group. Consider the inscription on an *ema* placed by members of the Matsushita Electric Company's Publicity Department at Chōmeiji in Shiga prefecture in 1987: "May we win the company production prize for the fifth time."[37]

Many Japanese businesses organize communal rituals in which employees join in worship of a deity (almost invariably a *kami*, for the Shinto gods are closely associated with issues of production) and pray for the company's success and prosperity. Indeed, many companies have developed links with specific shrines whose gods thus have become co-opted as guardian deities of the firm.[38] Company-sponsored rituals may be used to reinforce the employees' sense of identity with the company, to bring senior management together in communal rit-

Shrine on a modern business building

uals, and, most important for our purposes, to petition the company deity for practical benefits and its support in enhancing the company's fortunes. A recent book by a group of Japanese researchers studying this phenomenon examined forty-nine such companies and the shrines with which they were associated. It included many of the best-known names in Japanese business—such as Shiseidō, the leading cosmetics manufacturer, associated with the Seikō ("success") Inari shrine located on the roof of the company headquarters in the Ginza, Tokyo; the Toyota Car Company, which has "adopted" the Hōtō Shrine in the city of Toyota in Aichi prefecture (the shrine is popularly known as the Toyota Shrine); and the Tōshiba electrical group, whose main factories and offices are in the Yokohama-Kawasaki area and which has a number of relationships with shrines in the region.[39]

As economic activity in Japan has shifted from agriculture to business and industry, so too have Shinto shrines. Nowadays they are likely to be found on top of buildings, on factory grounds, and in office buildings as well as in the countryside. Because companies have become such a focus of modern communal life, Honda Sōichirō has suggested that "business companies are the new villages (*mura*) of industrial society that have replaced the old villages of agricultural society."[40] Company shrines even have their own annual observances (*nenjū gyōji*) and festivals attended prominently by top officials. The

Hitachi Company, for instance, has six regular ceremonies: in addition to occasions such as New Year's, they include observances of the anniversary of the founding of the company (July 16), fire prevention (December 1), and employee safety (July 1). Kumano Shrine serves as the company shrine, and branches have been established at most Hitachi facilities, including those of its subsidiary companies.[41] At factories where branch shrines have not been built, employees face in the direction of Kumano Shrine and carry out their observances on the designated days.[42]

While company religion resembles that of the *kō* associations insofar as employees form a ready-made (though not entirely voluntary) membership, it differs in that the organization itself becomes the object of respect and even reverence. Associations normally do not bother to perform a ritual in observance of the founding of the group, but companies do. Company officials can even take on sacerdotal functions—as the head of the Osaka Mitsubishi foundry does when he becomes the main officiant of the three annual *matsuri* held at the Tosa Inari Shrine located just beside the main gate.[43] While it might be said that a businessman/priest praying for the success of his company and the safety of his employees represents a secularization of sacred Shinto, he can also be seen as engaging in a kind of sacralization of secular business. This inseparability of the sacred and secular dimensions, as we have seen repeatedly, is a central part of the framework of practical benefits.

The Dynamics of Practice

Just as the practices for worldly benefits can be explained in terms of commerce, so too can companies use religious language and activities to give focus to important business issues. Our brief look at pilgrimage associations and the religious practices of companies—new villages that must have their Shinto shrines—points to the communal aspect of the pursuit of practical benefits. The ethical demands and the need for effort, discussed earlier in terms of the individual quest for benefits, are heightened in the communal context where such responsibilities affect the welfare of others as well as oneself.

As this outline has shown, the practices involved with purchase and acquisition are the most visible element of life at popular shrines and temples. In them we can see how people go about purchasing the benefits they desire and how they seek to attain fulfillment to their heart's content. The openness with which individual as well as corporate desires can be expressed is one consequence of the way in which Buddhist scriptures speak of the fulfillment of desire as a divine act that transcends the limits of human self-satisfaction. Benefits are not just sanctioned by the gods and the buddhas; they are provided by them. People must pay for what they get, though purchase invites complex considerations of value and questions about paying too much or too little. But once payment is made, the system, if it may be called that, sets in motion priests as intercessors as well as a wide variety of objects that are transferred, once the power of the deity has been consecrated in them, from temples and shrines to homes, cars, offices, schools, and other places and then taken back for renewal. Very little of this is abstract or fixed; the practices are concrete and dynamic. The petitioners are always in motion—quite vigorously so in the cases of pilgrimage and religious tourism. The practices for worldly benefits are caught up in this vigor because they are portable, especially when amulets are used, for amulets make it possible for the divine powers to go wherever the people go. Going to the gods is essential, but the gods also go with the people.

This efficiency and convenience do not come naturally. Practices must be maintained, revised, discarded, redesigned, promoted, and even forced cleverly onto people who might otherwise not be interested. We have said much about the importance of purchase, but there is an equally essential counterpart activity, the selling of benefits, that encourages purchase and creates the ambiance in which the culture of benefits can flourish. It is to this issue, and to the processes of creating and promoting the reputations of gods, buddhas, temples, and shrines, that we turn next.

6

Selling Benefits
The Marketing of Efficacy and Truth

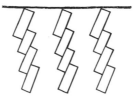

SINCE RELIGIONS DO NOT EXIST purely as teachings and practices apart from institutions, they survive and develop in ways necessary for the well-being of all organizations. Priests are aware that temples cannot exist without good finances—and that such support comes only with effort. If this-worldly benefits are to be purchased, they must be sold. Priests emulate the world of business in marketing these benefits, but they also use techniques of storytelling and preaching that developed in religious circles long before the appearance of commercial advertising. The possibility of combining traditional propagation methods with modern marketing is always there, but it takes the initiative of a good entrepreneur to transform potentiality into actuality.

Creating a Religious Department Store

In a December 1986 article in the *Asahi shinbun,* one of Japan's largest daily newspapers, Ishidō Ekyō, the priest in charge of the administrative office of Nakayama-dera in Takarazuka, commented on the close friendship between his grandfather (a former priest of the temple) and Kobayashi Ichizō, the founder of the Hankyū Railway and department store conglomerate. It is the Hankyū Railway line that connects Nakayama-dera, which is located only three minutes' walk from the Hankyū station of that name, with Osaka and the other cities of the Kansai area and has made it readily accessible to the large population of this region. Ishidō, while noting that this family friendship continued (he was a friend of the current head of the Hankyū organization, a scion of the founding family), drew an interesting parallel between his own family and the Hankyū founder: Kobayashi

had built a department store whereas his own family—as priests of
the temple—sought to build what Ishidō called a "temple department store" (*tera no depaato*).[1]

The priest went on to note that although Nakayama-dera is an extremely popular temple, receiving around 2 million visitors a year, it
faced a continuing need to diversify and find new ways of attracting
people into its precincts. Nakayama-dera's primary sources of religious fame and income, which comes from donations, the sale of
amulets, and fees for prayers and rituals performed there, relate to
the Nakayama Kannon's reputation in connection with the benefit of
safe childbirth and to the temple's position as one of the thirty-three
temples on the Saikoku pilgrimage route. But as Ishidō recognized,
these alone could not guarantee the temple's future: there was no as-
surance that the Saikoku pilgrimage would always draw in large numbers of pilgrims,[2] while changing social patterns were affecting the
numbers who might come to seek safe childbirth. Japan has, like other
industrialized countries, experienced a shift in its population structure and has witnessed an aging population and a declining birthrate
in recent decades: by the mid-1980s, when Ishidō's comments were
made, the rates had fallen to around 1.7 births per female.[3] This decline has had an effect on Nakayama-dera (and doubtless also on
other temples and shrines whose specialty is safe childbirth): fewer
births mean fewer people praying for safe childbirth. Hence the
temple has become aware of a gradual decline in the number of customers using this most central of its services, and this trend is likely to
continue.

Since the temple cannot depend on its staple support structures
(pilgrimage and safe childbirth) to assure its future prosperity, it
must find alternative ways of attracting support and customers. This,
Ishidō comments, it has done by a process of diversification and expansion of its areas of specialization and by capitalizing on the social
patterns within the contemporary market. The declining birthrate
and the smaller number of children per family, coupled with the general rise in prosperity in postwar Japan, have meant that greater attention and economic resources are being lavished on each child. In
religious terms this has meant greater expenditure per child on life-
cycle rituals such as *shichigosan,* the festival in autumn where parents
take their children (usually those aged seven, five, and three) to the
shrine or temple for a protective blessing. *Shichigosan* has, in late-
twentieth-century Japan, become an opulent affair mixing religious
rituals with social and consumerist display, and the institutions that
cater for it have benefited accordingly.[4] As an institution specializing
in the birth of children, Nakayama-dera could easily extend itself
by moving into postnatal spiritual care and has established its own

life-cycle rituals for the young—such as *hatsumiyamairi* (the first shrine visit, when the new baby is placed under the protection of the gods) and the *shichigosan* festival. While these two rituals are more normally observed at Shinto shrines, they are (like most calendrical religious events) not the sole preserve of Shinto. Both have been widely promoted by Buddhist temples as well—especially when, as with Nakayama-dera, they have a claim to the market because of their role as overseers of birth. Given that many parents pray to the Nakayama Kannon for the safe delivery of their child into the world, it is not surprising that they feel inclined to place the newborn child under the temple's protection through performing the *hatsumi-yamairi* rite and to continue that cycle of protection through the *shichigosan* ritual.[5]

Thus the temple has promoted its *shichigosan* rites in recent years, and this has served as a counterweight to the declining numbers of people visiting for safe childbirth reasons. It has, as Ishidō noted, diversified further by developing a natural forest reserve and a hiking trail that leads over the hills behind it to its inner temple (Okunoin) and, beyond that, to another of the Kansai region's famed *goriyaku* centers that we have encountered before in this book: Kiyoshi Kōjin. Ishidō, in mentioning these points, talks of the temple area as a recreation site as well as a religious center—a place where families can come and take in nature, hike, and of course pray.

Nakayama-dera has added other strings to its bow besides those mentioned in the *Asahi shinbun* article. It has, for example, become a participant in the Hankyū Ensen Saikoku *shichifukujin* pilgrimage (mentioned in Chapter 4), which was developed by the Hankyū Railway. It also has subtemples in its precincts catering for all manner of widely sought benefits such as educational success, and it actively promotes its various annual rituals and festive occasions and the benefits that can be accrued through them.[6] Moreover, it is actively involved in the practice of *mizuko kuyō* (memorial services for aborted fetuses)—one of the most thriving, if controversial, Buddhist temple activities in Japan in the past two or so decades. While some may consider it ironic that the temple thus caters for fetuses aborted in the womb (a practice which has led to criticisms that temples are thereby encouraging abortion) and also helps those in the womb to have a safe passage out,[7] both practices are in effect ways of caring for the fetus/child in its passage out of the womb into this world or (in the case of *mizuko*) to another one. Thus it is not surprising to find a temple dealing both with *mizuko* and safe childbirth within its precincts.

One might suggest, therefore, that Nakayama-dera is already a religious department store offering numerous services—from practical

benefits to receational activities that can provide for the well-being of
its clientele. One can also see how it has risen to the challenges of the
age and the changing social situation by expanding its services to
meet the new circumstances.

Marketing Reputation through Stories

Ishidō's comments, which relate to the marketing of religious services and the ways in which institutions promote themselves, provide
a suitable entry point into our next area of investigation. We have already discussed how benefits are purchased by petitioners through
their transactions with religious institutions. We now turn to the ways
in which the institutions themselves and their officiants encourage
these transactions by publicizing and selling benefits. In so doing we
examine how the reputations of religious institutions as providers of
benefits may be proselytized and how the benefits they offer may be
publicized.

Whether produced by temples and shrines themselves or written
by outsiders, stories are an important means for establishing the
reputation of a place and getting the word out to many people. In an
earlier age, before the development of advertising and marketing, literature that reached a wide audience through storytelling, drama,
and painting, as well as the written word, played a major role in enhancing the reputations of temples and shrines.

In the *Tale of Genji*, for instance, we hear the story of a young girl
from the nobility (whom we later discover to be Lady Tamakazura)
who, having been left by her mother in the care of a nurse and her
husband, had lost her position in society. She grew up in Higo, far
from the capital and when, aged twenty, she was brought back to
Kyoto to enter society there and find a good marriage, this task appeared difficult because of her lack of connections in the city. Those
who looked after her, including the vice-governor of Bungo province
(who was the oldest brother of the family that cared for her) sent her
to various religious institutions to pray for help: the vice-governor was
confident, he stated, that all would turn out well: "Our prayers will be
answered and she will be put back in her rightful place someday," he
assured his mother.[8] So saying he decided to send the girl on a pilgrimage to Hasedera, remarking of the temple: "It is known even in
China as the Japanese temple among them all which gets things done.
It can't help doing something for a poor lady back after all those years
so far away."[9] While visiting Hasedera the girl and her companions
encounter a former attendant of her mother's who now worked in the
household of Genji: the old attendant herself, having lost contact
with the girl, had prayed at the temple seeking to find her. In her joy

at finding her again after all these years, the attendant brings Lady Tamakazura to the attention of the Genji household and her position in society is thus established. The attendant also informs one of the temple priests that she must go on retreat to give thanks for this benefit of finding the girl, and he, delighted, replies: "Excellent. Our prayers over the years have been heard."[10]

The story expresses typical themes: a prayer for a thoroughly worldly desire of advancement, backed by a demanding religious practice (the pilgrimage, we are informed, was done on foot and was hard for a young woman unaccustomed to such exertions),[11] is met by an efficacious result. The joy of success is felt also by the priest and by the old attendant who engages in rites of gratitude to the deity because her own prayers have been answered. Although the "miracle" of this benefit is perfectly explainable—it is caused by the two parties happening to be at a popular pilgrimage site at the same time—it is the Hase Kannon, to whom both were on pilgrimage, that brought them together. Truly it had lived up to the reputation that had reached as far as China: it had "got things done." Doubtless, too, this story increased its reputation and made it more likely that others would come to visit it.

The development of a reputation depends not simply on getting things done, of course, but on that ability being made known to the public at large. It is here we see the fusion between the commercially pragmatic activities of temples and shrines, their claims to religious truth, and their assertions that they are places whose deities are active and caring entities who will listen to the prayers of petitioners. Without effective proselytization and propagation—in other words, without effective marketing—the deeds of their buddhas and *kami* will remain little known and shrines and temples will be unable to draw the crowds that enable them to flourish or, as examples such as Ichibata Yakushi tell us, to build religious organizations and networks. The more efficacious a deity or buddha appears to be in granting benefits, the more likely it is to attract customers. And the more satisfied they are, the more likely they will come back to the temple or shrine and develop a faith relationship and spread the word to their friends and acquaintances.

While the *Genji* story of the wonders of the Hase Kannon did not create its reputation, it did preserve and propagate it. The creation of reputation is normally accomplished through *engi*—the foundation stories we discussed in Chapter 1—that tell of the beginnings of a temple or shrine, usually as a consequence of a supernatural event. Augmenting the role of foundation stories have been tales of miraculous efficacy, which have frequently been woven into collections that were used as the basis of preaching and spreading the word about the efficacies of particular temples and shrines. Collections such as the *Hasedera Kannon genki* (Miraculous record of the Hasedera Kannon)—a collection whose dates are unclear but which developed after Lady Tamakazura had made her pilgrimage there—reinforced the reputation of that Kannon by relating fifty-two stories telling of Kannon's wondrous powers to cure illness and provide wealth, victory, and other benefits.[12]

Such collections, Yoshiko Dysktra suggests, were probably used by wandering professional preachers as a means of raising funds for the shrines and temples they served in the Heian and Kamakura periods. The necessity of raising funds in such ways was brought about by changing economic circumstances: the decline of aristocratic power and financial strength from the late Heian period onward led to a loss of patronage for the temples and shrines, and hence they were forced to start raising funds elsewhere. By enthusing the populace with tales of miracle and sanctity—and thus persuading them to make donations, procure amulets, and make visits to shrines and temples to pray to the sacred figures—the professional and itinerant preachers of the late Heian and Kamakura periods strove to provide a new economic basis for religious institutions.[13] Figures such as the *hijiri*, itinerant preachers who, as Shinno Toshikazu has shown, were affiliated with temples and shrines and served as mediators between them and the populace,[14] thus played a major part in spreading the reputations of shrines and temples. Donald F. McCallum has shown that they had a similar role in spreading the cult of Zenkōji and advertising the powers of its Amidist icon in medieval Japan.[15]

The spreading of miracle tales, whether by itinerant preachers or by temple priests, as well as the collecting and publishing of such stories, has contributed to the popularity of pilgrimage routes such as Shikoku. Miyuki Shōichirō argues that the existence of stories of *reigen* (miracles) and the hope of receiving them promoted the growth of this pilgrimage in the Tokugawa era.[16] Besides the collections of pilgrimage tales gathered together by itinerants such as Shinnen (Chapter 4), individual temples collected their own *reigenki*, or miracle tales, which affirmed the immanence and efficacy of their buddhas and Kōbō Daishi in aiding supplicants.[17]

The supply of miracle tales is not limited to the literature of the past, however. New stories are constantly being developed and told in Shikoku and elsewhere. At Hachijōji, a popular *shichifukujin* pilgrimage stop on Awaji Island, visitors are told of the virtues of the temple's *omamori*—a small, flat, black piece of stone engraved with a prayer inscription. As the priest informed his listeners (both publicly and in private, for he repeated the same things in an interview), such amulets are regarded by the locals as being highly efficacious. He spoke also of how, when the great Hanshin earthquake struck in January 1995, few people in the area had been injured or killed, though Awaji was the epicenter of the quake—in stark contrast to the five thousand or more killed and the many thousands injured a few miles away across the straits of Akashi in Kobe. This, the priest averred, was considered by the locals to be a result of the amulets' protective powers. Indeed, many claimed that their amulets had broken during the earthquake. The stone amulet had thus absorbed its impact—clearly demonstrating the *migawari* function of a buddha or deity in absorbing bad luck and protecting the owner of the amulet or talisman. This explication of the sacred and efficacious powers of the Hachijōji amulet was woven skillfully into a short sermon for the benefit of pilgrims to the temple. Naturally it encouraged them to purchase amulets.[18]

Largely produced and disseminated by priests, foundation stories and miraculous tales form a copious genre of literature shared by aristocrats and commoners alike. These stories constitute a kind of premodern media knowledge comprised of well-circulated stories that were no longer confined to a specific locale but were shared by a larger audience exposed to the word-of-mouth broadcasts of a multitude of itinerant monks and tellers of tales. Ordinary believers, too, are part of the network of stories. Their numbers increase with each telling of a new story about how someone was helped by the buddha or deity of a particular place.

Advertising through Events, Festivals, and Rituals

Apart from creating and propagating reputations through stories, religious institutions have been adept at drawing attention to themselves through the promotion of ritual events and festivals. In Chapter 1 we commented on many of these events—such as *hatsumōde* and the annual cycle of rituals and festivals (*nenjū gyōji*), as well as *ennichi*, which are both special prayer days and public markets. Here we draw attention to an event that has been widely used for promotion, especially by Buddhist temples, and that is the *kaichō*, literally the "opening of the curtain" to reveal at periodic intervals religious images that are otherwise hidden.

Many of the most important Buddhist images are of this sort—considered so sacred that they are normally shielded from public view except on certain festive occasions. The concept behind the practice of hiding icons, as Donald F. McCallum observes, is simple: "If people can see and worship the icon at any time they wished, the spiritual resonance of this activity would be devalued."[19] The secluding of the image fulfils another and perhaps more vital service for the temples, however. As McCallum comments, "in many ways the most effective fundraising technique available to a Buddhist temple is careful control of access to its most important icon."[20] By controlling access, temple authorities not only enhance the apparent powers and reputation of the image, and hence the temple, but they also can count on large crowds and income on the occasions when the image is open to public view. As McCallum notes, the *kaichō* is "a time when temples can hope for substantial donations."[21]

The term *"kaichō"* also referred to taking sacred icons to another location to display them to a public who ordinarily would not have seen them. This type of *kaichō* activity—which also provided the occasion for prayer, the seeking of benefits, and, of course, the garnering of funds by the temples—proved especially popular in Tokugawa times. As Kitamura Gyōen has shown, between 1654 and 1868 there were some 1,566 *kaichō* events in Edo alone.[22] Among the various icons that were transported and revealed to the faithful in different locations in this way was the Fudō of Shinshōji at Narita, which was displayed in Edo twelve times in this period.[23] McCallum gives accounts of how a replica of the Zenkōji Triad was transported around the country for similar purposes.[24] Statues from temples in Kyoto were brought to Edo in this period for *kaichō* displays, as well, and from these normally hidden buddhas from distant temples, it was believed, worshipers could acquire the same benefits as if they had gone to the temple itself.[25] The stated intention of such displays, Kitamura comments, was to allow the ordinary people to experience the powerful benefits of these images, but the reality, he wryly notes, was to raise money for the temples, usually to cover economic burdens such as repairs.[26]

The use of *kaichō* and other such spectacles was at times effective not just in the short term but also in creating long-term customs that were of benefit to temples. The case of Nozaki Kannon Temple in the northern Ikoma region, which was in the vanguard of institutions in that area in developing a clientele for itself, demonstrates how, through the skillful use of public events, a priest and institution were able to create a custom of religious veneration and pilgrimage. In the Genroku era (1688–1703), the temple began to hold *kaichō* exhibits and conduct lotteries as a way of encouraging customers. Soon large crowds began to arrive, and the temple, building on this success, then staged performances of *kabuki* and *joruri* (ballad dramas) as a means of strengthening the custom of *Nozaki mairi* (visits to Nozaki Kannon), a custom which they had created and which assured a steady clientele.[27]

Although *kaichō* events helped certain temples such as Zenkōji and Nozaki Kannon to become famous, even unknown village temples benefited from such activities. In his excellent study of a once-every-thirty-three-year *kaichō* ritual held in 1993 at Jingūji, a rural temple in Niigata prefecture, William M. Bodiford describes how temples and communities from the surrounding area cooperated to stage this special ritual, which touched not only on religious sentiments, but on feelings of nostalgia, social relations, and a sense of individual mortality.[28] While the event was a great success due to active community involvement, the head priest, Takeuchi Michio, was well aware that if the ritual had not been held, few people would have even noticed. The ceremonies, which took place over a period of thirty-three days, he insisted, "represent only the priests' attempts to maintain a temple tradition and do not reflect the villagers' desires or sentiments."[29] With the intersectarian help of priests in the area, Takeuchi and his group organized a variety of events and projects, the most critical of which was the direct fund-raising campaign (*kanjin*). The campaign committee sent to several thousand people a solicitation letter that began:

> One thousand twelve hundred years have passed since Jingūji's main image, a Kannon with eleven heads and one thousand arms, came here to become the protective deity of the Tsumari region. Throughout the ages this Kannon has been praised for responding to the prayers of local people and for granting numerous miracles to people in Tsumari and to people everywhere who have deep faith.[30]

Reminding people that they also needed to repay their indebtedness to their ancestors, the letter combined the key elements of the temple's foundation story, the power of its deity, and the benefits granted along with its plans for the series of ceremonies. Received by people who otherwise might not have cared about this special ritual, the letter was extremely effective: the campaign, which originally had set a goal of \$350,000, netted more than \$500,000 from some three thousand sponsors.[31]

On a smaller scale, the *kaichō* ceremonies at Tamon-in, a small Tendai temple in a rice farming community in Chiba prefecture, followed similar patterns. Suffering from ill health, the head priest, Ichishima Shōshin, was not feeling up to the task of staging the thirty-three-year Kannon *kaichō* ritual that was due at his temple in 1996. Being aware that the community would probably not even remember that it was time for this observance again, Ichishima felt spurred by a deep sense of obligation and faith and threw himself into the task of organizing the event with the help of his family and small temple staff. As word about the event spread, people offered unsolicited help and ample donations made it possible to undertake the expensive job of repairing the small temple building that housed the Kannon. Gratified by the tremendous support he had received, Ichishima thought his initiative was more than worth his efforts, especially when the climax of the nighttime ceremony was reached. As the doors to the outdoor shrine were slowly opened, the Kannon, which had not been seen for a third of a century, caught the full glare of the flood-lights in the courtyard and seemed to add its own illumination to the night. The large crowd in the courtyard spontaneously let out a long gasp of awe and reverence, and bowed to the ground. The offering box was so filled with coins that Ichishima, feeling a deep sense of gratitude to the community, donated its contents to a senior citizens group which later reported that the coins amounted to $1,300.[32]

Taking place only infrequently, *kaichō* are special events that aug-ment the usual ceremonies that attract people on a regular basis. Temple priests know that *kaichō* hardly form the basis for sustained support, but their very infrequency and special character go a long way toward the making of reputation. The *kaichō* at Jingūji sets it apart from other temples in the area and has even attracted the attention of a foreign scholar whose published report makes it known to a wider international audience. To reach a much larger group of people, therefore, temples and shrines use what businesses and other institutions use: mass media.

Contemporary Media

The practice of *kaichō*, opening normally hidden sacred images up to public view, continues to bring people to temples. But the other as-pect of Tokugawa *kaichō*—bringing sacred statues to places whose in-habitants would otherwise find it hard to visit in its home location—has ceased to be of much importance in the modern era when people can travel around freely and swiftly. Modernity, however, has brought shrines and temples new means of advertising their wares and benefits in such public places as train stations and billboards. On the Chūgoku expressway that leads into Osaka from the west of Japan, near the town of Senri a large billboard informs motorists they are only twenty kilometers from Ishikiri Shrine and the benefits it offers. Train stations and railway carriages are a popular spot for advertising: the Jishu Shrine in Kyoto, famed for its benefits of bringing couples together in love, makes use of the various rail companies in the Kyoto region in this way. Sometimes temples and shrines may take this pro-cess a stage further by organizing, in conjunction with railway com-panies, a combined promotion and visiting deal. Thus in April 1996 posters at Japan Rail's Osaka station (and many other locations in the area) advertised a *boke fūji kippu*—a prevention of senility rail ticket.

For the sum of 3,000 yen one could purchase a railway ticket that allowed for travel to and from two temples in the Kansai region that specialized in *boke fūji:* Ofusa Kannon at Sakurai in Nara prefecture and Abe Monju-in, also in the Nara region. The price included *ofuda* from these temples.[33]

Newspapers provide another medium for advertising: Daikannon Temple in Mie prefecture, home of a thirty-three-meter-high statue of Kannon able to help people attain good luck and protect them from misfortune, regularly advertised itself and its sacred "opening of good fortune pendants" (*kaiun pendanto*), inscribed with the text of the *Heart Sutra,* during the 1980s in Japanese newspapers.[34] At New Year, in particular, shrines and temples often advertise themselves and the benefits they offer, as well as any special rituals, in the newspapers and on television. In the mid-1980s, for example, a temple began to place a small advertisement in the Nagoya editions of a daily newspaper drawing attention to its *hatsumōde* rituals and services as a means of attracting customers. During the *hatsumōde* period after the ad had been placed, the priests at the temple discussed frequently among themselves whether the numbers visiting the temple had increased and whether the advertisement had had any effect.[35] Sometimes such advertisements are, like the Japan Rail ads, placed by transport companies in connection with shrines and temples. Such companies have played an important part in making shrines and temples more accessible in the modern era and developing a mass market for them.[36] An advertisement placed in the *Asahi shinbun* by a group of railway companies in the Tokyo region at the end of December 1992, for example, drew attention to the forthcoming *hatsumōde* rites of 1993. The advertisement gave a list of nineteen shrines and temples in the Tokyo region that could be accessed by different railway lines and cited the benefits they offered.[37] Among the places cited were many of the great benefit sites of the region that we have met already in this book, such as Shinshōji at Narita and Saijōji at Odawara.

Jishu Jinja, which calls itself the "Cupid of Japan," not only advertises heavily on trains but also through leaflets that make it possible to use another agent of modern communication: the postal service. Twenty kinds of amulets, ranging in price from 500 to 2,000 yen ($5 to $20) are pictured and described along with their respective shipping and handling fees. The leaflet contains a special tear-off request form that lists eighteen different benefits and instructs users to circle the ones they wish the shrine priests to pray for on their behalf. Another section calls for the petitioner's name, address, birthdate, and the name of the person, if any, for whom the prayers are being requested. In the space provided for notes or comments, the leaflet carries a request: if you do not wish to receive an *ofuda* or a certificate of the completion of prayers (*kigan shūryōsho*), please write "reply not necessary." The last section provides three choices, one of which should be circled: daily prayers for a whole year for 150,000 yen ($1,500); for a month for 15,000 yen ($150); or for a week for 5,000 yen ($50). At the bottom of this form for mail-order benefits is written the assurance that "even though prayers are requested by letter, the benefits are the same."[38]

New Technologies: Selling Benefits by Fax and Internet

The means by which benefits are sold do not, as we have seen, remain static. New technologies mean new ways of transmitting messages. This is evidenced by the ways in which Japanese religious institutions have adapted to new information technologies and media. Computers have become almost standard equipment for shrines and temples these days, as have facsimile machines: one can now fax requests for prayers and amulets to certain shrines and temples. The Dazaifu Tenmangū Shrine advertises a fax number to which one can send requests for academic success: the cost (in 1994) of this service was 3,000 yen ($30). According to a popular guidebook to prayer shrines and temples, this service has proved especially popular among students living far from the shrine. Those wishing to send their request by fax are asked to provide their name, age, address, and the school or college to which they seek entrance: when the fax is received, a prayer will immediately be addressed by shrine priests to the deity; within a week an *omamori*, an *ofuda*, and a certificate that the prayer was addressed as requested to the deity will be sent to the petitioner.[39] As Josef A. Kyburz has noted, the sale of this benefit by fax shows a subtle sales strategy: the fax number to be used for this purpose is 092-921-1010. In shrine advertisements this is read as "*o-kuni kuni ichiban no (gakkō ni) tōre tōre,*" which, as Kyburz notes, translates roughly as "Pass! Pass into the best (school) of the province, nay, the country!" The fax number itself thus evokes a sense of magical efficacy that is intensified by the imperative use of the verb (*tōre*).[40]

The latest arena into which Japanese religious organizations and institutions have penetrated for proselytization is the world of cyberspace. Although still in its infancy as a means of religious propagation and advertising, the Internet has become a growing new avenue through which religious organizations have been able to publicize themselves. It is widely considered that the new religions are the most technologically advanced and most in tune with the use of media techniques in Japan: new religions such as Agonshū, which prides itself on being one of the most up-to-date religions in terms of technological awareness and techniques, have certainly established an Internet presence.[41] Yet the older and allegedly less dynamic religions, along with some of their shrines and temples, have also been swift to get aboard the Internet bandwagon. Indeed, this is an area where the older religions may well be ahead of the new religions. Many major sectarian Buddhist organizations such as the Ōtani and Honganji branches of Jōdo Shinshū have home pages, as do Shinto organizations such as the Jinja Honchō, while a growing number of Shinto shrines and Buddhist temples have acquired an Internet presence, which they use as a medium for promoting themselves and selling benefits. Several of these institutions we have encountered already in this book, such as Saijō Inari, Kawasaki Daishi, and Izumo Taisha.

Given the ease with which entries may be modified in cyberspace, such home pages may change quite rapidly and now include increasing amounts of information and means of interacting with the shrine or temple. Kawasaki Daishi's home page, for example, in late summer 1996 contained an abbreviated version of the temple's foundation legend that provides the legitimation for the sacred power of the temple, a brief account of the powers of Kōbō Daishi, a section on visiting the temple giving a guide to the temple courtyard and buildings, along with a list of its yearly calendrical events (*nenjū gyōji*), including details on those coming in the next two months, and sections on the various talismans and protective charms available at the temple, ritual services, and their costs. It also offered brief details about Kawasaki Daishi's role in protecting automobiles and providing the benefits of traffic safety, as well as a section on the merits of the esoteric fire ritual (*ogoma no kudoku*) performed at Kawasaki Daishi to seek blessings and this-worldly benefits.[42] By early 1997 the entry had expanded to include more details on virtually every topic dealt with on the home page, such as a paragraph or more describing each calendrical event with pictures to illustrate each section or topic.

A number of additions had been made as well. Thus one could now (with the correct software) view the *goma* ritual and hear the Buddhist chants that accompany it and be taken on a guided Internet worship tour of the temple. In this tour the visitor is taken through the temple gates and instructed to conduct purificatory ablutions by washing her hands (in the pictures we see a young kimono-clad woman) at the temple fountain, to offer incense at the temple, and to purify her body and mind in the incense smoke. The visitor is then directed to the office where *goma* ritual prayers may be requested, to the *goma* ritual hall, and then to the main hall of worship. Here we are shown the monetary offering box and the woman placing a donation in it: it appears from the picture that she may be offering a banknote rather than coins. Her action is accompanied by the words "since our requests are many, we should make this amount of monetary offerings (*negaigoto ga ōi no de osaisen wa koregurai*)." After the offering one prays for good things to happen and is then directed to the place where one can get divination slips: the woman is shown reading hers, and afterward we are informed that we should hang the slips at the temple after reading them. The Kawasaki Daishi Internet site, then, presents details about the temple, how to get to it, the benefits it offers, the prices one has to pay, and encouragement to engage in religious actions such as prayers, purifications, and offerings.

At the Saijō Inari Internet site we find maps of the temple, lists of the various *nenjū gyōji* that take place at it, and a section discussing the acquisition of benefits at the temple.[43] This site illustrates how the reputation of the temple's deity as a provider of benefits has spread and attracted the faith of large numbers of people. Like Kawasaki Daishi's site, this home page presents a brief illustrated guide on how to visit and pray at the temple. It tells people to purify themselves before praying by washing their hands and mouths with water at the fountain, to go to the temple office (*kitō uketsuke*) to request the prayer services they wish to have done, and to pray at the main hall of worship as their petition is being put before the deities, making an act of obeisance (*gasshō*) and reciting the sacred mantra (*daimoku*) used at Saijō Inari.[44] Visitors are also told to go and pray at all the seventy-seven subshrines and temples within the Saijō Inari complex and to remember to light and offer incense at each of them. The section on benefits emphasizes that although the main hall of worship is guarded by a torii (Shinto gateway) and is itself built in Shinto style, the institution is in fact a temple (that is, Buddhist) and thus one should perform Buddhist-style prayer rituals when visiting. Ironically the institution is listed on Internet guides under the label "Shinto."[45] Reflecting the close interaction between tourism and religious institutions in Japan—in particular Saijō Inari's fame as one of the central tourist attractions in the area—the home page also provides a link to a site giving tourist information about the Okayama region in which the temple is situated.

While the Kawasaki Daishi and Saijō Inari Internet sites are at present largely informative, in that they advertise the institutions themselves and the services and religious goods they offer, others have taken their Internet presence a stage further by constructing interactive sites through which one can petition directly for benefits. At some sites one can access, download, and print out copies of talismans and lucky charms (available from a number of Internet shrine and temple sites such as that of the Takasu Shrine in northern Kyūshū).[46] Sometimes one can even make petitions and have special prayer services performed through the use of the Internet. The

World Wide Web home page of the Tamō Hachiman Shrine in Ehime prefecture, for example, informs visitors: "One can worship at Tamō Hachiman Shrine through the Internet. Whether needing to turn to the gods in times of trouble, or reporting to them times of happiness, please come and worship here one time, either on your own or with your friends and family."[47] One can even click on a computer icon that makes a clapping sound of the type one makes when actually praying at a Shinto shrine. Visitors are also informed that in worshiping at the shrine via the Internet they can also get amulets and talismans for various benefits such as traffic safety, academic success, and the first shrine visit of children via the Internet. Those interested in these services can progress to a subsequent page at the site where they can see images of four different amulets for such benefits as educational success and traffic safety: these are just examples of the various *omamori* and *ofuda* that have been sacralized by the shrine's priests (*tōjinja no shinkan ni yotte shingan shimashita*) and can be purchased from the shrine, via the Internet, for a monetary offering (*saisen*) of 800 yen each, postage included. To offer such a prayer and to order such amulets one fills in an electronic order form giving one's name, age, and address. By clicking on the appropriate box at the bottom of the form, the order is electronically mailed to the shrine.

The home page continues with sections on fortune-telling—brief predictions of the future based on astrology and star signs—and accounts of the various festivals and ritual events to be held at the shrine in the coming months. In autumn 1996, other offerings included a warning on the dangerous *E. coli* 0-157 bacterium, which had recently caused a number of food poisoning outbreaks in Japan; a map of how to get to the shrine; and information on the priest who created the home page (telling visitors, inter alia, what car he drives and that his father was also a priest and inviting them to e-mail him their comments). It also lists other Internet sites that might be of interest to visitors (including links to adult sites such as Penthouse and Playboy). In early autumn 1996 it also advertised prayers for election victory in the forthcoming general election. This particular posting by the shrine represents, as noted in Chapter 1, an example of how religious institutions are capable of making rapid responses to contemporary situations and, indeed, cashing in on them. The Tamō Hachiman Shrine is just one of a growing wave of religious institutions that have taken the uses of the Internet a stage further than simple advertising and publicity—to on-line interactive veneration and the purchase of charms and amulets.

Although Internet-based religious veneration (*intaanetto sanpai*) is currently in its infancy, it is growing rapidly. The speed with which some institutions have caught on to the new technology suggests that this will be an area of religious growth for a long time to come. At present it is a resource that only a few institutions have begun to exploit, but as priests become accustomed to using computers as they have become accustomed to placing advertisements in trains, buses, and newspapers and printing up temple and shrine leaflets for public distribution, this area of activity will only increase in size and scope.

As this-worldly benefits and the amulets symbolizing them become increasingly available to worshipers sitting at their computers far from the shrines and temples that purvey them, the geographical boundaries that have so far restricted the trade and catchment areas of shrines and temples will begin to disappear. This is unlikely to mean that people will stop visiting the actual shrines and content themselves solely with cyberspace veneration—for the numbers (and indeed age profiles) of those who use the Internet regularly is somewhat limited. However, in making themselves available on the Internet, religious centers may gain access to an audience (technologically motivated young computer aficionados, for example,) they might not be able to reach otherwise. Indeed a generation, or a class, of worshipers who access religious institutions only through their computers may develop.

There is, at present, an Internet site called Cyber Shrine—a pastiche of pictures from real shrines as well as depictions of various charms and talismans. It is not beyond the bounds of possibility that through the Internet we will see the development of virtual reality shrines and temples: not just "real" shrines that already exist and have created a second reality for themselves on the Internet, but the invention of a cyberspace institution that has no grounding in real buildings in the physical world. We have already seen the invention of a virtual reality Japanese pop star, named Kyoko Date, intended to appeal to the cyberspace generation and the dedicated computer aficionados who spend much of their time in cyberspace.[48] It is not hard to imagine a similar invention—a virtual reality shrine or temple dedicated perhaps to the this-worldly benefits and needs of the computer age (with perhaps talismans for protection against computer crashes and viruses)—being developed in the near future. Given the inventiveness of Japanese priests, their efficient use of media and advertising technologies throughout the ages, and the responsiveness of Japanese religious institutions to changing needs, such a development is to be expected.

In fact, a prototype of just such a virtual shrine is already on the Internet in the form of the Dai Uchū Jinja (DUJ): the Shrine of the Great Universe. Headed by the "Space Priest Sugimoto," the shrine is a New Age jumble of widely disparate elements that supposedly amount to a "custom 'Space Religion' for all the people on this

planet." The ultimate status seems to be that of "space comman-
der"—one who realizes, among other bits of esoterica, that the Dai
Uchū Jinja is nothing other than oneself. The description of how "sea
monkeys" can be discovered near Shinjuku train station is so out-
landish as to suggest that all this is nothing but a jest. And yet the possibilities of the Internet for creating a global spirituality bespeaks a
sincerity that is not uncommon among more ordinary religious leaders who wish to influence the world. While some of DUJ's activities are
entirely mundane, such as volunteering to help a group of farmers
plant rice, most of what it offers is on the bizarre side and uncharac-
teristic of the framework of practical benefits. Yet a prominent feature of this website is its "Digital *Ofuda* Database"—a listing of over
sixty Shinto shrines and Buddhist temples, each of which can be
clicked to call up their respective *omamori* or *ofuda* or to link one to
their home page if they have one. DUJ's objective in providing this
service is to enable people to realize happiness through worship of
ofuda. It offers this service without adding its New Age interpretations, except to say that although the *ofuda* should be ritually burned
at the end of the year, "once it is digitalized, nobody knows how to do
it." The listing is mostly of well-known shrines and temples organized
by prefecture. DUJ indicates its own location in the prefecture column with a question mark.[49] Existing only in cyberspace, offering digitalized talismans, DUJ is a harbinger of more to come.

Material Goods: Wholesale Suppliers

Reaching out to the general public as well as to prospective temple
clients, the manufacturers and suppliers of ritual implements, accou-
trements, and equipment have also appeared on the Internet. These
businesses sell supplies that are not resold, since they are used only by
priests and their temples, but they also offer at wholesale prices the
amulets, talismans, rosaries, and other objects that are retailed to the
public at the temple sales counters. Temples seldom manufacture objects of their own: they arrange with the wholesalers to have their
names printed on the objects they sell. Since the number of items
needed by temples and therefore offered by wholesalers is extremely
large, it is not practical to display entire inventories on the Internet.
Advertising therefore takes place primarily through catalogs containing detailed information on each item.

The catalogs are usually large-format, high-quality publications
filled with glossy color pictures and offer a wide variety of essentials
from neckties to cast bronze statues. Some companies serve single
sects; others are more ecumenical in their offerings. Kawakatsu Hōiten,
for example, serves Jōdo Shinshū temples and its catalog is, as ex-

pected, devoid of amulets.[50] Matsumotoya sells Sōtō Zen supplies that include work clothing, clerical robes, altars, bells, statues, incense burners, hanging scrolls (including one of the "three worthy buddhas" of the Sōtō tradition: Shakyamuni, Dōgen, and Keizan), and amulets ranging in wholesale prices from 30 cents to $1.30 each.[51] Shingon priests can order from a 250-page catalog issued by Suzuki Hōiten that offers pilgrimage clothing, ritual implements, scrolls of Kōbō Daishi, banners, and other supplies unique to Shingon Buddhism. The section on amulets is substantial and includes *ofuda* (a thousand pieces for 67,000 yen), demon-smashing arrows (*hamaya*), bumper sticker amulets for traffic safety, key chain amulets, *ema* plaques, pencils for academic success (set of four for 260 yen), and the Seven Gods of Good Fortune in figurine, painting, key chain, and *ema* editions.[52]

One of the largest wholesalers is the Izutsu firm headed by Izutsu Gafū, who is also a well-published expert on the history of clerical robes (*kesa*). Serving all the major Buddhist sects, the Izutsu catalog is brimming with items for every temple need imaginable—the section on amulets, talismans, and other objects of the practical benefits trade takes up nearly ninety pages. The subsection devoted just to *omamori* offers more than 275 versions covering a wide range of benefits; the designs, motifs, styles, and colors make for a varied and sometimes bewildering display. The traffic safety amulets outnumber the rest by far and include key chain, bumper, dashboard, rear view mirror, and seat belt versions. One of the more creative general-purpose amulets is the "Fragrance Calculator" (written in English)— a stainless-steel-faced calculator, the back (or front) of which can be inscribed with the *Heart Sutra,* the Seven Gods of Good Fortune, or the Eight Buddhas, infused with cedar, cypress, or incense fragrances.[53] Like Izutsu, Suiundō, which is headquartered in Tokyo, is pansectarian in service and specializes in large structures such as altars, statues, and even temple buildings. The costs of outfitting a temple are extremely high: an eighteen-inch-high gilded carving of Nichiren, for example, costs $14,000 for the standard grade and over $27,000 for the special grade, while an eight-foot-high bronze casting of Kannon can be bought for $92,000. Despite these high prices, Suiundō does a thriving business: from November 1993 to October 1994 it served over four hundred temples throughout the country by completing repair work and delivering goods ranging from large statues to rosary sets and had over a hundred major orders in process of completion.[54] While these figures represent only a small sampling of the wholesale side of the manufacture and marketing of religious goods, they support the view of an industry that is vigorous and healthy.

Unlike the catalogs, which are aimed solely at priests, the Internet postings are mostly for the general public and the home pages deal less with inventories and more with information and persuasion. The dominant theme is the importance of tradition (*dentō*) and how the wholesale suppliers themselves are its guardians as well as purveyors. Like the home pages set up by funeral companies,[55] which also provide instructive information to a public that is rapidly forgetting tradition, the wholesale suppliers have set an educational agenda for the Internet. The Kissyō company in Osaka, for example, explains the significance of having a Buddhist altar at home, the meaning of the posthumous names given to the deceased, what to expect of priests, how much to give them for their services (10 percent of one's monthly salary for a monthly service, 10 percent of one's yearly salary for an annual service), and even what to say when making the offering. The home page almost becomes homiletic as it preaches the everyday value of temples in people's lives. From birth to death, it insists, everyone has a relationship with temples as they receive services and blessings having to do with entering school, becoming an adult, getting married, having children, and dying. While Kissyō does not use the term "*genze riyaku,*" the services it mentions are precisely the worldly benefits offered by temples that therefore have an everyday value and a relationship with common people. Reminding all that "traditional Buddhism" also supports schools, hospitals, and other social services, the home page urges everyone to keep their thinking in line with that of traditional Buddhism.[56] On the Internet, the wholesale suppliers do their part to advertise, promote, and ensure continued patronage of Buddhist temples and the benefits they offer.

The Kobori company of Kyoto also makes a strong case for the preservation of tradition and the use of authentic objects (*honmono*) made with time-honored techniques. It invites the public to visit their production shop since seeing is better than just hearing or reading about something. But for all its insistence on how authentic and traditional its products are, the company makes it clear that they are constantly researching new techniques and products.[57] As in the wedding and funeral industries, it is important to develop clever new twists that do not violate the all-important "sense of tradition" (whatever that might be). As we have seen, innovation is a key element in the framework of practical benefits, one that can be developed by the wholesalers as well as the temples.

The *boke fūji* Kannon for the prevention of senility as a contemporary response to a growing social problem builds on this concept of tradition by playing on the traditional role of Kannon as compassionate benefactor capable of responding to the needs of all people whatever their circumstances. The Kannon for the prevention of senility, however, is not simply a response to a contemporary social concern developed by Buddhist priests and temples. A primary stimulus came from Gōtō Masahiro, the enterprising president of a Buddhist statue manufacturing company in Kyoto. Gōtō, having conceived of the idea, persuaded a number of Buddhist temples to take up the *boke fūji* theme, and his marketing agents have traveled around Japan drumming up support for the new image and its function, as well as cooperating with priests in various regions in establishing *boke fūji* pilgrimages. Advertisements for these statues have been placed in journals, magazines, and newspapers read at Buddhist temples — such as the Buddhist newspaper *Chūgai nippō,* which frequently carries advertisements from the manufacturers of religious items as well as a regular page on new developments in the world of religious goods.[58] Gōtō developed the idea of this statue because, he asserts, he wished to do something to help the elderly in the face of their worries about senility. In so doing, he says, he feels he is making a contribution to society.[59]

Though Gōtō may be sincerely concerned about such issues and may be keen to develop a Buddhist response to them, it is hard to take his proclaimed desires to help society at face value. He is, after all, a businessman and therefore concerned with profit and new ways of making his business more successful. Like the priests discussed in earlier chapters, who used the public rhetoric related to peace of mind and faith to legitimate their sales of amulets, Gōtō is clearly cloaking his business activities in the garb of public service. In his development of this statue, as well as the rapid assimilation by many Buddhist temples of the new form of Kannon, it is hard not to see some degree of manipulative exploitation of a social problem for fiscal gain — and perhaps even the creation of contemporary worries for religious profit. Similar concerns have, we noted earlier, also been raised in relation to the question about *mizuko kuyō,* as indeed they have over other areas in which religious movements offer solutions to problems or proffer the possibilities of amelioration. In the selling of benefits, as in the world of business, ethical questions may be tempered by economic prerogatives. The line between selling and manipulation, especially when the vendors themselves are concerned with questions of survival, may indeed become indistinct.

Competition and Survival

The business of practical benefits may be good, but businesses and temples know that such commerce can never be taken for granted — particularly in the highly competitive religious situation that exists in contemporary Japan. Just as priests must take the initiative for organizing *kaichō* ceremonies, and advertising them as effectively as possible, the wholesale suppliers know that their fortunes are tied to the temples and, more important, to the attitudes, inclinations, and understandings of the public. What worries them is the increasing cultural ignorance, especially among young people, who may easily abandon their patronage of traditional activities. Innovation is critical, therefore, and matters cannot be left entirely to tradition. But even when business is good, there is always the problem of ensuring that one is getting a fair share of it. We have already seen how Ishidō Ekyō, the chief priest of Nakayama-dera, saw the necessity of creating a religious department store to keep up with the competition from other temples.

What is striking about Ishidō's comments is the direct way in which he uses the analogy of a commercial enterprise—the department store—that relies for its continuing success on attracting customers and selling products. Department stores do this, of course, by numerous means: offering a wide range of services, advertising to develop a reputation for themselves, making themselves widely known, creating an image that affirms the value and quality of their product, developing customer loyalties through the services they provide, providing what their customers want and need, and staying in touch with the changing patterns of the market. In doing this, of course, they are engaged in competition for a share of the market with rival stores and enterprises.

All these techniques for selling their wares may also be utilized by religious institutions in their efforts to proselytize and to vend their services—a point made clear by the parallel Ishidō draws between the Hankyū Department Store and his temple. The analogy of temple as department store affirms what we have stated in earlier chapters: the business of religion is a commercial enterprise, and its products, whether as services offered in the performance of rituals, as non-material goods such as the promise of benefits, or as material goods such as amulets and talismans, are sold on the open market. We have seen, for example, how the income from sales of amulets and from donations to temples and shrines in the pursuit of practical benefits are often substantial and frequently crucial to the economic well-being of the religious institution and—especially in the case of large shrines and temples that can attract visitors on a national scale—even the organizations they belong to. A temple such as Ichibata Yakushi, which operates as the head temple of a sectarian organization, is able to support its branch temples because of its own fame as a center of worldly benefits. It is this aspect that enables it to support the social welfare activities that, as we noted in Chapter 3, are often carried out

Collecting the offerings at a large goriyaku temple

by such institutions. Major prayer temples such as Shinshōji (Narita-san) and Heikenji (Kawasaki Daishi), which belong to the Shingon Buzan sect, are able to provide their sectarian organization with a sizable income that can be disbursed to less well endowed temples in the sect and help subsidize other sectarian activities.

One of the key elements of success is the establishment and promotion of a good reputation grounded in a special service or product with which it remains associated. Nakayama-dera is exceedingly well known as a center for benefits. One basis of its appeal is the stature of a cultural and historical giant, Prince Shōtoku, who was led, according to the temple's foundation story, by a purple cloud (itself an auspicious sign) to the location where Kannon manifested herself. The site was thus linked to a popular and powerful deity and to a great historical figure. This link between place and a sacred figure whose spiritual power either sacralizes or confirms the location's sanctity is found repeatedly within the foundation legends of temples and shrines—as we have seen, for example, in the case of Kawasaki Daishi, whose founding legend unites the temple with Kōbō Daishi and the legends of Kurama. The powers of the Nakayama Kannon have been verified by various miracle stories and legends that attribute to her the powers to grant children and safe childbirth to petitioners. The two most widely reported of these stories relate to Toyotomi Hideyoshi, whose wife's faith in and prayers to the Nakayama Kannon were rewarded with the birth of a son, and to the mother of the Emperor Meiji, who prayed at the temple for the safe delivery of her child.[60] These miraculous tales enhance the temple's reputation for childbearing by linking it to two mothers who were important figures in Japanese history.

It is not surprising, then, that the Nakayama Kannon is the main choice of pregnant women in the Kansai region for acquiring protective talismans for safe childbirth, and visitors to the temple, especially on Sundays, cannot fail to note the numerous pregnant women and small children thronging the courtyards. Nakayama-dera is further blessed by its location, which is close to major urban centers such as Osaka, Kobe, and Kyoto and easily reached by local train services, yet on the edge of the hills of southern Hyogo prefecture that provide good hiking opportunities. Thus it draws on a large catchment area and offers a pleasant setting for a day out that includes a religious observance to assure petitioners that one of the most important events in life will take place without mishap.

Despite these advantages the priests at Nakayama-dera are well aware that market conditions and tastes can change. They know that their patrons do not come from an attached congregation but from the public at large and can, for any number of reasons, decide to go to other places that offer similar services or not to go at all. Even "brand names" cannot rely solely on reputation. Although petitioners may well return repeatedly to a shrine or temple from which they have received benefits,[61] the institutions know they cannot rely on this loyalty alone and must therefore keep attracting new clients.

This is especially the case for institutions that do not have a fixed clientele tied to it through social customs—such as loyalty to a community shrine or to a local temple that caters to one's ancestors. In modern times these institutions have had to seek alternative sources of support because of the increasing erosion of such socially conditioned ties. In rural areas, particularly, demographic changes have led to the decline or disappearance of their traditional communities. This problem is often quite severe. As Yonemoto Kazuhiro has shown in a discussion of Buddhist temples in the south-central parts of Shimane prefecture around Yokota-chō, the population is in decline and many temples are therefore struggling to keep going as the number of people and households affiliated to them declines. Indeed, many of the local temples are no longer able to support priests and have had to close in the past decade or so.[62]

Finding ways of attracting customers and keeping a flow of people passing through shrine and temple gates is thus a necessity, not just for opulence on the scale of a Nakayama-dera or a Kawasaki Daishi, but for survival. The promise of practical benefits is, as we have seen, one of the primary reasons that people flock to religious institutions. Naturally it has played a seminal role in enabling temples and shrines like Nakayama-dera to grow into economically powerful institutions. It also offers the hope of survival to temples and shrines faced with a clouded future. Such was the case with Kōya-dera, a small rural temple in Saga prefecture in Kyūshū that in the early 1990s was on the point of closure because of a declining local population. Then it was recruited into the newly formed thirty-three-stage Kyūshū *boke fūji* pilgrimage route and acquired a statue of the *boke fūji* Kannon, who offers the benefit of protection against senility. Since then the temple has managed to supplement its income through pilgrims' offerings and the sale of amulets and the like.

In their need to attract customers, temples and shrines are implicitly drawn into competition with each other, for they are aware that potential customers have neither the time nor the resources to visit every place that offers benefits relating to their needs. One response to the challenge of competition is to join with other temples to form a kind of cartel, such as the *boke fūji* pilgrimage circuit that Kōya-dera joined. Another is to develop one's temple, as Ishidō has done, to meet multiple and changing needs. Ishidō's recognition that Nakayama-dera has an economic focus not dissimilar to a real department store is framed by an understanding of the competition that exists in the benefits market. Although famed for its role in childbirth, Nakayama-dera cannot depend on a market monopoly. Other institutions may seek to build a reputation in the field themselves— perhaps through skillful sales campaigns and the reporting of answered prayers—and thus cut into its market. To prevent this from happening, it must find ways of keeping its name before the public and spreading its reputation as a provider of benefits. It must also, as Ishidō recognized, offer enough variety in terms of services and the like to not only attract people but ensure they enjoy their visit and want to return.

The competition in the benefits market has been made more intense by the growth of the new religions, which offer the hope of practical benefits and are very adept at publicizing their claims. As we noted in the Introduction, stories and testimonies of benefits that have been acquired through faith in the new religions form an important pillar of their recruitment strategies and success. And this again poses a challenge to the temples and shrines of the older religions, who must convince the public that they can continue to deliver the goods.

Marketing Truth

In examining the commercial dimensions of the sale of practical benefits—and the economic imperatives that underpin the activities of religious institutions in Japan—one has to recognize that eco-

nomics, marketing, and commercialization are part of the religious
process: they go hand in glove with the ethical and spiritual meanings
of religious practice that we have discussed in earlier chapters. No
doubt there are tasteful as well as reprehensible ways of doing business, but it is pointless to criticize religious establishments for their
economic involvements. These activities are essential to the well-
being of the temple or shrine and therefore to the continued practice of religion itself. The promise of practical benefits is not, in any
case, simply a matter of securing economic stability: it is also a prime
means of making faith and asserting religious truth. This point is emphasized in the Buddhist sutras we discussed in Chapter 2, such as the
*Sutra on the Merits of the Fundamental Vows of the Master of Healing, the
Lapis Lazuli Radiance Tathāgata,* which affirms the powers of Yakushi
to provide practical benefits and thereby proclaim that Buddhism is
a true religion. In promoting Buddhism's power to grant benefits, the
sutras are simultaneously proselytizing the values of Buddhism ("selling it to the wider populace") and affirming its inherent truths. The
letter of the king of Paekche does much the same in affirming that
Buddhism's ability to provide treasures to the heart's content establishes its claim to truth, not in any oblique or philosophically obscure
sense, but in direct relation to its power to satisfy wishes and fulfill
every prayer.

Similar themes are affirmed in the *Handbook for Believers* of the
Kōyasan branch of Shingon Buddhism—which, as we showed in
Chapter 3, in referring to the active role of Shingon in providing
practical benefits, described itself as "our religion of truth." Again,
the provision of benefits is used to demonstrate the inherent truths of
the institution that offers them: the whole process of promoting
benefits is intimately related to the truth claims that, whether advanced or implicitly affirmed by religious institutions and groups, are
at the very heart of their identity. A new religion that publicizes a story
such as Michiko's (see the Introduction) is in effect telling us here is
the proof that it is a true religion: it can deliver the goods by performing miracles and providing benefits of practical use to its followers. The priests of temples and shrines who claim that their *kami* or
buddha, or their amulets and prayers, can help avoid accidents, get
one into a good university, or cure an illness are telling us something
similar. The stories they use to create the reputations of specific
places and deities are in effect truth claims: here is a spiritual entity,
they say, that cares for people and whose spiritual powers work and
can help the living. In transmitting the miraculous stories associated
with Hideyoshi and the Emperor Meiji, Nakayama-dera is not merely
selling benefits and encouraging people to come and pray there; it is
making truth claims about the powers and efficacies of a deity who

has a record of responding to entreaties and delivering practical benefits. In such terms the Nakayama Kannon is a good proof of Buddhist truth. The promotion of truth claims—and the advertisement of the benefits and virtues that can be obtained at a particular site or from a particular deity—are thus part of the same process. Without testimonies and stories of miracles and benefits, places such as Nakayama-dera could not develop the sort of reputation that brings petitioners in: an advertisement rests on a sounder basis when the product is backed by evidence of truth. Truth is a practical and efficacious commodity only if it solves some kind of problem. Thus the selling of benefits is at the same time an advocacy of truth claims: spirituality and commercialization are in such terms inseparable.

Stagnation and Vibrancy

Throughout this book we have referred to religious institutions that have flourished because of their focus on this-worldly benefits. To name but a few (which themselves are but a small sampling of the wider picture) we could mention Hōzanji, Kawasaki Daishi, Nakayama-dera, Narita-san, Ichibata Yakushi, and Saijō Inari. Visitors to such places in the present day will no doubt be struck by the general air not just of activity—noise, incense smells, and so on—but of opulence. Such sites are by and large well off. They are able to build vast new structures (like Nakayama-dera's modern Believer's Hall), support large social welfare activities (as we saw in Chapter 3, Hōzanji supports social welfare institutions employing two hundred people and costing almost $7 million per year), help finance other major undertakings, and even bankroll the whole sectarian structure.

We do not claim that all religious institutions based on the promise and transmission of practical benefits are bound to become rich and famous. But the customary process—finding a particular benefit or set of benefits; developing a reputation by inventing or spreading legends and tales of miracle or by other forms of advertising; promoting that reputation through advertisements and the like; and actively proselytizing—represents one of the most direct and viable ways for a religious institution to flourish. Institutions such as Kawasaki Daishi, Saijō Inari, and Shinshōji, which have built their reputations over many centuries, have in the process become rich and nationally known. Some have continued to flourish in the modern age by becoming adept in newly popular areas of benefit—witness Shinshōji and travel safety. Other shrines and temples have, on the strength of a particular benefit, transformed themselves in even shorter spaces of time. Kōonji, the sixty-first temple on the Shikoku pilgrimage, has in the modern era moved from being perhaps the poorest to becoming the richest among the Shikoku temples—largely because of its active proselytization of the benefit of easy childbirth.[63]

Viewed from this angle it would thus appear that many of the common depictions of Japanese religious patterns in the modern age—which tend to associate vibrancy and dynamism with the new religions and to depict the older traditions of Buddhism and Shinto as being in decline and, indeed, largely static—are rather distorted. While in many areas the older religious traditions have become undermined—many Shinto shrines and Buddhist temples are closing or falling into disuse because of declining populations or lack of support—this decline has been associated with the social structures and support systems that underpinned these institutions. The erosions of social support for Buddhism are, in effect, those that affect *danka* (parishioner) temples, which depend on a parish membership structure; those affecting Shinto are similarly connected to *ujiko* (clan) social support structures, which are vulnerable to social change and shifting population structures. Buddhist sects, too, may be struggling to keep in touch with the changing patterns of religious behavior in contemporary society, especially as social ties weaken and people no longer feel the need to follow socially prescribed religious practices.

But when we examine the dynamics and orientations of Japanese religion in general—Buddhism and Shinto, as well as the new religions—we see a rather different picture. As we have seen, Shinto and Buddhist institutions have been able to create new religious responses to contemporary needs, to spot potential areas for new concerns, and to produce benefits, rituals, and amulets that address (and at times encourage) these needs. Along with the general and often rising tide of activity that surrounds the pursuit of practical benefits, such developments suggest a vibrancy and inventiveness that stand in sharp contrast to the prevalent image of stagnation. Moreover, the continuing engagement of temples and shrines in this process indicates that they have not yielded the center ground, in terms of religious dynamism or truth claims, to the new religions. Indeed, the new religions themselves have borrowed traditional means of indicating their veracity by emphasizing efficacy and experience in the realms of this-worldly benefits.

As we have seen in this chapter, the selling and propagation of practical benefits is an area of religious dynamism for Buddhist and Shinto institutions alike and remains at the heart of their assertions of truth and religious efficacy. This involvement, which has been central to the expansion of Buddhism in Japan, is crucial to the continuing existence and dynamism of these traditions both in the contemporary age and in the future. Given the general success that temples and shrines have achieved by promoting themselves in terms of this-worldly benefits, one should expect the emphasis on this-worldly benefits to continue. Not only have shrines and temples been adept at keeping themselves relevant and vibrant in these areas, but they have also shown an ability to seize and maintain religious initiatives in so doing.

Thus the widespread portrayal of established religion as moribund must be reconsidered. In reality, we suggest, it is when the established religions, especially Buddhism, have departed from their central (and sutra-validated) dynamic of this-worldly benefits—concerning themselves with the ritual etiquette of social structures and the maintenance of social order and formality and depending on a settled and parish-based clientele through the *danka* system—that they have run into problems of stagnation. When they have focused on individual aggrandizement and catered to the pursuit of worldly benefits, they have displayed an inventiveness and a capacity to attract attention that belie the image of decline.

7

Guidebooks to Practical Benefits

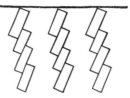

THE PUBLICITY and marketing strategies of priests and the temples and shrines they serve, the activities of companies selling religious amulets, the word-of-mouth proselytization that occurs as worshipers relate stories of their own good fortune—these are not the only sources publicizing the availability of practical benefits or creating a market for them. In this chapter we turn our attention to a further source of information on this matter: the numerous guidebooks that can be purchased at any bookstore. These guidebooks inform the general public about different forms of *genze riyaku* and where they may be sought, often drawing attention to particularly alluring aspects of the topic such as extraordinary forms of benefit or the lucky charms, votive tablets, talismans, and amulets associated with them.

While such guidebooks are a genre of popular literature produced, as a rule, independently of religious institutions by commercial publishers intent on making money for themselves, they often depend on the cooperation of religious institutions which in turn have a chance to publicize themselves and update the public on any interesting and new benefits that may be available. At the back of the 1993 edition of the annual *Nippon zenkoku goriyaku gaido* (All-Japan guide to practical benefits), for example, there is a short statement from the publishers inviting shrines and temples who wish to be included in the 1994 edition to provide them with information about any strange (*kawatta*) benefits, interesting *ema, omamori,* and similar goods they offer, along with maps, photographs, accounts of the shrine or temple's origins, and so on.[1] Some guidebooks also carry commercial advertisements: the *88 nenkan zenkoku jisha meguri* (1988 edition of the all-Japan tour of shrines and temples),[2] for instance, carries advertisements for sake breweries and manufacturers of shrine goods. Some guidebooks may even acquire sponsorship from shrines and temples for such services.

The guidebook business appears—from our visits to Japanese bookstores and acquisition of a large collection of such volumes over the past few years—to be a flourishing one that has acquired a mass-market niche, evidence in itself of the mass appeal of practical benefits and their marketability. While produced for commercial reasons, such guidebooks provide us with another lens through which to view the world of practical benefits. Here we examine some contemporary guides to *goriyaku* and discuss their content and meanings. In so doing we draw attention not so much to the standard forms of benefit (academic success, family safety, and so on), nor to the standard benefit-related commodities (the basic types of amulet, talisman, and so on), but to some of the especially strange (*kawatta*) benefits, as well as some of the more imaginative amulets and other representations that may be found.

A Nineteenth-Century Example

Although it is a subject worthy of research in its own right, this is not the place to give a detailed history of the genesis and development of such guidebooks. Essentially the roots of modern guidebooks, mass-marketed and produced as commercial ventures by major publishing firms, may be traced back to older collections of miracle tales and other such stories that sought to promote individual temples, shrines, and figures of worship, either individually or collectively. Thus collections that began to appear from the Heian era onwards—the *Hasedera reigenki,* for example, as well as the various guidebooks to pilgrimage routes such as Saikoku and guidebooks to "famous places" (*meishozue*) that flourished from the Tokugawa period onward and contained many references to temples and shrines—may be considered precursors of this genre. With the growing development of literacy in the Tokugawa era and the increasing mass market for books, various guidebooks to temples and shrines that could aid supplicants in their search for benefits began to appear on the market. By the early nineteenth century, specialized guidebooks of this sort had become available in Edo and Osaka informing people, for example, of places, gods, and buddhas who specialized in healing and preventing illness.[3]

One such collection was the *Jinja bukkaku gankake jūhōki shohen* (hereafter referred to as the *Jūhōki*), a guidebook authored by Hamamatsu Utaguni (or Kakoku) and published in 1816, which detailed the miraculous efficacies of local gods and buddhas.[4] Nobori Masao has drawn attention to some of the small wayside shrines with reputations for healing that are mentioned in Hamamatsu's text. His study is worthy of notice because both the text itself and the themes he extrapolates from it provide further insights into the world of benefits. As Nobori notes, many of the functions dealt with by the small wayside places mentioned in the *Jūhōki* relate to illnesses and conditions such as toothaches, headaches, and childbirth, which were not only matters of discomfort and concern to people in that era but remain so in the present day.[5] They are, we would add, themes that are frequently found in contemporary *goriyaku* guidebooks. By focusing on small shrines and statues, Nobori shows that it is not only the celebrated institutions that may be found on the map of benefits. Alongside the famed religious centers in cities such as Osaka there is a whole network of smaller institutions and figures of worship that contribute to the general religious ecology of the area. Many of these may offer similar benefits, and a number of different deities may well be venerated within the same area. Therefore, these institutions may well be competing with each other as well as with more prominent shrines and temples within their region, thus giving petitioners a number of options to choose from when seeking benefits.

For toothache alone the *Jūhōki* lists six small wayside locations where people could, in the earlier part of the nineteenth century, pray for relief from their physical sufferings—by worshiping before a statue of Yakushi in the (now-defunct) Umeda graveyard,[6] for example, or by visiting the Kitamuki (North-Facing) Jizō, a statue that has disappeared but was located at Kōbashi, possibly in the region of present-day Dotonbori.[7] For hemorrhoids and related complaints the guide provides five such wayside locations, including the Hirota Shrine in Naniwa ward in central Osaka, the Shin Kiyomizu Jizō in Tennōji ward (a statue that still exists but no longer attracts worshipers),[8] and a memorial stone to Akiyama Jiun Reijin in the courtyard of Kōshōji Temple in Fukushima ward.

Akiyama Jiun Reijin is worthy of mention here as an example of a human figure who, because of his personal strivings and his association with a particular affliction, has become transformed after death into a source of benefits. Originally a merchant in the sake trade in Edo, he suffered terribly from hemorrhoids. In his search to be cured of this affliction he turned to religious practices, took the tonsure, and became a monk in the Nichiren tradition. Nonetheless he continued to suffer for a further seven years until his death. On his deathbed, according to Joseph Kitagawa, he announced "his determination to become a god and save those who might suffer from the same ailment."[9] His spirit was enshrined first at the Nichiren temple Honshōji in Tokyo and then, as reports spread of miraculous cures experienced by hemorrhoid sufferers through his grace, at other Nichiren temples throughout Japan. Akiyama Jiun Reijin thus attracted a sizable number of worshipers during the Tokugawa period and was enshrined at numerous temples including at least six locations in Kyoto and five in Osaka.[10] Although the site dedicated to him and mentioned in the *Jūhōki* is no longer active, the cult has not died out entirely: Honshōji in Tokyo continues to be known for the benefit of curing hemorrhoids, and appears in various guidebooks and collections focusing on this-worldly benefits.[11]

The *Jūhōki* also deals with diseases that were often critical for those in earlier times, such as smallpox (now eradicated), as well as others that may still afflict people but have ceased to be so drastic in effect— diseases such as syphilis (which now may be readily treated medically) and measles. For these ailments the residents of early-nineteenth-century Osaka were offered a number of choices of wayside healing deities, including the deity Sarutahiko enshrined at the Mitsu Hachiman Shrine in Chūō ward and the *kasa* (bamboo hat) Inari that guarded the Osaka residence of the feudal lords of the Matsue domain.

In mentioning places that cater for uncomfortable bodily protrusions and maladies, the *Jūhōki* not only illustrates some of the earlier aspects of Japanese religion—an issue to which we return later in this chapter—but also draws our attention to the humor, often expressed in punning forms, that attended such benefits. Punning associations, as we noted earlier with the recent association between the Tobi Fudō and air travel safety, have been a recurrent element in the world of practical benefits—expressed, for example, in the case of Hirota Shrine, which is mentioned in the *Jūhōki* as a healing center for hemorrhoids. This shrine came to be efficacious, Nobori informs us, because of such punning associations. The shrine was in earlier times located within the *jiryō,* or temple estate and jurisdiction, of Shitennōji: the word "*jiryō,*" written with different ideograms, can be read as "healing (*ryō*) hemorrhoids (*ji*)." Moreover, the shrine's deity was a *kami* that protected the local area (*ji no kami*): by writing the sound "*ji*" (earth) with a different ideogram, the deity becomes the "god of hemorrhoids" (*ji no kami*).[12] The votive tablets at this shrine depicted a stingray which, because its malevolent properties were located in its tail, was often used as a symbolic motif in such circumstances. Such word associations and symbolic allusions demonstrate the role of sympathetic magic in the realms of providing benefits, but they also illustrate the wit and down-to-earth humor that are rarely far from the surface in Japanese religion, particularly in the world of benefits. They figure quite prominently in contemporary guidebooks, too, and play a role in creating an attractive aura associated with benefits and helping to take the sting out of painful situations by placing them in an amusing context.

Several of the shrines and figures of worship that figure in the *Jūhōki*, such as the Kitamuki Jizō, have subsequently disappeared, and this alerts us to the potential for change in the geography of benefits. The disappearance of such locations or their loss of popularity re-affirms the concerns raised in the previous chapter by the priest at Nakayama-dera: the world of benefits may be highly competitive, so shrines and temples must pay attention to changing circumstances if they are to survive and flourish. As shown by the number of small shrines and statues popular, according to the *Jūhōki*, in nineteenth-century Osaka but no longer so in the present day, it is clear that it is they, not the prestigious centers of worship that have been able to build up formidable reputations and clienteles, that are more likely to be at the mercy of such fluctuating fortunes.

The fluctuations in the market shown by the disappearance of for-merly popular places of worship also hint at the competition that is inherent in the world of practical benefits—a competition shown through the number of locations offering similar benefits in a given area. The degree of choice that may be offered to consumers within one geographical region is just as much an issue for present-day Japa-nese as it was for the citizens of Osaka in the early nineteenth century. Just as sufferers of hemorrhoids in Osaka had piles of places to choose from in seeking spiritual relief, so do modern petitioners have considerable scope in selecting the places where they will seek benefits. It is here that guidebooks play a role, alongside the factors mentioned in previous chapters, in influencing where petitioners may go and affording shrines and temples with a further means of publicity through which they can reach out to potential clients.

The *Jūhōki* shows us, too, that no figure of worship can expect to monopolize a category of benefits. A good example of this is found in the realms of healing: although Yakushi the Buddha of Healing may be considered a specialist in this realm, he did not, as demonstrated by the number of healing sites in nineteenth-century Osaka, have a monopoly in the matter. This buddha vied with other Buddhist figures of worship such as Jizō, as well as with Shinto deities, to pro-vide petitioners with cures for toothaches and other ailments. The same is true for other fields as well: Tenjin, for example, may be the most widely petitioned deity in the context of education, but he faces competition from the Buddha of Wisdom, Monju, as well as from other deities and buddhas. In one recent guidebook, for example, numerous Jizō and Fudō sites are noted for such benefits,[13] while even at Shinto shrines Tenjin does not always hold sway, as the example of the Azumamaro Shrine mentioned in Chapter 6 shows. Deities, like individual shrines and temples, must compete for their share of the market.

Contemporary Guidebooks

Many of the themes we have been discussing can be discerned in contemporary guidebooks as well. Here we just outline some of their general characteristics. Most *goriyaku* guidebooks are organized either on geographic principles or along the lines of categorizations of benefits; at times these two are used together.

Thus guidebooks organized primarily on geographic principles might cover the whole country by dividing it into regions and then listing and describing the various benefit-providing locations within each region. The *88 nenkan zenkoku jisha meguri* mentioned earlier, for example, covers the whole of Japan, region by region and prefecture by prefecture, in the normal order used in Japanese geography, starting from the north in Hokkaido and going south through the country to Kyūshū.[14] The *Nippon zenkoku goriyaku gaido,* also cited earlier, is an example of a guidebook focused on categorizations, listing places from across the country but in no geographical order, under six major subdivisions of benefits as follows: *ren'ai* (love, which includes such benefits as *enmusubi*); *gōkaku* (academic success); *kin'un* and *shōun* (fortune in acquiring wealth and victory, which also include *shōbai hanjō,* business prosperity, and success in gambling); *geijijōtatsu* (success in the development of skills and accomplishments); and the general category entitled *kaiun, shōfuku, ta* (opening of fortune, beckoning of good fortune, and other such things)—which includes as a subcategory *yakuyoke,* the prevention of misfortune.[15]

An example of a guidebook linking both formats is the *Fuku o yobu jisha jiten* (Dictionary of shrines and temples that summon fortune) produced by Kōdansha, one of Japan's main publishing firms, which is divided up into a number of sections, each catering to different categories of benefit, but with shrines and temples listed in each section in a standard Japanese north-to-south geographical order.[16]

Many guidebooks are specifically regional in focus—such as Yoritomi and Shiraki's guide to the *goriyaku* shrines and temples of the Kansai region (*Kansai goriyaku no jisha*), mentioned in earlier chapters, and the various guides to benefits in Tokyo, such as Naitō and Shimokawa's book discussed in Chapter 1, and the *Tokyo goriyaku sanpo* (A stroll through the practical benefits of Tokyo), to which we shall shortly turn.[17] Of these two Tokyo-based guides, the former is organized around categories of benefit and the latter geographically, going through the city ward by ward.

Some guidebooks target specific interest groups and the types of benefit they are most likely to seek, as with the *Jinja otera goriyakuchō* (Directory of *goriyaku* shrines and temples) published in 1989.[18] This book is clearly aimed at young college and postcollege people and focuses on three areas, Kyoto, the Tokyo-Kamakura area, and Nara—in other words, the country's main population center and three of its most important cultural centers full of well-known shrines and temples. These areas have become extremely popular among the young in recent years as settings for romantic travel. While this guidebook deals with practical benefits in Kyoto, Nara, Kamakura, and Tokyo in general, it focuses on areas of primary concern to the young: academic and examination success are featured prominently, while discussions of the attainment of skill (which might, in other contexts, deal with deities that could help in artistic accomplishments such as tea ceremony, poetry, and the performing arts) center especially on sports. Love and marriage also figure prominently, as does career success and the acquisition of wealth, all areas that speak to the ambitions of youth. Less prominent, though not entirely absent, are benefits associated with health—an area that the young, preoccupied by examination worries, excited by love and their first steps along the path of their careers, are likely to consider as more the province of older generations.

This guidebook also outlines several "date courses"—a concept that appears to have developed particularly in the 1980s but continues to flourish.[19] Date courses are itineraries that are suitable for romantic outings to shrines and temples where the deities are renowned for their ability to bring people together in love and guarantee happy marriages and lasting affection between couples. In this way the gods are utilized to bring two people together by giving them a common purpose and shared activity through a romantic day out visiting shrines and temples. The concept of date courses reiterates the blurred lines between entertainment and religion.

No matter how guidebooks are organized or what interest groups they target, there appears to be one form of categorization that has no place in them: sectarian and religious affiliation. We have not come across any guidebooks that separate *kami* from buddhas (or other entities) or that classify benefit-providing institutions by their religious or sectarian affiliation (that is, as Shinto shrines or Buddhist temples belonging to particular sects). Gods and buddhas, shrines and temples, exist together side by side in guidebooks. There is no attempt to differentiate by tradition or by category of being. This reaffirms the point made earlier in Chapter 4: it is in the realm of benefits that gods and buddhas are brought together under the same rubric. In the context of the guidebooks themselves and the provision of worldly benefits in general, such divisions between gods and buddhas, or Buddhism and Shinto, hardly appear relevant.[20]

Furthermore, contemporary guidebooks rarely differentiate between places or deities in terms of efficacy, and do not privilege some locations over others by suggesting that one site may be better than another for a particular benefit. They may describe temples, shrines, and deities as particularly efficacious or famous for certain benefits, but they do not as a rule indulge in comparisons between the levels of benefit that different institutions might produce or make value judgments by stating that Temple X is better than Shrine Y for education or health. The *Tokyo goriyaku sanpo,* for example, in introducing us to numerous sources of this-worldly benefits, informs us of the specific merits of each institution, rather than attempting to place them in a comparative perspective. While it may describe a prominent *goriyaku* location such as as Sensōji (Asakusa Kannon) as a "treasure house of *goriyaku* deities" (*goriyakusan no hōko*),[21] it devotes little more space to it than to other places in the city.

Occasionally guidebooks do comment on the status of different locations, but this is generally done in terms of the location's number of visitors rather than its power or efficacy. The *Nippon zenkoku goriyaku gaido* occasionally comments on a particular shrine or temple's status in its particular field of benefit—noting, for example, that the Jishu Shrine in Kyoto is the "number one place in Japan in terms of the number of lucky objects related to joining people together in love" (*enmusubi guzzu no kazu wa Nihon-ichi*).[22] Later, in the education section, the Dazaifu Tenmangū Shrine in northern Kyūshū, the parent shrine of Tenjin shrines in Japan, is described as the "top Tenjin" shrine.[23]

A more systematized form of ranking, based on the sumo wrestling *banzuke,* is made by Kōdansha's *Fuku o yobu jisha jiten.* The *banzuke* is a chart, published before every sumo tournament, that gives the rank and status (based on past performance) of each wrestler in the tournament. The *banzuke* of *riyaku* shrines and temples is similar: like the sumo *banzuke* it is divided into two halves, east and west, and gives the "eastern and western supreme grand champions" (the *yokozuna,* the highest rank in sumo wrestling, of the east and west), as well as the descending ranks from the *ōzeki* (the next level down from champion) and so on down the sumo scale to the *maegashira,* (the standard title of sumo wrestlers who fight in the upper echelons of the sport).[24] To give one example of this guidebook's rankings: under the category of the prevention of accidents (*kinanyoke*) there are four *yokozuna,* or supreme grand champions, the two eastern ones being Shinshōji (Narita-san) and Kawasaki Daishi, while the western *yokozuna* are the Kotohira Shrine in Shikoku and the Usa Shrine in Ōita prefecture in

Kyūshū. Asakusa Kannon is ranked as an *ōzeki* in this category, as are the Kashima Shrine in Ibaragi prefecture, the Munakata Shrine in Fukuoka prefecture, and the Kumano Nachi Shrine in southern Wakayama prefecture.[25]

The rankings are not, however, based on power and efficacy but on the number of people who visited each place for that particular benefit in the previous year (although, of course, one could suggest a correlation between perceptions of efficacy and numbers of visitors).[26] Thus places ranked at one level in one list might go up or down in another: Shinshōji, for example, may be a supreme grand champion in accident prevention but goes down one rank to *ōzeki* in the business prosperity chart.[27] While the guidebook may inform us of a center's importance, it does not compare it to others—for example, we are told of Shinshōji's fame in traffic safety and told how car buyers in Tokyo invariably visit it to get their travel safety amulets,[28] but nowhere is it suggested that Shinshōji is better than other places offering the benefits of travel safety. Nor are we advised that it would be better to go to this "supreme grand champion" of traffic safety rather than any of the other places mentioned in the book. Guidebooks take a generally neutral stance on such issues. Their focus is on drawing attention to the vast array of possibilities that are offered to petitioners seeking benefits.

By highlighting especially colorful and visually enticing manifestations and commodities associated with the pursuit of practical benefits, guidebooks draw our attention yet again to the commercial and visual dimensions of the *genze riyaku* business. Thus the *88 nenkan zenkoku jisha meguri* guidebook has three color spreads of what it terms the "goods" or commodities of practical benefits (*goriyaku no guzzu*). The first double-page spread shows an array of twenty-nine *ema* from different locations; the second shows fifty-five different types of amulets (ranging from the standard types described in Chapter 1, to bells, to *kumade* or rake-shaped *omamori* for "raking in" good luck and money, to lucky sets of chopsticks); the third presents a display of fifteen different types of talisman (*ofuda*).[29] We shall return to this point later when we describe one guidebook in greater detail.

Guidebooks and the Reporting of Miracles

Guidebooks further help temples and shrines to ply their trade by contributing toward the creation of feelings of expectancy in the minds of would-be petitioners through their frequent allusions to the various benefits, cures, miraculous events, and experiences said to have been gained by petitioners over the years at the locations they mention. Given that guidebooks are not intended as academic accounts of shrines and temples, nor as historical sourcebooks, and that they are often compiled by asking shrines and temples to provide the information they print, it is hardly surprising that they are generally short on precise detail and long on popular legends that affirm the incidence of benefits. Thus the *Tokyo goriyaku sanpo* narrates uncritically the legends and stories that link shrines and benefits together, describing, for example, why the temple Anyōji in Ōta ward is associated with the benefit of abundant breast milk for mothers by relating the tale (*densetsu*) of the Empress Kōmyō. According to this story, she suffered from a lack of milk after giving birth to the son of Emperor Shōmu. But in a miraculous dream she saw herself praying at a small Yakushi hall at this location (which according to its foundation story had been established in 710 by the Buddhist holy man Gyōgi), and as a result she began to produce milk and the prince grew up strong and healthy. In her gratitude to Yakushi, the guidebook informs us, the empress donated funds to turn what was a small hall of worship into a complete Buddhist temple. As a result of this story, the guidebook tells us: "It is said that those who worship here will receive [the blessing of] abundant breast milk, and the temple has become the focus of belief of mothers who had been distressed because their breast milk was insufficient."[30]

This site is by no means unique in its function. Breasts stand out prominently in the world of benefits, with various shrines and temples offering services relating to the production of abundant milk for nurturing children. At the *mama* Kannon ("*mama*" is written with the ideogram "*ma*," space, written twice, thus alluding to the loan-word "*mama*," mother) hall at Ryūonji at Komaki in Aichi prefecture, for example, a stone statue depicting two full female breasts is the focus for the prayers of expectant mothers seeking sufficient milk for their babies. The temple, which has a collection dating back to the early nineteenth century of votive tablets depicting female breasts, also provides related services connected to childbirth—from the benefit of conceiving children and the promise of safe childbirth to memorial services for aborted children.[31]

On the premises of the Ōkunitama Shrine in Fuchū City in Tokyo is a ginkgo tree, said to be about two thousand years old, which in earlier times was known for helping women produce breast milk if they rubbed the tree and then touched their breasts with the same hand. The tree is still associated with breasts, but the contemporary concern has shifted to the beauty of breasts. In the *Jinja otera goriyakuchō*, we read the following: "Whether they fall in love or not, women dream of creating beautiful proportions for themselves. They wish to achieve this for their whole bodies, of course, but first of all they want to raise up their breasts (*busto-appu*)."[32] A field visit to this shrine in

1993 revealed no sign of such activity, however, and a question to one of the priests elicited an emphatic denial of any such use of the venerable ginkgo tree.[33] It is possible that the priest was not willing to be truthful in his answer, but it is just as likely that the guidebook is fabricating this virtue for the tree at the shrine—or that, in attempting to cater to a youthful market, it might be making use of an old custom to appeal to a contemporary desire. Although not everything in the guidebooks is to be believed, we still need to keep in mind that by its very nature religious testimony has its fictive, incredible, and miraculous dimensions. Veracity is tied to assent. If enough people, believing the guidebook, agree that the ginkgo tree does improve the bustline, then that is the power the tree will come to have. Like other religious texts, guidebooks can create belief as well as report it.

Reporting the miraculous events of different places is a constant theme in the guidebooks. The *Tokyo goriyaku sanpo,* for example, talks repeatedly (although as a rule without attribution) of the occurrence of miraculous events (*reigen*) at—or the marvellous efficacy (*reigen arataka*) of—numerous locations and statues that have produced all manner of benefits. Thus we hear that the *yonaki* (night crying) Jizō at Jōkakuji has produced numerous miracles in which children have been cured of crying at night,[34] that the Erikake Jizō at Saibōji in Toshima ward has produced wonderful benefits connected with career advancement,[35] and that in the precincts of Yutenji Temple in Meguro ward there is a cave which is marvellously efficacious in preventing measles: infants who have been led through the cave, we are told, will not get the sickness or, if they do catch it, will suffer only a light dose.[36]

Some guidebooks do not just provide generalized stories of benefit and miracle but also give the testimonies of contemporary people who have experienced benefits at the shrines and temples they describe. The *Fuku o yobu jisha jiten* includes a number of testimonies in which the faithful talk about their experiences of benefits. Thus the actor Komatsu Hōsei tells of how, the day before he was due to appear on stage at the Nakaza Theater in Osaka, he lost his voice. Friends encouraged him to turn to the gods at this time of distress and visit the Mizumaki Fudō (Watering Fudō) located near the theater. He did so, he says, and the next day his voice was back to normal. Now when he visits Osaka he always makes a visit of gratitude to this Fudō and worships one of its talismans at home every day. He also states that when an actress he knew was feeling sick, he took her to worship there as well and she became better.[37] The writer Ikenami Shōtarō says that he always goes to pray for travel safety at the Samugawa Shrine in Kanagawa prefecture before going overseas and that, thanks to its help (*okage de*) he has never had an accident when traveling.[38] The actress

Osanai Minako records that she had previously not visited shrines and temples to pray to the gods. When her small child needed serious heart surgery, she was advised by those around her to go to Kawasaki Daishi to pray. Her child not only came through the surgery safely but does not even suffer from colds now. When time permits, she says, she makes visits of gratitude to the temple. She believes that her child's recovery and good health were a benefit from Kōbō Daishi (*Odaishi sama no go riyaku to shinjite imasu*).[39]

Such accounts provide further testimony to the benefits associated with particular places and show that real stories of experienced benefits play a continuing role in drawing people to shrines and temples. Again we note that people may pray for benefits due to the encouragement of friends and colleagues and that they may, when they feel they have benefited from such prayers, encourage others to do likewise. These testimonies, and hence the guidebooks themselves, reaffirm the importance of showing gratitude for what one has received: both Komatsu and Osanai make return visits of gratitude to their spiritual benefactors.

Unusual Benefits: The Example of the *Nippon zenkoku goriyaku gaido*

We will now look more closely at a recent guidebook, published in 1994, that illustrates many of the themes found in guidebooks in general. The *Nippon zenkoku goriyaku gaido* is produced by the publishing wing of one of Japan's main entertainment conglomerates, the Victor Entertainment Company. The company also produces and markets videos and computer games, manages pop and rock stars, and publishes magazines about rock and roll and other entertainments. Its production of this guidebook is a further illustration of the underlying links between entertainment, business, and religion that we have highlighted throughout the book.

The *Nippon zenkoku goriyaku gaido* (All-Japan guide to this-worldly benefits), as its title suggests, covers virtually the whole country (although it does not include entries for every prefecture, leaving out, for example, Kagoshima and Tokushima). By far the largest collection of locations it mentions are around the major population centers, especially Tokyo: of the 119 shrines and temples included in the book, 25 are in Tokyo and 22 are in Kyoto. Its focus on these places reflects to some degree the types of benefits most prominently featured in the book, such as love and education, while the mention of certain shrines and temples as places to visit on "date courses" (such as Yūshima Shrine in Tokyo and the temple Hasedera, popularly known as Iiyama Kannon in Atsugi in Kanazawa prefecture, which is described as a place for a "romantic date") shows that young Japanese are among those targeted by the book's publishers.[40]

The guide itself is attractively produced and is clearly intended to draw attention to the colorful aspects of shrine and temple visiting: its often lavishly and colorfully illustrated pages offer short descriptions of a shrine or temple, its history, principal claims to providing benefits, worship customs, festivals, and some of the more interesting benefits and customs related to these benefits. Accompanying the prose are photographs and pictures of some of the more eye-catching articles the sites purvey. Since the compilers of the guide seek out shrines and temples with "strange" (*kawatta*) forms of benefit, there is something of an emphasis on interesting objects. The Kanamara (also known as Kanayama) Shrine, mentioned in Chapter 1 and famed for its sexually related benefits with its AIDS-related protective themes, is featured: its five-monkey *ema* is prominently photographed along with some of the shrine's phallic amulets. Another popular shrine for love, the Enoshima Shrine dedicated to the female deity Benten in Kanagawa prefecture, is also featured: here emphasis is placed on its *ema* depicting a heart and on its seminaked statue of Benten, whom the guidebook describes as "having smooth white skin that even Rie-chan could not better."[41] The name Rie-chan refers to Miyazawa Rie, a well-known female singing star and actress who published a highly popular book featuring nude photographs of herself in the early 1990s.

Sexual themes are illustrated also by the Matsuchiyama Shōten Shrine in Tokyo, which provides the benefit of joining men and women together in sexual union: its votive tablets depict two giant intertwined daikon (long white radishes); one can also purchase daikon at the shrine to leave as offerings.[42] Similar phallic imagery is at work at the Kinone Shrine in Tottori prefecture, whose benefits of joining people together in marriage and producing succeeding generations of offspring are assimilated by purchasing and consuming the shrine's penis-shaped sweet cakes, which are lavishly photographed in the book in color.[43]

The Shiramine Shrine in Kyoto—which the guidebook says has been visited by former president George Bush—is highly popular with school and university football and rugby clubs, we are told, many of whom have placed large wooden *fuda* at the shrine seeking victory in national tournaments. Because of the ancient Shinto ritual game of *kemari* in which priests dressed in full Shinto regalia attempt to keep a ball aloft with their feet—a game played at the shrine every April and July—the shrine has acquired a reputation associated with ball-playing skills and is, according to the guide, the only place in Japan specializing in such benefits.[44]

Also in Kyoto we are introduced to the Ichihime Shrine with its five
female deities who protect women. Among its features are its "happy
card" amulets, which are shaped like credit cards. This shrine boasts
that it was the first in the country to use this now widely used format
for amulets. Another specialty of this shrine is an *omamori* that was
sold only during the year of the monkey (most recently in 1992).
Consisting of a pair of women's underpants with a picture of a monkey printed on them, it was, we are told, an efficacious protection
against "female illnesses" (*fujinbyō*).[45] Probably the reason for its association with the monkey was because the word for monkey, "*saru*,"
can also (written with different characters) mean "to go away" or "get
rid of."

Seeking help in breaking various vices and bad habits is a function
for which, as we saw with Hōzanji in Chapter 1, people may turn to
the gods. For cigarette smokers the appropriately titled Kahasan
Tabako Shrine near Mount Tsukuba north of Tokyo offers help. The
region produced the best tobacco leaves in Japan, and its farmers
would pray at the local shrine, beseeching the deity to safeguard the
crop: hence the shrine became associated with tobacco and acquired
its name, becoming Japan's only tobacco shrine. The shrine still holds
an annual festival widely attended by farmers, proprietors of tobacco
shops continue to pray for the flourishing of the tobacco business,
and it vends lucky metal charms shaped like pipes in connection with
this prayer. Due to the growing awareness of the health dangers of
smoking, the shrine has also developed another, and contradictory,
form of benefit: it has started to get petitioners coming to ask the
deity to support them in their vows to give up smoking.[46] Here we see
the flexibility of shrines, temples, and deities seemingly capable of
dealing with two contrary benefits related to each other.

In the same region, but closer to the town of Tsukuba, the Ichinoya
Yasaka Shrine is mentioned in the guidebook largely because of a
unique *omamori* sold at the shrine's annual festival in summer: a bulb
of garlic. The deity venerated here is a protector against illness, and
during its summer festival a garlic fair is held in the shrine's courtyard. (Garlic is a well-known herbal health remedy.) At this time the
shrine dispenses garlic *omamori* to petitioners. Although one can also
buy garlic in shops, it is the garlic obtained as *omamori*, the guidebook
tells us, that is truly efficacious in protecting against disease.[47]

Common Religion in a Modern City:
Tokyo goriyaku sanpo

There is another guidebook we wish to focus on, one from which
we have already extrapolated several elements, the *Tokyo goriyaku*

sanpo. The greatest concentrations of religious centers proffering benefits, we have suggested, appear to be around the major cities of Japan. On one level it may be rather obvious to say that the shrines and temples cited in guidebooks are found in the greatest numbers around the areas of highest population. Centers of benefits can, of course, only flourish if they have access to clienteles who will patronize them or need what they have to offer. Major population centers are not only able to provide the most concentrated clienteles, but perhaps the most varied ones, with consequently a broader array of needs and wishes than would be found in small villages and rural settings. The pressures and stresses of modern urban life themselves may well persuade people to seek the solace of practical benefits.

We focus on Tokyo here for the simple reason that standard perceptions of the nation's capital tend to revolve around issues of politics, economics and business, and its nature as a modern city. When Tokyo is discussed in religious contexts, it is usually in connection with the new religions—especially in the context of the "new" new religions (*shin shin shūkyō*). These are certainly a prominent part of that city's religious dynamism, but they are by no means its entirety nor even necessarily its most dynamic aspect. Even a cursory examination of Tokyo shows that it is a hive of activity connected to *genze riyaku*, with hundreds of temples, shrines, and statues of deities claiming the powers for themselves or being accredited in popular perceptions with the power to grant all manner of benefits from healing diseases to helping people succeed in business. In Chapter 1 we drew attention to this point when we outlined the contents of Naitō and Shimokawa's guide to the benefits of that city and hinted at the sheer scope of places proferring benefits there. While many of the benefits catered to "traditional" aspects of Tokyo life (dealing, for example, with established trades and crafts), they also included many of the "modern" forms of benefit, such as air travel safety. Modern urban environments such as Tokyo, besides demonstrating the enduring value of benefits, are equally the settings for the dynamic of renewal and regeneration inherent within the realm of practical benefits.

By taking—as the title of the *Tokyo goriyaku sanpo* puts it—a stroll (*sanpo*) through some of the locations of practical benefits in the capital, we can gain further perspectives on benefits in the contemporary world. While our excursion will follow the order of the guidebook in dealing with its shrines and temples, it will take a rather particular tack by continuing our examination of some of the less standard and more earthy dimensions of *genze riyaku*, in which bodily concerns and tribulations are expressed in religious settings.

The guidebook takes us through the city, in all listing seventy-six sites and benefit-granting deities, in each case providing one or two pages of text on the origins and foundation legends of the place, along with reports and assertions of each site's efficacy, illustrated by small black and white photographs. While the *Nippon zenkoku goriyaku gaido,* with its glossy photographs and concentration on matters such as love, appears to be aimed at a younger clientele, the *Tokyo goriyaku sanpo* clearly targets older generations: there are many references to sites of healing and descriptions of a number of shops that vend traditional Japanese foodstuffs such as *dango* (rice dumplings) and *senbei* (rice crackers).

In Meguro ward, close to Meguro station on the Yamanote loop line that circles the center of Tokyo, we find a cluster of temples offering intriguing benefits. At the Oshiroi Jizō at Banryūji Temple, for example, people can pray in order to become beautiful. Since this statue has "marvellous efficacy" in this respect, the guidebook asks us, why not try praying there yourself?[48] As we noted earlier, the *Tokyo goriyaku sanpo* tends to extol the efficacies and miraculous powers of all the deities and shrines it features. The guidebook makes similar comments about virtually every place it mentions, and frequently encourages people to pray at the place and try to experience the benefits it offers.

At the Tako (Octopus) Yakushi hall at Jōjuin Temple, itself only a step away from the Oshiroi Jizō, Yakushi is depicted astride an octopus: the iconography represents the legend that when the Buddhist priest Ennin (Jikaku Daishi, 794–864) was returning from China in the ninth century, a figurine he was taking with him went overboard during a storm. The figurine was brought safely to shore by an octopus, however, which carried it on its head, and was then carved into the form of Yakushi. The Tako Yakushi, because of the protruding shape of an octopus's head, is here specifically a healer of illnesses related to things that protrude (*deshapparu byōki*), such as hemorrhoids, warts, corns, and verrucae.[49] The octopus is linked to such complaints in yet another example of word associations, for "*tako*" (octopus), with different ideograms, also means callus or corn. The miraculous story of the octopus and the statue draws our attention once again to the ways in which legends of strange and miraculous happenings may provide the underpinnings of the world of benefits.

Other places dealing with concerns for health and the body include Yutenji in Meguro and its protection against measles; the Sekidome Jizō at Fukushuin, in Bunkyō ward, cures or protects one from coughs;[50] at Kōfukuji temple, in Sumida ward, one can acquire protection against whooping cough; and the temple of the Miminashi (Earless) Fudō, in Arakawa ward, is efficacious in dealing with both ear problems and sexual diseases.[51] At the Konnyaku Emma at Genkakuji Temple in Bunkyō ward, one can pray for cures from eye diseases. The link between this cure and the *konnyaku* (a Japanese foodstuff made from pounded devil's tongue plants) is provided by a typical story of miracle and piety. The story narrates how this statue of the Buddhist guardian of the nether regions, Emma, became popular and acquired its name. An old woman of great faith and piety in the Tokugawa era (like most such miracle stories, it has no dates beyond the most general), while herself suffering from eye problems, pitied the eyeless statue of Emma and hence offered her own right eye to the deity. Her offer resulted in a miraculous cure in which her sight was restored. To express her gratitude she gave up her favorite food, *konnyaku*, which she offered to Emma. As the rumor of her miraculous cure and her subsequent sacrifice spread in Edo, others came to offer *konnyaku* to Emma in the hope of similar benefits—and this has given the temple the name by which it is popularly known.[52]

Concerns with the body are manifold and at times extend beyond the usual physical problems. A specialized benefit is offered to women suffering from a particularly embarrassing personal problem at the Seiryū Shrine in Katsushika ward. Its reputation is for helping women who, as the guidebook somewhat coyly describes it, suffer from "not having hair in places where one ought to have it" (*arubeki tokoro ni ke ga nai*).[53] Such an embarrassment, we are told, can hardly be discussed with parents, close friends, or boyfriends, but a saving deity is at hand at the shrine to help such women face the future with confidence. The origins of this benefit can be traced to the misfortunes of a young lady from a wealthy family in the neighborhood who suffered from having no hair where "she ought to have some" in the Edo period. When she turned eighteen her parents, without her knowledge, arranged a meeting for her with a prospective suitor; she fell in love with him, and matters went as far as arranging the date for their marriage. The young girl, however, became increasingly depressed as the day approached and, lamenting her fate, flung herself into the Seiryū pond where she drowned. When her dead body floated to the surface, people became aware of her problem and started referring to the pond as "Hairless Pond" (*mumō ike*). However, the deity at the shrine must have had mercy on her soul, the story goes on, for suddenly the pond's surroundings, which had been bereft of grass, became luxuriant.[54] Thus the shrine deity, by showing mercy to the dead woman's spirit and bringing growth to what was bare, has become associated with helping others in a similar predicament. This story, besides illustrating a rather special form of benefit, shows how, within the dynamics of benefits, misfortunes may be transformed into grace and how the gods may intercede or be harnessed to prevent future generations from suffering. The death of the young girl at Seiryū pond has thus brought about the production of a this-

Ema for abundant breast milk

worldly benefit, and in this process the negativity of death has been superseded by the positive affirmation of life.

Love and its relationships are a common feature in the landscape of benefits. For those wanting to tie bonds of affection, Tokyo and its environs offer many love shrines—such as the Hie Shrine in Chiyoda ward with its stone statue depicting the two monkeys who are the spiritual messengers of the shrine deities. Since monkeys are believed to form strong bonding partnerships, they symbolize loving relationships. Here the statue of the two monkeys is prayed to for strength in love and also (again playing on the meaning of the word *"saru"*) for the power to get rid of any problems that occur in love.[55] The products of love are well catered for, too. There is ample provision for the benefit of safe childbirth, for instance, at the Suitengū Shrine in Chūō ward, where women can acquire a lucky *hara obi*—a sash traditionally worn around the stomach by pregnant women in Japan from around the fifth month of pregnancy onward, both as a sign of being pregnant and to protect the child in the womb and guard against cold.[56] The *hara obi* is put on on the first "day of the dog" (*inu no hi*) in the fifth month of pregnancy:[57] the association with dogs comes because they are believed to give birth easily and painlessly. After birth, too, Tokyo's shrines and temples care for mother and child by providing succor at temples such as Anyōji in the form of the benefit of abundant breast milk.

Rock sculpture at Yasui Kompiragū in Kyoto covered with requests for severing relationships

Solace is also offered when love goes wrong. The benefit of *enkiri* (sometimes pronounced *"engiri,"* cutting off relationships) is provided at the Enkiri Fudō temple at Machida, which can save women who wish to sever relationships with men who are causing them distress. Similar services are available at the Oiwa Inari Shrine in Shinjuku. Originally a guardian shrine to help women break away from unworthy men with whom they had unfortunately fallen in love, Oiwa Inari is now visited also by men suffering in a similar fashion from having fallen in love with unworthy women.[58]

Abstentions of many other types are covered in the guidebook. The Kotohira Shrine in Toranomon in Minato ward aids those who wish to give up alcohol or tobacco,[59] while the *sake-domachi* (giving up alcohol) Jizō in Shibuya ward provides us with another example of how misfortune in life can be transformed into the provision of benefits and aid to subsequent generations. Its origins emanate, we are told, from the story of a man called Raihei who lived in the area, which in the mid-Tokugawa era was rural. A hardworking teetotaler, Raihei constantly assisted his fellow villagers in their work, and to reward him and express their gratitude, they decided to give a feast on his behalf. Although he did not normally drink, he was so moved by their kindness that on this occasion he indulged—with the result that, on his way home, he lost his balance, fell into the river, and drowned. Later he appeared in a dream to one of the villagers, asking them to perform a memorial service for his spirit and erect a statue of Jizō that could give spiritual sustenance to those who suffered from problems with alcohol. Thus the roots of the *sake-domachi* Jizō's specialty are found in the misfortunes of one who suffered from the deleterious effects of alcohol, which itself features in the process of praying for release from its grip: petitioners should accompany their prayers with an offering (that is, a sacrifice) of alcohol to the deity.[60]

Protection (and it might be suggested that in seeking the benefit of abstention one is in effect asking for protection against a particular form of danger) is, of course, a major area in which benefits are sought, and here again the *Tokyo goriyaku sanpo* details some rather specialized forms. Dangers and fears need not be manifested only in the material waking world, for everyone depends on good sleep to keep them refreshed and healthy, and nightmares can cause grief, misfortune, and unhappiness. To counter this, the guide directs readers to the Gohyaku Rakan Temple in Meguro ward, which offers the benefit of eradicating bad dreams.[61] In the waking world the Rairyū Kannon at Kōmyōji in Ota ward offers protection against thunder and lightning,[62] while protection against theft and burglars can be sought from the Shibarare ("Shackled") Jizō at Nanzō Temple in Katsushika ward.[63] Dealing with the concerns of the modern corporate world is another area of protective activity for the gods and buddhas of Tokyo. The Kubitsugi ("Neck Joining") Jizō in Nerima ward offers protection against *kubikiri*—literally "neck cutting," or getting sacked from one's job.[64]

Naturally the guidebook offers numerous places where one can seek to improve one's life and skills in various ways—whether by offering the benefit of helping one's baseball team to win, a benefit provided at the Fukakawa Fudō temple in Etō ward,[65] or in improving one's musical and artistic skills, a beneficial function widely handled by Benten shrines and temples both in Tokyo and elsewhere throughout Japan.[66] Assistance is also at hand for those who want to improve their skills in one of Japan's most popular contemporary entertainments: karaoke. For this purpose one can call upon the services of the deity at Kitano Shrine in Bunkyō ward.[67]

The Religious Landscape

Both the *Nippon zenkoku goriyaku gaido* and the *Tokyo goriyaku sanpo* cover many more places than we have been able to discuss here. Besides demonstrating the scope of benefits that can be sought, and the often humorous nature of such benefits, both books engage actively in the business of promoting the search for practical benefits: why not, as the *Tokyo goriyaku sanpo* frequently asks, try praying to become beautiful, to become skilled at karaoke, or to deal with an uncomfortable physical problem? In such ways, guidebooks encourage the casual dimensions of seeking benefits and affirm, in their reproduction of miraculous stories and indications of the efficacy of the places they describe, the concepts behind the world of practical benefits, in which spiritual forces are believed to influence and transform the physical world. Most positively, perhaps, they reflect the underlying nature of Japanese religion, which affirms this world with a confidence that even misfortunes may be transformed into forces for the future good and help of the living. The suicide of the embarrassed young lady at Seiryū pond, and the unhappy drunken drowning of Raihei, thus produce positive results for the future: her death caused the god to express mercy and manifest a power that could be called upon by others in a similar plight; his death led to the establishment of a deity that could prevent others from suffering in the same way.

Guidebooks also highlight the continuing religious concerns with the body in all its imperfections and with the potential for magical processes—whether through sympathetic associations suggested by puns and wordplay or through the merciful intercessions of spiritual beings—to ameliorate the physical world, heal its wounds, and make it a better place. Such concerns with bodily malfunctions, and the notion that they can be cured with spiritual help, might appear to be little more than folkish and superstitious survivals from an earlier age. But the underlying themes they express are, as we have shown throughout this book, intimately connected to all levels of Japanese religion. The folkish, as we have noted, is not a separate domain from the supposedly highest realms of textual pronouncement and religious expression. If buddhas can produce riches to one's heart's content and produce the salve that wipes away suffering, they can—as the pragmatic petitioner might well reason—equally heal the pain of piles or make one's milk flow freely. Thus it is essential to recognize that such elements are not marginal to an ethical and logical system; they are central manifestations of a common religious process. The earthy and the magical are part and parcel of the fabric of contemporary Japan, not aberrations from it.

The guidebooks we have examined in this chapter emphasize just how prevalent *genze riyaku* is in the landscape of contemporary Japan. Even in Tokyo, as this account has shown, there is an extensive network of this-worldly benefits that is deeply embedded in the city's socioreligious infrastructure and forms a continuing strand in the city's social and cultural life. This network may not be as visible as the large office buildings of modern corporate Japan or, in religious terms, the offices and centers of the new religions that have flourished in the city. But it runs throughout the city, in back alleys and main thoroughfares, interweaving old and new themes together, providing the city dweller with access to benefits of every conceivable sort. Whatever the Tokyo dweller wishes to pray for—be it for a safe overseas flight for a loved one, for a child to grow strong, or for warts to be cured—people will not have far to go to do so. For the sites of practical benefits are an integral part of the city environment, just as they are part of the social, cultural, and religious world in which people live.

8
Conclusions

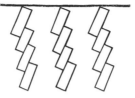

IN DISCUSSING the practical dynamics and conceptual meanings of *genze riyaku* we have dealt as much with commercialism, entertainment, and play as we have with questions of morality, spirituality, and doctrine. There is clearly a casual side to many of the issues and practices we have dealt with in this book, as well as a manipulative and coercive aspect in which gods may be cajoled into action for the benefit of petitioners. Just because behavior may at times be casual or commercial, however, does not render it invalid in religious terms: as we have shown in earlier chapters, the casual and relaxed, as well as the potentially manipulative, may be underpinned with serious meanings, motifs, and themes. The "casual religion" of popular shrine and temple visiting, therefore, should be taken seriously.

Many observers of religion in Japan have argued that the Japanese in general have a high level of religious participation—and are hence a religiously active people despite low levels of affirmed belief in religious doctrine—because of their adherence to custom and culturally ordained rituals, which are seen less as matters of belief and more as social injunctions. Thus Japanese religion has been widely portrayed in terms of etiquette, convention, social action, and cultural habit: turning to the gods not just in times of trouble but for reasons of custom, social convenience, and obligation. It is not surprising that *genze riyaku* has been largely disregarded as a frivolous sideshow in the study of Japanese religion rather than a reflection of serious religious values. Our approach, however, has been to take the casual seriously—not only because it exists but because it does so in complex and complementary relationships with serious religion.

The widespread participation in religious events in Japan, rather than simply promoting the pursuit of this-worldly benefits, is to a great degree *caused* by the pervasiveness of the conceptual and ritual framework of *genze riyaku*. The deeply regarded values embedded in the concept of this-worldly benefits, coupled with their general accessibility and their relevance to real-life issues and concerns, as well as to calendrical and life-cycle events, explain why Japanese religiosity, measured in terms of participation, has endured so well, especially when compared to many other industrialized countries. Hardly the superficial manifestation of aberrant superstition, the practical and conceptual framework of this-worldly benefits is the matrix within which much of Japanese religion thrives and must therefore be understood.

The pursuit of this-worldly benefits, along with its playful and casual sides, manifests moral dimensions, is embedded in social practices, and is affirmed in the textual sources and doctrinal structures of numerous religious organizations in Japan. As we noted in Chapter 6, the provision of benefits is used to demonstrate religious truth claims and to affirm the validity of specific religious traditions; as such it underpins a worldview and a religious sense of belonging and faith. Thus there is a reciprocal relationship between truth and benefits: scriptural and doctrinal truth legitimizes worldly benefits, which in turn validate the truth of scripture, doctrine, and, most important, institutional traditions.

Since the worldview epitomized by the seeking and selling of practical benefits in a religious context relies on spirit-oriented explanations and interpretations of events, it might appear to be antithetical to the scientific-rationalist worldview that underlies the modern education and political systems of Japan as a modern secular state. Yet praying for worldly benefits—although it has often been portrayed in a negative light by those who affirm a modern "rationalist" viewpoint and has been dismissed as being tinged with superstition and consigned to the wasteland of "false" religion—has much in common with the motivations and basic values expressed in secular societies.

Indeed, it is striking to note how closely the things sought through *genze riyaku* are aligned with the prevailing ethos of modern secular societies in what they seek for their citizens: happiness, assurances about the future, success, solace, and lives that can be lived as much as possible free from unforeseen problems and dangers. In Chapters 2 and 3 we saw how various religious values underlying practical benefits expressed the importance of prosperity in the community and nation. We saw, too, how the search for benefits was backed by a set of ethical constraints and values that emphasized hard work, duty, and diligence—values that recognized the obligations as well as the desires of the individual and therefore affirmed his or her social responsibility. Such ethics, rather than being out of touch with modern societies, are very much at their center: nothing is gained without commitment and striving; there is a price for everything; rewards follow from correct behavior. The pragmatic economic values and work ethics associated with Japan's postwar development are embedded in, rather than distant from, the normative values of Japanese religion as expressed in the concept and practice of this-worldly benefits.

Nevertheless, some might argue that the magical methods of practical benefits are inadequate mechanisms for obtaining the goals of well-being. Personal testimonies abound to the contrary, however. The tales of efficacy propagated by shrines and temples and repeated in guidebooks are themselves reiterations and affirmations of people's actual experiences with religious practices that produce worldly results. People repeat the practices for benefits because they appear to work just as well as rationalist technologies. In the petitioner's mind, these practices supplement rather than compete with rational technologies in the production of good results. Even if we attempt to explain away this behavior as self-delusion or a wrong ascription of causes—so that, for instance, the gods are given credit for curing a headache that actually went away of its own accord—we still need to recognize the function and significance of so-called superstition in modern society. Modernity, due to its own frustrations and failures, as we noted in Chapter 1, is itself a breeding ground for spirituality and superstition. While reason and magic may appear to be at odds with one another, they are not mutually exclusive: like the interactions between morality and magic discussed in Chapter 3, they may even feed off each other. Reason may be associated with modernity, but modernity itself can produce the need for magical solutions and the intercession of gods. Thus modernity and magic are bound together precisely because they are not sociologically inconsistent with each other. This is why we find students, businessmen, bureaucrats, housewives, and other modern, well-educated people engaged in the pursuit of worldly benefits in religious settings and through religious mechanisms. They see no terrible inconsistency between their religious and worldly views.

It is not surprising, then, that business companies geared to competition in the technologically grounded and rational world of economic complexity can adopt Shinto shrines and *kami* and that individuals, even when affirming adherence to modern rationalist ethics, find value in the meanings articulated within the practices of this-worldly benefits in dealing with their daily lives. The Japanese foreign service professional mentioned in Chapter 3, whose lack of belief in the *omamori* he had purchased for his sick son can be seen as articulating a "rationalist" viewpoint, nevertheless bought that *omamori*—and later admitted not just that he had done so because of his desire for his son's well-being, but that it might have had an effect on his son's recovery. Like students buying talismans or praying to the gods prior to examinations, which depend on their own ability to master forms of thinking rooted in the scientific rationalist system, this man recognized the limits of that system. He saw where a benefit-centered worldview could deal with his priorities, answer his needs, and fill a gap on an emotional level that his scientific worldview was ill equipped to deal with. What he faced was not just the question of rationality but the issue of chance, and it was an *omamori* rather than reason that allowed him to deal with that uncertainty. Chance plagues everyone, from highly educated technocrats to village farmers, and even after everything has been done to minimize the role of chance, it is seldom removed entirely as a factor that affects the outcome of surgery, taking an examination, being launched into space, planting rice, or playing pachinko.

Within the framework of practical benefits there is a common religious sentiment that speaks to everyone's needs at whatever level— whether pragmatic, transient, casual, sincere, or ascetic—they choose, wish, or need to engage with it. The commitment may be personal, self-directed, and austere, like the young woman's arduous journey of prayer to Izumo discussed in Chapter 5, or casual and minimal, like the purchase of an amulet while passing by a shrine, or group-centered, as when a member of a *kō* or company participates in a ritual supplication for benefits as part of a broad social organization. Need also conditions the manner of petition and the scale of desired result. In this system—as the king of Paekche well recognized when he first promoted Buddhism to the Japanese—there are treasures and fulfillment in which nothing is lacking. It is a spiritual care system with practical, this-worldly results in which all are equal: social status does not determine access, rewards, or merits. Although "value for money," as we have seen, plays a part in the ways people deliberate about seeking benefits, there are no barriers or exclusion zones to forbid anyone from asking for benefits or receiving them (since much of the process of receiving falls within the concerned person's framework of interpretation).

The recognition that people should be able to seek the benefits appropriate to their needs, and that none should be excluded from so seeking, has greatly influenced the Japanese religious environment. It has contributed, for example, to its generally nonexclusive nature: as has been frequently noted, there is a general sense that Japanese religion involves not a conflict between "this" and "that" (i.e., this but not that) but a potential utilization of various religious forms and traditions together in order to address different needs and social situations. We do not mean to imply here that conflict and exclusivity are not features of the Japanese religious landscape. (Indeed, we have elsewhere drawn attention to various manifestations and aspects of religious conflict in Japan.)[1] Certainly we recognize that some religious organizations and traditions in Japan have emphasized exclusivity. Rather, we are simply noting that the norm has tended far more toward pluralism. At the heart of this pluralism and sense of nonexclusivity lies the notion of *genze riyaku*. The interchangeability of *kami* and buddhas takes place in the world of *genze riyaku*, not in Shinto shrines or Buddhist temples where the main altars are reserved primarily for deities of their own kind. What exceptions we find, such as Inari and Benten, are still rooted in the conceptual and ritual framework of *genze riyaku*. This framework was central to the emergence of Buddhism as a vital religious entity in Japan—introduced as a new and powerful source of this-worldly benefits that could produce treasures to one's heart's content and used not so much to supplant the older religious order as to augment it.

This framework has played a major role in breaking down the barriers that distinguish the different traditions and ensuring open access to different figures of worship who are identified with particularistic religious frameworks. Some figures of worship can readily straddle the borders between Buddhism and Shinto, but even if they do not, their importance is related more to their reputation in providing benefits than to their identification with a specific religious tradition. Moreover, those who pray for benefits do not normally limit themselves to praying within the boundaries of one religious tradition but seek according to their needs: in this sense, there are no borders between religions. Rather, there are differentiations between types of benefit and the efficacy through which they can be met. This plurality is amply verified by studies on the religious sites of Ikoma, cited in earlier chapters, which show how petitioners made use of a variety of shrines, temples, deities, and buddhas in the region.[2] It is amplified also by the very nature of the guidebooks we discussed in Chapter 7: what frames them are the forms of benefits along with geographical location, not the figures of worship or the sectarian affiliation of the institutions.

Even religious movements that officially go against this basic plurality, or teach their members to retain a sense of exclusivity, may recognize the difficulties of enforcing this point in the face of inherited customs. Officials of movements such as Sōka Gakkai recognize that many of their members also attend religious occasions and petition for benefits in the shrines and temples of Shinto and Buddhism.[3] Awareness of the need for some form of plurality that accepts the pragmatic religiosity of this-worldly benefits is at the heart of the Jōdo Shin debates about reformation outlined in Chapter 2. In rejecting *genze riyaku*, the Jōdo Shin sect has caused many of its members simply to go elsewhere for the services that are denied them within their own temples. The discrepancy between their official teaching and actual practices suggests that had the Jōdo Shin sect been successful at enforcing its proscription against practical benefits, it might not have succeeded as much as it has in terms of institutional growth.

The normative religious tradition of practical benefits is not just a contributory factor to this general sense of nonexclusivity within the Japanese religious world: it is its dominant motivating force. Movements that express concepts associated with *genze riyaku* are world-affirming and have no problems with accepting the good things of this world and participating in the processes of worldly success. Thus they find themselves at ease with an informal system of religious and cultural values in Japan, a system that commands the support or tacit acceptance of the vast majority of Japanese people. The conceptual framework and rituals of practical benefits make up an informal religious complex, widely practiced throughout the country, that preserves and promotes a common set of values affirming health, wealth, success, and all the other virtues of materialism. As such it is a powerful and well-entrenched value system that may seem invisible because it is not organized into a formal structure and, moreover, is both pervasive and nonspecific.[4]

Once identified, however, this value system organized around practical benefits can be seen as a normative conceptual framework that pervades the country and articulates the values of modern as well as traditional Japan. It is the religion of Buddhism and Shinto at the highest scriptural levels, but it is at the same time a folk religion because it supports and is supported by Japanese people in all walks of life, dealing with their daily worries and their special concerns, from protecting their children to promoting their economic aspirations.

Throughout this book we have been concerned with describing the interlocking themes that are brought to life by the term "*genze riyaku*"—the ethical meanings, the textual sources, the practices, the commercial dimensions, the selling of religious truths—and showing how these all fit together within a common religious dynamic. We began the book with a story about the new religions and outlined how new religions have been attacked as aberrant for their focus on this-worldly benefits. In the ensuing pages we have hardly encountered the new religions at all, focusing instead on the older religious traditions of Shinto and Buddhism. This focus is deliberate. It is widely accepted that the new religions are centered on *genze riyaku,* and there are numerous studies of the new religions that touch on this topic (although, we should note, none that explores the topic in any great detail). By turning our attention to the mainstream, we have in fact demonstrated that the supposed aberrance of the new religions is nothing of the sort. That we can write a book about *genze riyaku* without mentioning (except as a frame of reference) the new religions is itself testimony to the prevalence of the topic in Japanese religion. Far from being perversions or frightful superstitions, the new religions accord, in terms of their focus on *genze riyaku,* with the general tenor and focus of Japanese religion—continuations rather than aberrations of the Japanese religious tradition. What marks them is not their emphasis on practical benefits per se but the ways in which they present them and make them available, as well as the interpretations and rituals that surround these benefits. As such the new religions—or at least the vast majority that are world-affirming—simply present another angle on the themes at the heart of the common religion of Japan.

The provision of this-worldly benefits, as we have seen, is a service found almost everywhere in Japan—as illustrated by the sheer number of institutions that cater for its every form. Though sanctioned by a wide range of formal institutions, it is an informal system that allows its practitioners to pick and choose the forms of religious action they will undertake and the deities they will petition, but at the same time it places them within a moral framework of responsibilities. It caters to every need from peace of mind to career success, from acquiring a spouse to begetting children, from aspiring to a safe family life to hoping that one's children succeed in their studies, enter good universities, and then progress up the ladder of success in business while remaining free from diseases and safe from accidents. It underpins the economic structure of Japanese religious institutions while providing them with the means (grounded in scripture and formal rituals) to assert their truths and religious validities. It affirms an ethical structure that offers security and allows people to buy out chance and at the same time provides a focus for social identity. In short, the religion of practical benefits permeates and upholds the religious traditions of Japan and is at the very core of its common religion.

Notes

Introduction

1. The term "new religion" (*shin shūkyō*) refers to those religions that have developed in Japan from the latter Tokugawa era onward outside the mainstream of Shinto and Buddhism, though they incorporate elements from these and other traditions. See, for example, Inoue et al. (1996) and Reader (1991a: 194–233).

2. Michiko's story is in fact a composite we put together from a number of similar testimonies found in the magazines, books, and catalogs of several new religions, including Mahikari, Sōka Gakkai, and Agonshū. We have drawn here on leaflets and pamphlets of believers' testimonies—such as *Tekazashii*, published by Mahikari, and Agonshū's collections of "miracle stories," *Sugobutsu hōtō: Kiseki no taikendanshū* (undated pamphlets published in the late 1980s)—and on oral testimonies from Sōka Gakkai believers at meetings in Canada and directly from members in Japan. See also Richard Anderson (1988; 1994) for detailed examples of narrative experiences, including benefits and efficacious results, from a number of new religions. We use a composite story because such themes are common to a number of new religions.

3. See Hardacre (1986:34), who argues that to see *genze riyaku* as solely material benefits is not only derogatory but inaccurate.

4. Inoue et al. (1996:216) and Earhart (1982:174).

5. Cited by Inoue et al. (1983:8).

6. Ibid., p. 9.

7. Kikumura (1978:69–70).

8. Asai (1968:162–169).

9. Inoue et al. (1983:9).

10. Arai (1985:239).

11. Schopen (1997:1–22).

12. Miyake (1974).

13. Shinno (1991); Miyata and Tsukamoto (1994).

14. See, for example, the various surveys conducted by public organizations such as NHK and the numerous commentaries by Japanese scholars on such surveys: general outlines of these surveys (and the questions that are therefore as-

sociated, by Japanese scholars, with religion) can be found in Swyngedouw (1993) and Reader (1991a).

15. Sharf (1995:452).

16. Ibid., p. 453.

17. Among other works, we should mention Sharf's own article (1995) as well as William M. Bodiford's (1993; 1994; 1996) and Bernard Faure's (1991; 1996) work on Sōtō Zen.

18. Reischauer and Jansen (1995:215).

19. Ibid.

20. See, for example, Ōmura (1988), Reader (1991a), and the debate between Anderson (1991) and Reader (1991b).

21. Reader (1991a) offers an overview of such surveys. For further details see Iida (1986), Kaneko (1988), Kōmoto (1988), and Swyngedouw (1993).

22. Reischauer and Jansen (1995:215).

23. Here, as elsewhere in the book, we use the term "ritual" not merely to refer to formal, organized contexts but to indicate behavior and actions that follow a ritualized format. See van Bremen (1995) for further discussion.

24. Dai Edo tankenkai (1994:24–25).

25. Kōdansha (1980:183).

26. The terms "established" and "mainstream" are widely used in relation to Shinto and Buddhism to denote that the religious traditions have been associated with the social structure and belonging to the community (Shinto) and household (Buddhism).

27. Kōdansha (1980:97).

28. Faure (1987:25–55, esp. 50–51). The close relationship between austerities and benefits has also been examined by William M. Bodiford (1993:116–117).

29. Gendai shimbutsu kenkyūkai (1993:27 and 273).

30. On Saijōji's size and position in the sect see Gendai shimbutsu kenkyūkai (1993:27) and Saijōji (undated temple leaflet collected April 24, 1996).

31. Inari, although commonly identified with the Shinto tradition, is not necessarily a Shinto deity. As Karen Smyers (1993) has shown, Inari can be venerated in Shinto and Buddhist contexts, and many of the best-known Inari centers of worship are in fact Buddhist institutions, such as Myōgonji and Saijō Inari in Okayama prefecture.

32. Kōdansha (1980:186).

33. The Sōtō sect's handbook for priests (Shūryō hikkei) lists, besides the two head temples of the sect and their two branch temples, only twenty-one such training temples for monks and four special training centers for nuns (senmon nisōdō); see Sōtōshū shūmuchō (1978:75–79).

34. Daiyūsan Saijōji kaisō roppyakunen hōsan jimukyoku (1984:9).

35. Interview at Saijōji, April 24, 1996. A priest had made similar comments to us on a previous visit to Saijōji on November 30, 1981.

36. Aston (1956: p. 2, 66).

37. One should perhaps add a caveat here that there have been, in comparison to studies of Buddhism or indeed the new religions, few major studies of Shinto. Nelson (1996), which discusses genze riyaku activities at a Shinto shrine in Nagasaki, is a recent useful addition to the literature.

38. Bunkachō (1994:2–45) summarizes all the legally recognized religious organizations classified under the rubric of Shinto in Japan and outlines their doctrines.

39. Bunkachō (1994:19).

40. See, for example, Kōmoto (1988) on the levels of participation in death-related rituals. The numerical size of the various Pure Land Buddhist sects centered on Amida (Jōdo and Jōdo Shin)indicates the importance of this promise of otherworldly salvation.

41. Among the studies of ancestors are Smith (1974) and Takeda (1971).

42. See, for example, Tenrikyō (1985:75–81).

43. See Blacker (1975) for a general discussion of Japanese attitudes to spirits and healing, as well as Reader (1991a). Davis (1980) is perhaps the most comprehensive account of the role of healing in the new religions.

44. Interview, Daimanji, Sendai, January 1, 1982.

45. Votive tablet seen at Kokawa-dera, Wakayama prefecture, June 12, 1988. The writer was a female who gave her name but no age or address.

46. Imai (1993:4).

47. Arai (1985:262).

48. Honmon Butsuryūshū pamphlet (undated), p. 3.

49. This simplification of the temple's foundation story is abbreviated here to illustrate the link between faith and benefits. For a further discussion of foundation legends as a means of promoting benefits see Chapter 6.

50. Bunkachō (1994:86). See also Saijō Inarikyō hōsha (1979) for a general explanation of the temple, its connection to Inari, and the role of Inari. This discussion is also based on information provided by priests at the temple during a visit there in October 1994.

51. Bunkachō (1995:78).

52. Interview at Ichibata Yakushi with Rev. Mishima, June 16, 1995.

53. Shimazono (1992). See also Reader (1993a:236) for a discussion of Shimazono's work.

54. See Hayami (1983:48–51) and Yoritomi (1984:35–36).

55. See, for example, Nakamura (1973), Dykstra (1976), and Yoritomi (1984: 63–76).

56. Undated temple pamphlet (collected in 1987).

57. Matsumoto (1985:9–10).

58. Ibid., pp. 12–13.

59. Duffy (1992:3).

60. Ibid., p. 2.

61. Thomas (1971).

62. See, for example, Ambros (1995).

63. Ibid., pp. 19–28.

64. Duffy (1992:3).

65. See, for example, Collcutt (1981).

66. This is, for example, a major theme in the works of Miyake Hitoshi (1974; 1981; 1989), Sakurai Tokutarō (1968), and Hori Ichirō (1968), to name but three leading figures in the study of religion in the postwar era.

67. The former is more closely translated as "folk belief" but may also be glossed as "folk religion." In recent years it has become more common to use the

second term (*minzoku shūkyō*) rather than the first (*minkan shinkō*), but this is to some degree dependent on one's academic perspective. For a discussion of the differences between these two terms see Shinno (1991; 1993).

68. Even in Miyake's (1989) theoretical study of folk religion, perhaps the most comprehensive work of its kind, although he does pay attention to aspects of religious art and the like, there is scant reference to texts or liturgical traditions as formative elements in Japanese religious views.

69. Pye (1996:264–265).

70. Ibid., p. 264.

71. We mean this in the sense in which Levy-Bruhl (1926) constructed his analysis of primitive religious mentalities, which was founded on notions of pre-literacy, and in the ways in which Taylor (1963) has developed Levy-Bruhl's views and talked of a primal view involving a sense of cosmic oneness.

72. Duffy (1992:3).

73. Ibid.

74. This is not a topic that can be discussed at any length here, but studies of the factors behind the rise of new religions commonly imply that stagnation and lack of spiritual dynamism within the established religions have been a major cause of the growth of these new movements. See, for example, McFarland (1967).

75. On the issues of tradition and nostalgia, see, for example, Reader (1987), Robertson (1991), and Ivy (1995).

76. Allen (1990:229).

77. This point is made, for example, by Pye (1977).

78. See, for example, Kino (1981), Kanaoka (1981), and Takagami (1980). The extent of their sales can be judged by the fact that such books are frequently reprinted due to demand: Kanaoka's book was first published in 1973 and by 1981 was in its eighth printing; Takagami's, first published in 1952, was by 1980 in its twenty-fourth printing.

79. Among these categories we could include members of Japan's ethnic minorities, such as the Koreans living in Japan, who generally have their own religious centers, practices, and shared rites, including calendrical rites (see Iida 1988 and Kino 1990), as well as movements such as the Jehovah's Witnesses whose members do not participate in common Japanese religious activities. The exclusivist groups that have emerged within the Japanese context (such as Sōka Gakkai), even though their members withdraw from participation in common rituals and the like, tend to develop their own versions: thus a member of Sōka Gakkai can perform a *hatsumode* (first religious visit of the year) rite at a Sōka Gakkai center. Exclusivity does not therefore necessarily mean rejection so much as adaptation and making formerly common rituals specific to a particular group. See Reader (1991a:8–9 and 245, n. 19). Seeking this-worldly benefits is very much part of Sōka Gakkai's religious activity and to this extent shares in the common religion of Japan.

80. Davis (1992:15–27 and 272, n. 2).

81. By "saint" we refer to figures such as Kōbō Daishi—miracle-working holy figures who are, in essence, humans who have become transcendent spiritual figures.

82. See, for example, Shinno (1991) and Goodwin (1994).

83. See Ikei (1985:225–227). Although it is generally considered that the term was first used by Ōmura Eishō, we have not been able to track down its first appearance in print.

84. A partial exception has been Hardacre (1986:34), who argues for a re-interpretation of the idea of *genze riyaku* and later (p. 134) suggests that a reorienting of the self is part of the process of *genze riyaku*.

Chapter 1: Benefits in the Religious System

1. Kabanoff (1994:101–102).

2. Ibid., p. 100.

3. Ibid., pp. 121–122.

4. See Kabanoff (1994:99–100) for a discussion of Kankiten's names.

5. Murata (1995:194). It is not uncommon for the main benefit-granting figure at a temple to be different from the main image of worship, and Hōzanji is in no way unique.

6. Shūkyō shakaigaku no kai (1985); Shiobara (1987).

7. Iida's comments are made in Shūkyō shakaigaku no kai (1985:35–36).

8. Chōgosonshiji temple leaflet (undated).

9. Murata (1995:194).

10. Yoritomi and Shiraki (1993:126–127).

11. See Chapter 3 for an example of what happens when one fails to treat Kankiten correctly and an example of this deity's dangerous powers.

12. On the Hōzanji *ema* and their inscriptions see Holtom (1938) and Reader (1991c), who discusses the changing content of the messages.

13. Murata (1995:195).

14. The temple has published a number of collections of stories and miracle tales affirming the provision of benefits at Hōzanji, including the volume *Taishō Kankiten risshōki* (Hōzanji 1966). See also Chapter 6.

15. Murata (1995:185). He notes that on the road up to the temple there are rows of stone lanterns donated by grateful petitioners.

16. On several occasions when Ian Reader visited the temple, he observed *hyakudo mairi* being performed barefoot.

17. This is an estimate (based in part on temple information) that was given in the Shūkyō shakaigaku no kai volume and has been repeated elsewhere (as in Yoritomi and Shiraki 1993:127). It is extremely hard to get precise figures on shrine and temple visiting in Japan; figures such as those at *hatsumōde* are made by the police and normally are based on estimates. See Murata (1995:194–204).

18. Between us we have made five visits to Hōzanji: one by Tanabe in midweek when the temple was quiet and four by Reader on Sundays or major ritual occasions, including once at the New Year period in 1988.

19. These events are listed in Yoritomi and Shiraki (1993:127). The Buddha's birthday is normally celebrated on April 8 in Japan, but in some places it is celebrated a month later.

20. For an extended discussion of the whole cycle of events and formal and informal ritual that frame the New Year period, see Reader (1994).

21. Given that some people make several shrine and temple visits, two-thirds might be an exaggeration. Many nowadays travel overseas or to holiday destinations such as Tokyo Disneyland during this period, but not nearly so many as go

to shrines and temples. According to the *Fukushima minpō* newspaper (January 3, 1993), some 5,380,000 people in all went to leisure sites during the first three days of the year, the top location being Tokyo Disneyland with 190,000 visitors—a number far smaller than the 3.5 million who went to Meiji Shrine. The *Yomiuri* newspaper survey of religious activity in 1984 showed that 65 percent of its respondents took part in *hatsumōde*. See Bunkachō (1995:14).

22. See, for example, the newspaper *Fukushima minpō*, January 5, 1993, p. 3, which reported record numbers of *hatsumōde* participants and attributed the turnout to good weather and the wish to seek the gods' help in times of uncertainty.

23. The figures for 1994 come from the magazine *Yoke* 12(66) (1994): 9.

24. Shūkyō shakaigaku no kai (1985:39).

25. Ibid., pp. 38–81, especially p. 40. The connection with the *mizu shōbai* business probably stems from the association of Kankiten (who is iconographically depicted as two figures embracing) with the notion of union. Kankiten has been widely seen as a deity who can help in matters relating to sex. Sexual union—or at least the promise of sexual encounters—is an underlying theme of the *mizu shōbai* business (Allison 1994).

26. Bunkachō (1994:188).

27. See Reader (1991a) for a discussion of this point. See also Ōmura (1988), Kōmoto (1988), and Kaneko (1988).

28. Many details of the 1983 NHK survey are available in English in Swyngedouw (1993).

29. Naitō and Shimokawa (1984).

30. Ibid., p. 17.

31. See Naitō and Shimokawa (1984:76–104) for coverage of the shrines, temples, and benefits of Taitō ward.

32. Extended interviews with two pilgrims from Osaka in Shikoku between November 11 and 14, 1990.

33. This is the most widely visited Ebisu shrine in the region, but many Osakans visit Imamiya Ebisu Shrine in southern Osaka.

34. Interview with a female Japanese student, Hawai'i, October 1996.

35. Miyata (1987:1–2).

36. Ohnuki-Tierney (1984:138) notes that it is still common for women in Japan to wear a sash known as an *iwata obi* around the stomach during pregnancy: of 106 women who answered her questionnaire at an Osaka hospital, 81 had got such a sash from Nakayama-dera—testimony to the extent to which this temple is seen in the region as *the* temple to visit on such occasions.

37. Officially the institution is known as Seichōji and is a Buddhist temple: Kiyoshi Kōjin as a *kami* (Shinto deity) provides us with one of the rare cases where a deity rather than a Buddha figure is venerated as the main focus of worship at a Buddhist institution.

38. On Kiyoshi Kōjin see Yoritomi and Shiraki (1993:104–105).

39. Interview at Kawasaki Daishi, January 8, 1993, with Rev. Fujita Ryūjō.

40. Reader (1991a:190–191).

41. Interview with Rev. Ueyama, Saidaiji, Okayama prefecture, April 25, 1996.

42. Chiba (1988:92).

43. Ibid.

44. This is not the first instance in which the *kami* have been invoked in connection with the space age. As Jan Swyngedouw (1993:59) has pointed out, the Shinto *kami* have been invoked in connection with the launching of Japanese communications satellites from the space center on the Japanese island of Tanegashima.

45. http://www.netwave.or.jp/~hachiman/.

46. Shrine leaflet written by Nakamura Hirohiko, chief priest of Kanamara Shrine (April 1992).

47. Ibid.

48. See Young and Ikeuchi (1995).

49. For further discussion of these points see Reader (1995:14–15).

50. On the cult of faith in Kōbō Daishi in general see Hinonishi (1988). On Kōbō Daishi and pilgrimage see Reader (1993b).

51. See, for example, Reader (1996a:281–282), which describes the activities of a group of people who are mostly members of the Ōtani branch of Pure Land Buddhism and who nonetheless have helped construct a hall of veneration to Kōbō Daishi and whose veneration of him transcends their official sectarian concerns.

52. Interview at Kawasaki Daishi, January 8, 1993. We thank Rev. Fujita Ryūjō for his information on Kawasaki Daishi.

53. This term was first used by Gary Ebersole (1991:3–16).

54. Shinno (1991) and Goodwin (1994) both discuss the role of *hijiri* in publicizing temples and show how legends and myths affirming religious power played a crucial role in this process.

55. See, for example, Nii and Nakajima (1982:25).

56. Ian Reader (research on Shikoku, in progress).

57. Interview with Fujita Ryūjō, January 8, 1993. *Engi* are rarely static and fixed stories: as inventions and means of proselytization, they can assume a number of forms. At Kawasaki Daishi that appears to be the case: the legend related here is based on an oral version told by Rev. Fujita, which focuses primarily on the carving of the statue by Kōbō Daishi in his forty-second year, and an account of it in Chiba (1988:102).

58. Takahashi (1979:5–6).

59. *Japan Times Weekly* (January 7, 1991) and *Fukushima minpō* (January 5, 1993).

60. In Shinto shrines (as in some new religions) the ritual is generally known as a *hitakisai,* but the ritual format (priests incanting ritual prayers and consigning wooden sticks on which requests have been made to the flames) is quite similar.

61. This is our translation of the Japanese text under this title on the Kawasaki Daishi home page of the Internet (http://www1.sphere.ad.jp/daishi/). The same text appears in various leaflets produced at the temple.

62. For a general overview of such objects see Reader (1991a:175–182); for *ema* see Reader (1991c:23–50). Besides Shinto shrines and Buddhist temples, many new religions use *ema* as a means of conveying requests to the deities they worship or, at times, to the spirit of their founder who, in many new religions, may be regarded as a source of benefits.

63. We use the term "privatized" here in the sense in which it is commonly used in the sociology of religion—to indicate personal and individualized expressions of religious meaning and action.

64. Takizawa et al. (1979:151). The volume presents a photograph of such a prayer ritual for the Seibu Department Store in January 1967. The temple also has photographs of prayer services for the police force, and temple priests on January 8, 1993, confirmed that this ritual continues to be held regularly.

Chapter 2: Scripture and Benefits

1. Visit to Todoroki Fudō, June 13, 1993.
2. Watson (1993:99).
3. Ibid.
4. Ibid., p.102.
5. Watanabe (1966:283).
6. McCullough and McCullough (1980:533).
7. Ibid., p. 534.
8. Ibid., p. 771.
9. Nihon Bukkyō kenkyū kai (1970:43).
10. McCullough and McCullough (1980:533) and Watson (1993:22).
11. Kim (1990:153).
12. Tamura (1960:58).
13. Kohno (1996:24).
14. Kanaoka (1981:123–129).
15. Satō (1971:33 and 63).
16. Ibid., p. 101.
17. Rhys Davids (1963:10).
18. Ibid., p. 29.
19. Ibid., p. 33.
20. Ibid., p. 34.
21. Ibid., p. 31.
22. Ibid., pp. 31–33.
23. Ibid., pp. 49–50.
24. Hare (1961:24).
25. Ibid., p. 27.
26. Ibid., pp. 31–32.
27. Ibid., pp. 37–38.
28. *Hua-yen ching*, T10:430a–c.
29. Ibid., p. 429c.
30. Pye (1990:106).
31. *Hua-yen ching*, T10:391b.
32. Fujii (1993:235–284).
33. Ibid., p. 264.
34. Ibid., p. 252.
35. Ibid., p. 255.
36. Ibid., pp. 273–274 .
37. Iijima (1995:60–61).
38. Ibid., pp. 79–82.
39. Ibid., pp. 84–86.

40. Ibid., pp. 85–86.
41. Sueki (1995:14).
42. Ōchō (1969:453–461).
43. Watson (1993:103).
44. Ibid., p. 267.
45. Ōchō (1969:465–466).
46. Watson (1993:286 and 288).
47. Ōchō (1969:474).
48. Ibid., p. 485.
49. As if to emphasize the point we made in the Introduction about the need for a study of this topic, very little (apart from scholars such as Fujii who attempt to explain the topic away) has been published on the subject in the years between the first and second editions of *Nihon shūkyō no genze riyaku*.
50. Tsuruoka (1970:36–51).
51. Birnbaum (1979:149).
52. Ibid., p. 153.
53. Ibid., pp. 167–168.
54. Ibid., p. 176.
55. Gomez (1996:69–76).
56. Birnbaum (1979:209).
57. Sōtōshū shūsei chōsa iinkai (1984:10–40).
58. Reported in Sasaki (1988:17).
59. Ibid., pp. 13–35.
60. Ibid., p. 20.
61. Ibid., p. 25.
62. Ibid., p. 32.
63. See our comments in the Introduction, and see also Shimazono (1992).
64. Sasaki (1988:26); emphasis added.
65. Ibid., p. 28; emphasis added.
66. Nara (1995:19–42).
67. Ibid., p. 22.
68. Takakusu (1969:183).
69. Ibid., p. 198.
70. Nara (1995:36).
71. Takakusu (1969:178) .
72. *Kyōgyōshinshō*, T83: 599b.
73. Aston (1956:144).
74. Ibid., p. 200.
75. Ibid., p. 348.
76. Ibid., pp. 119–122.
77. Ibid., p. 133.
78. Shiraishi Mitsukuni cited by Philippi (1990:2).
79. Philippi (1990:3).
80. Aston (1956:154).
81. Ibid., p. 177.
82. See Philippi (1990:17–83).
83. Joseph Kitagawa in preface to Philippi (1990:xxvii).
84. See, for example, Uda (1963).

85. Bodiford (1994:25–27).
86. Uda (1963:348–349).
87. Ibid., pp. 350–352.
88. Uda (1963:347–348).
89. Davis (1992:298).
90. Kanzaki (1995:18–20).

Chapter 3: Buying Out Chance

1. This is a pseudonym for a female Japanese academic colleague of ours.

2. These are common themes expounded in the literature on sickness and misfortune in the new religions. Thus the views of Mahikari that germs are only a surface explanation of what is wrong—and that true investigations into the causes of illness require an understanding of spiritual matters causing the germs to afflict a particular person (see Davis 1980)—reflect this underlying spiritual worldview.

3. Hoshi kuyō pamphlet, Kōyasan (undated).

4. The term "moral luck" is used by Western philosophers to indicate the idea that moral actions are subject to the vagaries of luck and therefore good intentions followed by right actions do not always produce moral results. See Williams (1981) and Statman (1993). Martha Nussbaum (1986:25) speaks of Greek tragedy in terms of "good people being ruined because of things that just happen to them, things that they do not control." Whereas Williams uses "moral luck" to mean that morality is affected by luck, we use the term to indicate that luck is affected by morality.

5. Tan (1989:10–11).
6. Kalupahana (1975).
7. Ibid., p. 89.
8. Wilson and Dobbelaere (1994:24).
9. Ibid., p. 23.
10. Gomez (1996:188).
11. LaFleur (1992:15).
12. *Ikoma Shōten* 75 (May 16, 1996):1.
13. Ibid., p. 4.
14. Davis (1980:37).
15. Yoritomi and Shiraki (1993:14).
16. Interview in Mathews (1996:172).
17. Tan (1991:27); emphasis added.
18. Oates (1995:11).
19. Etori (1994:28–29).
20. Hara (1992:100).
21. Arai (1988:61–62).
22. Hori (1968:47).
23. Alberto Villoldo cited in McCarry (1996:34).

24. See the comments about education *omamori* (many of which are purchased for students by close relatives, especially mothers and elder siblings) in Reader (1991a:189).

25. Ibid., p. 54.
26. Ueda (1988:17–42).

27. Yoritomi and Shiraki (1993:11–14).

28. Oda (1976:98–100).

29. Shūkyō shakaigaku no kai (1985:130) discusses how visitors to Ishikiri Shrine may be making visits of gratitude after having received benefits as a result of a previous visit.

30. Narita-san brochure (undated).

31. Shūkyō shakaigaku no kai (1985:77).

32. Yoritomi and Shiraki (1993:34–35).

33. Hagiwara and Sutō (1985:104).

34. Ichihime Jinja brochure (undated).

35. Gendai shimbutsu kenkyūkai (1993:1–6).

36. Iwashimizu Hachiman Shrine, which enshrines Hachiman, originally an imperial deity, was established by the imperial household in the ninth century and continues to receive visits from its representatives during important festivals and ritual events.

37. Kawasaki Daishi (1993:3).

38. Sōtōshū shūmuchō (1980:48–50).

39. Nakajima (1980:435).

40. Matsumoto (1980:254).

41. Reader (1991a; 1991b); see also Anderson (1991).

42. T17: no. 786, p. 726a.

43. Honda (1985:20).

44. Interview in Toronto, November 24, 1993.

45. Tan (1991:20).

46. Interview at Zenkōji, Nagano, May 1996.

47. As noted in the Introduction, *shinkō* is translated both as "faith" and as "belief" in Japanese.

48. Cognition is a problematic term because of the many levels of thought it can embrace. It might be said, for instance, that a statement about how an amulet can keep one healthy has to involve cognition since the statement is intelligible, but we prefer to consider this an example of affective belief since the level of rational or systematic explanation is relatively low. Affective belief is characterized by low-level cognition.

49. Cahill (1995:204).

50. For a discussion of the role of images in thinking and Buddhism see Tanabe (1992:147–152).

51. Gendai shimbutsu kenkyūkai (1993:5).

52. Ibid., p. 8.

53. Arai (1988:105).

54. See, for example, Reader (1991c).

55. Staal (1979:2–22).

56. Buruma (1996:32).

57. Nakao (1983:30–31).

58. Cited in Shūkyō shakaigaku no kai (1985:40).

59. Ibid., p. 67, n. 45.

60. Yoritomi and Shiraki (1993:17).

61. Interview in Tokyo, May 1996.

62. Oda (1976:105–106).

63. Shimizutani (1986:161–162).
64. Saitō (1982:160).
65. Kasahara's position is taken from Kasahara (1976:75–89).
66. Ibid., pp. 84–85.
67. Sasaki (1990:234).
68. Oda (1976:18–21 and 54–58). In his foreword to Oda's book, the late Professor Yoshito Hakeda of Columbia University certifies Oda's explanations as being true to Shingon teachings.
69. Toganoo (1935:147–148).
70. Cited in Mathews (1996:169).
71. Miyasaka (1983:7).
72. Gorai (1983:19–20).
73. Katō (1983:31–32).
74. Ibid., p. 41.
75. Kanzaki (1995:38–44).

Chapter 4: The Providers of Benefits

1. Morris (1967:172–173).
2. Interviews conducted during a visit to Kurama in May 1996.
3. Undated and unpaginated brochure from Mount Kurama collected in May 1996.
4. This summary of the foundational story of Kuramadera is based on Kuramadera kyōmubu (1995:5–21).
5. Undated and unpaginated brochure from Mount Kurama, collected in May 1996.
6. Smyers (1996:99).
7. For example, the guidebook *Nippon kamisama zukan* edited by the Shūkyō minzoku kenkyūjo (1996) has a long section (pp. 182–215) on different localized Jizō throughout Japan, including several of those mentioned here.
8. This song is translated in LaFleur (1992:63–64).
9. See the picture in Hiro and Morimura (1990:142).
10. Smyers (1996:92).
11. Ibid., pp. 88–98.
12. Ibid., p. 89, n. 12.
13. Ibid., p. 90.
14. Ibid., p. 96.
15. Ibid., p. 91.
16. Translated in Tsunoda et al. (1958:80).
17. Matsunaga (1969:217).
18. Translated from the *Honchō kōsōden* in Matsunaga (1969:220).
19. Nakamaki (1983:265).
20. Bukkyō minzoku gakkai (1986:212).
21. Earhart (1974:50).
22. Shinmura (1970:1162).
23. Some scholars deny that Sarutahiko is of Taoist origin and see it as a native Japanese deity that only took on the name Kōshin. See Nihon Bukkyō kenkyūkai (1970:32–33).

24. Sakurai (1968:38–40).

25. Saganoi's comments were made in a symposium published as "Shimbutsu shūgō to shimbutsu kakuri o megutte" in Shintō shūkyō gakkai (1992:42–43 and 94).

26. Mihashi's comments can also be found in "Shimbutsu shūgō to shimbutsu kakuri o megutte" in Shinto shūkyō gakkai (1992:32–33).

27. Ibid., p. 68.

28. Ibid., p. 74.

29. Ibid., pp. 68–70 and 105.

30. Satō (1990:115).

31. Undated and unpaginated flyer from the Narita-san Shinshōji temple in Narita, Chiba prefecture.

32. Abe (1992:199); Yoritomi (1995:5).

33. Naganuma (1991:54–65).

34. Abe (1992:128).

35. Kida (1976:61–70). Kida holds that Saburō is Kotoshiro no Mikoto, but Naganuma (1991) disputes this.

36. This description is cited in Kida (1976:239).

37. Sugata (1992:55).

38. Ibid., p. 182.

39. See, for example, Hirose (1993), Tatsukawa (1993), and Shūkyō minzoku kenkyūjo (1996).

40. These details of the various paintings of the *shichifukujin* are taken from Kida (1976:74–95).

41. Satō and Kaneko (1989:29).

42. Ibid., pp. 33–48.

43. T16: no. 665, pp. 430c–431a.

44. Aston (1956:114).

45. For an excellent reproduction of this scene see Akiyama et al. (1968: pl. 24–25).

46. Satō and Kaneko (1989:100–109).

47. This poem is cited in Satō and Kaneko (1989:126).

48. Ibid., p. 129.

49. T8: no. 245, p. 832b–c.

50. This web page is found at: http://www.cha.or.jp/~hatada/sitifuku.html.

51. Shiraki (1995:13).

52. For the compositions and histories of these pilgrimage routes see the appropriate entries in Shiraki (1995), Ozeki (1993), and Satō and Kaneko (1989).

53. Yoritomi and Shiraki (1993:176–177).

54. Iwai (1974:183–197).

55. Ibid., pp. 174–175.

56. Ibid., pp. 104–105.

57. For a full outline of Ishikiri's reputation and specialization in these areas see Kiseki (1973).

58. See, for example, Gendai shimbutsu kenkyūkai (1993:214–215) and Sugata (1992:132).

59. Yoritomi and Shiraki (1993:32–33).

60. Ibid., pp. 80–81.
61. Ibid., pp. 136–137.
62. Saitō (1984:470).
63. http://ss4.inet-osaka.or.jp/~kissyo/naze.html.
64. For a detailed study of the Kōbō Daishi legends see Shirai (1986); for belief in Kōbō Daishi in general see Hinonishi (1988).
65. Arai (1988:84 ff).
66. Ibid., p. 86.
67. See Reader (1996a:276–279) for a discussion of this point. As well as collections of pilgrimage miracle tales dating from the latter part of the seventeenth century—such as the *Shikoku henro kudokuki* gathered and published in 1689 by the ascetic Shinnen Yūben (Reader 1996a:277)—there are a number of modern collections including Kōbō Daishi Kūkai Kankōkai (1985), which recounts miracle tales from the Shikoku and the Shōdoshima pilgrimages.
68. Interview at Kōyasan in March 1990.
69. Lecture at Kōyasan on September 24, 1994.
70. Arai (1988:172).
71. Ibid., pp. 170–171.
72. See, for example, Yamasaki (1988), Kiyota (1978), and Hakeda (1972).
73. Arai (1988:175).
74. See Reader (1996a:283–284) and Saitō (1984:470) for further comments on this point.
75. Interview with head priest of Hikō Shrine, Yawata, October 1995.
76. Nye (1990:3).
77. Hubbard's welcome is quoted by Nye (1990:161).
78. Nye (1990:154).
79. Bright (1949:66); Baldwin (1995:122).

Chapter 5: The Dynamics of Practice

1. On matchmaking and *miai* see Edwards (1989:39 and 58–66).
2. This story was originally told to Dorothy Reader by a close friend in Kobe in 1985: the woman in question subsequently succeeded in her quest, meeting a prospective husband and becoming engaged and later married.
3. Smith (1992:245).
4. The linking of the words "play" and "pay," to signify the relationship between the two, was first made by the anthropologist Nelson Graburn, who also linked these terms to the importance of ludic activities in the title of his study of Japanese tourism: *To Pray, Pay and Play: The Cultural Structure of Japanese Tourism* (Graburn 1983).
5. The notion of ritualized optimism is taken from Malinowski's (1974:90) essay on magic, science, and religion, where he states that "the function of magic is to ritualize man's optimism, to enhance his faith in the victory of hope over fear." It is not necessary to regard the seeking of practical benefits solely in terms of magical practices—as noted in Chapter 3, for example, ethical considerations are also significant—but the issues Malinowski outlines, in terms of hope and optimism, are central to the whole process of practical benefits.
6. Likewise, we would note, the practice of *mizuko kuyō* involves a vital public dimension: placing an *ema* addressing the dead fetus, often with the name of

the child and mother on it, at temples is virtually a public declaration of having had an abortion.

7. Honda's remarks appeared in a general feature on praying at shrines and temples in the magazine *Denim*, January 1993, pp. 64–65.

8. This tale appears frequently in the legends of Kōbō Daishi. See, for example, Saitō (1988) for an overview of these legends; see pp. 54–57 for the prevalence of such water-related legends.

9. Interviews in Takamatsu, Shikoku, November 13, 1990.

10. See Reader (1991a: chaps. 6 and 7), which deals extensively with activities at temples and shrines and the diverse ways in which people interact with shrines, temples, gods, and buddhas. Nelson (1996) provides further descriptions of practices in the context of a Shinto shrine.

11. Kōdansha (1980:264).

12. This reiterates the points made by K. Peter Takayama in his supplementary remarks (pp. 248–250) to Swanger (1981) about the importance of social love as a factor in the uses of *omamori*.

13. Averbuch (1997).

14. In his study of amulets, H. Byron Earhart (1994:618–619) refers to this process as a "transfer" of the power of the buddha or *kami* to the amulet object.

15. See Swanger (1981) for a general discussion of the more common forms of *omamori*. On the Tagata Shrine charms and talismans see Chiba (1988:26).

16. Fieldwork observations at Kawasaki Daishi, January 8, 1993.

17. Swyngedouw (1993:54).

18. As a rule Shinto shrines are less likely to suggest that their objects could be placed in a Buddhist altar: this, we consider, is because the Buddhist altar, as a memorial altar to the ancestors, is associated with death and thus, in Shinto eyes, ritually impure.

19. Tenjin shinkō henshū iinkai (1981). This book was on sale at Kitano Tenmangū Shrine.

20. Ibid., p. 148.

21. Tenjin shinkō henshū iinkai (1981:148).

22. These instructions are written on the paper bags in which talismans and amulets are handed to purchasers at these shrines. Similar instructions may be found at shrines and temples throughout Japan.

23. See Reader (1994) for an extended discussion on these issues and the rituals of New Year in general.

24. For more details on *ema*—their history, their designs, the messages written on them, the ways they operate in relation to practical benefits—see Reader (1991b) and Iwai (1974; 1983).

25. Reader (1991b:41–42).

26. On pilgrimages in Japan see Reader (1996a), Shinjō (1982), and Shinno (1992; 1996).

27. On the significance and symbolism of death images in the Shikoku pilgrimage see Reader (1993b).

28. Interview with Iwatsubo Shinkō, Osaka, April 24, 1996, plus research at Hachijōji, April 30, 1996. For further information on the *shichifukujin* pilgrimages in present-day Japan and their role as summoners and providers of benefits, see Satō and Kaneko (1989) and Ozeki (1993).

29. For a discussion of these issues see Reader (1993b). They form a prevalent theme in many works about Shikoku (see Miyazaki 1985), especially those relating to the pilgrimage folklore (see Takeda 1972).

30. We thank Rev. Aki Hiroshi of Gokurakuji in Tokushima prefecture for allowing Ian Reader to conduct this survey at his temple, which was carried out on *osamefuda* left at the temple between January and early March 1991. Reader (1996a:274) presents a preliminary report on these findings.

31. Maeda (1976) and Kaneko (1988) both provide data from surveys showing that practices associated with the deceased such as visiting graves (*haka mairi*) increase with age. See Reader (1991a:251).

32. These observations are based on Oda (1984:62) and information given us by representatives of the island's pilgrimage association (Shōdoshima Reijō-kai) in March 1991.

33. This poster is one of many such seen by Ian Reader during his research on pilgrimages in Japan and which will form part of a wider project he is doing on pilgrimage: this one was photographed during a visit to Shōdoshima in April 1987. Not all of the 350 people listed were physically present in the party, for it is a common practice to represent someone else (*daisan*) when participating in the pilgrimage: the banner mentioned 350 pilgrims including *daisan*.

34. See, for example, Smyers (1993:467–475) where she discusses the formation and activities of *kō* centered on Inari and major centers of Inari worship.

35. Collcutt (1988:256).

36. Ueda (1981:42).

37. Reader (1991b:38).

38. Jinja shinpōsha (1986); see also Swyngedouw (1993:57–59).

39. Jinja shinpōsha (1986:40, 78, and 68 respectively).

40. Honda (1985:24–26).

41. Ibid., p. 29.

42. Jinja shinpōsha (1986:67).

43. Honda (1985:28).

Chapter 6: Selling Benefits

1. This article appeared in the Kansai editions of the *Asahi shinbun* on December 5, 1986.

2. As Maeda (1971) has shown in his analysis of Tokugawa-era pilgrimage, the number of pilgrims may fluctuate from era to era depending on various circumstances, including economic conditions.

3. Long (1990:87).

4. See Reader (1991a:62 and 71).

5. A comment along these lines was made to one of the authors by a priest at Nakayama-dera on November 15, 1987, at the hall of worship where the temple's *hatsumiyamairi* rituals are conducted.

6. Reader (1991a:149–153) and Nakayama-dera (1986).

7. See, for example, Werblowsky (1991) and LaFleur (1992) for discussion of the issue of *mizuko kuyō* and some of the debates that surround it.

8. Seidenstecker (1981:394).

9. Ibid., p. 394. Ambros (1995:21–22) cites Lady Tamakazura's pilgrimage to Hasedera as an example of Heian-era female pilgrimage with this-worldly purposes.

10. Seidenstecker (1981:395).

11. Ibid., pp. 394–395.

12. Dykstra (1976:117). Dysktra is unable to date the origins of this text exactly but shows it cannot have been before 1192; evidence she cites from other Japanese scholars indicates that a date early in the thirteenth century is the most likely (p. 121).

13. Ibid., pp. 119–120. For a detailed and extensive study of the economic issues behind these campaigns, as well as the role of itinerant priests and the campaigns they carried out, see Goodwin (1994).

14. See Shinno (1991:281–285) for further discussion of this point and the seminal role of the *hijiri* in Japanese religion.

15. McCallum (1994:79–86).

16. Miyuki (1996:17).

17. For the incidence of miracle tales in Shikoku, especially collections of tales at individual temples such as Tatsueji (the nineteenth site on the pilgrimage), see Shinno (1980:161–196).

18. Fieldwork visit to Hachijōji, April 29, 1996.

19. McCallum (1994:169).

20. Ibid.

21. Ibid.

22. Kitamura (1992:2).

23. Ibid.

24. McCallum (1994:170–171).

25. Miyata (1987:139).

26. Kitamura (1992:3).

27. Shūkyō shakaigaku no kai (1985:18).

28. Bodiford (1994:3–36).

29. Ibid., p. 14.

30. Ibid., p. 17.

31. Ibid., p. 20. The letter, of course, was not the only appeal made. Bodiford describes the other efforts that went into this successful campaign.

32. Interview with Ichishima Shōshin on May 31, 1996.

33. This poster was on display in the Japan Railway station at Osaka and various other stations in the Kansai region during April 1996.

34. Such an advertisement was carried in the *Mainichi shinbun*, October 18, 1983.

35. This temple was Tōganji in Motoyama in Nagoya, where Ian Reader spent several *hatsumōde* periods between 1984 and 1988.

36. See Reader (1991a:161–167) for more comments on this issue.

37. *Asahi shinbun*, December 29, 1992, p. 18.

38. Jishu Jinja leaflet collected in 1992.

39. Victor Books (1994:42–43).

40. Kyburz (1996:272). It is not uncommon for Japanese advertisements to read telephone numbers in such ways, using shortened or alternative readings to express catchy meanings. In this case, the word "*gakkō*" (school) is not articulated in the reading of the number itself. Originally the talismans were sent back to the petitioner by fax. But as Kyburz notes (p. 272), this caused objections by the Jinja Honchō (the umbrella organization of Shinto shrines), which argued that such talismans were inauthentic because they had not been blessed by a priest. Now,

from the entry in the guidebook, it appears that the shrine has got round this objection by receiving the requests by fax but sending the talismans by mail.

41. On Agonshū and media technologies see Reader (1988). Agonshū's Internet site can be found at http://www.agon.org/.

42. http://www 1.sphere.adjp/daishi/.

43. http://www.icity.orjp/inari/. This site appeared in 1996.

44. Since the temple is a Nichiren Buddhist institution, the prayer recited is the *daimoku* (Namu myōhō renge kyō) used by Nichiren.

45. At least this is the case with the Internet search engine (Yahoo) we used when first accessing Saijō Inari's home pages: it is listed as Shinto at the following location: http://www.yahoo.co.jp/Society-and-Culture/Religion/Shinto/.

46. This shrine has a page dedicated to the reproduction of one of its *ofuda*, which can be downloaded and printed out: this particular *ofuda* is also available on the Cyber Shrine site, which provides photographs and information about various shrines.

47. The Tamō Hachiman Shrine pages are located at http://www.netwave.or.jp/~hachiman/.

48. On the invention of the cyberspace pop star Kyoko Date see "Virtual Reality Replaces Human Characters" (May 16, 1996) at http://www.iipl.com.sg/genVtext/vrl.htm.

49. http://www.duj.net.

50. Kawakatsu Hōiten catalog (1995).

51. Matsumotoya catalog (1992).

52. Suzuki Hōiten catalog (1995).

53. Izutsu catalog (Fall 1995).

54. Suiundō catalog (1995).

55. See, for example, the home page for Sekise at http://www.sekise.co.jp/sougi/index/html.

56. http://ss4.inet-osaka.or.jp./~kissyo/.

57. http://www.taihei.co.jp/kobori/.

58. See, for example, *Chūgai nippō* (October 18, 1990) for such a *boke fūji* advertisement. The paper has a regular feature entitled *Gyōkai nyūsu* (news from the business world) that features new religious items for sale.

59. His comments were made in a documentary entitled the *Goddess of Mercy for the Prevention of Senility,* made and produced by Japan's national broadcasting company NHK and issued in an international edition in 1990. For further comment and details see Reader (1995:12–13).

60. These temple legends are recounted in the temple's own guide; see Nakayama-dera (1986:15). See also Reader (1991a:149).

61. See, for example, Shūkyō shakaigaku no kai (1985:128–131).

62. Yonemoto (1995:202–212).

63. This comment was made in Statler (1984:195).

Chapter 7: Guidebooks to Practical Benefits

1. Victor Books (1994:154).

2. Chiba (1988). This volume, generally produced annually by the Hinode publishing company, is not connected with Victor Books' annual *goriyaku* guide cited in note 1.

3. Tatsukawa (1993:14).

4. As the last term in the title, "*shohen*," implies, this was the first edition of the guide: a second edition with additional sites was published two years later. See Nobori (1994:108).

5. Ibid., p. 109.

6. This graveyard was disestablished in 1869 after the Meiji Restoration; ibid., p. 110.

7. Ibid., p. 110.

8. Ibid., p. 114.

9. Kitagawa (1966:174).

10. These details about Akiyama Jiun Reijin have been taken from Nobori (1994:114).

11. It is, for example, included in the Kyōhan Books *goriyaku* map of Tokyo, which provides a guide to the locations of over two hundred shrines and temples in the Tokyo area related to the local train and subway services. See Kyōhan Books (1989).

12. Nobori (1994:113).

13. Kōdansha (1980).

14. Like most guidebooks it does not mention the southern island prefectures of Okinawa. Because of Okinawa's geographical distance from the rest of Japan and its somewhat different religious structure, related both to indigenous Okinawan traditions and to its Chinese heritage, the island is often considered to be outside the mainstream of Japanese religion and is frequently ignored by mainland Japanese in such contexts.

15. Victor Books (1994:6).

16. Kōdansha (1980).

17. Dai Edo tankenkai (1994).

18. Shinbutsu goriyaku kenkyūkai (1989).

19. At least this is the era when we first became aware of the concept of a date course in such settings. In 1985, Ian Reader heard about date courses from a number of young Japanese students he taught in Kobe, who informed him that they were a recent phenomenon. A family friend described how she and her boyfriend went on a New Year's Day date course in Kyoto, where she prayed for her brother's success in the university entrance examinations and for her own emotional happiness.

20. Such hypothetical divisions are so irrelevant that at least one guidebook dispenses with any terms that might suggest there are differences. Instead of using terms such as *shinbutsu* (which, while classifying the gods and buddhas together, still implies a possible differentiation of types), the *Nippon kamisama zukan* treats all the benefit-providing figures of worship as "*kami*," including figures normally considered under the rubric of *butsu* or *bosatsu* ("buddha" or "bodhisattva"), such as Kannon, Jizō, and Yakushi. See Shūkyō minzoku kenkyūjo (1996).

21. Dai Edo tankenkai (1994:150).

22. Victor Books (1994:8). The loanword "*guzzu*" (literally "goods" or objects) refers clearly here and elsewhere in the book to lucky objects and charms in general.

23. In Japanese the awkward term "*toppu obu tenjin*" is used; ibid., p. 42.

24. For general background on sumo see Reader (1989:288–289), which describes its ranking system.

25. Kōdansha (1981:162).
26. Ibid., p. 15.
27. Ibid., p. 18.
28. Ibid., pp. 164–165.
29. Chiba (1988:6–10).
30. Dai Edo tankenkai (1994:29).
31. Shūkyō minzoku kenkyūjo (1996:26–27).
32. Shinbutsu goriyaku kenkyū kai (1989:95).
33. Field visit on June 6, 1993.
34. Shūkyō minzoku kenkyūjo (1996:45).
35. Ibid., p. 90.
36. Ibid., p. 19.
37. Kōdansha (1980:47).
38. Ibid., p. 171.
39. Ibid., p. 233.
40. Victor Books (1994:94).
41. Ibid., p. 32.
42. Ibid., p. 110.
43. Ibid., pp. 34–35.
44. Ibid., p. 73.
45. Ibid., p. 77.
46. Ibid., p. 125.
47. Ibid., p. 131.
48. Dai Edo tankenkai (1994:11–12).
49. Ibid., pp. 12–13.
50. Ibid., pp. 123–124.
51. Ibid., pp. 181–183.
52. Ibid., p. 122.
53. Ibid., p. 200.
54. Ibid., pp. 200–202.
55. Ibid., pp. 67–68.
56. See Ohnuki-Tierney (1984:183–184).
57. Dai Edo tankenkai (1994:62–63).
58. Ibid., pp. 57–58.
59. Ibid., pp. 59–60.
60. Ibid., pp. 31–32.
61. Ibid., p. 14.
62. Ibid., p. 26.
63. Ibid., p. 197.
64. Ibid., pp. 106–108.
65. Ibid., pp. 171–173.
66. Ibid., p. 140, for example.
67. Ibid., pp. 124–126.

Chapter 8: Conclusions

1. See the volume of essays we edited on this topic (Reader and Tanabe 1994) and the introduction we wrote for that collection.
2. Shūkyō shakaigaku no kai (1985:131).

3. For comments on this point, based on discussions with Sōka Gakkai officials in the 1980s, see Reader (1991a:8–9). Here we are speaking in general terms and recognize that in some parts of the religious spectrum there are religious groups, and members of religious organizations, who regard praying at shrines and temples, even at socially and customarily accepted times such as New Year, as unacceptable breaches of their exclusivist perceptions. Even so, we contend that these are the exceptions that affirm the general rule.

4. As such it can be seen to resemble aspects of the invisible religion of Thomas Luckmann (1967) and the *mienai shūkyō* (invisible religion) of customs and etiquette discussed by Ōmura Eishō (1988), but it contains more doctrinal and ethical underpinnings and more emphasis on practice (that is, on active religious components) than does the passive notion of invisible religion.

Bibliography

Abe Masamichi. 1992. *Nihon no kamisama o shiru jiten.* Tokyo: Nihon bungeisha.

Akiyama Terukazu et al. 1968. *Emakimono.* In *Genshoku Nihon no bijutsu,* vol. 8. Tokyo: Shōgakkan.

Allen, R. E. (ed.). 1990. *The Concise Oxford Dictionary of Current English.* 8th ed. Oxford: Clarendon Press.

Allison, Anne. 1994. *Nightwork: Sexuality, Pleasure and Corporate Masculinity in a Tokyo Hostess Club.* Chicago: University of Chicago Press.

Ambros, Barbara. 1995. "Journeys into Liminality: Pilgrimages of Noblewomen in the Mid-Heian Period." M.A. thesis, Harvard University.

Anderson, Richard. 1988. "Taiken: Personal Narratives and Japanese New Religions." Ph.D. dissertation, Indiana University.

———. 1991. "What Constitutes Religious Activity? (I)." *Japanese Journal of Religious Studies* 18(4) (December): 369–372.

———. 1994. *Taiken: Nippon shin shūkyō no taikendan foukuroa.* Translated by Doki Takaichirō and Tōdō Okuto. Tokyo: Gendai Shokan.

Arai Ken. 1985. "Gendai no shin shūkyō." In Hori Ichirō (ed.), *Nihon no shūkyō.* Tokyo: Taimyōdō.

Arai Yūsei. 1988. *Kōyasan Shingonshū danshintō hikkei.* Kōyasan: Kōyasan Shingonshū Kyōgakubu.

Asahi shinbun.

Asai Endō. 1968. "Sōka Gakkai no shutsugen to mondaiten." In Mochizuki Kankō (ed.), *Kindai Nihon no hokke bukkyō.* Kyoto: Heirakuji shoten.

Aston, W. G. (trans.). 1956. *Nihongi.* London: Allen & Unwin.

Averbuch, Irit. 1997. "Performing Power: On the Nature of the Japanese Ritual Dance Performance of Yamabushi Kagura." *Journal of Ritual Studies* 10(2) (in press).

Baldwin, Neil. 1995. *Edison: Inventing the Century.* New York: Hyperion.

Birnbaum, Raoul (trans.). 1979. *The Healing Buddha.* Boulder: Shambhala.

Blacker, Carmen. 1975. *The Catalpa Bow: A Study of Shamanistic Practices in Japan.* London: Allen & Unwin.

Bodiford, William M. 1993. *Sōtō Zen in Medieval Japan.* Honolulu: University of Hawai'i Press.

————. 1994. "Sōtō Zen in a Japanese Town: Field Notes on a Once-Every-Thirty-Three-Years Kannon Festival." *Japanese Journal of Religious Studies* 21(1) (March): 3–36.

————. 1996. "Zen and the Art of Religious Prejudice: Efforts to Reform a Tradition of Social Discrimination." *Japanese Journal of Religious Studies* 23(1–2): 1–27.

Bright, Arthur A. 1949. *The Electric Lamp Industry.* New York: Macmillan.

Bukkyō minzoku gakkai (ed.). 1986. *Bukkyō minzoku jiten.* Tokyo: Shinjinbutsu Ōraisha.

Bunkachō (ed.). 1994–1995. *Shūkyō nenkan.* Tokyo: Gyōsei.

Buruma, Ian. 1996. "Japan: In the Spirit World" (review of Ian Littlewood, *The Idea of Japan: Western Images, Western Myths;* Deborah Boliver Boehm, *A Zen Romance: One Woman's Adventures in a Monastery;* and John K. Nelson, *A Year in the Life of a Shinto Shrine). New York Review of Books,* June 6, p. 32.

Cahill, Thomas. 1995. *How the Irish Saved Civilization.* New York: Doubleday.

Chiba Tadaki (ed.). 1988. *88 nenhan zenkoku jisha meguri: daremo ga shiritai go riyaku tokuhon.* Tokyo: Hinode Shuppan.

Chūgai nippō.

Collcutt, Martin. 1981. *Five Mountains: The Rinzai Monastic Institution in Medieval Japan.* Cambridge, Mass.: Harvard University Press.

————. 1988. "Mt. Fuji as the Realm of Miroku." In Alan Sponberg and Helen Hardacre (eds.), *Maitreya, the Future Buddha.* Cambridge: Cambridge University Press.

Dai Edo tankenkai (ed.). 1994. *Tokyo go-riyaku sanpo.* Tokyo: Hakubikan Shuppan.

Daiyūsan Saijōji kaisō roppyakunen hōsan jimukyoku (ed.). 1984. *Daiyūsan Saijōji kaisō roppyakunen hōsan.* Kanagawa: Daiyōsan.

Davis, Winston B. 1980. *Dojo: Magic and Exorcism in Modern Japan.* Stanford: Stanford University Press.

————. 1992 *Japanese Religion and Society: Paradigms of Structure and Change.* Albany: State University of New York Press.

Duffy, Eamon. 1992. *The Stripping of the Altars: Traditional Religion in England 1400–1580.* New Haven: Yale University Press.

Dykstra, Yoshiko (trans.). 1976. "Tales of the Compassionate Kannon: The Hasedera Kannon Genki." *Monumenta Nipponica* 31(2): 113–146.

Earhart, H. Byron. 1974. *Japanese Religion: Unity and Diversity.* 2nd ed. Encino: Dickenson.

————. 1994. "Mechanisms and Process in the Study of Japanese Amulets." In Okada Shigekiyo (ed.), *Nihon shūkyō e no shikaku.* Osaka: Tōhō shuppan.

Ebersole, Gary. 1991. *Ritual Poetry and the Politics of Death in Early Japan.* Princeton: Princeton University Press.

Edwards, Walter. 1989. *Modern Japan Through Its Weddings.* Stanford: Stanford University Press.

Etori, Akio. 1994. "Not Immune to Hard Work." *Look Japan* 39(456)(March): 28–29.

Faure, Bernard. 1987. "The Daruma-shū, Dōgen and Sōtō Zen." *Monumenta Nipponica* 42(1)(Spring): 25–55.

————. 1991. *The Rhetoric of Immediacy: A Cultural Critique of Chan/Zen Buddhism.* Princeton: Princeton University Press.

———. 1996. *Visions of Power: Imagining Medieval Japanese Buddhism.* Princeton: Princeton University Press.

Fujii Masao. 1993. *Sosen saishi no girei kōzō to minzoku.* Tokyo: Kōbundō.

Fujimoto Shinsei (ed.). 1966. *Taishō Kankiten risshōki.* Tokyo: Oishōten Daifukuseiji.

Gendai shimbutsu kenkyūkai. 1993. *Goriyaku shojiten.* Osaka: Nenshōsha.

Gomez, Luis O. (trans.). 1996. *The Land of Bliss: The Paradise of the Buddha of Measureless Light.* Honolulu: University of Hawai'i Press.

Goodwin, Janet R. 1994. *Alms and Vagabonds: Buddhist Temples and Popular Patronage in Medieval Japan.* Honolulu: University of Hawai'i Press.

Gorai Shigeru. 1983. "Nihon Bukkyō to jujutsu." In Daihōrin henshūbu (ed.), *Jujutsu kitō to genze riyaku.* Tokyo: Daihōrinkaku.

Graburn, Nelson. 1983. *To Pray, Pay and Play: The Cultural Structure of Japanese Tourism.* Aix-en-Provence: Centre des Hautes Études Touristiques.

Hagiwara Hidesaburō and Sutō Isao. 1985. *Nihon shūkyō minzoku zuten: inori to sukui.* Vol. 1. Kyoto: Hōzōkan.

Hakeda Yoshito. 1972. *Kūkai: Major Works.* New York: Columbia University Press.

Hara Mitsuju. 1992. *Togenuki Jizō-sama.* Tokyo: Bukku kurabu.

Hardacre, Helen. 1986. *Kurozumikyo and the New Religions of Japan.* Princeton: Princeton University Press.

Hare, E. M. (trans.). 1961. *The Book of the Gradual Sayings.* Vol. 3. London: Pali Text Society.

Hayami Tasuku. 1983. *Kannon shinkō.* Tokyo: Hanawa Shobō.

Hinonishi Shinjō (ed.). 1988. *Kōbō daishi shinkō.* Tokyo: Yūsankaku.

Hirose Hisaya. 1993. *Shibai hanjō no kamigami.* Tokyo: Tōyō keizai shimpōsha.

Holtom, Daniel C. 1938. "Japanese Votive Pictures (the Ikoma Ema)." *Monumenta Nipponica* 1:154–163.

Honda Sōichirō. 1985. *Nihon Shinto nyūmon.* Tokyo: Nihon Bungeisha.

Hori, Ichiro. 1968. *Folk Religion in Japan: Continuity and Change.* Chicago: University of Chicago Press.

http://ss4.inet-osaka.or.jp./~kissyo/

http://www l.sphere.adjp./daishi./

http://www.agon.org/

http://www.duj.net

http://www.icity.orjp/inari/

http://www.iipl.com.sg/genVtext/vrl.htm

http://www.netwave.or.jp/-hachiman/

http://www.sekise.co.jp/sougi/index/html

http://www.taihei.co.jp/kobori/

http://www.yahoo.co.jp/Society-and-Culture/Religion/Shinto/

Ichihime Jinja brochure (undated).

Iida Takafumi. 1986. "Gendai shūkyō no shakai shinri." In Manba Hisaichi (ed.), *Shakai shinrigaku o manabu hito no tame ni.* Tokyo: Sekaishisōsha.

———. 1988. "Folk Religion Among Koreans in Japan: The Shamanism of the 'Korean Temples.'" *Japanese Journal of Religious Studies* 15(2–3) (June–September): 155–182.

Iijima Yoshiharu. 1995. "Genze riyaku no kami to wa nani ka." In Yamaori Tetsuo (ed.), *Nihon no kami,* vol. 2. Tokyo: Heibonsha.

Ikei Nozomu. 1985. "Hanzai to taishū bunka." In Nakamura Shōichi and Nakano Osamu (eds.) *Taishū no bunka*. Tokyo: Yūhikaku.

Ikoma Shōten 75 (May 16, 1996).

Imai Enmyō. 1993. "Introduction." In Yoritomi Motohiro and Shiraki Toshiyuki, *Kansai goriyaku no jisha*. Osaka: Toki shobō.

Inoue Nobutaka et al. 1983. *Shin shūkyō kenkyū chōsa handobukku*. Tokyo: Yūzankaku.

——— (eds.). 1996. *Shinshūkyō kyōdan jinbutsu jiten*. Tokyo: Kōbundō.

Ivy, Marilyn. 1995. *Discourses of the Vanishing: Modernity, Phantasm, Japan*. Chicago: University of Chicago Press.

Iwai Hiromi. 1974. *Ema*. Tokyo: Hōsei Daigaku Shuppankyoku.

———. 1983. "Ema tenbyō." In Iwai Hiromi (ed.), *Ema hisshi*. Tokyo: Nippon Hōsō shuppan kyōkai.

Izutsu catalog (Fall 1995).

Jinja shinpōsha (ed.). 1986. *Kigyō no jinja*. Tokyo: Jinja shinpōsha.

Jōdo Shinshū Honganji-ha, Education Department (trans.). 1982. *Jōdo Shinshū Handbook for Laymen*. Kyoto: Honganji International Center.

Kabanoff, Alexander. 1994. "The Kangi-ten (Ganapati) Cult in Medieval Japanese Mikkyō." In Ian Astley (ed.), *Esoteric Buddhism in Japan*. Copenhagen: Seminar for Buddhist Studies.

Kalupahana, David. 1975. *Causality: The Central Philosophy of Buddhism*. Honolulu: University of Hawai'i Press.

Kanaoka Shūyū. 1981. *Hannya shingyō*. Tokyo: Kōdansha bunko.

Kaneko Satoru. 1988. "Gendaijin no shūkyō ishiki." In Ōmura Eishō and Nishiyama Shigeru (eds.), *Gendaijin no shūkyō*. Tokyo: Yūhikaku.

Kanzaki Noritake. 1995. *Kamisama hotokesama gosenzosama: Nipponkyō no minzokugaku*. Tokyo: Shōgakkan.

Kasahara Kazuo. 1976. *Gendaijin to Bukkyō*. Tokyo: Hyōronsha.

Katō Seiichi. 1983. "Shingon mikkyō ni okeru juhō no imi." In Daihōrin henshūbu (ed.), *Jujutsu kitō to genze riyaku*. Tokyo: Daihōrinkaku.

Kawakatsu Hōiten catalog (1995).

Kawasaki Daishi. 1993. *Kawasaki Daishi Yakuyokereki*. Kawasaki: Kawasaki Daishi.

Kida Sadayoshi. 1976. *Fukujin*. Tokyo: Hōbunkan shuppan.

Kikumura Norihiko. 1978. *Shinran jiten*. Tokyo: Tokyodō shuppan.

Kim, Young-ho (trans.). 1990. *Tao-sheng's Commentary on the Lotus Sutra: A Study and Translation*. Albany: State University of New York Press.

Kino Kazuyoshi. 1981. *Hannya shingyō o yomu*. Tokyo: Kōdansha gendai shinsho.

Kino Yōko. 1990. "Zainichi shāman no shūkyō girei: sosen saishi no jirei kenkyū." *Ritsumeikan sangyō shakai ronshū* 26(3): 115–153.

Kiseki Kazuji. 1973. *Ishikiri: denbo no kamisan*. Osaka: Rokugatsusha.

Kitagawa, Joseph M. 1966. *Religion in Japanese History*. New York: Columbia University Press.

Kitamura Gyōen. 1992. "Edo no shinkō: kaichō." *Bukkyō to bunka* 11:2–7.

Kiyota Minoru. 1978. *Shingon Buddhism: Theory and Practice*. Los Angeles: Buddhist Books International.

Kōdansha (ed.). 1980. *Fuku o yobu jisha jiten*. Tokyo: Kōdansha.

Kohno Jiko. 1996. "Making Each Day Count." *Dharma World* 23(September/October): 23–24.

Kōmoto Mitsugu. 1988. "Gendai toshi no minzoku shūkyō—kakyō saiken to chinkon." In Ōmura Eishō and Nishiyama Shigeru (eds.), *Gendaijin no shūkyō.* Tokyo: Yūhikaku.

Kuramadera kyōmubu (ed.). 1995. *Kuramasan shoshi.* Kyoto: Kuramasan shuppanbu.

Kyburz, Josef A. 1996. "Magical Thought at the Interface of Nature and Culture." In Pamela J. Asquith and Arne Kalland (eds.), *Japanese Images of Nature: Cultural Perspectives.* London: Curzon Press.

Kyōhan Books (ed.). 1989. *Shutoen jinja bukkaku goriyaku mappu.* (Map.) Tokyo: Kyōhan Books.

LaFleur, William R. 1992. *Liquid Life: Abortion and Buddhism in Japan.* Princeton: Princeton University Press.

Levy-Bruhl, Lucien. 1926. *How Natives Think.* London: Allen & Unwin.

Long, Susan O. 1990. "The Society and Its Environment." In Ronald E. Dolan and Robert L. Warren (eds.), *Japan, a Country Study.* Washington: Library of Congress.

Luckmann, Thomas. 1967. *The Invisible Religion.* New York: Macmillan.

Maeda Takashi. 1971. *Junrei no shakaigaku.* Kyoto: Minerva Books.

———. 1976. "Ancestor Worship in Japan: Facts and History." In W. H. Newell (ed.), *Ancestors.* The Hague: Mouton.

Mainichi Shinbun.

Malinowski, Bronislaw. 1974. *Magic, Science and Religion and Other Essays.* London: Souvenir Press. (Essay first published in 1925.)

Mathews, Gordon. 1996. *What Makes Life Worth Living? How Japanese and Americans Make Sense of Their Worlds.* Berkeley: University of California Press.

Matsumoto Hideo. 1980. "Negai ni ikiru." In Sōtō tōkaidō kyōkasentā (ed.), *Oriori no hōwa,* vol. 3. Tokyo: Sōtōshū shūmuchō.

Matsumoto Jitsudō. 1985. *Kankiten shinkō e no michi.* Osaka: Hōzanji. (First published in 1952.)

Matsumotoya catalog (1992).

Matsunaga, Alicia. 1969. *The Buddhist Philosophy of Assimilation: The Historical Development of the Honji-Suijaku Theory.* Tokyo: Sophia University

McCallum, Donald F. 1994. *Zenkōji and Its Icon.* Princeton: Princeton University Press.

McCarry, John. 1996. "Peru Begins Again." *National Geographic* 189(5)(May): 5–40.

McCullough, William H., and Helen Craig McCullough (trans.). 1980. *A Tale of Flowering Fortunes.* Vol. 2. Stanford: Stanford University Press.

McFarland, H. Neill. 1967. *The Rush Hour of the Gods: A Study of New Religious Movements in Japan.* New York: Macmillan.

Miyake Hitoshi. 1974. *Nihon shūkyō no kōzō.* Tokyo: Keiō tsūshin.

———. 1981. *Seikatsu no naka no shūkyō.* Tokyo: NHK Books.

———. 1989. *Shūkyō minzokugaku.* Tokyo: Tokyo Daigaku shuppan.

Miyasaka Yūshō. 1983. "Kaji kitō jumon no imi." In Daihōrin henshūbu (ed.), *Jujutsu kitō to genze riyaku.* Tokyo: Daihōrinkaku.

Miyata Noboru. 1987. *Edo saijiki.* Tokyo: Yoshikawa Kōbunkan.

Miyazaki Ninshō. 1985. *Shikoku henro: rekishi to kokoro.* Osaka: Toki Shobō.

Miyuki Shōichirō. 1996. "Shikoku henro shi kenkyū yosetsu: henro no minshūka to shohan no henroseisaku." In Shinno Toshikazu (ed.), *Seiseki junrei* (vol. 2 of *Kōza Nihon no junrei*). Tokyo: Yūsankaku.

Morris, Ivan (trans.). 1967. *The Pillow Book of Sei Shōnagon.* 2 vols. New York: Columbia University Press.

Murata Jūhachi. 1995. "Ikoma mōde—Kankiten no maneki." *Bukkyō,* 31(4): 194–204.

Naganuma Kenkai. 1991. "Ebisu kami saikō." In Kitami Yoshio (ed.), *Ebisu shinkō.* Tokyo: Yūsankaku shuppan.

Naitō Masatoshi and Shimokawa Akihito. 1984. *Tokyo no jisha.* Tokyo: Ryōhoku shuppan.

Nakajima Ikufū. 1980. "Jitafuni no riyaku." In Sōtō tōkaidō kyōkasentā (ed.), *Oriori no hōwa,* vol. 3. Tokyo: Sōtōshū shūmuchō.

Nakamaki Hirochika. 1983. "Jinja to Shintō." In Miyata Noboru (ed.), *Kami to hotoke.* Tokyo: Shōgakkan.

Nakamura, Kyoko Motomichi. 1973. *Miraculous Tales from the Japanese Buddhist Tradition: The Nihon Ryōiki of the Monk Kyōkai.* Cambridge, Mass.: Harvard University Press.

Nakao Takashi. 1983. "Eien no yasuragi no en." In Kusunoki Noriyoshi (ed.), *Zenkoku jisha meguri.* Tokyo: Hinode shuppan.

Nakayama-dera (ed.). 1986. *Nakayamadera no shiori.* Takarazuka: Nakayama-dera.

Nara, Yasuaki. 1995. "May the Deceased Get Enlightenment! An Aspect of the Enculturation of Buddhism in Japan." *Buddhist-Christian Studies* 15:19–42.

Narita-san brochure (undated).

Nelson, John. 1996. *A Year in the Life of a Shinto Shrine.* Seattle: University of Washington Press.

NHK International. 1990. *Goddess of Mercy for the Prevention of Senility.* Video documentary.

Nihon Bukkyō kenkyū kai (ed.). 1970. *Nihon shūkyō no genze riyaku.* Tokyo: Daizō shuppan.

Nii Hiromasa and Nakajima Yoshimine. 1982. *Odaishisama.* Kōyasan: Kōyasan shuppan.

Nobori Masao. 1994. "Jinja bukkaku gankake jūhōki shohen ni miru shōshi to chiryō." In Miyata Noboru and Tsukamoto Manabu (eds.), *Minkan shinkō to minshū shūkyō.* Tokyo: Yoshikawa shōbunkan.

Numata Kenya. 1995. *Shūkyō to kagaku no neo paradaimu.* Osaka: Sōgensha.

Nussbaum, Martha. 1986. *The Fragility of Goodness: Luck and Ethics in Greek Tragedy and Philosophy.* Cambridge: Cambridge University Press.

Nye, David E. 1990. *Electrifying America: Social Meanings of a New Technology.* Cambridge, Mass.: MIT Press.

Oates, Wayne. 1995. *Luck: A Secular Faith.* Louisville: Westminister John Knox Press.

Ōchō Enichi. 1969. *Hokke shisō.* Kyoto: Heirakuji Shoten.

Oda Masayasu. 1984. "Shōdoshima ni okeru utsushi reijō no seiritsu." *Jinbun chiri* (Kyoto University), 36(4): 59–73.

Oda Ryūkō. 1976. *Mikkyō kitō no himitsu.* Tokyo: Hō shuppan.

Ohnuki-Tierney, Emiko. 1984. *Illness and Culture in Contemporary Japan: An Anthropological View.* Cambridge: Cambridge University Press.

Ōkawa Ryūhō. 1995. *Jinsei seiko no hissaku.* Tokyo: Kōfuku no Kagaku shuppan.

Ōmura Eishō. 1988. "Gendaijin no shūkyō." In Ōmura Eishō and Nishiyama Shigeru (eds.), *Gendaijin no shūkyō.* Tokyo: Yūhikaku.

Ōmura Eishō and Nishiyama Shigeru (eds.) 1988. *Gendaijin no shukyo.* Tokyo: Yuhikaku.

Ozeki Chikayasu. 1993. *Shichifukujin meguri: omairi no reishiki to kokoroe.* Tokyo: Sanshindō.

Philippi, Donald (trans.). 1990. *Norito: A Translation of Ancient Japanese Ritual Prayers.* Princeton: Princeton University Press.

Pye, Michael. 1977. "The Heart Sutra in Its Japanese Context." In Lewis Lancaster (ed.), *Prajnaparamita and Related Systems: Essays in Honor of Edward Conze.* Berkeley: University of California and Berkeley Institute of Buddhist Studies.

———— (trans.). 1990. *Emerging from Meditation.* Honolulu: University of Hawai'i Press.

————. 1996. "Aum Shinrikyō: Can Religious Studies Cope?" *Religion* 26: 261–270.

Reader, Ian. 1987. "Back to the Future: Images of Nostalgia and Renewal in a Japanese Religious Context." *Japanese Journal of Religious Studies* 14(4): 287–303.

————. 1988. "The Rise of a Japanese 'New New Religion': Themes in the Development of Agonshū." *Japanese Journal of Religious Studies* 15(4): 235–261.

————. 1989. "Sumo: The Recent History of an Ethical Model for Japanese Society." *International Journal of the History of Sport* 6(4): 285–298.

————. 1991a. *Religion in Contemporary Japan.* Honolulu: University of Hawai'i Press.

————. 1991b. "What Constitutes Religious Activity? (II)." *Japanese Journal of Religious Studies* 18(4): 373–376.

————. 1991c. "Letters to the Gods: The Form and Meanings of Ema." *Japanese Journal of Religious Studies* 18(1): 23–50.

————. 1993a. "Recent Publications on Japanese Religions: The Work of Shimazono Susumu." *Japanese Journal of Religious Studies* 20(2–3): 228–248.

————. 1993b. "Dead to the World: Pilgrims in Shikoku." In Ian Reader and Tony Walter (eds.), *Pilgrimage in Popular Culture.* Basingstoke: Macmillan.

————. 1994. "The Japanese New Year: Transitions, Festivities, and Religion." In Reiko Mochinaga Brandon and Barbara B. Stephan (eds.), *Spirit and Symbol: The Japanese New Year.* Honolulu: Honolulu Academy of Arts and University of Hawai'i Press.

————. 1995. "Social Action and Personal Benefits in Contemporary Japanese Buddhism." *Buddhist-Christian Studies* 15:3–17.

————. 1996a. "Pilgrimage as Cult: The Shikoku Pilgrimage as a Window on Japanese Religion." In P. F. Kornicki and I. J. McMullen (eds.), *Religion in Japan: Arrows to Heaven and Earth.* Cambridge: Cambridge University Press.

————. 1996b. *A Poisonous Cocktail? Aum Shinrikyō's Path to Violence.* Copenhagen: NIAS Books.

Reader, Ian, and George J. Tanabe Jr. (eds.). 1994. Special edition on Conflict and Religion in Japan. *Japanese Journal of Religious Studies* 21(2–3).

Reischauer, Edwin O., and Marius B. Jansen. 1995. *The Japanese Today: Change and Continuity.* Enlarged ed. Cambridge, Mass.: Harvard University Press.

Rhys Davids, T. W. (trans.). 1963. *The Questions of King Milinda.* Pt. 1. New York: Dover.

Robertson, Jennifer. 1991. *Native and Newcomer: Making and Remaking a Japanese City.* Berkeley: University of California Press.

Saijō Inarikyō hōsha (ed.). 1979. *Saijōsama no hanashi.* Okayama: Saijō Inarikyō hōsha.

Saitō Akitoshi. 1984. "Kōbō Daishi shinkō ni kansuru jittai chōsa." In *Bukkyō bunka ronshū* 4:400–479.

———. 1988. "Kōbō daishi densetsu." In Hinonishi Shinjō (ed.), *Kōbō daishi shinkō.* Tokyo: Yūsankaku.

Saitō Tsuneharu. 1982. *Nippon goriyaku kikō.* Tokyo: Arachi shuppansha.

Sakurai Tokutarō. 1968. *Shimbutsu kōshōshi kenkyū.* Tokyo: Yoshikawa kōbunkan.

Sasaki Shōten. 1988. "Jōdo Shin and Folk Religion: Toward a Post-Modern Jōdo Shin 'Theology.'" *Bulletin of the Nanzan Institute for Religion and Culture* 12:13–35.

———. 1990. "Posuto modaun kyōgaku e no shiken." In Ōmura Eishō, Kaneko Satoru, and Sasaki Shōten (eds.), *Posuto modaun no Shinran.* Kyoto: Dōbōsha.

Satō Makoto. 1990. "Shimbutsu shūgō no shoyōsō." *Tōyō gakujutsu kenkyū* 20(4): 111–121.

Satō Taishun. 1971. *Hannya shingyō kōwa.* Fukui: Fukkōkaku.

Satō Tatsugen and Kaneko Wakō. 1989. *Shichifukujin.* Tokyo: Mokujisha.

Seidensticker, Edward (trans.). 1981. *The Tale of Genji.* Harmondsworth: Penguin.

Sharf, Robert. 1995. "Sanbōkyōdan: Zen and the Way of the New Religions." *Japanese Journal of Religious Studies* 22(3–4): 417–458.

Shimazono Susumu. 1992. *Gendai kyūsai shūkyōron.* Tokyo: Seikyūsha.

———. 1995. "In the Wake of Aum: The Formation and Transformation of a Universe of Belief." *Japanese Journal of Religious Studies* 22(3–4): 381–415.

Shimizutani Kōshō. 1986. *Junrei no kokoro.* Tokyo: Daizō shuppan.

Shinbutsu goriyaku kenkyūkai (ed.). 1989. *Jinja otera goriyakuchō.* Tokyo: KK rongu serizu.

Shinjō Tsunezō. 1982. *Shaji sankei no shakaikeizaishiteki kenkyū.* Tokyo: Hanawa shobō.

Shinmura Izuru. 1970. *Kōjien.* Second edition. Tokyo: Iwanami Shoten.

Shinno Toshikazu. 1980. *Seikatsu no naka no shūkyō: junrei no minzokushi.* Tokyo: NHK Books.

———. 1991. *Nihon yugyō shūkyōron.* Tokyo: Yoshikawa kōbunkan.

———. 1993. "From *Minkan-shinkō* to *Minzoku-shūkyō*: Reflections on the Study of Folk Buddhism" (trans. Paul Swanson). *Japanese Journal of Religious Studies* 20(2–3): 187–206.

——— (ed.). 1996. *Kōza Nihon no junrei.* 3 vols. Tokyo: Yūsankaku.

Shintō shūkyō gakkai (ed.). 1992. "Shimbutsu shūgō to shimbutsu kakuri o megutte." *Shintō shūkyō* 146.

Shiobara Tsutomu (ed.). 1987. *Nihon shūkyō fukugōteki kuzo to toshiyumin to shūkyō kōdō ni kansuru jisshōteki kenkyū*. Osaka: Osaka Daigaku jimbun kagaku.

Shirai Yūko. 1986. *Kūkai densetsu no keisei to Kōyasan*. Tokyo: Dōseisha.

Shiraki Toshiyuki (ed.). 1995. *Shichifukujun jumpai*. Osaka. Toki shobō.

Shūkyō minzoku kenkyūjo (ed.). 1996. *Nippon kamisama zukan*. Tokyo: Hamano shuppan.

Shūkyō shakaigaku no kai (ed.). 1985. *Ikoma no kamigami*. Osaka: Sōgensha.

Smith, Robert J. 1974. *Ancestor Worship in Contemporary Japan*. Stanford: Stanford University Press.

———. 1992. "Review of Ian Reader, *Religion in Contemporary Japan*." *Journal of Japanese Studies* 18(1): 243–246.

Smyers, Karen. 1993. "The Fox and the Jewel: A Study of Shared and Private Meanings in Japanese Inari Worship." Ph.D. dissertation, Princeton University.

———. 1996. "'My Own Inari': Personalization of the Deity in Inari Worship." *Japanese Journal of Religious Studies* 23(1–2): 85–116.

Soapberry Seed Sutra (Ch.: *Mu-huan-tzu ching;* Jp.: *Mokugenshi-kyō*) T17: no. 786.

Sōtōshū shūsei chōsa iinkai (ed.). 1984. *Shūkyō shūdan no ashita e no kadai*. Tokyo: Sōtōshū shūmuchō.

Sōtōshū shūmuchō (ed.). 1978. *Shūryō hikkei*. Tokyo: Sōtōshū shūmuchō.

——— (ed.). 1980. *Seishin e no joshō*. Tokyo: Sōtōshū shūmuchō.

Staal, Frits. 1979. "The Meaninglessness of Ritual." *Numen* 36(1): 2–22.

Statler, Oliver. 1984. *Japanese Pilgrimage*. London: Picador.

Statman, Daniel (ed.). 1993. *Moral Luck*. Albany: State University of New York Press.

Sueki Fumihiko. 1995. "Two Seemingly Contradictory Aspects of the Teaching of Innate Enlightenment (*hongaku*) in Medieval Japan." *Japanese Journal of Religious Studies* 22(1–2): 3–16.

Sugata Masaki. 1992. *Nihon no jinja o shiru jiten*. Tokyo: Nihon bungeisha.

Suiundō catalog (1995).

Sutra on the Yoga Rosaries of the Diamond Peak (Jp.: *Kongōchō yuga nenju kyō;* Ch.: *Chin-kang-ting yü-ch'ieh nien-chu ch'ing*) T17: no. 789.

Suzuki Hōiten catalog (1995).

Swanger, Eugene R. 1981. "A Preliminary Examination of the Omamori Phenomenon." *Asian Folklore Studies* 40:237–252.

Swyngedouw, Jan. 1993. "Religion in Contemporary Japanese Society." In Mark R. Mullins, Shimazono Susumu, and Paul L. Swanson (eds.), *Religion and Society in Modern Japan*. Berkeley: Asian Humanities Press.

Takagami Kakushō. 1980. *Hannya shingyō kōgi*. Tokyo: Kadokawa bunko.

Takahashi Ryūten. 1979. "Sono toki, go honzon wa buji." In Takizawa Mamoru et al. (eds.), *Kawasaki Daishi fukkō sanjūnen no ayumi*. Kawasaki: Kawasaki Daishi henjō gyōsho.

Takakusu, J. (trans.). 1969. *Amitāyur-dhyāna-sūtra: The Sūtra of the Meditation on Amitāyus*. In E. B. Cowell (ed.), *Buddhist Mahāyāna Texts*. New York: Dover.

Takeda Akira. 1972. *Junrei no minzokugaku*. Tokyo: Iwasaki bijitsusha.

Takeda Chōshū. 1971. *Minzoku Bukkyō to sosen shinkō*. Tokyo: Tokyo Daigaku shuppan.

Takizawa Mamoru et al. (eds.). 1979. *Kawasaki Daishi fukkō sanjūnen no ayumi.* Kawasaki: Kawasaki Daishi henjō gyōsho.

Tamura Yoshiro. 1960. "Religion and Modern Life II." *Contemporary Religions in Japan* 1(3): 40–67.

Tan, Amy. 1989. *The Joy Luck Club.* New York: Ballantine.

———. 1991. *The Kitchen God's Wife.* New York: Ballantine.

Tanabe, George J., Jr. 1992. *Myōe the Dreamkeeper: Fantasy and Knowledge in Early Kamakura Buddhism.* Cambridge, Mass.: Harvard University Press.

Tatsukawa Shōji. 1993. *Byōki o iyasu chiisana kamigami.* Tokyo: Heibonsha.

Taylor, John V. 1963. *The Primal Vision.* London: SCM Press.

Tenjin shinkō henshū iinkai (ed.). 1981. *Gakumon no kamisama: wakariyasui Tenjin shinkō.* Tokyo: Kamakura shinsho.

Tenrikyō (ed.). 1985. *The Doctrine of Tenrikyō.* Tenri: Tenrikyō Church Headquarters.

Thomas, Keith. 1971. *Religion and the Decline of Magic.* New York: Scribner's.

Toganoo Shōun. 1935. *Himitsu jisō no kenkyū.* Kōyasan: Kōyasan daigaku shuppan bu.

Tsunoda, Ryusaku, et al. (eds.). 1958. *Sources of Japanese Tradition,* vol. 1. New York: Columbia University Press.

Tsuruoka Shizuo. 1970. "Kodai minshū Bukkyō no genze riyaku." In Nihon Bukkyō kenkyū kai (ed.), *Nihon shūkyō no genze riyaku.* Tokyo: Daizō shuppan.

Uda Toshihiko (ed.). 1963. *Shin zassai norito taisei.* Tokyo: Meibunsha.

Ueda Kenji. 1981. "Shinto." In Ichirō Hori (ed.), *Japanese Religions: A Survey by the Agency for Cultural Affairs.* Tokyo: Kōdansha.

———. 1988. *Shintō no chikara.* Tokyo: Tachibana shuppan.

van Bremen, Jan. 1995. "Introduction: The Myth of the Secularization of Industrialized Societies." In Jan van Bremen and D. P. Martinez (eds.), *Ceremony and Ritual in Japan: Religious Practices in an Industrialized Society.* London: Routledge.

Victor Books (ed.). 1994. *Nippon zenkoku goriyaku gaido.* Tokyo: Victor Books.

Watanabe Tsunaya (ed.). 1966. *Shasekishū.* In *Nihon koten bungaku taikei,* vol. 85. Tokyo: Iwanami shoten.

Watson, Burton (trans.). 1993. *The Lotus Sutra.* New York: Columbia University Press.

Werblowsky, R. J. Z. 1991. "Mizuko kuyō: Notulae on the Most Important 'New Religion' of Japan." *Japanese Journal of Religious Studies* 18(4): 295–354.

Williams, Bernard. 1981. *Moral Luck: Philosophical Papers 1973–1980.* Cambridge: Cambridge University Press.

Wilson, Brian, and Karel Dobbelaere. 1994. *A Time to Chant: The Sōka Gakkai Buddhists in Britain.* Oxford: Clarendon Press.

Yamamoto, Kosho. 1963. *An Introduction to Shin Buddhism.* Ube City: Karinbunko.

Yamasaki Taikō. 1988. *Shingon: Japanese Esoteric Buddhism.* Boston: Shambhala.

Yonemoto Kazuhiro. 1995. "Furusato no tera ga kiete iku." In *Obōsan to issho: bessatsu Takarajima,* no. 218. Tokyo: Takarajima.

Yoritomi Motohiro. 1984. *Shomin no hotoke: Kannon, Jizō, Fudō.* Tokyo: NHK Books.

————. 1995. "Shichifukujin no shimbutsu tachi." In Shiraki Toshiyuki (ed.),
    Shichifukujin jumpai. Osaka: Toki shobō.
Yoritomi Motohiro and Shiraki Toshiyuki. 1993. *Kansai goriyaku no jisha.* Osaka:
    Toki shobō.
Young, Richard, and Ikeuchi Fuki. 1995. "Religion in the Hateful Age: Reflec-
    tions on Pokkuri and Other Geriatric Rituals in Japan's Aging Society."
    Japanese Religions 20(2): 167–200.

Index

About the Authors

IAN READER received his Ph.D. from the University of Leeds in 1983. Among his publications are *Religion in Contemporary Japan*, *Pilgrimage in Popular Culture*, and *A Poisonous Cocktail? Aum Shinrikyō's Path to Violence*. He is at work on a book manuscript on Japanese pilgrimage. Dr. Reader is on the faculty of the Scottish Centre for Japanese Studies, University of Stirling, Scotland.

GEORGE J. TANABE, JR., holds a doctorate in East Asian Languages and Cultures from Columbia University. His publications include *The Lotus Sutra in Japanese Culture* (co-edited with Willa Jane Tanabe) and *Myoe the Dreamkeeper*. Professor Tanabe is currently researching the funeral industry in Japan. He is professor of Japanese religion and chairman of the Department of Religion at the University of Hawai'i.